D1393460

A191

/ DPC

(Fer)

RESOURCES:
Environment & Policy

HAROLD BRIDGES LIBRARY
S. MARTIN'S COLLEGE
LANCASTER

Books are to be returned
the last date belo.

20

1853961507

John Fernie is a senior lecturer in economic geography at Huddersfield Polytechnic. He has taught and researched extensively in Canada and the United States since 1978, including a one-year Fulbright exchange professorship at Arizona State University in 1981/82. His main interests are in the field of energy resource management, especially in relation to nuclear energy issues in the United Kingdom and the United States. He is author of *A Geography of Energy in the UK*, a contributor to other books on energy and has written many articles on energy topics.

Alan S. Pitkethly is a lecturer in resource management at Huddersfield Polytechnic, having researched innovations in Scottish water management, and taught and researched resource topics in the Department of Economics, Heriot Watt University, Edinburgh, and the Department of Geography, University of Edinburgh. He too has taught in Canada. As well as being responsible for a range of resource courses at the Polytechnic, he teaches an option in recreation and leisure management.

RESOURCES: Environment & Policy

John Fernie
and
Alan S. Pitkethly

P·C·P
Paul Chapman
Publishing Ltd

Copyright © John Fernie & Alan S. Pitkethly 1985
All rights reserved

First published 1985
by Harper & Row Ltd

Reprinted in this edition
by Paul Chapman Publishing Ltd
144 Liverpool Road
London N1 1LA

No part of this publication may be reproduced, stored in a retrieval
system, or transmitted, in any form or by any means, electronic,
mechanical, photocopying, recording or otherwise, without the prior
permission of Paul Chapman Publishing Ltd.

British Library Cataloguing in Publication Data

Fernie, John
   Resources environment & policy.
   1. Natural resources —— Management
   I. Title   II. Pitkethly, Alan S.
   333.7   HC55
ISBN 1 85396 150 7

Printed and bound by Athenaeum Press Ltd,
Newcastle upon Tyne.

B C D E F G 7 6 5 4 3 2

Contents

Preface

Since the 1960s and the rise of environmentalism, there has been a plethora of texts on resources. Why add another to a long list? This book was written for two reasons: first, there is a need for a *general* teaching text on resources and resource management and secondly, it was felt that a different approach to understanding resource issues and problems was necessary. The underlying theme of this book is that all resource problems – overpopulation, hunger, poverty, fuel shortages, deforestation – are fundamentally *institutional* problems which warrant institutional solutions. The success or failure of resource management is intrinsically tied up with institutional structures – the pattern of agencies, laws and policies which pertain to resource issues. Consequently, problem recognition and the determination to solve basic resource issues depend upon the attitudes and behaviour of groups involved in the decision-making process.

Resource management is about power and politics. To change the status quo, fundamental shifts in the balance of power among vested interests who influence policy are required. This helps to explain the failure of the 'South' in its quest for a new international economic order, the persistence of corporate imperialism and the difficulties which face the environmental movement in a world recession.

The book falls into two parts. Part One introduces the reader to the debate on resources and population, resources and the existing world order. There follow chapters on energy, commodities, food, water and forestry and wilderness which are discussed in terms of patterns of supply and demand, problems, issues, strategies, futures and the need for management. The latter theme is taken up in Part Two which is concerned with decision making, institutional structures and case studies of policy in practice.

John Fernie wishes to record his appreciation to Suzanne for all her help in the preparation of the manuscript. Many thanks to Steve Pratt for his cartographical skills. We would also like to thank our students who for several years have acted as guinea pigs to our ideas. This book is dedicated to them.

Acknowledgements

The author and publishers would like to thank the following for permission to reproduce copyright material:

Ann Arbour Publishers for Figure 9.2 from Canter, L.W., 1979 *Water Resources Assessment - Methodology of Technology Sourcebook*

Annual Review for Figure 9.5 from *Energy*, Vol. 6 1981

The Association of American Geographers for Tables 10.1, 10.2, 10.3 from Calzonetti with Eckert 1981 *Finding a Place for Energy*

The British Geological Survey for Tables 4.3 and 4.4 from Institute of Geological Sciences 1982 *World Mineral Statistics*

The British North American Committee for Tables 11.2 and 11.3 from Mikesell, R.F., 1979 *New Patterns of World Mineral Development*

CBS Educational and Professional Publishers for Figure 12.1 from Hopkins R.F., Pearlberg R.L., Wallerstein M.B., 1982 *Food in the Global Arena*

Ceres May June 1981 for Table 5.2

Ceres March April 1982 for Table 5.4

Cornell University Press for Table 4.6 from Mikdashi, Z., 1976 *The International Politics of Natural Resources*

The Central Scotland Water Development Board, Percy Johnson - Marshall & Partners and Robert Cuthbertson & Partners for Figures 14.3 and 14.5

Finance and Development for Figure 3.2 from Goodman, R., December 1980 *Managing the demand for energy in the developing world*

Food and Agriculture Organization of the United Nations for Figures 5.1, 5.2, and Tables 5.1, 5.3, 5.5. from 1982, *The State of Food and Agriculture*

Forest Service, US Department of Agriculture for Figures 13.1, 13.2 and Tables 13.1, 13.2 from Hendee, J.C., *et al Wilderness Management*

Fortune for Table 11.1 from 1979 *50 Largest Industrial Corporations in the World*

The Geographical Magazine for Tables 7.1a and b from Sewell, W.D., *Water Across the American Continent*

George Allen & Unwin for quotation from Parker, D.J., and Penning-Rowsell, E.C., *Water Planning in Britain*

HMSO for Table 10.4 and Figure 10.2 adapted from the Central Office of Information publication *Nuclear Energy in Britain*

HMSO for Table 12.3 from the *Royal Commission on Environmental Pollution 7th Report, Cmnd 7644*

Institution of Mechanical Engineers for Table 4.5 from the Materials Forum

John Wiley & Sons Ltd for Figure 8.1 from Sewell and Coppock *Public Participation and Planning* and Tables 9.1 from O'Riordan, T, and Sewell, W.R.D., *Project Appraisal and Policy Review* and Table 12.6 from Tarrant 1980, *Food Policy*

Macmillan, London and Basingstoke, for Table 11.6 and 11.7 from Stopford, J.M., *et al* 1980 *The World Directory of Multinational Enterprises*

The Monthly Review Press for quotations from Michaelson, K., 1981 *And the poor get children: radical perspectives on population dynamics*

The *New Internationalist* for Table 12.2

The Oxford University Press for Table 12.5 from *The World Bank Development Report 1982*

Pan Books for Figure 1.1 from *The Brandt Report 1980*

Penguin Books for Tables 4.2, 6.1, 6.3, and Figure 11.1 from *The Global 2000 Report to the President 1982*

Pergamon Press for Table 7.2, from Biswas, A.K., *United Nations Water Conference: Summary 1978* and Tables 7.3, 7.4, 7.5, 7.6, 7.7 from *United Nations Water Development and Management 1978*

Pulp and Paper for Table 6.2

Science for Table 4.8

Shell Briefing Service for Tables 3.3 and 3.5

Sierra: The Magazine of the Sierra Club for Table 13.1

South for Table 11.4 and 11.5

TRRU for Tables 13.3 and 13.4 from *The Economy of Rural Communities in the National Parks of England and Wales 1981*

UCS Publishing for Figure 10.1 from Coffin, B., *Nuclear Power Plants in the US: Current Status and Statistical History*

United Nations for Tables 3.1, 3.2, 3.8, 3.9 from *The Yearbook of World Energy Statistics 1979*

US Geological Survey Bulletin for Figure 1.2

US Geological Survey Circular for Figure 9.3

Westview Press Inc., Colorado for Figure 5.7 from Valdes, A., *Food Insecurity for Developing Countries 1981*

PART ONE:
RESOURCE STUDIES

1   Concepts of Resources

1.1 Introduction

Over the past two or three decades there has been a considerable change in the way resources are regarded. War in the Middle East and the Iranian Revolution have raised the question of whether a resource such as oil can be made permanently and securely available. The growing list of endangered species has raised the question of whether man's progress on planet Earth can be limitless. Soil erosion and the sterilization of lakes by acid rain have reinforced fears that there might be resource-based limits to a good life on Earth.

More and more people are recognizing the value of unspoilt countryside, of nature and of recreational pursuits, such as climbing or angling. These values seem increasingly threatened by commercial developments of various kinds. Developments in communications, travel and world diplomacy have made it increasingly obvious that the benefits derived from consumption of the world's resources are unequally shared. The larger part of humanity may be classified as 'have nots' anxious to improve their situation by 'development'. This is often regarded by the richer nations as good for business, but when the existing order of things has been challenged, sometimes forcibly, as a threat to their legitimate interests.[1] Control over resources gives power. Loss of control threatens a loss of power. Politics is about power. At home and abroad political arguments over the control and development of resources increasingly dominate the political agenda and public concern.

In the first part of this book, the problem of resources is viewed in a global perspective, highlighting the differences between the so-called 'North' and 'South' (Fig 1.1), terms which are largely synonymous with 'rich' and 'poor', 'developed' and 'developing' countries, perhaps even with 'winners' and 'losers'. In recent years the importance of a 'North–South' dialogue has been increasingly recognized.[2] Dialogue on trade relations, economic aid and the political interaction between manufacturing countries chiefly of the 'North', and the rest of the world, all of which are in many respects dependent on decisions made in and by the 'North', has brought a new focus to resource studies. In 1980 the Brandt Commission took the view that resource technology was effectively in the hands of large transnational corporations, who were also responsible for a large share of world investment and world trade in raw materials and manufactures:[3]

Because of this economic power Northern countries dominate the international economic system – its rules and regulations, and its international institutions of trade, money and finance. Some developing countries have swum against this tide, taking the opportunities which exist and overcoming many obstacles; but most of them find the currents too strong for them. In the world, as in nations, economic forces left to themselves tend to produce growing inequality.

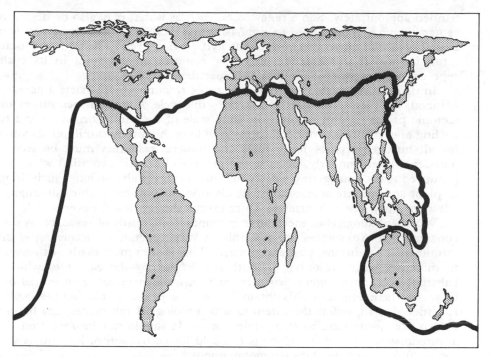

Figure 1.1 Peter's Projection of 'North' and 'South'
Source: Dr Arno Peters, University of Bremen

The intervention of international law, said the Commission, would be necessary to protect the weak. If this is so, or even if a large number of nations believe it to be so, then resources and resource management will remain in the forefront of global attention as they have been over recent decades.

It is the purpose of this book to introduce the context, the background and the basic ideas of this important global debate. The approach adopted is an institutional one, concentrating on the actors, agencies and policies that make resources available or condition their availability. Nevertheless, definitions of different subclasses of resources are a useful starting point.

1.2 The Nature of Resources

The terms 'stock', 'resources' and 'reserves' span a range of meaning: from all materials potentially available for use, to those definitely capable of development.[4] *Stock resources* are the sum total of materials to be found in the environment – anything and eveything with mass, inert or biological, plus all forms of energy, kinetic, physical and chemical. Useful purposes have so far been discovered or developed for only a part of such stock. *Resources* have purpose and value, and are defined in cultural, economic and ecological terms. Resources may be classified as renewable or non-renewable. Renewable resources are expressions of one form or another of energy. For example, solar energy is converted by the process of photosynthesis to provide short-term field crops or long-term timber harvests, giving a renewable and sustainable yield if husbanded appropriately. Some renewables, such as water, may also be described as *flow resources*, a term used to emphasise that these occur as part of a cycle or closed system of movement such as the hydrological cycle. The term is a useful reminder that if use is made of a flow resource at one point in its cycle, repercussions elsewhere should be anticipated.

In defining renewable and non-renewable resources there exists a paradox. Minerals are themselves part of a cycle – the cycle of erosion, deposition and tectonic processes. But because the time scale of such transformation and re-cycling of elements into mineral forms is so long (hundreds of millions of years) for all human purposes fossil fuels and mineral resources must be seen as non-renewable. Similarly, because the process of genetic evolution which has produced today's staggering variety of living things is also so long, such things as plant and wildlife species must be classified as non-renewable, although, if left alone, they renew themselves. Once extinct they are lost for ever.

Whether biological or inert, an important characteristic of resources is their concentration. Substances are available in varying amounts according to en-vironmental conditions, past and present. This is seen most easily with regard to minerals, where resource deposits are defined by the extent to which a substance occurs in higher densities, or in a form more easily separated out, then elsewhere. Higher yields obtainable in some places (or the fact that a yield is achieved at all) define the extent to which biological substances may become a resource appropriate to that environment. It should not be forgotten that approximately 20% of the globe is too cold for cultivation of humanly useful biota, 20% too dry and 20% too mountainous.[5]

Resources are subjective phenomena, a view emphasized by Zimmerman.[6] The phrase 'Resources are not: they become', frequently encountered in ex-amination papers, invites us to consider the extent to which the concept of resources requires discussion of how substances become available for use, the advantage of one location of occurrence as opposed to another, or one substance as opposed to another, and how the use itself came to be regarded as important.

The concept of social action is necessary to the definition of resources since it is the nature of a particular society at any one time that defines and creates a demand for a particular substance, and for storing and communicating know-ledge of its properties and its location. It is a particular society that creates the capacity to utilize the end product. Uranium, for example, was a substance of little or no value until knowledge of nuclear reactions became available and the appropriate technology to apply it to purposes of weaponry or power produc-tion were developed. These purposes are also socially defined. Alternatively, the value of some substances may disappear. Shale reserves in central Scotland were regarded in the late 19th and early 20th centuries as valuable sources of kerosene and other oil products until the availability of cheaper and easier-to-use imported crudes made their working uneconomic. The waste products, huge tips of tailings, scarred the landscape for decades until these too came to be of value as hard core for motorway construction in the 1960s. It is because resources are socially defined that it is appropriate to label historical epochs in material or energy terms: the Stone, Bronze and Iron Ages, and more recently the Steam Age (19th century), the Atomic Age or the Plastic Age (now).

The history of resources is the history of civilization around the world. Today, in the dominant urban-industrial culture of Western Europe and North America, few people are immediately occupied in the direct handling of re-

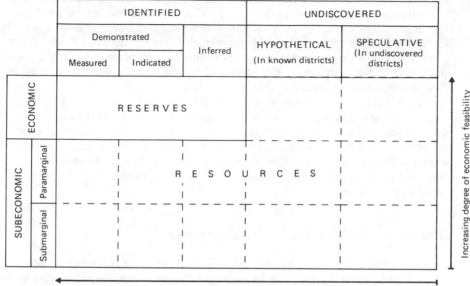

TOTAL RESOURCES

	IDENTIFIED			UNDISCOVERED	
	Demonstrated		Inferred	HYPOTHETICAL (In known districts)	SPECULATIVE (In undiscovered districts)
	Measured	Indicated			

Figure 1.2 Classification of Mineral Resources, The 'McKelvey Box'
Source: US Geological Survey Bulletin 1450A, 1976

sources, although many people depend on 'downstream' employment in their processing, distribution or marketing. Most of the raw materials of value to this society do not originate locally. Resource studies must therefore include study of transport technology, storage and trade. Most importantly, trade now dominates resource availability. Hence barriers to trade, particularly those of political origin, loom large. The term *strategic resource* has emerged in recent years in recognition of the fact that, under certain circumstances, the import of important raw materials may be disrupted to the great disadvantage of the home country. This makes stockpiling, the development of indigenous resources or substitutes and a resource-orientated foreign policy not only worthwhile but matters of some importance.[7]

Finally, looking to the future, there are resources that have achieved the status of *reserves* – raw materials for future development. These are of course defined in the context of today's techniques of discovery and current economic and technological conditions. Various classifications of reserves have been devised, particularly with regard to mineral resources. One such system is presented in Figure 1.2, 'McKelvey's Box'.[8] This is a matrix with columns defined from right to left in terms of an increasing degree of geological certainty as to the chemical composition, concentration, orientation and extent of certain deposits as well as constraints on access to them. Rows are defined in terms of profitability, with reference to markets, production costs and the availability of feasible processing techniques. The best possible case is to be found in the top left-hand corner, with a fully demonstrated and measured deposit which is economic to work. Deposits may then deteriorate by stages, through to the lower right-hand corner, where it is possible to conceive of a submarginal deposit in a district yet to be explored, i.e. a presently uneconomic concentration, the location of which has not yet been identified. The terms 'paramarginal' and 'submarginal' within the subeconomic category refer to the extent to which it is thought possible that changes in market demands or prices, or changes in the cost effectiveness of retrieval and processing techniques might come about in future to make the working of deposits feasible in financial terms. Paramarginal measured deposits might merely require an increment of change, such as occurred with oil prices in the early 1970s, making the exploitation of North Sea and Alaskan reserves feasible.

Such potential resources as those in the marginal categories are most difficult to define. If extraction costs fall without prices following suit, the number of deposits classified as measured and economic reserves is likely to grow. The technical improvements that can make economic reserves out of unprofitable assets are difficult to predict; it involves assessment of the likelihood of practical innovation in a very large number of fields of scientific enquiry and technological application.

1.3 The Use and Exploitation of Resources

In recent times there has been an explosion of interest in resources of one sort or another. In fuel, food, consumer goods and recreational pursuits, some people currently enjoy the use of more resources than previous generations even dreamt of. Others have fears over the future availability of resources: Will there be another energy crisis?; Will sugar or coffee run short in the supermarkets? Yet others have personal worries over the effects of resource-related developments on their way of life. The slogan of one New Zealand fringe party is apposite here:[9] 'We do not inherit the Earth from our parents – We borrow it from our children.' The ways in which resources are valued, made available and used are inherited, but worries have been increasingly expressed as to the extent to which 'more of the same' is now appropriate as a strategy for the future. Such themes are developed in Chapter 2. For the moment it is important to recognize the extent to which Zimmerman's subjective and functional approach to the conceptualization of resources invites us to consider major changes in social attitudes to resources, past, present and future. In the latter context, the environmental group Greenpeace have recently commissioned professional advertising in an attempt to remove one category of resource from society's list altogether. The result reads:[10]

'It takes up to 40 dumb animals to make a fur coat. But only one to wear it. If you don't want animals to be gassed, electrocuted, trapped or strangled, don't buy a fur coat.'

Whether this attempt to ridicule the deeply embedded view of the fur coat as a sensual status symbol will succeed remains to be seen. If it did succeed it would represent a most remarkable change in the values of human civilization and it would remove perhaps the oldest resource-based industry, hunting, from the economic agenda, with serious consequences for many small traditional communities.

A resource is anything that people in society value and can use. Firey has developed the idea of the crucial role of value judgements in the definition of resources by identifying three kinds of value judgement: economic, ecological and cultural.[11] Resources currently in the *economic* system are raw materials whose discovery, exploitation, processing and marketing is a source of profit and employment to many. Each step requires investment, often of staggeringly large proportions; to attract funds, a premium in the form of a high rate of return is often necessary, particularly when risks are high. These economic values bring several themes to resource studies. The operation of market laws determines the actions of resource businesses or public management. The trend towards huge enterprises of a transnational character with near monopoly powers over the market and a great deal of influence over the terms and conditions of supply gives rise to the theme of 'corporate imperialism' in the international geopolitics of resources (Chapters 3 and 4). Some resources have no market price and were regarded as 'free' until it came to be recognized that their consumption has adverse effects on others, perhaps on society as a whole, perhaps even threatening the future of the planet.

Cultural values bring with them an equally important array of relevant themes. Technology makes resources available but it can also make them redundant by finding cheaper substitutes. Technology can also be bad for your health: the human consequences of exposure to radiation, carcinogenic dust or harmful chemicals are often only discovered years after exposure. Growing materialism, especially in Western society where happiness is too often defined in terms of the contents of a bottle or access to a credit card, has fuelled an enormous growth in the demand for resources. More recently, a counter-culture has emerged, albeit affecting as yet only a relatively affluent minority, emphasizing the aesthetic value of the wilderness, of wildlife and the majesty of nature.[12] The political expression of such values through pressure groups has served to contain the production of resources but only to a limited extent.[13]

Ecological values further define and condition ideas about resources. Ecologists speak in terms of 'the web of life', of 'carrying capacity', 'limits to growth', and 'organic growth'.[14] The term 'web of life' serves to describe the interdependence that is now recognized to exist between plants, animals and the various characteristics of the physical environment. Each habitat produces a living response, and interference with either side of the equation must be expected to have certain consequences. Increasingly, people have come to the view that the human race ignores this interdependence at its peril. The extent to which a renewable resource may be cropped whilst sustaining its renewability is termed the 'carrying capacity'. This concept has been increasingly applied to human endeavour: are our economic and recreational activities appropriate to the capacity of our environment to sustain them? From here it is a short step to the notion that there are 'limits to growth', meaning that beyond a certain point further expansion of our activities causes environmental damage which is so costly to rectify that it draws a declining rate of return, to the extent that eventually all growth will be halted by the collapse of the necessary environmental support systems.[15] 'Organic growth' is suggested as a more viable alternative.[16] An organic thing, such as an oak tree, tends to grow slowly at first, then spurt to maturity in a phase of rapid growth; thereafter remaining at roughly the same size, in harmony with its environment. The growth of the human individual conforms to this pattern, and it has been suggested that human society should do likewise (Chapter 2).

Marxists and others argue that *people* are the ultimate resource. Marxists argue that all things of value are created by the labour and intellect of people. Similarly, liberal economists say that people are potential markets for goods and sources of talent, ideas and innovations.[17] In recent years, however, doomsday soothsayers have promoted the view that too many people are not so much a resource but a threat to the existing order of things, or more correctly, too many people of the wrong sort (in their eyes): the poor and the peasants of non-Western societies. Such views serve to place the relationship between population and resources, in the context of ecological ideas of 'limits to growth' and a 'global carrying capacity', at the centre of moral thought and international political activity.

1.4　The Actors in Resource Development and Use

In a sense everyone is an actor on the resource stage, either as a consumer or a voter. Relatively few individuals produce resources for others, but, generally, resources are the province of organizations. There is a hierarchy of sub-national, private organizations, regional public organizations, national and in-ternational organizations. Some actors are developers. Their role is to make resources available. Others are experts or technicians skilled in the means of so doing. Another set of actors, again to be found at all levels, are regulators. It is their job to make sure that the activities of developers do not exceed limits set in the interests of others, a task that invariably falls to governments because legal authority to enforce compliance is required. Definition of the relevant laws, performers, developers, experts and regulators is the task of later chapters.

At a global level, the United Nations organization has provided the forum and institutional setting for a great deal of activity seeking to help the recog-nition of resource problems, help the dissemination of possible solutions and alleviate stress and distress around the world. Meanwhile, the transnational corporations that dominate the supply of many major resource commodities represent, in the eyes of some, the pinnacle of achievement of capitalist effi-ciency of organization,[18] and in the eyes of others the greatest threat to human liberty and equality of opportunity presently faced by mankind. At the national level, governments have developed policies in the interests of their own national use of resources.

It is evident that resource studies have to be very wide ranging and embrace themes borrowed from a wide variety of disciplines. The view that resources reflect the values of society has been heavily emphasized here. In that light we now turn our attention to recent thinking[19] about the relationship between population, resources and the environment.

2 The Population and Resources Debate

2.1 Introduction

The theme of man's relationship with his environment is an old one,[1] but in recent decades it has acquired a new twist from the view that man might ultimately destroy his environment, and hence himself, unless urgent action on population, resources and environmental issues is taken. Two themes permeate recent literature. The first is that there are limits to the number of people that can be supported by a given resource base – in modern terms a concept of 'carrying capacity' for humans. The second is that growth in population elsewhere threatens to overrun home populations or undermine their position of supremacy and superiority. This can be called the geopolitical theme.

The prospect of widespread starvation and misery because of over-population is often referred to as the 'Malthusian spectre' after Thomas Malthus whose essay *A Summary View of the Principle of Population* has been widely quoted at various times.[2] Briefly, Malthus envisaged population inevitably growing at an exponential rate whereas the means of subsistence could be increased only at a much slower, arithmetic rate. It was therefore unavoidable that, unless 'preventative', voluntary checks on population growth were adopted, the 'positive' or inescapable checks of poverty, disease and death would 'naturally' regulate the levels of population back into balance with the means of support. Malthus urged the adoption of fertility control through the postponement of marriage to a relatively late age, thus ensuring a 'reasonable' rate of human reproduction (with the nutritional standards of the day, perhaps a total fertility rate of 2 or 3 children per family before the end of the fertile period, always assuming the observance of chastity outside marriage).

Malthus's pleas for such limits to population growth went largely unheeded by the people of England and Wales until the end of the 19th century when the birth rate began to fall towards replacement levels. The reasons for this fall in fertility are unclear in the context of a lack of detailed reporting of the motivations and actions of common folk. However, falling levels of child mortality as a consequence of better nutrition, a high degree of urbanization, social legislation restricting the capacity of children to earn their keep and dissemination of ideas of family planning, all appear relevant.[3]

Indeed, by the 1930s discussion of population problems in Britain and North America concerned the dangers of too low a rate of growth.[4] However desirable that children are born only if wanted, attention was being increasingly drawn by the leaders of Western civilization to the implications of a low birth rate and a static or even declining population. Their belief was that the power of a nation was directly related to its numerical strength and Imperial Japan and Nazi Germany, by way of justification for the invasion and forceful subjugation of neighbouring nations, argued that a large, strong nation was entitled to appropriate other people's territory. Contemporary quotations make the point:[5]

The habit of counting the cost [of children] will doubtless grow ... nations under western civilisation may ... lose their supremacy in world affairs and ... be invaded by people from other parts of the globe.

and:[6]

... in differing rates of population increase we find the major threat to world tranquility. The bulk of the mineral resources and the main unsettled lands of the earth are controlled by non-growing populations.

Historically, then, two fears pervade debate on population and resources: the spectre of society being destroyed from within as starving millions claw at each other for a share of a cake which is insufficient for all, and the spectre, even if things are in balance at home, of being invaded by a neighbour under that same pressure. For the parent of a well-nurtured pair of children, little could be more alarming than the idea that the 'good life' for which he or she had so carefully worked and planned could be destroyed by the irresponsibility of others at home and abroad.

By 1970, after a 'baby boom' in the immediate post-war years and the early 1960s, fertility in these countries again stood at barely above replacement level. Standards of living were unprecedentedly high for the majority of people. Things looked good for the new generations. Their parents had fought World War II in defence of a way of life which, as a result of the victory, dominated the world. But that victory had not been complete, and it had been sustained at a cost. War had forged a rival culture in Soviet communism. As tensions between the two great powers grew, the power to destroy the whole planet by a nuclear confrontation emerged. Concern for the future of humanity came to be voiced as the nuclear arms race gathered momentum. Kennedy and Khrushchev squared up to each other over Cuba in 1962. Soviet and American space missions beamed back to earth pictures of our small planet, instantly provoking a widespread re-appraisal of its vulnerability. In the West, the quality of life came under increasing scrutiny as mobility and leisure time were enhanced[7] by the unprecedented prosperity of the post-war period.

There emerged three views as to the role of population growth in such a changing social context, each reflecting different ideological leanings. Marxists believe that stresses attributed to 'overpopulation' are, in fact, reflections of inadequate social, economic and political structures. Some believers in the free market, on the other hand, believe that an increasing population will eventually stimulate innovation and economic expansion. A more conventional view holds that because in non-peasant societies children are unproductive they siphon off investment. Excessive population growth acts as a drag on economic development.

The purpose of this chapter is to briefly consider such ideas in the context of the general population–resources debate which has been taking place over the last two decades. Before doing so, however, it is useful to review current demographic trends. These are considered in full elsewhere[8] as are current views as to population policies.

2.2 Population Trends

2.2.1 Fertility

No human society exhibits the level of biological fertility that is theoretically attainable: everywhere fertility is socially controlled.[8] Nevertheless, substantial differences exist between nations. On the one hand, the advanced industrial countries have in recent years shown a remarkable decline in crude birth rates, while the nations of the 'South' have shown falling crude birth rates but only from a value that might be described as 'very high' to one that is still 'high'. Throughout Western Europe, crude birth rates hover around 11 or 12 per thousand. In the United States the figure is 16, and in Canada 15 per thousand. This compares with values in the mid-30s in tropical and central America and throughout Asia. In Africa average values lie in the high 40s. (Table 2.1).[9]

A number of factors appear to underly such differences. Some of these factors are structural; some are apparently related to lifestyle. Crude birth rates include males and females not able to bear children. In developed countries

Table 2.1: Crude birth rates in the major regions of the world and selected countries (per thousand). Source: H.R. Jones, Population Geography, Harper & Row, 1981, pp. 280–283

World	28		
Less Developed Countries	32	More Developed Countries	16
Northern Africa	42	North America	16
Egypt	38	Canada	15
Western Africa	49	United States	16
Ghana	48	Middle America	38
Nigeria	50	Mexico	37
Eastern Africa	48	Nicaragua	47
Kenya	53	Caribbean	28
Rwanda	50	Cuba	18
Tanzania	47	Jamaica	29
Middle Africa	45	Tropical South America	36
Central African Republic	42	Colombia	29
Zaire	46	Venezuela	36
Southern Africa	39	Temperate South America	24
South Africa	38	Argentina	26
Namibia	44	Northern Europe	13
South-West Asia	40	United Kingdom	12
Iraq	47	Sweden	11
Saudi Arabia	49	Western Europe	12
Middle-South Asia	37	West Germany	9
Bangladesh	46	Netherlands	13
India	34	Eastern Europe	18
Pakistan	44	East Germany	14
South-East Asia	36	Poland	19
Indonesia	35	USSR	18
Philippines	34	Southern Europe	15
East Asia	18	Greece	16
China	18	Spain	17
Japan	15	Oceania	20
		Australia	16

Table 2.2: Total fertility rates for the major regions of the world and selected countries (children per female). *Source:* Jones, op cit, 1981, pp. 280–283

World	3·8		
Less Developed Countries	4·4	*More Developed Countries*	2·0
Northern Africa	6·2	*North America*	1·8
Egypt	5·3	Canada	1·9
Western Africa	6·8	United States	1·8
Ghana	6·7	*Middle America*	5·3
Nigeria	6·9	Mexico	5·2
Eastern Africa	6·6	Nicaragua	6·6
Kenya	8·1	*Caribbean*	3·8
Rwanda	6·9	Cuba	2·5
Tanzania	6·5	Jamaica	3·7
Middle Africa	6·0	*Tropical South America*	4·6
Central African Republic	5·5	Colombia	3·9
Zaire	6·1	Venezuela	4·9
Southern Africa	5·2	*Temperate South America*	2·9
South Africa	5·1	Argentina	2·9
Namibia	5·9	*Northern Europe*	1·8
South-West Asia	5·8	United Kingdom	1·7
Iraq	7·0	Sweden	1·7
Saudi Arabia	7·2	*Western Europe*	1·6
Middle-South Asia	5·5	West Germany	1·4
Bangladesh	6·3	Netherlands	1·6
India	5·3	*Eastern Europe*	2·3
Pakistan	6·3	East Germany	1·8
South-East Asia	4·7	Poland	2·3
Indonesia	4·1	USSR	2·4
Philippines	5·0	*Southern Europe*	2·3
East Asia	2·3	Greece	2·3
China	2·3	Spain	2·6
Japan	1·8	*Oceania*	2·8
		Australia	2·1

there are more elderly women than there are in the less developed; the crude expression of births per thousand is therefore artificially low in comparison. An alternative measure, which is free of this structural problem, the 'Total Fertility Rate' (TFR), indicates the average number of children that would be born to each woman in the reproductive age group if mothers exhibited the current average birth characteristics of their society[10]. However, this statistic continues to reveal substantial differences, with values for Western Europe of around 1·7 and North America 1·8 per thousand, but of 4·5 or more in South America, 5·5 or more in much of Asia and 6·5 or more per thousand in Africa. There is thus a great deal of differentiation of fertility around the world. (Table 2.2.)

Similar differences are evident when comparing historical periods in the evolution of the 'developed' countries. The term 'demographic transition' has been coined to describe transformations from high rates of both birth and death to low rates of both, by way of a period of rapid population growth in which death rates fall faster than birth rates[11]. In this light, many see the present rapid growth rates of many of the less developed countries as a temporary phase to be endured until the transition is complete, thus following the pattern of the developed nations.

There is no guarantee that the transformation of fertility rates required for that to happen will be achieved. Jones has summarized the factors relevant to earlier transitions in terms of processes of urbanization, industrialization and secularization.[12] With urbanization, the extended family, composed of parents, aunts, uncles and grandparents, is said to give way to the nuclear family, placing the entire burden of young children on the parents or even, in effect, on only one, diminishing the attraction of large numbers. With industrialization, the opportunity for children to contribute their labour to family income is considerably delayed. Compulsory education (a requirement for an efficient work force, albeit, in global terms often curtailed at the age of twelve) and restrictions on child-labour in the interests of safety, almost double the age at which a child might become a net contributor to family fortunes – to fourteen or even twenty, as compared with eight on a peasant land holding.

In general, urbanization has also forced the implementation and development of measures of public health, designed to contain the danger of spreading infectious disease. These, alongside better understanding of nutritional needs and the development of programmes of pre- and anti-natal care, have reduced the incidence of infant mortality. Higher living standards and greater proximity of medical care have tended to reduce the need to have several pregnancies to ensure the survival of at least one offspring.

Industrialization also brings greater opportunities for the full-time employment of women, away from any possibility of simultaneously child minding, adding an extra disincentive to large families (but also, more positively, offering women opportunities for more economic independence and, perhaps, more personal fulfilment through job satisfaction). Industrial pursuits have changed and do change. This dynamism is reflected in greater social mobility. It is possible for a young person to 'get ahead' by being prepared to move between firms and places – but only, perhaps, if the benefits of children and a stable family life are sacrificed for career advancement, at least in the early years. Delaying the first birth until parents are in their late twenties considerably increases the probability of a family of only one or two children.

Education has become an important part of 'doing well', and this education has increasingly been secular, free from the religious doctrine that a family is blessed in proportion to the number of its children. Secular education reinforces a change in values away from having children and towards material reward and social standing beyond the family circle. Most modern urban-industrial countries have developed systems of welfare, so that the individual need not rely totally on his family for care in the event of accident or illness, widowhood or retirement by virtue of old age. Hence the insurance value of a large family is reduced.

Thus far, little has been said of the most obvious possible cause of falling fertility – contraception – for the very good reason that for birth control to be effective, there must be a wish not to conceive. In the UK the birth rate began to fall dramatically well before contraceptives became widely available and relatively convenient to use.[13] Where there is a will there is a way: in the past most usually coitus interruptus, involving no 'technology' at all, just motivation. Clearly, the current availability of sex education, contraception and advice makes the choice of few children easier, but the availability of the means does not, by itself, create the demand for it. Fertility levels, it would seem, are inseparable from wider economic and social considerations.[14]

It appears that currently low fertility levels in the UK, Europe and the USA result from a kind of cost-benefit calculation, reflecting the spread of materialistic values in Western society. On the other hand, in peasant, rural societies, the prevailing idea seems to be 'my children are my wealth'. This is because of the extra work children can do, the security for old age or accident they provide, and the lack of opportunity to acquire wealth without the direct investment or sale of labour. In developed societies, people wish themselves and their children to enjoy a standard of living, including substantial leisure and recreation, that is best afforded and secured by birth control. In this context, if it is true that economic development increases the standard of living and that that standard reflects modern Western values, then the slogan 'development is the best contraceptive' may well be apt.

Clearly, then, fertility appears to be socially controlled and the socio-economic structure of any particular society is important in predicting birth rates. The population–resources debate is therefore understandably linked with questions such as the industrialization and urbanization of society; of principles of social organization such as socialism or capitalism; and of 'development', meaning likely trends in patterns of employment, income and life style.

2.2.2 Mortality

The pattern of mortality also shows a distinct division between developed and less developed countries. Death rates in the developed nations vary between 7 and 12 per thousand whilst those of the less developed regions are typically around 20 per thousand in Africa and Asia (Table 2.3). A structural problem with the crude death rate statistic is once again apparent, however, in the paradox that many less developed countries have very low rates (for example, most Caribbean countries report values of 5, 6 or 7 per thousand). This is a reflection of very high fertility, which in turn means that a very high proportion of the population is below the age of twenty-five (between forty and fifty per cent), which further means that, excluding accidents or infant mortality, there is little 'exposure' to possible causes of death. A better measure of the extent to which populations enjoy full and healthy lives is their life expectancy at birth, expressed in years.[15] This figure is the average lifetime of the whole population. The longer most people live, the larger this figure will be. On the other hand, the more child deaths there are, the lower the average value.

Differences between 'North' and 'South' are demonstrated much more clearly in this way. In Europe, North America and Japan, values of over 70 years are the norm, in South America values in the 60s are most common, in the 50s throughout Asia, and in Africa, figures in the 40s are common. As with fertility, much of the world currently displays patterns of mortality now consigned to the history books of developed countries, where mortality rates have fallen over the last hundred years or more, largely through the eradication of infectious diseases, particularly those leading to high mortality amongst children. A number of causal factors have been identified and reviewed: higher standards of living in the form of improved nutrition and improved availability of key consumer goods; medical advances; public health developments and the possibility of a change in the character of the infections themselves.[16]

Warmer climates and lusher vegetation means that there are many more

Table 2.3: Crude death rates for the major regions of the world and selected countries (per thousand). *Source:* Jones, 1981, op cit, pp. 280–283

World	11		
Less Developed Countries	12	*More Developed Countries*	9
Northern Africa	13	*North America*	8
Egypt	10	Canada	7
Western Africa	19	United States	9
Ghana	17	*Middle America*	7
Nigeria	18	Mexico	6
Eastern Africa	19	Nicaragua	12
Kenya	14	*Caribbean*	8
Rwanda	19	Cuba	6
Tanzania	16	Jamaica	7
Middle Africa	20	*Tropical South America*	9
Central African Republic	19	Colombia	8
Zaire	19	Venezuela	6
Southern Africa	11	*Temperate South America*	9
South Africa	10	Argentina	9
Namibia	15	*Northern Europe*	11
South-West Asia	16	United Kingdom	12
Iraq	13	Sweden	11
Saudi Arabia	18	*Western Europe*	11
Middle-South Asia	16	West Germany	12
Bangladesh	20	Netherlands	8
India	15	*Eastern Europe*	11
Pakistan	16	East Germany	14
South-East Asia	13	Poland	9
Indonesia	15	USSR	10
Philippines	10	*Southern Europe*	9
East Asia	6	Greece	9
China	6	Spain	8
Japan	6	*Oceania*	9
		Australia	8

suitable habitats for vectors and micro-organisms of disease in the 'South' as compared with the 'North', and hence it seems easier to contemplate complete control in temperate lands. There is little doubt that one major factor in combating the spread of infectious disease has been the 'public health movement' which has led to measures of regulation and inspection designed to ensure the supply of wholesome, uncontaminated water supplies, the hygienic preparation, distribution and storage of food, the proper disposal of wastes and rotting organic matter, and the outlawing of damp, densely occupied accommodation. The benefits of such measures had spread to the major part of Europe and North America by the early decades of this century but, as is discussed in Chapter 7, much remains to be achieved, especially with regard to proper water supply in many parts of the world.

The advances and spread of modern medical care have also been a major factor in falling rates of mortality over recent decades, particularly in the 'South'. The creation of systems of health centres and the dissemination of antibiotic drugs and vaccines, often supported by the United Nations World Health Organization, have been spectacularly successful in many applications. Detailed analysis of the earlier fall in Europe suggest, however, that the contribution of the medical profession was by no means the most significant factor.[17] Instead, it would appear that advances in standards of living appear responsible for the major fall in rates of mortality from infections long before any effective modern treatment became available.

It seems that a substantial reduction in the incidence of malnutrition radically reduced mortality at the same time as consumer goods, such as more and better clothes and bedding, became more widely available, promoting a much greater degree of personal hygiene. It would appear that it is the poor who are hungry, and it is the hungry who die, along with their children, of infectious disease. Thus, there appears to be a relationship between 'development' and mortality as well as 'development' and fertility. The reader is warned, however, that McKeown reaches this conclusion by systematically demolishing other potential explanations for falling mortality, thus leaving no alternative to the hypothesis that:[18]

the health of man is determined essentially by his behaviour, his food and the nature of the world around him, and is only marginally influenced by personal medical care.

Some considerable support for this view is provided, however, when current major causes of death in the UK are examined. These are heart attacks and cancers of one type or another. There is mounting evidence that these diseases are related to diet, lifestyle, place and type of employment. There appears to be a relationship between a lack of physical work or exercise, an over-rich diet and heart disease. The tobacco smoker is definitely more likely to encounter either cancer or heart disease. Employees of certain industries appear to incur a greater risk of cancer. Further support for McKeown's claims comes from a comparison of trends in heart disease between the UK and the USA. In the UK, an elaborate National Health Service is in fact preoccupied with treating the symptoms and after-effects of disease. In the USA enterprising firms and public health programmes have energetically promoted an alteration of diets and the widespread adoption of exercising pursuits, such as jogging, with the result that a downward trend in heart disease has occurred.

The principal causes of death endured in the 'South' seem to stem from deficiencies in nutrition and public health. As with trends in fertility, again it would appear that the phrase 'development is good for your health' may be true, if better diets and environmental health facilities follow. But in the 'North' the principal causes of death appear to be related to work, environment and lifestyle, raising the truly ironic possibility that what has hitherto been seen as the 'good life', orientated towards an ever greater accumulation and consumption of goods, may be self-destructive.

2.2.3 Migration

In global terms, few international migrations are of significant size to influence the geography of the 'population problem' although the impact of massive migrations to North America and Australia in the 19th century should not be forgotten. Virtually all countries now have strict quotas and rules of entry, severely restricting the free movement of peoples from one part of the world to another. The importance of modern international migration lies in their tendency to be forced, arising either through expulsions (Asians from Uganda in

1968 or foreign workers from Nigeria in 1983) or through people fleeing from
an unacceptable régime (the Vietnamese boat people and the Kampuchean
exodus to Thailand). Wars and droughts have also engendered a mass movement of refugees suffering from poverty, malnutrition and ill-health. Such
movements, often substantial, create severe problems for humanity as a whole,
notwithstanding the efforts of a wide range of relief agencies, and create local
instances of the worst effects of population pressure on environments and
peoples.

In quantitative terms, the most significant migration has been the move to
the cities of vast numbers of the rural poor in the 'South'. If present trends
continue, by the end of the century more people will live in cities than in rural
areas. Most metropolitan areas have been growing in population at very high
rates, ranging from 5 to 12% per annum. The trend is most firmly established
in South America, but African capital cities are also expanding rapidly.[19]

Loraine quotes the case of Lagos, Nigeria. Lagos is one of Africa's fastest
growing cities with a forecast of twenty million inhabitants by the first decade
of the 21st century and with half of its population under the age of fifteen.[20]

Already the malign effects of overpopulation dominate Lagos – massive overcrowding,
inadequate housing, appalling sanitation, soaring infantile mortality rates, chaotic traffic,
pervasive water shortages, ubiquitous power cuts, port facilities clogged or stretched
beyond endurance. How much worse will all this be in twenty years from now?

The flight from the countryside in part reflects economic conditions there. But
it is also indicative of the extent to which cities offer a symbol of hope for the
future, especially through education. The implications of a large and lively
urban population attracting the major part of their government's attention are
dealt with in our discussion of rural development policy in Chapter 12 and the
problems of water supply are considered in Chapter 7.

A number of themes have been outlined that can fairly be called population
related problems. A significant development of the 1960s was the extent to
which such themes became intertwined with questions of resources and the
quality of the environment, and in particular with the future of both in the face
of rapid population growth, which peaked in global terms at around 2% in the
late 1970s although now at around 1·7% per annum.[21] This, however, merely
represents the difference between a doubling of world population in 41 years
as compared with the previous 25 years.[22] Inevitably, questions arose as to
whether twice as many people could be accommodated in little more than a
generation without causing serious resource and environmental consequences
for those of us already here.

2.3.1 The Doom Decade

Among the first things to capture public attention was the environmental effect
of modern agricultural practices. In 1965, there appeared an evocative narrative
by Rachel Carson, *Silent Spring*. This was one of the first popular ecologies,
identifying the insecticide DDT as a highly dangerous threat to the web of
life[23]. The prospect of a world without natural wildlife was raised. Birds surviving direct ingestion of DDT were said to be rendered sterile. Nature reserves
and bird sanctuaries could be poisoned by run-off from elsewhere. Domestic

livestock could also be affected, and Carson claimed that every meal Americans eat potentially carried with it chlorinated hydrocarbons as the spraying and dusting of crops became universal. Could the human nervous system, chromosomes and genes stand up to such an onslaught? Carson thought it better not to wait and see. She advocated immediate research into, and development of more natural means of pest control by harnessing the predators that already exist in natural ecosystems.

Not only food was seemingly contaminated. Water was also tainted. Among the many popular paperbacks which appeared in the mid-1960s highlighting environmental pollution, *Disaster by Default* by Frank Graham, which appeared in 1966,[24] provided a catalogue of polluting incidents and practices. Graham and others argued for more effective control over industry and municipalities to safeguard the water resources of the United States.

Other aspects of the environment received similar study – air pollution, urbanization, noise pollution and the despoilation of the wilderness. These issues raised the question of the purpose of continued economic growth. *Moment in the Sun* by R. and L. Rienow is typical[25] of the reaction against the expansion of consumer goods production. How long could such prodigious consumption last before raw materials became scarce? Shades of Malthus were here combined with the geopolitical theme of concern over population growth abroad. The Rienows came right out with it:[26]

We find our glowing future shadowed not only by our abnormal appetite but by the fecundity of people the globe over. Can the US be comfortable in a world of agony, asks population expert [sic] Dr Isaac Asimov. A more vital question might be: How safe will this food rich nation be, with the half-starved hordes of the world straining at every boundary? How long will paper treaties contain them?

Scientific advances, widely thought to have undermined the strictures of Malthus, would not help this time, it was argued. It was science and technology that were putting such strain on the resource base of the 'good life'. Americans were reminded that they accounted for 5½% of the earth's people but consumed half of its total product. In one year Americans consumed enough big trees to build a ten-foot boardwalk thirty times around the world at the equator.

There were no material solutions to the impending resource crisis:[27]

Only a powerful social effort involving the abandonment of aggrandisement as the national creed – in short, the acceptance of a totally new code of values – can bring us into equilibrium with our environment and perhaps prolong our moment in the sun.

Such arguments reached their zenith in what might be called the 'Ehrlich phenomenon'. Paul and Anne Ehrlich published two works[28] on *Human Ecology* and *The Population Bomb* encapsulating what has come to be called the neo-Malthusian view. The basic argument was that the world was already overpopulated and the trend of developments unsound from an ecological point of view. Population levels had overshot the carrying capacity of the planet so that life could now be sustained only by consuming capital resources, fossil fuels and other non-renewable resources, and by poisoning ecological systems. Because of overpopulation, the life support systems of the planet were being poisoned, which would in the long run change the pattern of weather and affect food production. Greater competition for dwindling resources would precipitate tensions so great that nuclear war might be triggered. And that would be that. The message was clear: the world must repent before it was too late. But how?

One major response came from an unlikely source. In 1968 Aurelio Peccei, an Italian businessman, formed the 'Club of Rome', an international group of business people, civil servants, academics and politicians.[29] Although it was not made particularly clear at the time, this group were concerned to bring to the attention of the world's leaders the nature of the 'world problematique' (by which they meant the interrelated issues of population growth, environment and moral decline). Looking for ways of moving the hearts and minds of men, they produced computer models and mathematical formulae giving reasonably credible predictions of what might happen if current trends continued unabated.

One of these exercises became an international best-seller: *The Limits to Growth*.[30] The basic thesis of this report was that because our environment, the earth, is finite, the growth in human population and the spread of industrialization could not continue indefinitely. Malthus with numbers, one might say. But there was more to it than that. The figures fed into the computer model were adjusted to simulate policies that might be adopted to stave off the predicted 'overshoot and collapse'.

In the initial run of the model no major changes in physical, economic or social relationships were assumed. But later runs accommodated the possibility of technical and other changes, albeit crudely. The initial run predicted overshoot and collapse of the world system because of a diminishing resource base. In the second run it was assumed that unlimited resources as nuclear energy replaced fossil fuels and enabled lower grade non-renewable materials to be developed economically. In this run, the limit to growth appeared in the form of mounting pollution levels leading to widespread environmental degradation, ecological collapse and the consequent failure of food supplies. In a third run it was assumed that strict measures of pollution control were introduced. These averted the pollution crisis of the previous run, but overshoot and collapse occurred once again because of food shortage, the limit of agricultural land having been reached. In a fourth run, therefore, it was assumed that the land question was being tackled by universal adoption of techniques designed to greatly improve the productivity of available land. Such techniques are known collectively as the Green Revolution and are discussed in Chapter 5. But agricultural and industrial growth, thus set free from constraint, overshot and again brought ecological collapse, notwithstanding controls over pollution. It seemed, then, that there were limits to growth even if appropriate technical advances in the spheres of non-renewable resources, pollution control and food production were forthcoming.

Finally, the model was run assuming a rapid halt to population growth. A limit to growth was still predicted before the year 2100 through the medium of three simultaneous crises: over-use of land leading to erosion and other forms of environmental damage so that food production fell; non-renewable resources being depleted to the point of scarcity; and a rise in levels of pollution. However, after a period of crisis and distress, when per capita income and food consumption fell, a lower level of sustainable living could be achieved.

The message was clear: there were limits to growth, and only population limitation could make any real impact in averting 'overshoot and collapse', although technical advances in resource production, pollution control and food production would also be necessary.

Not surprisingly, such startling conclusions provoked a widespread critical reaction. Much comment concerned the assumptions made in the model and the quality of the data that had been processed. Clearly, any such endeavour is liable to the 'GIGO' effect: if garbage is fed in, garbage will be printed out. Equally, it is an impossible task to model the workings of the global economy and various lifestyles adequately. A run of the model in reverse, using the data and the model to predict the present from a point in the past failed to reveal anything recognizable. From the debate that followed the publication of *The Limits to Growth*, however, three fundamental points emerge. First, it is note-worthy that the debate took place at all. Such themes apparently struck a chord in the hearts and minds of many people. Second, it brought into focus the question of the utility of the two great ideologies of Western civilization – free enterprise and Marxism. Devotees of the free market system pointed out that new demands, levels of income and unprecedented industrial activity would stimulate technological innovation at an increased rate. Had technical progress, in response to lower levels of economic growth, not been astonishingly rapid in recent decades? Why should this not continue under the influence of the even greater levels of stimulus predicted? On the other hand, many a Marxist must have welcomed the publication of the work with a knowing smile. Was this predicted overshoot and collapse not the final crisis of over-production that Marx had predicted? Would this not mark the end of capitalism as a form of social organization?

Not only Marxists read this message. A number of works at around the same time called for a restructuring of social organization and hence contri-buted to the general debate on population, resources and the future of mankind. Notable among these was E.F. Schumacher's *Small is Beautiful*.[31] Also signi-ficant was the growing ecological movement, as represented by the Ecological Magazine's special issue, *Blueprint for Survival*.[32] In *Small is Beautiful*, concern over the implications of modern technology was raised. The essential problem according to Schumacher was one of the choice of scale. The trend was towards large enterprises that were wasteful and inefficient in their use of resources and the environment. Better use of both would follow the adoption of a small scale of organization for living and production because of closer contact with the realities of resource use and environmental degradation. Similarly, *Blueprint for Survival* envisaged a viable future through the acceptance of 'natural limits' and respect for all living things – the ecocentric point of view. An end should be put to population growth, the discharge of all toxic substances, the apparently insatiable growth in energy consumption, and the overconcentration of people through urbanization. Instead, we should adopt low impact technol-ogies, environmentally acceptable production processes and a 'steady state eco-nomic system' compatible with maximum resource self-sufficiency in a society decentralized into autonomous tribal units. The social culture of Western civi-lization should switch from an emphasis on growth and materialist acquisition to one of social well-being and the 'quality of life'.[33]

Thus far, however, little had been said of the major part of humanity, which does not live in the West or the Soviet bloc. Surely this dimension of the global futures debate could not be ignored? Indeed it could not. Working on behalf of the United Nations (UN), Leontief had developed another world model and in 1973 published his predictions as to the effects of the UN's 'International Development Strategy' then being promoted.[34] It seems that existing plans for the UN's 'Second Development Decade' would be insufficient to cope with levels of population growth. Unlike *The Limits to Growth*, Leontief felt that resource endowment would be adequate to support economic development around the world at relatively high rates, although pollution and environmental degradation might become serious problems if appropriate measures of management were not taken. In fact,[35] 'the principal limits to sustained economic growth and accelerated development are political, social and institutional'. A better functioning of institutional structures was necessary. This primarily involved changes in 'North–South' relations, specifically in the terms and conditions of trade.

This was the theme that came to dominate the global futures debate. We return to it below. Meanwhile, the geopolitical theme of 'them against us' also entered the debate in such forms as Robert Heilbroner's view of *The Human Prospect*. He saw the key problem as:[36]

The descent of large portions of the underdeveloped world into a condition of steadily worsening social disorder, political apathy intermingled with riots and pillaging when crops fail – ruled by dictatorial governments serving the interests of a small economic and military upper-class and presiding over the rotting countryside.

That population pressure would increase the gap between rich and poor nations had been a prominent prediction of all models. Nuclear blackmail and wars of redistribution, as predicted by the Ehrlichs, must be anticipated.[37]

We are entering a period in which rapid population growth, the presence of obliterative weapons and dwindling resources will bring international tension to dangerous levels for an extended period.

From the coming ecocatastrophe engendered by gross imbalance between population, resources and the degrading effects of economic growth on the common environment, only two outcomes were possible: anarchy or totalitarianism. Only authoritarian régimes were likely to be able to cope with problems arising from the central environmental issues of the future. Things were serious.

2.3.2 The Institutional Response

Such warnings as these were not confined to popular literature. Through their connection with 'development' and economic growth, the issues of global population, resources and environment took the stage at the United Nations with increasing frequency during the 1970s. In 1971 a meeting on 'Development and Environment' was convened in Fouvex, Switzerland, at which the connections between economic growth in the developing countries and the global environment were explored. How could industrialization be achieved without disastrous environmental side-effects? And how could the costs of the new environmental policies now being advocated by the growing environmental movement of the developed countries be defrayed without worsening the terms of trade (increasing the costs of imports) for the developing countries? Signs that these issues could be tackled successfully allowed the now celebrated 'Stockholm Conference' to proceed.

The United Nations Conference on the Human Environment took place in Stockholm in June 1972 and was attended by 113 governments, most of the membership of the United Nations. The notable exceptions were the countries of the Soviet bloc. The agenda had been under preparation since 1970 and involved problems of urbanization, natural resources, pollution of land and sea, as well as the environmental implications of industrialization and the conservation of wildlife and its habitat. At the end of the day a declaration was produced and an action plan of 109 recommendations accepted.

Although often vague and characterized by compromise to the point of near meaninglessness, these have shaped action since. Perhaps most important was the resulting tendency to divide the issues into their specialist parts and to continue investigating and discussing them. The United Nations Environmental Programme (UNEP) was established to act as 'the environmental conscience of the UN system',[38] coordinating the environmental activities of UN agencies and other international organizations and stimulating activity on the part of individual national governments.

A series of conferences dealing with specific issues followed: on population at Bucharest in 1974, on food and agriculture at Rome in 1975, on international economic cooperation at Paris in the same year, and in 1976 on trade and development in Nairobi, on the human habitat in Vancouver and the law of the sea in New York. Clark and Timberlake have reviewed progress over the 1970s.[39] They see a mixed result, with some substantial progress in the conservation of wildlife, more national parks, a world conservation strategy and conventions on trade in endangered wildlife and animal products. Concern over pollution has stimulated a worldwide campaign for better drinking water, but oil pollution at sea has worsened and the seriousness of the problem of acid rain is said to be increasing. The basic problem remains, however: that of meeting 'the inner (minimum) limits of basic human needs' without violating the outer limits of the planet's resources and environment. The question is not so much 'What to do?' but 'How to do it?', as detailed studies of population, resources and environmental problems continue to shed light on the inadequate institutional structures which mankind has thus far developed. There is now growing agreement that environmental ills are not caused by absolute shortages of resources, or even by 'over-population', but by economic maldistribution and social maladministration.

Of course, the United Nations has not been the only forum for exploring the future. In both the United Kingdom and the United States, reports have appeared with a view to advising government. In Britain, the Cabinet Office of the Labour Government (1974–1979) published a discussion paper on world trends in population, resources and pollution and their implications in 1976.[40] The main problem foreseen for the United Kingdom was that of obtaining and paying for imported raw materials, particularly food and energy. The result of rapid population growth in the developing countries was seen as a principal future change, with the population of the developed countries falling from 30 to 20% of the total by the year 2000 to an ultimate level of as low as 10%. The long term limits to expanding food production in the developing countries were seen as energy-related, although in physical terms the world could meet its needs for the next thirty or forty years. However, because of economic, social and political problems leading to maldistribution and less than optimal production, this situation was unlikely to be realized.

The official British view was that in the long term, only the universal adoption of anti-natal policies was likely to prevent mass starvation. New technology and research could be expected to keep pollution levels in balance. Increasingly improved and extended monitoring would ensure that pollutants

were less frequently allowed to reach danger levels, except as a result of unforeseen developments, accidents or social or economic disruption.

Such themes also figure prominently in the *Global 2000 Report* commissioned by President Carter in 1977 but not published until 1982.[41] The principal conclusions of this report are that serious stresses involving population,
resources and environment are clearly visible ahead, although not becoming
pressing until next century. Nevertheless, bearing in mind the relatively long
lead and lag times required for new developments and policies:[42]

Vigorous, determined new initiatives are needed if worsening poverty and human suffering, environmental degradation, and international tension and conflicts are to be
prevented.

The worrying news, according to this view, was that:

... there are no quick fixes. Problems of population resources and the environment are
inextricably linked to some of the most perplexing and persistent problems in the world
– poverty, injustice and social conflict.

Repeatedly, problems of economic and social administration emerge as the root
cause of principal elements of concern over global futures. This was in line
with the alternative views to those of the Ehrlichs and *The Limits to Growth*
and these are now reviewed.

2.3.3 Alternative Views

It was not long before the stunning message of the doom purveyors became
the subject of widespread and detailed critical analysis. For example, The
Social Science Research Council in Britain supported, with others, work by the
Science Policy Research Unit at the University of Sussex enquiring into questions of modelling the future and the derivation of likely future scenarios.[43] In
the volume that resulted, *Thinking about the Future*, detailed and convincing
criticisms of the forecasting and techniques of computer simulation appeared.
Subsequently, the team took a look at the substantive issues.[44] Notwithstanding
the fact that political upheavals of major significance such as two world wars,
the Vietnam war and the Russian Revolution could never have been predicted,
the team were able to put together their own array of futures.

They found it impossible to integrate the three major sectors of food, energy
and materials into a generalized approach while retaining rigorous methodological accuracy. Indeed:[45] 'While we have cast our net perhaps more widely
than some others, we have caught no new fish'. Nevertheless, their studies
suggested that physical limits in the provision of food were not the main problem now, and need not be in future. The energy sector did face serious problems but, once again, not of physical limits.[46] Even here, in 'the most difficult
sector, the desirable future is not beyond our reach'. The regional distribution of resources was likely to cause more problems than overall worldwide
shortages.

What was important about the global futures debate was the ideological
stance of the viewer. Several different viewpoints could be developed: 'conservative', 'Malthusian', 'environmentalist', 'radical' or 'technological determin-
ist'. The Malthusian and environmentalist viewpoints have already been indi-

cated in the previous sections. In this section, the other views are noted. Technical optimism as a world view may be represented by Herman Kahn, whilst an optimistic conservative view is represented by Julian Simon, and Karen Michaelson bears the 'radical' standard.

Herman Kahn undertook a series of studies on global futures at the Hudson Institute, New York.[47] He thought that limits to growth were most likely to arise from psychological, cultural or social limits to demand, or from incompetence. He saw the main problem as the fact that:[48]

... science and technology – which in western civilisation removed poverty, illiteracy, hunger, frequent and severe disease, and short life spans for the majority of people, and created for them instead relative affluence, improved health and medical care, longer life expectancy and a sense of increasing power – now appear to some groups to raise a general threat to the continuation of our civilisation.

He argued that scientific and technical progress could not and should not be stopped. What was needed was a greater alertness and greater attention to the mistakes and undesirable impact of innovations. It could and would be done:[49]

... most predictions of damage hundreds of years from now tend to be incorrect because they ignore the curative possibilities inherent in technologies and economic progress.

Similarly optimistic is the 'conservative' view of Julian Simon in his book *The Ultimate Resource*. He too argues that the application of technology, the result of the stimulation of competition and demand in a free market economy, would continue to benefit and improve the condition of mankind. In his eyes the fundamental resource is people. More people create a larger market for food and services, stimulating development, innovation and improvement. More people bring more talent and intellect to bear on present problems, thus making their solution more likely. Population growth, therefore, does not pose a permanent threat but, on the contrary, brings with it the very tools needed to overcome obstacles and improve the standard of living. He says:[50]

History since the industrial revolution does not support the simple Malthusian model. No negative relationship between population growth and economic growth is revealed. ... the on-balance effect of additional persons is positive, an attractive 'investment' compared to other social investments.

Simon might be called conservative because of his belief in the utility of the present world economic system. He says that in the short run all resources are limited. In the short run, a greater use of any resource means pressure on supplies. But the long run is a different story:[51]

The standard of living has risen along with the size of the world's population since the beginning of recorded time. And with increases in income and population have come less severe shortages, lower costs, and an increased availability of resources, including a cleaner environment and greater access to natural recreation areas.

He sees no reason why such trends should not continue. Simon does say, however, that very high rates of population growth in the least developed countries may overload the capacity of society to cope; moderation is called for.

The radical view of the population-resources debate is quite simple. As Michaelson has put it:[52]

Contrary to much of classical economics, surplus population – that is, the number of people who are unemployed or underemployed – arises not because of natural increase outstripping resources but because the accumulation of capital, which this very population makes possible, allows investment in such things as automated machinery, which makes the people superfluous.

Further, Marxists view the relationship between capitalism and the natural environment as a parasitic one.[53] Capitalists are envisaged as expropriating the 'free goods' of resources, clean air and water for their own profit, while not adding anything in return. Hence the analogy with a parasite, something that takes from its host without contributing any benefit to it. The radicals see the problem in terms of removing capitalism and replacing it with a system that allocates the means of earning a living – jobs, land or resources – on a different basis. Socialist and Marxist régimes have attempted to do this but it is not possible to point to any existing examples of astounding success, with the possible exception of China.

Sandbach has briefly examined socialist policy with regard to environmental problems in China.[54] Admittedly, there was no specifically environmental policy in China before 1970 but economic development policies had included strategies of low-level technology, land reclamation and the like which had beneficial effects on resource and pollution problems. He is impressed, as have others been, with regard to the relative success of population policy.

2.4 The Geopolitics of Population–Resource Issues

It is difficult to avoid the conclusion that the population–resources debate was seen by many to be a question of ideology: the free market system versus its Marxist critics. This theme is not merely of academic interest, as ideological struggles for the hearts and minds of men continue around the world and the superpowers face up to each other in nearly every corner of the globe. For some, these politics pose a threat to the investment climate for resource production, for others they form a basis for starting a movement towards a higher standard of living for the mass of humanity. These politics create the circumstances for mass misery as confrontation moves to local wars and disruption.

2.4.1 Imperialism

Much of the politics of unrest around the world revolves around the concept of imperialism. Marx saw imperialism as an essential phase in the development of capitalism. As profits are reinvested and more and more capital goods are used to produce goods, it becomes increasingly difficult to make profits unless either the costs of capital can be reduced or the rate of exploitation of labour increased. Marx saw colonies as satisfying these two needs. The role of the colonies, according to this view, was to provide cheap raw materials and provide a new, controlled mass market for goods.

Whether Marxist views have any substance or not, the capitalist world does reflect an international division of labour, with the 'North' the principal source of manufactured goods and the 'South' being heavily involved in the production of raw materials. The role of the colonial empires in the commodity trades is discussed in Chapter 4. Of interest here is the inclusion in the radical view of the global future of the notion of the evil effects of economic imperialism. These are also considered with regard to population. Michaelson says:[55]

While the demand for higher quality labour in the industrialised world resulted in a reduced fertility rate (known as the demographic transition), the penetration of industrial capitalism into the Third World had quite the opposite effect. A number of factors – taxation, land expropriation, the introduction of the plantation system, and so forth – all freed the peasantry for wage labour. At the same time, there was an increased demand for low quality labour as the tertiary sector expanded and the labour of children was increasingly valuable. As mortality declined with the introduction of immunisation programmes and rudimentary health care services, fertility rose to meet the new demands of labour; these processes worked to produce an increase in overall population in many Third World nations.

If the effect of economic imperialism has been to create a pool of cheap labour and dispense with higher paid workers at home, why worry? Again, Michaelson has an answer:[56]

... an abundance of cheap labour in the Third World, coupled with extensive unemployment and poverty, is also dangerous to capitalism. For while they are needed for capitalist expansion and accumulation, the masses of unemployed may voice their discontent by trying to wrest control over their life circumstances from those in power. Rather than lose control of economic resources, the ruling elite proposes to control the numbers of the population of the poorer classes. It is an inherent contradiction of capitalism that the same system which proposes population control programmes also, by its control over individual lives, sets the conditions for high fertility, extensive labour migration, and other distortions of capitalist development.

The ideological conflict of interpretation of global problems of population and resources also has real and continuing substance.

2.4.2 The Global Futures Debate (2): Towards a New International Economic Order

In 1974 a successor to *The Limits to Growth* appeared from the Club of Rome. Entitled *Mankind at the Turning Point*, the results of a regionally disaggregated projection were presented.[57] Two gaps, steadily widening, now appeared to be at the heart of 'mankind's present crisis':[58] the gap between man and nature; and the gap between 'North' and 'South', rich and poor. This text was less pessimistic than *The Limits to Growth* on resources. The long-term availability of resources should not be taken for granted but it now seemed that planned population growth, at reducing levels, was a feasible future. But, even with a slowing of population increase, and without severe resource scarcities, it seemed likely that the gap between rich and poor nations would widen to the point of the regional collapse of South-East Asia. This would be followed by a 'domino effect' throughout the rest of the world economic system.

Mankind was at the turning point, for if such a catastrophe was to be avoided, the rich would have to slow their rates of growth and allow the 'South' the expansion that could be sustained within ecological limits. A central concept to the thesis was that of 'organic growth'. This is how an oak tree grows, slow at first, then sprinting to maturity, to be followed by a relatively long period of steady state. This rhythm of growth was what regions of the world should aspire to. Those regions that were economically mature should be content to adopt and adapt to a steady state. The 'South' could then enter its sprint to maturity. What should not happen was the continuation of undifferentiated (exponential) growth everywhere.

Such a transition would require a new world economic order and cooperation in allocating respective roles to regions of the world – something never seen before. Cooperation could avoid catastrophe. Global issues required global action. Questions then arose as to the exact nature of such action, and as to how cooperation could be achieved.

In 1976, the Club of Rome published its answers under the title *Reshaping the International Order*.[59] This text was even less pessimistic on the question of physical limits, stating that it was now accepted that fears concerning the exhaustion of natural resources may well have been exaggerated. This time there was no computer model featured and the emphasis was on the institutional arrangements that might save mankind. A major role was foreseen for the United Nations in coordinating bargaining between the producers of raw materials and their consumers with a view to transferring economic growth away from the rich 'North' to the poor 'South'. The 'North' and 'South' should develop industries in which they had clear comparative advantages, and alter patterns of trade towards living in symbiosis in the future. The dependency of the economies and peoples of the 'South' should be reduced through action on a wide variety of fronts. Typical of the approach were the recommendations for the mineral resource sector.[60] Three objectives had to be achieved:
(1) producer countries should receive a much fairer share of the final retail price of their raw materials; (2) price stabilization should be introduced through internationally agreed mechanisms; (3) an international structure of institutions should be established to work towards a real world market and world taxation policy for minerals. Action on these fronts would remove the obstacles to economic development led by mineral exploitation in countries of the 'South' and involve a massive transfer of resources and profits away from the 'North'.

A similar approach came from another body in 1980. The Brandt Report, entitled *North–South: A Programme for Survival*,[61] represented the views of an independent commission on international development issues. The central idea of the report was that a massive promotion of the economic development of the 'South' was in the best interests of the rich countries of the 'North'. It was a much more pragmatic approach than that of the Club of Rome. Action was urged to transfer substantial resources to the poverty belts of Africa and Asia. Intensified agricultural development was necessary to alleviate the hunger of 800 million people. The earnings of commodity producers needed strengthening and the value adding (and employment generating) stages of processing and manufacture required relocation. Reform of international monetary and development financing was necessary, as were controls over the investment decisions of transnational corporations, all to create a stable investment climate on which a future could be built. Overall, there were several reasons for 'Northern' participation in a 'North–South' dialogue. There was a moral imperative to tackle disparities of wealth and quality of life. A new rapport between 'North' and 'South' could stimulate export markets and revive world trade. The danger of default on the part of existing 'Southern' borrowers was very real: it could only be permanently staved off through a negotiated re-ordering of world trade, otherwise the financial systems of the 'North' could fall into chaos. Finally, a geopolitical threat existed in the form of a spectre of ideological confrontation in a morass of economic stagnation and environmental degradation.

The British Prime Minister, Mrs Margaret Thatcher, found[62] 'a great deal in the Brandt Commission's Report with which the British Government agree'. But she went on to deny the fundamental assumptions on which the report had been built, saying:[63]

It is no longer realistic to speak of rich industrial countries and poor Third World countries; there are marked degrees of poverty and of prosperity within both worlds, and they are not determined by geography. The term 'North–South', implying as it does a simple division of needs and interests, is an inadequate and often misleading description of the complex inter-relationship that now exists between countries in a wide variety of economic circumstances.

This interrelationship required stability. That meant not altering the status quo to any great extent. Instead, the industrialized countries could make a contribution by returning to rapid economic growth. This would require the fight against inflation to be given top priority (hence increases in commodity prices should be avoided). Private investment in development must be encouraged (not constrained through adverse regulation of transnational corporations). The oil exporting countries should use their income to help other developing countries ('South–South' dialogue).

In the light of this view it came as no surprise that the international conference on the Brandt Commission's ideas at Cancun, Mexico, in 1982 failed too make any headway, especially since the Reagan administration took a similar line. The views of governments, perhaps naturally more concerned with their own domestic interests, appear to contrast markedly with those of academics on the nature of the relationships presently existing on planet earth.

For example, Nigerian geographer Mabogunje has defined 'North–South' relations as being of the 'core'–'periphery' type. Until 1945:[64]

the global relationship between the centre and the periphery was seen within the benign context of the international division of labour in which the centre specialised in the production of industrial goods and the periphery in the production of agricultural and other primary commodities such as minerals.

Since then trends have worked towards a relationship of more and more unequal exchange. The 'North' has expanded the value of its exports while the value of commodity returns has remained stable or fallen in real terms. The transnational corporations have emerged as a dominating form of institutional structure, reinforcing the superior bargaining power of the 'centre', because, among other things, of their central location within the global communications network and better access to information and finance. The periphery has responded in three ways, each of which has given calls for a new international order a real political impetus, often using the United Nations as a forum for calls for progress. First, the 1960s saw a wave of nationalizations and joint ventures in an attempt to gain more control through ownership. Mabogunje says there was an average of 45·5 nationalizations annually between 1960 and 1969, rising to 93·3 over the following period 1970 to 1974.[65] Second, various strategies of technology transfer have been applied, with the establishment of national research institutes, government ministries of technology, industrial development banks and programmes of overseas training. A major constraint here, noted by Mabogunje, however, is the extent to which transnational corporations hold patents to processes and guard them well. Third, there has been a growing appreciation of the advantages of regional economic groupings on the lines of the European Economic Community and the development of commodity producer associations. The latter have hardly been successful, however, as discussed in Chapter 4. Notwithstanding what leading politicians of the 'North' say, there are very real trends supporting the notion of a need for a new, less confrontational, 'North–South' dialogue.

The Brandt Commission produced a second volume in 1983.[66] In the year since its original report the world economy had stagnated. The industrial countries had aimed to control inflation and protect their currencies. Recession had dramatically reduced commodity earnings in the 'South'. Debt service repayments had risen in line with Northern interest rates. New proposals were[67] '... directed to averting world economic collapse and the subsequent chaos and human suffering and to creating conditions leading to world economic recovery'. The need for action was urgent. Prospects for the future looked grim.

The 'North–South' debate provides essential background for the view of global resource trends and issues that follows in subsequent chapters. It also explains, in its transition from initial worries over adverse impacts of undifferentiated and rapid economic growth to its more recent phase of concern over the global effect of recession, why the environmental and resource issues arose and now appear to be momentarily in decline. More immediate spectres of distress have grabbed the headlines – unemployment and economic depression. Like those concerning the 'North–South' dialogue, issues of environment and resources are still there; they have merely been obscured by more immediate preoccupations closer to home.

3   Energy

3.1.1 In all ecosystems, as indeed in all studies of resource processes, the role of energy is crucial. Without the input of energy from the sun, life could not exist; the movements of air and water in the atmosphere are driven by this source, and even non-renewable sources of a geological nature have been formed as a result of solar energy.[1]

Solar radiation plays the most important role in our energy system. Throughout time man has refined his technology to harness this energy in its various forms. Simmons identifies two main kinds of energy sources – 'equilibrium' and 'non-equilibrium' sources of energy.[2] In the first, energy flows would be present without man's interference. The conversion of solar energy by photosynthesis, energy in winds, waves and water, gravitational energy in the form of tidal currents and the heat from the earth's crust (geothermal energy) – these are equilibrium sources of energy. Such energy forms are fairly ubiquitous although only a limited number of sites have been commercially developed.

By contrast, non-equilibrium sources are relatively concentrated and localized. These could only have been developed with human technology. Fossil fuels, which have slowly accumulated throughout geological time, yield their energy upon combustion. Nuclear energy is released as a result of the fission of the uranium isotope U235. Technological innovation has facilitated the rapid development of such non-equilibrium sources of energy. However, non-equilibrium resources are finite in nature, and man's insatiable appetite for these energy forms has placed a strain on our economic and political systems. Only now has man reached a crossroads on his developmental pathway. In the transition to a renewable and/or nuclear fusion future, the geopolitics of supply and demand for non-equilibrium resources will remain a key issue in world affairs.

3.2.1 Patterns of Demand and Supply

Man has thus turned full circle in the exploitation of energy sources. Primitive man used only solar energy, in the form of plants for food and wood for fires. Industrial man, substituting machinery for labour, developed non-equilibrium sources of energy. His successor – 'post-industrial man' – may hope ultimately to utilize his technological expertise to tap equilibrium resources.

The past two centuries have been the most significant in the growing demand for various energy forms to fuel increasingly complex economic systems. The substitution of coal for wood and water as a source of fuel and power resulted in the development of heavy industry in coalfield areas. Coal's dominant position in the energy market was not seriously challenged until the 1950s.

Table 3.1: World consumption of commercial energy. *Source:* UN, 1981, 1979
Yearbook of World Energy Statistics

	Coal %	Oil %	Natural Gas %	HEP/Nuclear %	Total (*million metric tons coal equivalent*)
1929	80	15	4	1	1,713
1955	56	30	12	2	3,056
1960	51	32	15	2	4,019
1965	42	38	18	2	4,992
1970	35	43	20	2	6,512
1975	32	44	21	3	7,529
1979	31·5	44	21	3·5	8,709

Even then, many countries sought to rebuild their war-torn economies by investing in coal. Indeed, Britain's early commitment to nuclear power in the mid-1950s was a response to an impending 'energy gap' in the 1970s that could not be met solely by coal expansion.

The full potential of the Middle East oil reserves was not realized until the early post-war period. Concessions to the oil majors proved lucrative. Reserves were abundant and the marketing skill of the transnationals lured the West with the prospect of cheap oil for the foreseeable future. The transition to an oil-based economy had begun (Table 3.1). Oil was cheap, clean, flexible, easy to store and distribute. Coal was bulky, dirty, difficult to transport and in many cases uncompetitive with oil. Coal quickly lost many of its clients and was relegated mainly to serving the power-plant and coking-oven market. Oil and natural gas largely replaced coal in the domestic, industrial and transportation sectors. With the discovery and development of Soviet, Dutch and North Sea gas reserves, natural gas – always a competitive fuel in North American markets – began to make a major impact in Europe. By the first 'energy crisis' of 1973/ 74, oil and gas accounted for two-thirds of the world's consumption of energy. The initial quadrupling of oil prices by between 1973 and 1975 and subsequent significant price rises following the Iranian Revolution in 1979 have prompted Western governments to reduce their dependence upon imported oil. The dislocation of the world economy as a result of oil price increases has produced a lower rate of growth in energy demand in the 1970s. Continuing recession and slackening of demand have given Western governments the opportunity to invest in coal and nuclear technologies for future energy supplies, whilst conservation measures and further development of oil and natural gas reserves have reduced their dependence on OPEC oil. A more detailed outline of the patterns of demand and supply by region is presented in Table 3.2. Responding to the cheap energy of the period between the late 1950s and the early 1970s, Western economies fuelled their growth on increased oil consumption. This growth in turn accentuated North America's appetite for energy. In 1979 the US consumed 32% of the world's oil, 22% of its coal, 45% of its natural gas and 35% of its electricity with only 5½% of the world's population. The geo-political ramification of this growth in energy demand will be discussed in more detail later in the chapter. Table 3.2 illustrates North America's increased reliance on imports to meet domestic energy demand[3] and Western Europe's widening import gap. At the other end of the scale, centrally planned economies

Table 3.2: Production, trade and consumption of commercial energy. *Source:* 1979
Yearbook of World Energy Statistics UN, 1981

Region	Year	Production (mmtce)	Trade (mmtce)*	Consumption (kilograms per Capita)
World	1955	3,296		1,143
	1960	4,305		1,368
	1965	5,409		1,544
	1970	7,150		1,781
	1975	8,214		1,879
	1979	9,560		2,019
N. America	1955	1,366	−68	7,393
	1960	1,494	−127	7,644
	1965	1,817	−158	8,661
	1970	2,335	−190	10,673
	1975	2,251	−382	10,627
	1979	2,378	−554	11,305
Rest of America	1955	224	+111	455
	1960	312	+156	563
	1965	399	+196	676
	1970	459	+167	857
	1975	416	+48	998
	1979	516	+60	1,129
Western Europe	1955	546	−175	2,174
	1960	542	−302	2,411
	1965	552	−576	2,919
	1970	538	−943	3,679
	1975	630	−950	3,869
	1979	801	−975	4,253
Centrally Planned	1955	756	+20	816
Economies	1960	1,338	+53	1,308
	1965	1,599	+89	1,412
	1970	1,996	+88	1,500
	1975	2,601	+102	1,797
	1979	3,164	+170	2,027
Africa[1] (Developed)	1955	28	−38	1,871
	1960	34	−42	1,946
	1965	43	−76	2,221
	1970	49	−146	2,241
	1975	57	−203	2,457
	1979	77	+47	2,376
Africa (Developing)	1955	5	−10	64
	1960	22	−1	77
	1965	165	+126	119
	1970	438	+383	129
	1975	380	+303	168
	1979	513	+392	193
Middle East[2]	1955	–	−2	827
(Developed)	1960	–	−2	918
	1965	–	−5	1,694
	1970	7	−1	1,986
	1975	7	+2	2,391
	1979	–	+11	2,275

Table 3.2—*contd*

Region	Year	Production (*mmtce*)	Trade (*mmtce*)*	Consumption (*kilograms per Capita*)
Middle East	1955	237	+204	673
(Developing)	1960	388	+320	1,057
	1965	618	+523	1,699
	1970	1,038	+918	3,098
	1975	1,476	+1,311	3,177
	1979	1,619	+1,423	3,723
OPEC	1955	422	+370	196
	1960	654	+569	327
	1965	1,071	+948	356
	1970	1,745	+1,582	355
	1975	2,058	+1,848	509
	1979	2,346	+2,089	565
Far East[3]	1955	46	−18	673
(Developed)	1960	55	−54	1,057
	1965	56	−139	1,699
	1970	51	−337	3,098
	1975	36	−415	3,177
	1979	39	−457	3,723
Far East	1955	63	−4	87
(Developing)	1960	92	−9	115
	1965	120	−26	148
	1970	169	−35	168
	1975	248	−24	211
	1979	321	−38	257
Oceania[4]	1955	24	−14	2,449
	1960	29	−17	2,720
	1965	39	−23	3,347
	1970	70	−16	3,850
	1975	111	+6	4,403
	1979	133	+15	4,582

[1] Customs Union of South Africa: S. Africa, Botswana, Lesotho, Namibia and Swaziland. Africa (Developing) is the remainder of Africa.
[2] Israel; Middle East (Developing) is the remainder of the Middle East.
[3] Japan; Far East (Developing) is the remainder of the Far East.
[4] Oceania includes Australia, New Zealand, Guam, Fiji, French Polynesia, New Caledonia, Papua New Guinea, Wake Island, Samoa, American Samoa, Christmas Is., Kiribati, Pacific Is., Cook Is., Solomon Is., Tonga, Vanuata Nauru and Niue.
* (million metric tons coal equivalent) A negative value indicates that a region has a net trade deficit in energy; a positive value indicates a trade surplus.

have maintained an export surplus, and OPEC members, especially those in the Middle East have increased their share of the world export market.

Table 3.2 illustrates only patterns of *commercial* energy production and consumption. Although this gives an indication of energy trends throughout the world, it underestimates the role of *non-commercial* energy production in the developing countries. Over 60% of the energy needs of these countries is met by non-commercial biomass in the form of wood, crop and animal residues.[4] Similarly, the data for per capita consumption of energy do not reveal these significant amounts of non-commercial energy consumed by developing nations. For example, Bangladesh consumed 38 kilograms/coal equivalent per capita in 1979 compared with the US figure of 11,361.[5] Indeed, the US and Canada are the greatest consumers of commercial energy in the developed world – per capita figures are almost double that of the USSR and the UK, and 3 times greater than that of Japan.

In terms of the pattern of energy supplies, most of the world's energy is produced for local or regional markets. This has led to a geographical concentration of supplies of particular fuels. For example, the USA, USSR and China produce around 60% of the world's coal, and the USSR and USA produce two-thirds of the world's natural gas.[6] Only in the case of oil have the constraints of distance been overcome by technological advance, most notably with the advent of the supertanker. Hence, a mere 8% of the world's coal and 12% of the world's natural gas is traded internationally compared with 54% of world oil.[7]

In the case of coal, the physical bulk of this fuel has restricted its market potential, with only high value coking coal being internationally transhipped to any great extent. International trading of steam coal is mainly confined to short-distance transfers such as from Poland to other European countries and from the USA to Canada. The future success of world coal producers in energy markets will therefore be dependent *inter alia* upon the upgrading of infrastructure facilities to handle an increase in the coal trade (see 3.3.2).

In much the same way, natural gas has not had the same worldwide impact as oil despite representing 21% of world primary energy consumption. Gas supply systems are capital intensive and inflexible; and

the most significant difference between oil and gas is that per unit of heat delivered natural gas is technically more difficult and costly to transport than oil over the same distance, other factors being equal. Moreover, this cost disparity increases with distance and applies to both transportation of gaseous natural gas by pipeline and liquefied natural gas (LNG) by ship.[8]

Consequently, most natural gas traded on the international market travels only relatively short distances to neighbouring countries (the Netherlands, Norway and the USSR to Western Europe, Canada to the US) by pipeline. Only 2·5% of the market is made up of long-distance LNG shipments from North Africa to Europe and the US, and from the Middle East and South-East Asia to Japan.[9] However, trade in this and the heavier gases – ethane, propane and butane – is expected to become more buoyant in the future, with Japan and the USA being the main recipients of liquid energy gases.[10]

The conversion of primary energy to electricity also suffers from transportation constraints. Hence, for reasons cited above, coal and natural gas are converted as close as possible to areas of extraction, whereas oil and nuclear power are more flexible. For example, in both the US and the USSR nuclear plants have been built in areas deficient in fossil fuels but high in demand for electricity. At an international level, nuclear development is more associated with the transference of controversial technologies rather than the geographical constraints of fuel inputs (see 3.3.3).

3.3.1 Issues in Energy Development

The Geopolitics of Oil

It has been shown in the previous section that oil is a more flexible fuel than either coal or natural gas and that its relative cheapness, cleanliness and availability made it an internationally traded commodity. Supplies, however, have always been politically vulnerable. Western corporations, seeking concessions throughout the globe during the last century, have therefore invariably marshalled government support to secure their objectives.[11]

In the post-Second World War era, however, corporate imperialism began to wane just at a time when the industrialized 'North' became very dependent upon oil, especially the oil of the politically volatile Middle East. Table 3.3 highlights this problem. North America, almost self-sufficient in oil in 1950, has become increasingly reliant upon imports; similarly, in Western Europe and Japan the 'import gap' has been widened by the increased export surpluses of the Middle East and Africa. This degree of dependence upon such a narrow geographical area has inevitably led to political tension, with oil being the source of the conflict. OPEC was formed in 1960 at the instigation of Venezuela in response to a 10% reduction in oil prices in 1959. The cartel increased its membership to thirteen countries by the time of the first 'energy crisis' but unity of purpose in a group with so many different geographical, cultural and economic interests has been difficult to achieve. Lack of unity meant that OPEC did not seriously challenge the power of the oil majors during its first decade of existence. Indeed, the oil companies survived a six-day, Middle East war in 1967 and the real price of oil products fell by 50% in the 1960s.[12] The situation began to change in the early 1970s. The more militant members of OPEC, under the leadership of Col. Qadhafi of Libya, began to press for higher prices and greater participation in existing oil concessions. In January 1973, the oil companies agreed to some of these demands, an initial weakening of their stance. However, the situation altered quickly in the aftermath of the Yom Kippur war later that year. The Arab embargo to the US and other Israeli

Table 3.3: World oil production and consumption by areas (million barrels per day). *Source:* Shell Briefing Service, November 1979, 'Background to oil'

	Production			Consumption		
	1950	1973	1978	1950	1973	1978
North America	6·2	13·6	13·3	6·6	19·6	21·4
Caribbean, South America	1·8	4·7	3·6	0·6	2·6	3·1
Middle East	1·8	21·0	21·3	0·2	1·3	1·9
Africa	–*	5·9	6·1	0·3	1·2	1·5
Western Europe	0·1	0·5	1·8	1·3	15·2	14·3
Japan	–*	–*	–*	0·1	5·5	5·4
East, Australasia	0·2	2·3	2·8	0·4	3·0	3·8
USSR, Eastern Europe and China	0·8	9·9	13·9	1·2	9·1	12·2
World total	10·9	57·9	62·8	10·7	57·5	63·6

*Negligible.

allies placed sufficient pressure on the oil market to cause a three- to four-fold rise in oil prices throughout this 'energy crisis'. After the initial turmoil and dislocation of economies which this action generated in the industrialized 'North', the oil market began to settle down. With OPEC producing an average of 30 million barrels a day from 1974 to 1978 the real price of oil began to fall. In 1978 political instability in the Middle East in the form of the Iranian Revolution again threw the oil market into chaos.

In retrospect, the hike in oil prices in the wake of the Iranian Revolution can be mainly attributed to panic buying, rather than to any oil supply shortage. Prior to the Revolution, Iran had been the world's second largest exporter of crude oil, its 5 million barrels a day accounting for 18% of total OPEC exports.[13] By the end of 1978, Iranian exports had ceased, yet fears of widespread shortages proved unfounded. In fact 1979 was a record year for world oil production and OPEC produced over 1 million barrels a day more than in 1978 mainly through the efforts of Saudi Arabia, Iraq, Nigeria and Kuwait (see Table 3.4).

Why did prices increase by between 150 and 200% from late 1978 to mid-1980 in a period of world oil surplus? The Iranian situation precipitated a crisis of uncertainty – uncertainty over future supplies. In a matter of months the oil market was transformed from a buyer's to a seller's market. Buyers scrambling

Table 3.4: Crude oil production for major exporting countries (1973–1983, million barrels per day). *Source:* US Department of Energy, 1981–1984, Monthly Energy Reviews

	1973	1974	1975	1976	1977	1978	1979	1980	1981	1983
USSR	8·42	9·02	9·63	10·17	10·7	11·22	11·47	11·72	11·80	12·04
United States	9·21	8·77	8·38	8·13	8·25	8·71	8·55	8·6	8·56	8·66
Saudi Arabia	7·6	8·48	7·08	8·58	9·21	8·3	9·53	9·9	9·82	5·09
Iran	5·86	6·02	5·35	5·86	5·67	5·24	3·17	1·66	1·33	2·43
Iraq	2·02	1·97	2·26	2·42	2·35	2·56	3·48	2·51	0·99	1·01
Venezuela	3·37	2·98	2·35	2·3	2·24	2·17	2·36	2·17	2·11	1·79
China	1·14	1·31	1·49	1·74	1·88	2·08	2·12	2·11	2·02	2·09
Libya	2·18	1·52	1·48	1·93	2·07	1·99	2·09	1·79	1·15	1·08
Nigeria	2·05	2·26	1·78	2·07	2·09	1·9	2·3	2·06	1·43	1·24
Kuwait	3·02	2·55	2·08	2·15	1·98	2·14	2·5	1·66	1·14	1·08
United Arab Emirates	1·53	1·68	1·66	1·94	2·0	1·83	1·83	1·71	1·5	1·15
Indonesia	1·34	1·38	1·31	1·5	1·69	1·64	1·59	1·58	1·61	1·39
Canada	1·8	1·7	1·42	1·3	1·32	1·32	1·5	1·42	1·29	1·39
Mexico	0·45	0·58	0·72	0·8	0·98	1·22	1·46	1·94	2·31	2·69
Algeria	1·07	0·96	0·96	1·02	1·1	1·16	1·15	1·01	0·80	0·68
United Kingdom	0·01	0·01	0·02	0·25	0·77	1·08	1·57	1·62	1·81	2·29
Total OPEC*	30·96	30·68	27·13	30·71	31·23	29·8	30·93	26·89	22·63	17·60
Arab Members of OPEC†	17·98	17·68	15·96	18·52	19·15	18·46	21·09	19·05	15·8	10·36
World	55·83	55·88	52·99	57·40	59·61	60·40	62·40	59·46	55·60	52·82

*The 13 members of OPEC are Algeria, Iraq, Kuwait, Libya, Qatar, Saudi Arabia, United Arab Emirates, Indonesia, Iran, Nigeria, Venezuela, Ecuador and Gabon.
† Arab members are Algeria, Iraq, Kuwait, Libya, Qatar, Saudi Arabia, and the United Arab Emirates.

for available oil overheated the market. Spot market prices tripled from around $13 a barrel in late 1978 to $40 a barrel in the autumn of 1979; producer governments began to levy surcharges and premiums on their official prices (in some cases with justification as they had increased production to meet the Iranian shortfall in supplies).

The events of this period further diminished the role of oil majors and put Saudi Arabia into the enviable position of being able to dictate the flow of the oil market almost at will. The oil majors that fared best at this time were those with access to the increased volumes of Saudi crude (Exxon, Mobil, SOCAL and Texaco) at the expense of others (such as BP) which had been excluded from Nigeria and was heavily involved in Iranian supplies. Overall, the Iranian crisis culminated in the decline of oil majors in all areas of the oil business. In terms of production, the 'Seven Sisters'' direct access to crude oil through ownership has fallen from 61 to 25% between 1970 and 1979. During the same period our own governments' share of crude oil production, through the partial or total take-over of concessions, has increased from 5 to 65%.[14] Whilst the changing control of production may have been considered inevitable as a result of OPEC demands in the early 1970s, the oil majors have also seen their role as suppliers of oil rapidly undermined in the 1970s. During this decade their share of the non-communist world's oil trade outside North America was eroded from 60% to just over 40%.[15] Much of this loss occurred after the Iranian crisis. The tight market situation led OPEC members to reduce their dependence on the oil majors. Indeed, Western consumers – most notably the import-dependent Japanese – began to buy direct from producing governments.[16]

The 1980s witnessed further political instability in the Middle East in the form of the Iran–Iraq war which began in September 1980, simmered throughout the early 1980s and escalated in May 1984. The West has always feared that inter-state warfare could jeopardize oil exports from the Persian Gulf, and Iran has threatened to block the Straits of Hormuz on several occasions during the war. Despite the political tension in the Middle East, OPEC's influence has declined in the oil market throughout the 1980s culminating in a $5 reduction in its 'official' market price to $29 a barrel in Easter 1983 – the first time a price cut had been initiated in its history.

The main reasons for the weakening of OPEC's position are:

a) a temporary drop in demand owing to the recession;
b) the loss of markets through consumers switching to alternative fuels and the imposition of conservation measures – a policy adopted by Western governments;
c) the rise in production from non-OPEC countries. OPEC's share of a declining world market fell from 51% in 1979 to 33% in 1983, with Mexico and the UK being fourth and sixth respectively in the world-producer league table (Table 3.5);
d) the drawing down of stocks by the oil companies because of price reductions on the spot market.

By mid-1984, OPEC's position in the oil market had stabilized with production levelling out at 17 to 18 million barrels a day and prices firming on the spot market. This stabilization can be attributed to continued unrest along the Persian Gulf and a modest economic recovery in the US. Indeed, Wilbanks

Table 3.5: Reserves of oil (million barrels).
Source: Shell Briefing Service,
November 1979, 'Background to oil'

Saudi Arabia	113,284
Kuwait	71,400
USSR	58,438
Iran	44,966
Iraq	34,392
United Arab Emirates	31,904
Mexico	28,407
USA	27,804
Libya	27,304
China	20,025
Venezuela	18,228
Nigeria	12,273
United Kingdom	10,191
Algeria	9,575
Indonesia	7,824
Canada	5,784

implies that the US could face another 'energy crisis' by 1986/87 if world oil consumption and effective production capacity move closer in line with each other.[17] He argues that this is a distinct possibility as consumption increases with economic recovery, stocks are drawn upon and existing production capacity is more fully utilized. A political 'event' could easily transform the situation from one of surplus to one of scarcity and create another crisis. In the long term, much oil remains to be discovered throughout the globe, but over two-thirds of known reserves are in OPEC territory. Table 3.5 shows the overwhelming predominence of Middle Eastern countries, especially Saudi Arabia and Kuwait. Bearing this in mind, the oil glut of the early 1980s is a product of short term conditions. The West, despite its present diversity of oil suppliers, will continue to be dependent upon OPEC oil.

3.3.2 King Coal Revived?

Until the 1960s most industrialized nations of the world, with the notable exception of the US, relied heavily upon coal. The advent of clean, cost-competitive oil led to a rationalization of the coal industry throughout the world. Initially, older collieries were closed, but the rapid erosion of coal markets resulted in further closures on economic grounds. In the UK alone, collieries were closed at the rate of one per week in the mid 1960s.[18]

In the 1970s the growing strength of OPEC and corresponding oil price increases gave coal a second chance. Major coal producing nations began to re-invest in coal, especially the US, USSR, China, and Australia, which together account for 88% of ultimate world reserves (Table 3.6). There is no question about coal's long term future. Known reserves ensure supplies for countries even with a large increase in demand. 'Proven' reserves discovered in the lee of the 1973/74 crisis have grown at a much faster rate than coal production.[19] This contrasts markedly with oil.[20] Despite coal's apparent long term future – illustrated by the World Coal Study[21] – short term difficulties will be

Table 3.6: Coal production and reserves of major coal producing countries.
Source: D.J. Spooner, January 1981, The geography of coal's second coming, Geography and Shell Briefing Service, May 1980, Coal: Energy for the future

	Coal Production (mtce)			Proven Reserves (btce)	Ultimate Reserves (btce)
	1975†	1985*	2000*		
USSR	614	851	1100	110	4,860
United States	581	842	1340	167	2,570
China	349	725	1200	99	1,438
Poland	181	258	300	60	140
United Kingdom	129	137	173	45	190
West Germany	126	129	145	34	247
India	73	135	235	12	81
Australia	69	150	300	33	600
South Africa	69	119	233	43	72
Canada	23	35	115	4	323

† Actual
* Estimated

encountered in securing markets, in addition to the social, economic and political problems associated with the changing geography of coal production.

In terms of demand, the World Coal Study (WOCOL) envisages a doubling or tripling of coal use and a three- to five-fold increase in the world coal trade by the end of the century. These forecasts are based on the assumption that OECD energy demand will increase by 1·75% to 2·5% per annum and, in the more optimistic forecasts, that constraints will be imposed on other supply alternatives, for example, oil supply limitations and nuclear delays. These assumptions can be examined in the light of events since publication of the report: energy demand remains depressed in the OECD nations; two significant coal producers, the UK and the US have endorsed their commitment to nuclear expansion; and oil prices have fallen in response to a world oil surplus.

According to WOCOL's most conservative expectations, coal-fired generating capacity would double by the end of the century, coking coal requirements would show a modest increase and the industrial use of coal would double by the year 2000. Total industrial, residential and commercial use of coal was expected to grow from 14% of OECD's coal use to between 17% and 26%. These forecasts are highly optimistic. Due to the recession, electricity demand has fallen in some countries. In several countries, for example the UK and France, nuclear plants are being ordered in preference to coal-fired stations. Neither does the other main market for coal – coking coal – hold out much prospect for future growth. Even in buoyant times, the steel industry had been improving its fuel efficiency and thus its demand for coking coal had been reduced. Now, OECD members are faced with overcapacity and the rationalization of their steel industries. Hence, steel provides a contracting, rather than a stabilizing or growing market for coal.

Other markets for coal show little promise of growth in the short term. Countries in the report which projected the largest increases in the use of coal in industry were Canada, the US, France and the UK. However, early signs of growth were not discernible. In the UK a Confederation of British Industry (CBI) survey showed that firms did not intend switching to coal.[22] In the US, coal use in the industrial sector declined by 18% from 1973 to 1979.[23] Much of the optimism concerning new market opportunities in the industrial, residential and commercial sectors was based on the development of Coalplexes – large plants designed to convert coal to liquid or gaseous fuels. British research is well advanced in this area, with an SNG demonstration plant at Westfield, Fife and a liquefaction plant at Point of Ayr in North Wales. Nevertheless, official forecasts do not foresee synthetic fuels making a great impact until the next century. Similarly, a change of administration in the US effectively slowed down the Synfuels programme commenced by President Carter: the Synthetic Fuels Corporation has to rely on private, rather than federal finance. In view of these recent developments, significant market penetration in the domestic, industrial and commercial sectors is unlikely.

The accuracy of WOCOL's forecasts will be greater in non-OECD nations. Centrally planned economies have a history of coal use. The Chinese, in particular, are expanding coal production to fuel their industrial growth. Furthermore, the non-oil producing nations of the Third World which incurred escalating oil import bills have begun to develop indigenous coal reserves. India's planned expansion is indicative of this trend (Table 3.6). The newly industrialized countries are also likely to take advantage of the growth in the coal trade, especially countries poor in domestic energy sources.

The growth in demand forecast by WOCOL may not materialize at levels that justify the original investment proposed by coal producers in the early 1970s with the purpose of reducing oil dependence. In addition, problems have been encountered in winning coal from new areas. In the USSR more and more coal has been discovered further east. In the US the cheaper low-sulphur coal lies in the western states. It is estimated that by 1985, 76% of the net increase in coal production in N. America, the USSR and in Europe since 1973 will have been from 'distant' coal basins.[24] This increasing spatial disparity between supply and demand has necessitated massive investments to upgrade existing transportation systems.[25]

A recent survey of new mining capacity in the US gives an indication of the scale and geographical significance of new mining investment.[26] Of the 404 mines[27] which will provide 647 million tons of new capacity by 1987, 169 surface mines will produce 70% of the total additional capacity. Around three-quarters of this capacity is located west of the Mississippi. This western bonanza is not confined to coal, but affects other mining interests too. Overall, the proliferation of new power plants, slurry pipelines, and perhaps in the future, synfuel plants, will place additional pressure on the western USA's most scarce resource – water. Competition for water can only aggravate relations between the farmer and the mining companies. Already, the traditional rural way of life in parts of the 'wild west' has succumbed to the impact of the boom. Rapid growth of small communities has created social and economic disruption of local economies, and potential coal communities are being cautious not to be afflicted by the 'Gillette syndrome'.[28] Even in a small country like the UK, the National Coal Board (NCB) has been experiencing opposition to its expansion plans as new reserves are discovered in parts of rural England previously immune from the ravages of industrialization. The lack of demand for coal in Britain has made it exceedingly difficult for the NCB to justify expansion in these new areas. Indeed, the NCB has been exporting between five and ten million tonnes a year to reduce the cost of maintaining record stocks of unwanted coal.

The role of the NCB as a coal exporter highlights the short-term difficulties facing high cost producers in a recession. Along with other major coal producing nations, the UK embarked upon an investment programme to expand its productive capacity. However, languishing demand, especially with the collapse of the coking coal market, has meant that demand is out of phase with supply. By 1983, stocks had reached 53·3 million tonnes and annual production was 120·9 million. The NCB's programme of pit closures, bringing capacity back into line with demand, has been met with fierce resistance from the miners' union, most of whose membership began a protracted strike in March 1984. In contrast to the social disruptions caused by coal expansion, the miners are attempting to preserve 20,000 jobs and the livelihood of their communities in the hope that demand will pick up in the long term. The crux of the problem is the level of subsidization which government is willing to bear as compared with its food policy (Chapter 12) and nuclear strategy (Chapter 10). A House of Lords' Select Committee has shown that UK production costs are lower than those of other EEC coal producers and that UK subsidization is considerably less per tonne (five and a half times less than that of Belgium and France).[29] Nevertheless, the future of the coal industry will be decided according to the fiscal priorities of the government.

The world coal trade amounted to 200 million tonnes in 1977, which is only 8% of world production. WOCOL expected this trade to increase by three to five times, to between 550 and 930 million tonnes by the year 2000.[30] Most export potential lies in the low-cost, surface mines of the US, Australia and South Africa. The extent to which this increased volume of trade is realized depends on the nature of demand and the upgrading of port capacity to handle coal freight traffic. South Africa's prominence as an exporter can be attributed to expansion of the port at Richards Bay.[31] Undoubtedly, Australia and the US have the best export potential, and plans to construct new coal terminals and develop existing port capacities are well underway. The exact volume of exports may be determined by government policy. For example, in the US, present export opportunities are largely related to a lack of domestic demand despite government initiatives to increase coal use.[32] If domestic markets were to pick up, this would impair export growth. This uncertainty may explain the indecision over the size of the investment proposed for some of the east coast ports. Coal producers have been reluctant to invest in projects to expand capacity in Baltimore from 14 million to 80 million tonnes and the creation of a new 15 million-tonne port at Marley Neck, Maryland.[33]

There are too many uncertainties to be able to accurately predict the volume of world coal trade and the level of coal production in specific countries by the year 2000. The main weakness of the WOCOL forecasts is their over-optimistic demand projections. The coal industry will experience short-term difficulties in securing markets, particularly in a recession. Hence, WOCOL's supply forecasts may also be premature. Nevertheless, world coal consumption will increase. The US, USSR and China will be the main coal producers, and the US, Australia and South Africa will increase their exports to energy deficient nations, particularly Japan, France and Italy.

3.3.3 The Nuclear Dilemma

Nuclear power is the most controversial of all the energy supply technologies. Concern has been expressed over a number of issues, ranging from cost and safety to the dangers of proliferation and the problem of discarding wastes without threatening the welfare of future generations. On the other hand, most Western governments and the public utilities operating nuclear plants claim that nuclear power is the cheapest, safest form of energy production with less impact on the environment than other methods of producing energy. The debate on the pros and cons of nuclear energy is now firmly on the political agenda of many countries, resulting in the fall of the Social Democrats in Sweden, referenda in Switzerland, Austria and Denmark and civil disobedience in France, Germany, the US and the UK. The history of nuclear power has been short and troubled.

Before discussing the growth of the industry, it is necessary to unravel the intricacies of the nuclear fuel cycle. The discovery and mining of uranium ore is the first stage of the cycle (Figure 3.1). The ore is then processed into uranium oxide (U_3O_8) – better known as yellowcake – before being purified into uranium metal which is made into natural uranium fuel for use in either the British Magnox reactors or the Canadian CANDU reactors. To improve efficiency in fuel output per kilogram of uranium, the more compactly designed

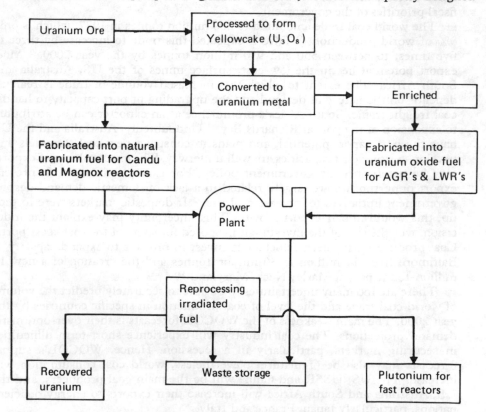

Figure 3.1 The Nuclear Fuel Cycle

Advanced Gas Cooled Reactor (AGR), Pressurized Water Reactor (PWR) and Boiling Water Reactors (BWR) were developed during the 1960s. These reactors use uranium oxide fuel. In all these reactors, nuclear fission occurs through the bombardment of the uranium isotope U235 by stray neutrons. The ensuing controlled chain reaction produces heat which is mainly used for electricity generation. At the same time, the heavier isotope U238 does not undergo fission but, on capturing a neutron, it transforms into the fissile plutonium 239. As U235 only occurs as 0·7% of natural uranium, fission can only be efficiently sustained through either the slowing down of the neutrons by the use of a moderator or the enrichment of U235 to 2 to 3%.[34] The AGR's and the US-designed light water reactors require both enriched uranium oxide fuel and a moderator because of high neutron absorption in their designs.

The most controversial aspects of the fuel cycle occur after the electricity generation stage. When after a few years the uranium fuel becomes irradiated the spent fuel is removed from the reactor to nearby storage ponds. Once the radiation level is sufficiently reduced, the fuel is transported to a reprocessing plant. There the fuel elements are separated to recover uranium, for further conversion to fuel, and plutonium which can be used in the Fast Breeder Reactor (FBR). The remaining wastes are then either released into the environment or stored depending on their level of radioactivity. Although 99·9% of all nuclear wastes lose their radioactivity within ten years,[35] it is the small amounts of highly radioactive waste which have to be stored for posterity that have aroused public concern. To date, the technology for transforming these liquid wastes into more manageable form – vitrification or producing synthetic rocks – has yet to be perfected. And more research is required to determine the reception areas for the ultimate disposal of these wastes. The self-sealing properties of clay and salt rocks have been explored by West Germany and the US, whilst the hard crystalline 'shield' terrain offers better prospects for Britain and Canada. Waste disposal, however, has excited much opposition. No one wants nuclear waste as a neighbour for life, and it is probable that wastes will be stored in geologically quiet areas of the ocean floor.

Plutonium is recovered during reprocessing for use in FBRs. Unlike the previous generations of fission reactors, which burn uranium, the FBR 'breeds' more uranium/plutonium fuel than originally used. FBR technology would improve energy efficiency by 50 or 60 times compared with burner reactor technology. Engineering problems have still to be resolved. A compact core has to be designed to achieve a high neutron density as fission is caused by fast neutrons. The fuel is enriched to 15–20%, no moderator is required and a coolant (usually sodium) has to be used to remove heat quickly from the core. FBR programmes are well behind schedule and are still at the demonstration stage, except in France.

With the current problems related to fission technologies, the futuristic technology of nuclear fusion now looks an even more distant solution to our energy problems than it did a decade ago. At the present level of technology, the heat input required to fuse the abundantly available hydrogen isotopes, deuterium and tritium, is often greater than the energy released.

Nuclear technologies were developed during World War II primarily by Britain and America and subsequently spread to other 'Northern' industrialized nations. Countries adopted this form of power largely as a reflection of their wartime experience in nuclear research and development (R&D) and their domestic energy needs. After the war, the three participants in the wartime Manhattan Project – the US, Canada and the UK – began to develop their nuclear programmes independently. Whilst Canada embarked upon a civilian nuclear programme, the US and Britain concentrated their efforts on improving the efficiency of nuclear weapons. In contrast to the US, however, Britain experienced fuel shortages in the immediate post-war years. The creation of the UK Atomic Energy Authority in 1954, the announcement of a civilian nuclear power programme the following year and the generation of the world's first commercial electricity from the Calder Hall Station in 1956, made Britain the world leader in civilian nuclear power development. By 1952 the following plants had been commissioned: a uranium refinement and fuel fabrication factory at Springfields, near Preston, an enrichment plant at Capenhurst, Cheshire, and a reprocessing plant at Windscale, Cumbria (see Figure 10.2). As early as 1959 Britain was producing power from a demonstration FBR at Dounreay, northern Scotland. The only missing link in the fuel cycle was a lack of indigenous uranium supplies; hence it was understandable that Britain should attempt to use its imported supplies as efficiently as possible.

By the late 1960s, Britain's nuclear supremacy had been lost to the US. Whilst Britain experienced technical difficulties with its second generation of nuclear reactors – the AGRs – the US began to develop their light water reactors. The PWR in particular began to be accepted as the standard design for other countries' nuclear programmes. They were constructed, under licence, throughout the Western world. At the same time the US had a virtual monopoly of the market in the enriched uranium needed to supply fuel for these reactors. This predominance was broken by the USSR in the 1970s. The main consumers of imported enriched uranium – Western European nations – are now developing their own enrichment facilities. Urenco Centec, a joint Dutch, British and German combine, is developing a new gas centrifuge technology.

Meanwhile, the French are independently developing their enrichment capacity. The lack of domestic supplies of energy in France and its overwhelming dependence on Middle Eastern oil[36] prompted the French government to introduce a 'crash' nuclear programme. By 1985 France will be foremost in nuclear power operation in Europe and may seriously challenge the US as world leader by the end of the century. The French are involved in all aspects of the fuel cycle. Although possessing uranium reserves, they are still dependent upon imports, and the commitment to the FBR and reprocessing is an attempt to utilize their own supplies more efficiently. The growth of nuclear generated electricity in France in the 1970s is shown in Table 3.7. Only Japan, another country devoid of indigenous energy resources, has developed its nuclear generating capacity at a similar rate. The Japanese, however, do not have the benefit of an integrated domestic fuel cycle. They are dependent upon US enriched fuel and US light water reactors and their nuclear waste is sent to France and the UK for reprocessing. The political ramifications of this dependence could impede the growth of the Japanese nuclear programme.[37]

Other European countries have been developing their nuclear programmes using light water reactors (with the exception of Britain). Germany and the UK, two of the main nuclear powers in Europe during the 1970s, have scaled down their original nuclear programmes. In Germany, delays in many projects can be attributed to concern over the ultimate disposal of radioactive wastes.

Table 3.7: Nuclear electricity generation by non-communist countries (billion gross kilowatt-hours). *Source:* US Department of Energy, March 1984, Monthly Energy Review

	1973	1974	1975	1976	1977	1978	1979	1980	1983
Argentina	0	1·0	2·5	2·6	1·6	2·9	2·7	2·3	2·5
Belgium	0	0·1	6·8	10·0	11·9	12·5	11·4	12·5	24·1
Canada	18·3	15·4	13·2	18·0	26·8	32·9	38·4	40·4	53·0
Finland	0	0	0	0	2·7	3·3	6·7	7·0	17·4
France	11·6	14·7	18·3	15·8	17·9	30·5	39·9	61·2	144·2
India	1·9	2·4	2·5	3·2	2·8	2·3	3·2	2·9	2·9
Italy	3·1	3·4	3·8	3·8	3·4	4·4	2·6	2·2	5·8
Japan	9·4	18·1	22·2	36·8	28·1	53·2	62·0	82·8	106·5
Netherlands	1·1	3·3	3·3	3·9	3·7	4·1	3·5	4·2	3·6
Pakistan	0·5	0·6	0·5	0·5	0·3	0·2	(s)	0·1	0·2
South Korea	0	0	0	0	0·1	2·3	3·2	3·5	9·0
Spain	6·5	7·2	7·5	7·6	6·5	7·6	6·7	5·2	10·7
Sweden	2·1	1·6	12·0	16·0	19·9	23·8	21·0	26·7	40·5
Switzerland	6·2	7·0	7·7	7·9	8·1	8·3	11·8	14·3	15·5
Taiwan	0	0	0	0	0·1	2·7	6·3	8·2	18·9
United Kingdom	28·0	34·0	30·5	36·8	38·1	36·7	38·5	37·2	50·0
West Germany	11·9	12·0	21·7	24·5	35·8	35·9	42·2	43·7	64·7
Non-Communist World (Excluding US)	100·7	121·1	152·7	187·3	207·8	263·6	300·1	354·4	569·7
United States	88·0	104·5	181·8	201·6	263·2	292·7	270·7	265·3	313·6
Total Non-Communist World	188·7	225·6	334·5	388·9	470·9	556·3	570·8	619·7	883·3

Note: Totals may not equal sum of components due to independing rounding. Figures are for gross electrical generation. Net figures are generally less than gross figures by about 5%, which represents the energy consumed by the generating plants themselves. (s) = Less than 0·05 billion gross kilowatt-hours.

In the UK, indecision over the choice of reactor design for the next generation of power plants has been one of the main factors creating uncertainty within the industry. Ironically, the UK government is evaluating the nationalized electricity utility's proposal to build PWRs under licence from Westinghouse. The first reactor, proposed for Sizewell, is the subject of a public inquiry. This comes at a time when the US nuclear industry is at its lowest ebb in terms of financial credibility and public confidence following the Three Mile Island accident of 1979. Both these issues are discussed at some length in 10.4.2 and 10.4.3. Although the Reagan Administration has lifted the ban on reprocessing and tried to stimulate the ailing industry through the promise of fiscal incentives and regulatory reform, the private sector has not responded. Even the ill-fated FBR at Clinch River, Tennessee was finally cancelled in 1983 when the Republican-dominated Senate declined to appropriate $1·5 billion to keep the programme active.

The main reason for President Carter's original ban on reprocessing was the fear of nuclear proliferation. In 1974 India conducted a 'peaceful' explosion with imported Canadian equipment. This made 'Northern' powers more cautious about exporting 'sensitive technologies' – enrichment, reprocessing and heavy water refinement – to the 'South'. Despite the 1968 Nuclear Non-Proliferation Treaty (NPT), the 1978 US Non-Proliferation Act and the action of the Uranium Institute to monitor the spread of nuclear technologies, the number of 'Southern' nations embarking upon nuclear power programmes continues to rise[38] (Table 3.7). Many of these countries are newly industrialized countries (NICs) which are developing nuclear power to foster their industrial expansion and lessen their dependence on imported oil. Some, for example India, Pakistan, Argentina and Brazil, have not signed the NPT and see the concern over the dangers of proliferation as a smoke screen designed to restrict the transfer of technology to the 'South'. In any case, the 'North' – in particular the US – has been active in the export market. With orders dwindling at home, the 'South' offers the best opportunity to maintain a viable domestic power manufacturing industry.

In order for any country to embark upon a nuclear power programme, availability of uranium supplies is a prerequisite. Many of the Third World countries cited above have indigenous uranium reserves which have been barely exploited. Most of the world's uranium production is concentrated in a handful of countries (Table 3.8). Although the US is by far the largest producer, it consumes most of this uranium in its own nuclear programme. France – the world's fifth largest producer – still needs to import (mainly from Niger) for its expanding nuclear programme. The other countries in Table 3.8 are thus the free world's main exporters. Table 3.8 underestimates the role of Australia which will probably be the world's main exporter by 1990.

In the late 1970s much concern was expressed over the availability of uranium to fuel nuclear programmes. On the one hand, two major suppliers – Canada and Australia – had frozen their exports in the mid-1970s due to the fear that their uranium was being used for military rather than civilian purposes. On the other hand, the OECD/International Atomic Energy Agency (IAEA) forecast that uranium supplies may become scarce by the 1990s in view of the West's commitment to nuclear power.[40] This pessimistic outlook gave the proponents of FBRs ammunition in their campaign to develop this fuel-efficient technology as quickly as possible. Already by the early 1980s, however, pessimism seems unfounded. The bottom has fallen out of the uranium market.

Table 3.8: Uranium production in 1979 (metric tons) *Source:* UN, 1981, 1979 Yearbook of World Energy Statistics

World	37,953
United States	14,500
South Africa Customs Union*	8,887
Canada	6,900
Niger	2,300
France	2,180
Gabon	1,800
Australia	710
Others	676

* All estimates, except South Africa of which Namibia accounts for 3,692.

The initial forecasts of nuclear energy's contribution to the Western economies by the year 2000 were excessively optimistic. Nowhere is this more aptly illustrated than in the US where uranium output has been cut by one-third as production costs increased and prices collapsed. Rotting uranium mills in Wyoming, Colorado and New Mexico bear testimony to the most recent boom-and-bust period in this industry's volatile history.

3.3.4 Renewables – renewed prospects?

Renewable energy sources occur as either 'radiation from the sun which can appear as ambient heat, as energy transferred to the wind, to the ocean waves, to water at high levels deposited from clouds or as energy stored in plant materials', or through 'the earth's rotation which through complex interactions between the sun, earth and moon can appear as tidal energy'.[41]

As fossil fuels become scarcer, these equilibrium sources of energy will be developed with renewed vigour in the 21st century. The transition to renewable energy sources will require an upgrading of existing technologies and the development of appropriate storage facilities. The main difficulty with renewable energy sources is that they produce heat and power intermittently. The sun does not shine, the wind does not blow and the tides do not ebb and flow just when their energy is required by man. To store heat, water, rocks and pebbles are the most common materials in use at the present time. Research into the use of chemicals to absorb heat at high temperatures and then release it at lower temperatures would reduce heat loss and the size of storage area required.[42] Storing electricity, however, is a bigger problem than storing heat. The only practical method in use is conventional batteries, which are bulky and expensive. Batteries other than the lead acid battery are being developed, and surplus electricity can be used for the electrolysis of water to produce hydrogen which is easier to store and distribute.

Although storage is a difficult problem to overcome, renewable energy sources do have the advantage of flexibility of application. Renewable energy appliances can range from the solar-electric irrigation pump of 20 kW to the large, aerogenerator of 1–3 MW supplying electricity to the grid system. Furthermore, in some cases the basic technologies have been known for centuries and only require modification for 20th-century uses. Geographical constraints make some of these renewable energy sources site-specific; others have worldwide rather than regional implications.

Geothermal energy, wave power, tidal energy and Ocean Thermal Energy Conversion (OTEC) are renewable energy sources which would come into the site-specific category. Geothermal energy, in the form of 'high enthalpy' power from hot aquifers, has been developed in only a few countries of the world where magma is found relatively close to the earth's surface (around the rim of the Pacific Basin). Although of regional significance, the total world generating capacity is equivalent to only *one*, large conventional power plant![43] Of more wide-ranging importance will be the utilization of 'low enthalpy' energy in the form of heat, rather than power from cooler reservoirs. The world's spa resorts were developed from early times because of the therapeutic properties of their hot water. Now, thermal springs will be developed according to the temperature of the water and the proximity of the site to an available market. It is possible, of course, to found a new community to take advantage of this energy service.

Although geothermal energy has already been exploited to some degree, wave power, tidal power and OTEC projects are still very much at the research rather than the development stage. Tidal power offers the most potential in the near future, although there are only a few sites in the world where tidal ranges are sufficiently high (13 to 16 metres) to generate enough electricity to justify the high development costs involved.[44] The only commercial plant in operation is at La Rance near St Malo in France. Opened in 1966, this scheme is tiny compared to the size of the projects envisaged for the Bay of Fundy in Canada and the Severn Estuary in south-west England.[45] In view of the question mark over the safety of the Severn Road Bridge, it is possible that a barrage may be constructed as a multi-purpose venture in the foreseeable future.

Both water and wind energy were used for centuries to pump water to irrigate and grind grain into flour. Upon the advent of steam power, many of these plants became redundant. Water power, however, in the form of hydro-electric power (HEP), became the most significant of all renewable energy resources in the 20th century. Although the best sites for HEP development have already been exploited in the developed world,[46] there is considerable untapped potential to be realized, especially in the developing countries (see Table 3.9).

As to wind power, many rural communities that have become dependent upon increasingly expensive fossil fuels, may return to a more sophisticated version of a technology used by their ancestors. This could happen in the Great Plains of the US, an area that has the greatest wind energy potential in the country.[47] Hill top sites and coastal or offshore zones also provide opportunities for harnessing the wind. The energy crisis has given aerogenerators a second chance in the market place. Although small-scale windmills offer prospects to dispersed, rural settlements, most research and development has centred upon reviving the use of large-scale aerogenerators in 'windmill farms'. A large number of experimental wind machines were built in the two decades before the cheap energy era. At present, utility companies, with Government support, are testing various designs and sizes of aerogenerators, monitoring their performance and economic feasibility. It is probable that the first commercial windmills in the 100- to 200-foot rotor range will be commissioned in remote areas where

Table 3.9: Development status of HEP sites in 1977 (thousand kilowatts).
Source: UN, 1981, 1979 Yearbook of World Energy Statistics

	Operating sites	Under construction	Planned	Other Probable
North America (Developed)	109,743	25,722	6,063	140,874
Other America (Developing)	36,324	41,110	111,902	133,686
Africa	11,603	4,624	11,065	53,755
Middle East	3,773	5,986	10,683	18,100
Far East	42,901	14,052	54,797	66,549
Centrally Planned Asia	16,800	–	4,889	–
Centrally Planned Europe	53,376	14,700	4,169	–
Western Europe	118,292	13,343	37,867	24,226
Oceania	9,482	2,600	5,670	20,660
World	402,294	122,137	247,105	457,850

utilities incur high costs in supplying electricity. This is indeed the case in Orkney in Scotland and Culebra Island in Puerto Rico where wind power will replace expensive oil-generated power.

Biomass and direct solar energy have the best potential of all renewable energy resources for the future. Clearly, some areas are geographically better suited for exploitation than others, but the differential rate of development in countries throughout the world is a function of land availability, land-use competition and the relative costs of other energy sources.

Problems in capturing this energy become apparent when seasonal variations or even the diurnal range of solar radiation levels are taken into account. For example, the ratio of summer to winter insolation levels is high in high latitudes compared to the more uniform figures achieved in equatorial latitudes. Hence, countries in north-west Europe have limited potential for solar space heating and solar power stations; here, the most likely impact of solar technologies will be in the fields of water heating and photovoltaic cells. Although the less developed countries are more favoured with high insolation levels, much of the technology to harness energy from the sun is being patented in the North. The US, Japan and France – all major energy importers – have been investing heavily in solar R.&D. These countries have operational solar power stations, the largest being the 10 MW plant at Barstow, USA. These stations work on the principle of focusing the sun's rays on an array of reflecting mirrors (heliostats). The reflected sunlight is concentrated upon a receiving tower which converts water into steam to generate electricity. The French are developing small, low output stations, such as the one in Corsica (300 kW) for the needs of rural communities. This would be an appropriate technology for developing countries with high insolation levels. On an even smaller scale, the French are world leaders in the manufacturing and marketing of solar engines. Already, French-designed engines have been used for cooling and water pumping in African and Mexican villages.

As most of the R.&D. into solar energy is being pursued in the industrialized 'North', the technologies receiving most active interest are the flat plate collectors for water heating and photovoltaic cells for electricity production. The advantage of solar cells is that they can be built at a variety of scales according to the amount of power required. Since their early applications in photography and in the space programme, the costs of production have fallen considerably. In the early 1980s, their most appropriate application was in small power plants in remote locations or for specialized uses (telecommunications, light buoys); however, it is felt that further breakthroughs in the efficiency and mass production of cells could make them cost competitive for other uses by the late 1980s.[48] Of all the types of solar equipment manufactured at the present time, solar flat plate collectors have made the greatest impact in the market place. Low grade heat is in constant demand throughout the year for a variety of uses. Solar heat can therefore be a worthwhile investment to supplement conventional water heating systems. The boom in sales of solar water heating systems has been particularly marked in the US, where federal and state tax credits have stimulated growth.

It was mentioned earlier in this chapter that biomass was the main source of energy in many developing countries. In recent years developed nations, especially those with energy deficits, have reconsidered the tapping of energy stored in organic materials such as crops and organic wastes. Theoretically, the potential world energy yield from biomass could satisfy demand;[49] in practice the poor efficiency of photosynthesis requires large acreages to be devoted to energy production.[50] In countries with existing pressures on the land, biomass production would increase land-use competition.

The use of wood for fuel and the use of biogas plants for methane production are the most common biomass applications. Wood – the main source of world energy prior to the Industrial Revolution – is still an important resource in the developing countries. Although fast-growing species such as acacias, albizias and eucalyptus have been introduced into tropical areas, extensive deforestation of tropical areas has often led to soil erosion and aggravated firewood crises in countries poorly endowed with forest cover, such as Niger and Mali[51] (see Chapter 6). By contrast, countries such as the US, Canada and Brazil have the potential to exploit large tracts of unharvested forest. These countries have been experimenting with the technology required to produce methanol from wood to make it cost competitive with methanol produced from natural gas.

The production of methane by fermenting organic wastes anaerobically (without air or oxygen) was practised in Europe during World War II. Upon the return of peacetime conditions, interest waned in Europe and the process was adopted instead by countries with more favourable climate conditions and appropriate agricultural systems such as India.[52] In India and Kenya, where deforestation is a problem, biogas programmes are being introduced into village communities at a rapid rate. For example, in India 81,000 fermentation plants have been constructed, with the prospect of 580,000 plants operational by 1983.[53] Only China, with 7 million biogas plants producing 200,000 barrels per day of oil equivalent, exceeds the Indian total.

In the post-1973 era, much attention has focused upon the conversion of organic materials into alcohol to reduce dependence upon imported oil. The fermentation of crops with a high starch and sugar content to yield ethanol has commanded most interest.[54] Sugar cane offers the best potential because of its high rate of energy conversion, but maize, cassava, sorghum, pineapples and even potatoes can also be used in this process. The lure of this familiar technology is that it can produce results in a short period of time. For example, by 1981 'gasohol' had captured 1% of total gasoline sales in the US.[55] Alcohol blended fuels are a mixture of 90% unleaded gasoline plus a mixture of methanol and ethanol. The alcohol content can be raised to 20% without the need to redesign engines. Indeed, in Brazil car manufacturers are expanding their fleet of cars designed to use hydrated ethanol alone (95% ethanol and 5% water).[56]

The Brazilian experience with ethanol is quite unique and can not be easily applied to other countries. For example, only 2% of her land area would be required to substitute ethanol for all her present oil imports; however, this 2%, or 160,000 square kilometres, would constitute a much larger percentage of land in most other countries. Figure 3.2 highlights the countries which can justify ethanol production. The developing countries with surplus agricultural production and dependence upon imported energy have the strongest incentive to develop biomass programmes: for example, Brazil, Thailand, Philippines and Sudan.[57] This contrasts with Bangladesh and Pakistan where biomass production may alleviate the oil importation situation but aggravate food shortages. The more fortunate oil-exporting developing countries – Mexico, Nigeria and

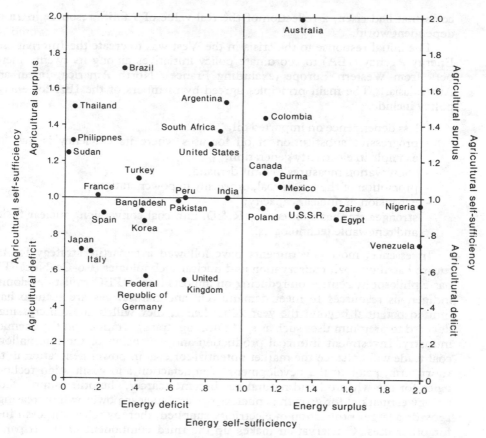

Figure 3.2 Alcohol Production from Biomass Energy and Agricultural Self Sufficiency
Ratios for Selected Countries
Source: R. Goodman, December 1980, Managing the Demand for Energy
in the Developing World, *Finance and Development*

Venezuela – can use their oil revenues to either buy imported food or to expand
agricultural production at home. In either case, there is little incentive to
venture into ethanol production. In the developed world, a similar situation
prevails, with energy-deficient France and the US developing biomass
programmes.[58]

3.4.1 Investment Strategies

Until the oil crisis of 1973/74, Western governments tended to operate a
laissez-faire energy policy based upon the cost competitiveness of available
fuels. As a result of the availability of low cost oil from the Middle East,
Western economies were geared to using imported oil supplies. Quadrupling
of oil prices in the winter of 1973/74 caused the West to review its energy
strategies. Energy was no longer cheap. Not that the financial costs of producing OPEC oil had risen significantly; they had not. It was the 'political'

costs that had risen, a reflection of the real value of a finite resource in an oil dependent world.

The initial response to the crisis in the West was to create the International Energy Agency (IEA) to coordinate policy initiatives among its twenty members from Western Europe (excluding France), North America, Japan and Australasia.[59] The main principles agreed by members of the IEA for energy policy included:

- less dependence on imported oil;
- progressive substitution of oil for uses where its efficiency is low, for example in electricity generation;
- conservation measures to limit demand;
- promotion of the use of coal, especially in power stations;
- expansion of nuclear capacity;
- stronger emphasis on energy R.&D. into coal conversion, nuclear fusion and renewable technologies.

In essence, most governments have followed a tripartite strategy for the future based on coal, conservation and nuclear technologies (Co-Co-Nuc). The basic philosophy centres on reducing oil imports from OPEC whilst developing indigenous resources to meet demand. Oil and natural gas are seen to have limited potential beyond the year 2000; hence, they will become increasingly devoted to premium uses such as space heating, transportation and the chemical industry. Investment into coal production and expansion of the international coal trade will enhance the market potential for coal in power generation in the short term, prior to the development of liquefaction and gasification technologies for use when oil and natural gas become scarce. The other supply technology earmarked for growth is nuclear power. Nuclear power will increasingly provide a larger proportion of electricity supplied, thereby releasing fossil fuels for other uses. Conservation makes up the third component of the tripartite strategy or Co-Co-Nuc. Unlike the coal and nuclear options, conservation technologies require less capital investment to maintain the balance between energy supply and demand. Nevertheless, many of the emergency measures introduced during the 1973/74 crisis have been phased out. Governments have preferred to play a passive role in persuading consumers to save energy. The price mechanism has been the main instrument of government policy along with establishing minimum energy efficiency standards and incentives for investment into energy saving technologies.

It would be difficult to quantify the role that conservation has played in dampening energy demand in the West since 1973. Sluggish economic growth during the recession has tempered energy demand especially in the energy intensive industries, such as iron and steel. Hence, a combination of factors has caused many national governments to downgrade their forecasts of energy demand by the end of the century. This is fortuitous in that original supply forecasts do not look attainable over the same period.

The IEA advocated that national governments should develop their indigenous reserves to ensure greater security of supplies. It is clear that the quest for energy self-sufficiency will be easier for some countries than for others. The relative weighting of Co-Co-Nuc in each nation's strategy is a function of dependence on OPEC oil and the availability of domestic resources. Energy-rich countries such as the US, Canada and the UK have the enviable task of choosing the appropriate 'energy mix' from a range of available options. At the other extreme, nations such as Japan and France were more vulnerable to OPEC action because of their reliance on imported oil. Their vulnerability was accentuated by a lack of indigenous power resources. Not surprisingly both countries have ventured down the nuclear road at a faster pace than some of their Western counterparts.

The economic dislocation experienced by industrialized countries due to rising energy prices has overshadowed the acute problems being faced by the non-OPEC countries of the developing world. Developing countries only account for 12% of world commercial energy consumption[60] but their populations and their economies are growing faster than those of the 'North'. It is envisaged that the non-OPEC developing countries will increase their share of world oil consumption from 10% in 1980 to between 35 and 40% by the year 2000 as they pass through the most energy-intensive stage of their economic development.[61] Whether some of these countries can now afford to undertake ambitious development plans is in doubt due to the escalating oil prices of the 1970s.

Much of the economic growth in developing countries was fuelled by imported oil. Consequently, the oil bill for non-OPEC nations rose dramatically from $8 billion to $51 billion between 1973 and 1980.[62] During the same period oil imports, as a proportion of total imports, rose from 12 to 22%, thereby diverting investment from other sectors of the economy.

Some developing countries have been able to absorb the price increases better than others. The newly industrialized countries (NICs) have much greater export earnings potential and a better developed energy infrastructure than the poor developing countries. The NIC's can therefore absorb increased energy costs and diversify supply much easier than the poor countries which lack sophisticated electricity grid systems and are often dependent on petroleum as their main form of commercial energy. According to Turner, their plight has been made worse by the friction between OPEC and the oil companies because the multinationals have less incentive to supply small markets. The net result of this action is that the poorer countries are forced to deal directly with oil producing governments or to buy on the more expensive spot market.[63] Commercial energy consumption in the non-OPEC developing countries is projected to grow from 12·4 million barrels a day (mbd) to 22·8 mbd from 1980 to 1990 (Table 3.10). At the same time, production is expected to rise from 7·8 to 15·2 mbd, resulting in a widening of the 'energy gap' by 3 mbd.

In the light of projected trends, non-OPEC developing countries have formulated strategies to reduce their dependence upon imported oil – the fuel responsible for the widening gap (Table 3.10). The World Bank has assisted these countries in formulating an energy strategy, in addition to providing most of the public funding for exploration and development. The energy programme from 1981 to 1985 will account for 17% of total bank lending; however, this is not considered sufficient for the investment needs of the developing countries.[64] Most of the investment is earmarked for electric power projects (58%) but oil and natural gas projects have substantially increased their share compared with earlier years.[65]

Of the developing countries, the NIC's have followed the approach of their 'Northern' counterparts. Countries such as South Korea, Taiwan, Brazil, Argentina, Mexico and India are committed to nuclear expansion and further

Table 3.10: Primary commercial energy in developing countries, 1980 and 1990 (million barrels of oil equivalent).
Source: R. Goodman, December 1980, Managing the demand for energy in the developing world, *Finance and Development*

| | 1980 | | | | 1990 | | | |
| | Less developed countries | | Oil importing developing countries | | Less developed countries | | Oil importing developing countries | |
	Production	Consumption	Production	Consumption	Production	Consumption	Production	Consumption
Oil	13·2	9·2	2·0	6·5	19·4	15·4	3·6	11·4
Gas	3·0	2·1	1·5	1·4	5·2	3·0	2·6	2·6
Coal	2·5	2·6	2·4	2·5	3·7	3·8	3·3	3·4
Hydro	1·9	1·9	1·5	1·5	4·1	4·1	3·2	3·2
Nuclear	0·1	0·1	0·1	0·1	1·2	1·2	1·0	1·0
Other*	0·3	0·8	0·3	0·4	1·9	3·1	1·5	1·2
Total	21·0	16·7	7·8	12·4	35·5	30·6	15·2	22·8

* Includes alcohol and other non-conventional primary energy sources.

development of their indigenous fossil fuel reserves. In the field of conservation, savings can be made with the introduction of modern energy-efficient equipment in new industrial plants coupled with improvements in existing production processes. Hence, the Co-Co-Nuc strategy is partly relevant to the developing world. It is not really pertinent to rural areas where most of the energy consumed is non-commercial energy. Hence, conservation measures can only have a marginal effect as little energy is wasted. Although appropriate solar and biomass technologies would increase energy supplies and reduce pressure on traditional scarce resources such as firewood, most of the rural poor still cannot afford the capital outlay for these technologies.

3.5.1 The Need for Management

If the ultimate goal of energy resource management is to ensure fuel supplies at an acceptable cost to consumers, then the 1970s brought into sharp focus the weakness of existing policies. The political cost of oil supplies has changed the framework for energy decision making. Internationally, the IEA members have agreed to pool oil supplies in times of emergency, and the US – the world's largest consumer of oil – has built up its Strategic Petroleum Reserve to ensure continuity of supply in the event of further political crises.[66] These short-term measures will give nations a breathing space in which to develop their own energy reserves and lessen their dependence upon OPEC oil.

Within the context of domestic energy production, key management decisions are being taken. Energy projects require long lead times; hence, accuracy of long term forecasting is a prerequisite for maximizing the timing of investments. Most energy policies formulated immediately after the 1973/74 crisis assumed higher rates of economic growth than have been achieved to date or are likely to be realized in the future. On the supply side, the first schemes designed to achieve self-reliance were over-optimistic. Objectors at public hearings invariably question the need for particular projects in view of sluggish demand and the downgrading of forecasts from one year to the next.

In essence, the key to effective energy resource management is a clear definition of the objectives of national policy. If greater self-sufficiency is a desired goal, the following questions must be answered:

- what is the desirable energy supply mix?
- what is the role of conservation technologies?
- what will be the economic, social and environmental costs of these decisions?
- what will be the impact of energy investment on other aspects of the economy?

In the long run, countries committed to developing their indigenous resources will have to decide upon which energy future is most acceptable to their society. Already, referenda have been carried out in countries and provinces throughout the world on the issue of nuclear power.[67] The nuclear issue illustrates some of the problems in reconciling national and local government policy objectives. It may be national policy to 'go nuclear' but the chosen sites for nuclear installations (especially waste disposal facilities) could be rejected by local planning authorities. The problem of national versus regional goals for energy development has been more marked in recent years as exploration for fossil fuels has moved into areas previously immune from energy-related activity. Public hearings have therefore focused upon social and environmental costs in addition to the economic and technical feasibility of particular energy projects. If national objectives override local opposition, the prime aim of resource management is to ensure minimal environmental disruption during resource exploitation. Energy decision making will be discussed more fully in Chapter 10.

3.6.1 Energy Futures

The future is very uncertain, but of one thing we can be sure – the world is not about to run out of energy. There are still plentiful reserves waiting to be exploited. Whether and how soon they are tapped will depend partly on the state of technology, but mainly upon the level of prices prevailing on the world market.[68]

This assertion is far removed from the pessimistic forecasts of the 1970s which predicted impending 'energy gaps', the rapid depletion of oil reserves and thus the urgent necessity to develop alternative sources of energy.[69] (The American CIA's study forecast that oil demand would overtake supply by 1983!) Most forecasts were based on the assumption of continued high rates of economic growth that have never materialized. The net result of transition from low cost to high-cost energy economies is that energy demand has remained depressed in the industrialized countries with most growth being experienced in the developing world.

Adjustment to the realities of the new energy situation has delayed the move from fossil-fuelled to self-sustained economies based on nuclear and renewable energy sources. It is unlikely that oil will relinquish its share of the world market in the manner predicted in the 1970s. The development of small marginal fields, the use of enhanced recovery techniques and the eventual exploitation of unconventional oil deposits – shales, tar sands and heavy oil – will ensure continued availability of oil. If shortages do occur before 2000, this will be due to political factors rather than any physical scarcity of oil and gas. Odell and Rosing have shown that the oil companies have changed their views with regard to the availability of oil reserves since the 1973/74 crisis.[70] Prior to 1973, the oil majors exuded confidence about supplying oil for the foreseeable future. In the wake of the crisis, this optimism turned into extreme pessimism, with forecasts that production would peak by the late 1980s. In view of the downturn in demand for oil since 1973, the volte-face by the oil companies is merely a reflection of their exclusion from specific oil provinces rather than any physical shortage of oil. Furthermore, Odell and Rosing chastise governments that overtax the oil companies and stifle their motivation to explore. In essence, they argue that there would be enough oil to satisfy world demand well into the next century if the institutional framework was conducive to development.

According to the World Coal Study, coal will act as a bridge to the future. Indeed, coal has much greater long-term potential than oil and gas. It was argued in section 3.3.2, however, that forecasts of coal demand and the international market for coal were very optimistic. Recession has hit those industries which constitute the prime markets for coal – the steel industry in particular, and to a lesser extent the electricity supply industry. Other potential markets, such as the domestic, industrial and commercial heating markets, are reluctant to be weaned away from oil and gas. With stabilization of oil prices in the early 1980s, the switch to coal will be deferred for as long as possible.

The 1973/74 crisis was originally seen by the nuclear power industry as a boon. If oil was no longer cheap and readily available, nuclear power would plug the 'energy gap'. Problems with reactor design, safety standards and escalating costs during a period of moderate demand have dampened some of the optimism concerning the nuclear option. The US, which has the largest programme in the world, suffered further setbacks to its nuclear plans as a result of the Three Mile Island accident in 1979, which cast doubt on the desirability of building PWRs under licence in other countries. Fortunately, a slackening of demand has given the nuclear industry more time to ensure greater reactor reliability and to seek an acceptable solution to waste disposal.

Whilst the nuclear industry has not fulfilled expectations since 1973, conservation and renewable technologies have begun to make a significant impact in the market place. For example, few forecasters would have predicted in the early 1970s that in the US firewood would supply twice as much delivered energy as nuclear power by the early 1980s.[71] High energy prices have stimulated efforts to improve energy efficiency and encouraged growth in solar and biomass technologies. Nevertheless, the oil glut of the early 1980s has limited investment to the most cost effective technologies. The future of the world's energy resources will largely be dependent upon the level of prices prevailing on the world market, the cost competitiveness of supply alternatives and the political security of supplies.

4   Commodities

4.1.1 Introduction

At the end of the 1970s, exports of primary products, excluding oil, still represented nearly half the value of exports of developing countries. Thirty per cent of the developing countries depended on non-oil primary commodities to earn 70 per cent or more of their export earnings, and they included some of the poorest countries of the world.[1]

The plight of these poorest countries has been aggravated in the decade since the energy crisis by spiralling energy bills and declining demand for their raw materials abroad due to the continuing world economic recession. Countries such as Uganda – 96% of its exports are coffee – and Sudan, 39% dependent on cotton, have been caught in a web of debt. But even their problems have been overshadowed by the scale of the indebtedness of middle-income, aspiring countries whose indebtedness has threatened the international banking system.[2] The only successful policy objective to materialize from this situation has been 'Northern' governments' achievements in controlling inflation, gained at the expense of poor 'Southern' countries where the lowest commodity prices for over 30 years have been received.

    The evolving relationship between 'North' and 'South' with regard to the political ramifications of commodity development, especially the role of *strategic* minerals considered vital to the well-being of the 'North', is an important theme in this chapter. Transnationals, backed by their own governments, have met with increased resistance to their operations from 'Southern' governments that have sought more control of their resources and better prices and terms of trade for their commodities. The quest for a new international economic order found expression through commodity development. The policy responses by both 'Northern' and 'Southern' governments to this dynamic situation will be discussed here as a primer to a more thorough analysis of UN and other initiatives at harmonizing 'North–South' relations in Chapter 11. What will become clear from this aspect of the 'North–South' debate is the necessity for better management at an international level. The world is *not* going to run out of commodities, but in a political climate of distrust, capital investment will not be forthcoming to ensure supplies of 'hard' commodities for the future if an upturn in demand should occur. Before dealing with these issues in more depth, it is first necessary to identify the types of commodity utilized by modern societies and to monitor their pattern of supply and demand.

4.1.2 Types of Commodity

In its widest possible sense the term 'commodities' would cover the resources discussed in Chapters 3 and 5. However, certain primary products warrant special treatment because of their importance in international trading and the

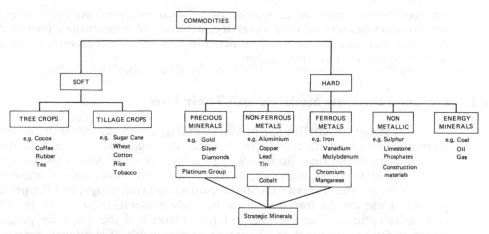

Figure 4.1 Types of Commodity

need for organized market institutions, such as the London Metal Exchange (LME), London Commodity Exchange, New York Commodity Exchange (COMEX) and the Chicago Board of Trade, to establish trading prices.

In classifications of commodities, the first major distinction is between what are commonly known as *hard* and *soft* commodities or, more appropriately, non-renewable and renewable commodities (Figure 4.1). Soft commodities are associated with plantation agriculture and cash cropping, whereby crops are grown for export rather than indigenous consumption. Within this group a distinction is made between *tree crops* and *tillage crops*. The latter can be more responsive to the vagaries of market price fluctuations than tree crops which have longer production cycles when new investment decisions are taken. Hard commodities are the raw materials that provide the basis for modern industrial processes. A general classification of these commodities is shown in Figure 4.1. *Energy minerals*, discussed in Chapter 3, and *non-fuel minerals*, which can be further sub-divided into *precious minerals*, *ferrous*, *non-ferrous* and *non-metallic minerals*, provide a broad typology of mineral commodities. Within these groups, minerals will come in all shapes and sizes with varying values, for example uranium and platinum are low-volume, high-value minerals compared with many of the non-metallics – sand, gravel, salt – which are high-volume and low-value materials. Blunden sub-divides the non-metallic group into *ubiquitous* non-metalliferous minerals and *localized* non-metalliferous minerals on the basis of their place and unit values[3]. For example, most of the materials used in the construction industry are high-volume, low-value minerals that incur high transport cost penalties and are therefore exploited in proximity to market demand. The localized minerals, on the other hand, are more geographically dispersed in occurrence, are of higher value and can therefore bear higher transport costs to more distant markets. These non-metals include potash and salt for the fertilizer and chemical industries and china clay for pottery and paper making.

A final categorization which has been identified by 'Northern' governments is that of *strategic minerals*. Minerals can be strategic in the sense that national security is threatened if they are denied for industrial (notable defence) purposes. From a range of studies on possible strategic minerals, four groups are consistently identified as worthy of political consideration by 'Northern' governments because of their necessity, difficulty of substitution, import dependence and possible political vulnerability of supply – chromium, manganese, cobalt and the platinum group[4].

4.2.1 Demand for Commodities and Their Uses

The importance to civilization of commodities, especially minerals, is highlighted by the nomenclature of epochs commemorating man's use of his natural environment: Stone Age, Bronze Age, Iron Age, Nuclear Age. This ingenuity in the use of available materials varies in time and space. As was shown in Chapter 1, resource use is a function of culture and technology, and the present pattern of use can be traced back to the early exploration period of the 15th and 16th centuries. The discovery of new plants and the quest for precious minerals sowed the seeds of 'corporate imperialism'[5]. Traditional tastes and demands changed to accommodate new products, and the companies involved, from the first trading firms to the present day multinationals, were strongly involved in the marketing of new commodities.

Western Europe was a willing consumer of tropical produce from newly discovered colonies in Africa, Asia and America. Tea, coffee, cocoa and the intoxicating rum from fermented sugar became established beverages. Cotton and jute formed the basis of a thriving textile industry. The advent of the automobile encouraged the exploitation of rubber on a large scale. However, soft commodities have been subjected to substitution, the whims of changing tastes and market saturation in an increasingly affluent modern Western society. Industrial raw materials – cotton, jute and rubber – face competition from oil-based synthetic fibres. Beverages have reached a market hiatus with low income elasticities in the 'North'. Sugar and tobacco have been the targets of health food campaigns, especially in the US. All of which points to a stabilization of demand for many soft commodities in the 1970s and 1980s.

By contrast, mineral commodities would almost certainly experience growth if there were a slight upturn in the economy. In the early 1980s, however, demand remained depressed and real prices for some commodities reached record lows despite production cut-backs and stock reductions by consumers. Until the recession began to bite in the late 1970s, world consumption[6] of metallic minerals had grown at a spectacular rate, especially in the period after World War II. Between 1950 and the mid 1970s, the average, annual rate of growth was around 6%, with aluminium and the newer alloying minerals, such as nickel, chromite, molybdenum and titanium, achieving the highest growth rates[7]. Table 4.1 summarizes the evolution of the use of minerals from the traditional metals of the pre-20th century period to the modern ferrous-alloys developed to meet the needs of an industrial society.

Table 4.1: Timescales of large-scale consumption of selected minerals

Pre–20th century	'Traditional' base metals – iron ore, lead, zinc, copper and tin; manganese
1900–1945	Chromium, nickel, aluminium, molybdenum and tungsten
Early post-war	Cobalt, silicon, titanium
1951–to date	Zirconium, vanadium, columbium

Copper, iron and aluminium have been the three most important base minerals to civilization. Copper was critical to early civilizations because it was the only metal which occurred in a workable form for early man to smelt it for making tools and ornaments. Its main use since the turn of this century has been in electrical appliances because of its high electrical conductivity and as an alloy in shipbuilding because of its resistance to salt-water corrosion. Modern civilization, however, has been founded on iron and steel since the discovery by Darby in 1709 of how to smelt iron from coke. Further technological breakthroughs in the conversion of iron to steel in the 19th century laid the basis for the mass consumption society of the 20th century. The time lag from innovation to wholesale adoption can be half a century. This was the case for Darby's innovations. In the case of bauxite, the technology for extracting alumina and reducing it to aluminium was known in the 1880s, but not applied on a large scale until the 1920s. The lightness and durability of aluminium gave it a multiplicity of uses; but many decades passed before aluminium broke into world markets. Now its properties are indispensable to the aerospace and automobile industries in addition to having widespread applications in the housing and consumer goods sectors.

The remaining minerals listed as 20th century minerals with respect to their applications in Table 4.1 are either non-metallic – zirconium, silicon – or alloying metallic minerals. The latter were known as 'minor' minerals, often found in association with the key metals, but their increased use in the automotive, aerospace, general engineering and electrical industries has labelled many of them as critical strategic minerals for defence purposes. As these industries required steels that could withstand greater pressures and higher temperatures, chromium, cobalt, tungsten, vanadium, molybdenum, titanium and columbium were developed as alloying elements to improve the properties of steel. Some of these metals have other specialized functions: chromium as a protective, corrosion resistant surface, tungsten carbides for use in machine and mining tools and cobalt for its magnetic characteristics.

The use of zirconium and silicon in the post World War II era highlights the rapid transition to a 'high tech', post-industrial society. Zirconium – used as fuel cladding in Pressurised Water Reactors (PWRs) – and of course, uranium, were of little value to society until the creation of nuclear fission in 1942 and the rapid development of nuclear technology in the post-1945 era. The ubiquitous silicon is now a key element in the ceramics, aerospace and electronics industries – all of which are post World War II developments.

In terms of demand for these minerals, the industrial 'North' is the greatest consumer, with the US capturing the major share of the market. In 1978 its demand for minerals was as great as of its demand for fuels. The US consumed around one-quarter of world production[8]. This appetite for the world's mineral wealth has resulted in the US and other industrialized, developed countries becoming dependent upon imports for a large share of their domestic consumption of specific minerals (see Table 4.2). The USSR is much more self-sufficient in minerals than its 'Northern', capitalist counterparts; hence, continuity of supplies is a key geopolitical issue in the international mining industry, a point which will become apparent in the next section on the patterns of supply.

Table 4.2: Mineral imports as a percentage of mineral consumption, 1976.
Source: Council on Environmental Quality, 1982, *The Global 2000 Report to the President*

	United States	European Economic Community	Japan	USSR*
Bauxite	88	50	100	44
Chromium	90	95	95	0
Copper	16	99	93	4
Iron Ore	35	85	99	0
Lead	12	85	78	24
Manganese	100	99	90	0
Nickel	61	90	95	0
Tin	75	90	90	22
Zinc	60	74	63	13

* 1975

4.2.2 Patterns of Supply

a) Hard Commodities

'The prize in the struggle between the winners and losers among the developed capitalist countries was the low-cost, high-profit minerals of the underdeveloped countries. Unfortunately for the Third World, their economies and military power were not enough developed to stave off the predatory foreign powers, and in the nineteenth and twentieth centuries they were overwhelmed, either taken as outright colonies or as neocolonies.'[9]

Tanzer views the evolutionary pattern of mineral development as a geopolitical process in which the quest for minerals is equated with the desire for economic, military and political power. Great Britain – the 'workshop of the world' – relied on its own domestic reserves to fuel its industrial and military machinery throughout the 19th and 20th centuries.[10] Other aspiring nations, especially France and Germany, also developed their indigenous resources, but by the late 19th century most Western powers began to depend on their colonies to augment supplies. World War I and World War II weakened Western European states and the US took up the mantle of the dominant economic and political force in the capitalist world.

By the end of World War II, most mining was still heavily concentrated in the developed world. However, unprecedented economic growth, the advent of a consumer society and the arms race associated with the Cold War caused a search for rich, high-grade ores in the 'South' to supplement the rapidly depleting quality ores of the 'North'. Low labour costs, higher grade quality ores and improvements in transportation, led to the development of minerals in Zaire, Zambia, Guinea and South Africa in Africa; Chile, Brazil, Peru, Jamaica and Guyana in the Americas; and Malaysia, Thailand, Indonesia and New Caledonia in Asia. The pace of development in these countries has slackened during the past decade as mining companies, fearing expropriation of their assets, have channelled the bulk of new capital investment into 'safe' countries, notably the US, Canada, Australia and South Africa and into politically amenable 'Southern' countries such as Brazil and Chile (since the overthrow of Allende).

Although recent trends show a shift back to developing 'Northern' reserves, world mine production of sixteen key minerals in 1980 shows the importance in global markets of the developing countries (Table 4.3). For example, the OECD and the communist countries account for around 66% and 25% respectively of world demand[11] compared with the mineral export surplus situation of the developing countries. The planned economies of the communist countries, which have the objective of self-sufficiency, are clearly in a much healthier position regarding import dependence than the OECD, where molybdenum, and to a lesser extent zinc, lead, mercury and nickel are the only minerals on which dependence on 'outside' economic blocs is low and is unlikely to change in the future because of healthy reserves within OECD countries. In addition, the two mineral-rich communist powers - the USSR and China - have liberalized their trading policy with the West in the past decade by exporting fuels and minerals in return for technology and 'hard' currency to further their development plans.

Table 4.4 gives a more detailed breakdown of mine production by country rather than by economic/political bloc and illustrates the overwhelming concentration of production in a handful of countries for the key minerals identified in Table 4.3. Although the geographical distribution of mineral ores is spread across the earth,[12] the concentration of mining activity is a reflection of the evolution of the mining industry and its economic/political justification for exploiting specific areas and countries.

The alarming implication of Table 4.4 for the OECD countries is not so much the concentration of production in so many Third World countries but the significance of the USSR and South Africa as major producers. The political ramifications of dependence on those countries are obvious, and the situation is unlikely to improve because known reserves are also tied up there. For example, the Materials Forum of the UK identified eight minerals which they considered strategic because of the vulnerability of supplies through political instability or even industrial action in one company or mine.[13]

Table 4.5 shows the percentage of reserves tied up in particular countries:

- 97% of chromium in South Africa and Zimbabwe;
- 80% of manganese in South Africa and the USSR;
- 98% of the platinum group in South Africa and the USSR;
- 77% of columbium in Brazil;
- 47% of tungsten in China;
- 75% of cobalt in Third World countries; (21% in communist countries).

It is not surprising that most of the OECD countries have refused to sign the Law of the Sea Treaty on the grounds that the sections on deep-sea mining are against their interests, and those of the multinational companies. The richest prize on the seabed is manganese nodules which contain two out of the eight strategic mineral identified in Table 4.5 - manganese and cobalt - in addition to large reserves of nickel and copper. The Western multinationals have the technical expertise, the financial support and the political backing, not to harvest these minerals for the benefit of mankind as suggested by the UN, but to give the industrialized West a non-political source of scarce, key minerals (the Law of the Sea negotiations will be discussed in Chapter 11).

Table 4.3: Share of world mine production of 16 minerals, 1980. *Source:* British Geological Survey 1982, *World Mineral Statistics 1976–1980*

Commodity	OECD	Comecon	China	South Africa	Yugoslavia*	Albania†	Developing Countries
Bauxite	37·0	11·0	1·9	–	3·4	–	46·7
Chromium	5	26·2	–	35·9	–	11·6	21·3
Columbium Group	11·9	–	–	–	–	–	88·1
Cobalt	17	10·9	–	–	–	–	72·1
Copper	29·3	21·0	2·1	2·6	1·5	0·1	43·4
Iron Ore	33·2	27·8	8·3	2·9	N	N	27·8
Manganese	9·1	37·4	6·1	21·6	0·1	–	25·7
Mercury	38·0	35·3	10·8	–	–	–	15·9
Lead	45·7	21·4	4·4	2·4	3·4	–	22·7
Molybdenum	75·7	9·8	1·8	–	–	–	22·7
Nickel	38·9	24·6	1·5	3·4	N	1·1	30·5
Platinum Group	6·9	47·6	–	45·5	N	–	–
Tin	6·7	8·3	6·4	1·3	–	–	77·3
Tungsten	30·2	17·5	26·2	–	–	–	26·0
Vanadium	22·2	28·2	12·7	35·8	–	–	1·1
Zinc	51·6	22·1	2·4	1·3	1·5	–	21·1

N = negligible.
* Yugoslavia has a special status in OECD and participates in some Comecon bodies.
† Albania withdrew from Comecon in 1961.

Table 4.4: Concentration of mineral production of 16 minerals in 1980. *Source:* British Geological Survey 1982, *World Mineral Statistics 1976–1980*

Commodity	Degree of Concentration (No. of Countries)	(%)	Principal producing countries (%)
Bauxite	7	76	Australia (30), Jamaica (13), Guinea (13), USSR (7), Surinam (5), Brazil (5) and Guyana (3)
Chromium	3	74	South Africa (36), Albania (12), and USSR (26)
Columbium Group	1	83	Brazil
Cobalt	4	70	Zaire (45), Zambia (10), USSR (6) and Australia (9)
Copper	6	67	US (15), USSR (15), Chile (14), Canada (9), Zambia (8) and Zaire (6)
Iron Ore	7	77·5	USSR (27), Brazil (13), Australia (11), China (8), US (8), Canada (6) and India (4·5)
Manganese	6	87	USSR (37), South Africa (22), Brazil (8), Gabon (8), India (6) and China (6)
Mercury	4	82·5	USSR (33), Spain (17·5), Algeria (16) and US (16)
Lead	5	55	USSR (16), US (15), Australia (11), Canada (8) and Peru (5)
Molybdenum	4	95	US (63), Chile (12), Canada (11) and USSR (9)
Nickel	4	65	Canada (26), USSR (19), New Caledonia (12) and Australia (8)
Platinum Group	2	93·5	USSR (48) and South Africa (45·5)
Tin	5	75	Malaysia (27), Thailand (15), Indonesia (14), Bolivia (12) and USSR (7)
Tungsten	5	64	China (26), USSR (17), Canada (7), Bolivia (7) and Australia (7)
Vanadium	5	94	South Africa (36), USSR (25), China (13), US (12) and Finland (8)
Zinc	5	54	Canada (17), USSR (16), Australia (18), Peru (8) and US (5)

Table 4.5: Reserves of strategic minerals in 1978. *Source:* Materials Forum, Strategic Minerals and the United Kingdom, 1981, Institute of Mechanical Engineers

Chromium		Manganese	
Country	*Reserves (%)*	*Country*	*Reserves (%)*
South Africa	67·6	South Africa	42·8
Zimbabwe	29·8	USSR	37·9
USSR	0·6	Australia	8·7
Finland	0·3	Gabon	4·6
India	0·2	Brazil	2·4
Brazil	0·2	India	1·5
Others	1·3	Others	2·1

Cobalt		Vanadium	
Country	*Reserves (%)*	*Country*	*Reserves (%)*
Zaire	30·0	USSR	73·4
Communist Countries	21·0	South Africa	18·3
New Caledonia	18·0	Chile	1·4
Philippines	13·0	US	1·1
Zambia	8·0	Finland	0·5
Australia	3·0	Others	5·3
Canada	2·0		
Others	4·0	Molybdenum	

Tungsten		*Country*	*Reserves (%)*
		US	43·3
Country	*Reserves (%)*	Chile	31·2
China	47·0	USSR	8·6
Canada	11·0	Canada	7·5
USSR	8·0	Peru	2·9
US	6·0	Others	6·5
North Korea	5·5		
Turkey	4·0	Columbium	
Australia	4·0	*Country*	*Reserves (%)*
Other Communist Countries	2·5	Brazil	76·6
South Korea	2·0	USSR	6·3
Bolivia	2·0	Canada	5·5
Burma	1·5	Zaire	3·8
Others	6·0	Nigeria	3·0
		Others	4·6

Platinum Group	
Country	*Reserves (%)*
South Africa	73·0
USSR	25·0
Others	2·0

b) Soft Commodities

Most of the internationally traded soft commodities were discovered by European colonialists and developed on agricultural plantations. Indeed, corporate imperialism had its roots in the slave-based revolution from 1450 to 1750.[14] The foundation of European prosperity was derived from slave-based tropical production, which generated sufficient wealth for Britain and other developed nations to 'take off' into industrialization. The trade between Europe, Africa and the Americas, in which slaves were transported on the vital second leg of the triangular journey, the middle passage, fostered coastal development of plantations in the South-east USA, Caribbean and north-east Latin America. Sugar was in much demand in Northern Europe in the 17th century and was therefore grown where climatically feasible. For example, Portugal used slaves from its African colony of Angola to work the cane plantations, gins and refineries developed in Bahia, north-east Brazil prior to shipping the refined product back to the mother country.

Most colonial activity at this time, however, centred upon the Caribbean, where the West Indies and Antilles islands provided Western Europe with sugar, coffee, cotton and tobacco. The British American colonies were not particularly fruitful at this time. They were too cold for sugar cane. Tobacco was grown on the vast estates in Virginia and Maryland. Further south and west the Spanish and French introduced sugar and cotton plantations. The overall pattern of the slave economies varied according to soil fertility and slave availability. Slave revolts were endemic in the Caribbean and, coupled with soil exhaustion, produced a type of plantation capitalism which shifted from one area or country to others nearby.[15]

After the abolition of slavery in the 19th century, the colonial powers turned their attention to Asia and Africa. Already, the British Empire stretched eastwards to India. The Dutch had had a well-established mercantile position in the East Indies from the early 17th century. By 1712, coffee plantations were introduced in Java and the Dutch built up a 'culture system' superimposing other cash crops – coffee, tobacco and spices – upon the indigenous pattern of shifting cultivation. On annexing Burma and Malaya, the British developed tree crop commodities, notably teak and rubber, the latter introduced from the Amazon at the turn of the century.

The main scramble for possessions, and by implication for commodities, occurred in Africa between 1880 until the commencement of World War I. The effect of colonialism was to create a threefold categorization of farm produce where only one existed in the past,[16] namely:

a) new export crops were introduced – coffee, cocoa and tea;
b) local crops were grown for export – groundnuts, palm oil and cotton;
c) local crops were grown for indigenous consumption – yams, millet and cassava.

Colonial administration would then direct capital and R. & D. onto the cash crops with most export potential, neglecting the basic food crops for local consumption. The emphasis on cash crop production continued after independence because of its value as an earner of foreign exchange. The importance of coffee to Uganda and cotton to Sudan were mentioned earlier; Ghana, the Ivory Coast and Cameroon are respectively, 56%, 38% and 37% dependent on cocoa for export earnings.[17]

The neo-colonial pattern of the post-1945 era has favoured the 'North', especially the US. As population grew in the 'South' and the demand for food crops increased, countries of the 'South' which had been net exporters of grains have progressively become more dependent upon the 'North' (and the US in particular) for staple commodities while they continued to export 'luxury' commodities.[18] For example, in 1980/81, the 'North' produced two-thirds of the world's wheat harvest of 445 million tonnes, and of the 92 million tonnes traded internationally 61% was imported by 'Southern' countries.[19]

The historical legacy of colonial production systems is still very much in evidence. Most tropical soft commodity production remains concentrated in specific areas and countries. For example:

- *Rubber* production in South-East Asia (Malaysia (42%), Indonesia (23%) and Thailand (13%)).[20]
- *Jute* production in the Indian subcontinent (India (31%), Bangladesh (24%).[21]
- *Coffee* production throughout the tropical world, with Brazil (33%) and Columbia (12%) dominating production and export quotas (25% and 17% respectively).[22]
- The *tea* export market is derived from India (23%), Sri Lanka (22%), China (10%) and Indonesia (6%).[28]

Two commodities influenced strongly by 'Northern' production are cotton and sugar. The US has grown cotton since the days of the slave trade. The USSR and China are the world's main cotton producers. Consequently 1ZMAR – a group of 'Southern' producers (excluding China) – have only 30% of the world export market.[24] The case of sugar is interesting: plantations were developed by European colonialists to meet demands for sugar cane from the 17th century onwards. However, the increased share of sugar beet, at the expense of cane,[25] has removed the 'South's' monopoly to the extent that they produce only 55% of the world's sugar production.[26] In this instance, the demise of the 'South' is illustrated by the example of the EEC, formerly a net importer of sugar, which has now subsidized its beet farmers to produce a marketable surplus. It accounted for 25% of the sugar traded in the world market in 1982.[27]

Problems and Strategies

4.4.1(a) The Problems

The 'South's' quest for a new international economic order since UNCTAD IV (United Nations Conference on Trade and Development) in Santiago in 1972 was intrinsically tied up with its demands for a new approach to the pricing, control and trading of commodities. The successful action of OPEC in 1973 and the commodity price boom of 1973/74 raised hopes in the 'South' of a change in the international commodity rules. However, by early 1983 this optimism had turned into outright pessimism as prices collapsed, international agreements faltered and adherence to the status quo was the order of the day.

(i) Price Instability

Unstable commodity prices have been a key issue in discussions between 'North' and 'South' for a long time. It is in the interest of both to secure price stabilization – the 'South' to maintain foreign exchange earnings for their development, the 'North' to secure a guaranteed flow of supplies to fuel their industries. Despite this apparent compatibility, commodity prices are much less stable than the price of manufactured goods. McNicol shows that between 1951 and 1975, the coefficient of variation for the prices of fifteen commodities was around twice that of manufactured goods.[28] Whilst this analysis depicts a general trend for several commodities, much variation exists between one type of commodity and another. The vagaries of market prices for soft commodities are mainly a function of weather and other natural hazard conditions around the globe. For example, the sudden spurt in coffee price levels in 1975 happened in the wake of severe frosts which decimated much of the Brazilian crop. In 1983 the bush fires in the Ivory Coast caused price rises for cocoa because of the fear of impending shortages.

In the case of hard commodities, the state of the world economy is the main determinant of demand/supply and therefore of prices, but other forces are also at work. It has been suggested that fluctuations in prices according to surplus/scarcity conditions are magnified by speculation on the commodity exchanges. Hence, traded metals such as copper, lead and zinc appear to experience greater short-term price volatility than those for which producer prices are the norm.[29] The magnitude of the rise and fall in copper prices, especially in 1974/75 when prices varied from £1,400 to £500 per tonne, has been attributed to the copper companies' peculiar pricing policy. For example, the markets for nickel and aluminium are tightly controlled by a few multinationals. Prices, and therefore profits, are much more stable than with copper which is controlled by a much larger oligopoly constituted of multinationals, smaller, private independents and nationalized corporations.[30]

(ii) Problems of Control and Ownership

In addition to fluctuations in the price of their commodities, 'Southern' producers have experienced deteriorating terms of trade and a lack of marketing power. They have been unable to capture a major share of the high-value, refining or processing stage of raw materials production. It is estimated that the cut received by the developing countries is around 25% of final consumer prices.[31] The Brandt Commission suggested that this situation has evolved for soft commodities because of the weak bargaining position of farmers in relation to marketing/trading organizations. Their developed country counterparts have formed cooperatives and associations to ensure a fairer return on their produce.[32] The degree to which minerals are processed in producing countries or other 'Southern' countries is a function of the type of mineral, of the structure of the industry and of the relative costs of production and distribution. For example, the most profitable stage of the production process for copper is extraction, whereas most other raw materials (the notable exception being oil) generate greater profits in the later stages of production. This fact, coupled with a high degree of state-owned production in the main developing countries has resulted in 75% of mined copper being processed in the producing countries.[33] By contrast, most processing of iron ore and bauxite occurs in the developed world, although the high energy and labour costs involved has led to more projects being developed in the 'South' in recent years, namely, aluminium smelting in Brazil and Venezuela and steel production in Liberia and Brazil.

Some developing countries tried to shape their own commodity destiny through nationalization of the transnationals' assets in a surge of nationalistic fervour in the post-independence era, especially in the 1960s. Between 1956 and 1972 over 20% of the multinationals' mining assets were expropriated.[34] Furthermore, 'creeping expropriations' in the form of higher taxation or re-negotiated contracts have dissuaded many of these companies from investing in the richer, more abundant ores of the 'South'.[35] For example, one survey of North American mining companies in the mid-1970s showed that 80% of their exploration activity had been confined to the developed countries. Another survey, of fourteen European mining firms, revealed that from 1961 to 1977 their share of exploration expenditures in developing countries fell from 57 to 19%.[36]

The relationship between transnationals and host governments is a problematic one. The transnationals have the experience, capital and technology to mine the lucrative reserves of the developing countries. The developing countries, even when they nationalize the mines, remain dependent on external assistance to finance the market and the product. It was shown earlier that much of current copper production capacity in developing countries is state-owned, but these companies continue to use the transnationals as agents to market their copper in the main consuming countries of the 'North'.

(iii) Terms of Trade

A major grievance of the developing countries is the international trading environment within which they sell their commodities. Even if indigenous processing were expanded, access to 'Northern' markets is discouraged through the use of protectionist tarrifs. For example, the US, EEC and Japan are generally amenable to the importation of unprocessed commodities. But they impose a scale of levies on processed products according to the stage of production. For example, the unweighted average of tariffs facing developing countries that export cocoa products into ten industrial countries was 2·6% for cocoa beans, 4·3% for processed cocoa and 11·8% for chocolate products.[37]

Hence the 'rules of international trade' have relegated many 'Southern' countries to the role of exporters of primary raw materials and importers of finished, manufactured goods. Historically, the price of commodities has risen much more slowly over time than the price of manufactured products. Thus the 'terms of trade' between the 'South' and the 'North' (unit index of exports divided by unit value index of imports) has been constantly deteriorating. Between 1953 and 1975 the terms-of-trade index for commodities (excluding oil), based at 100 in 1970, fell from 109 to 84.[38] Fidel Castro attributed the declining buying power of 'Southern' countries to the adverse terms of trade. In his speech to the summit of non-aligned countries in 1983, he pointed out that:

- in 1960, 6·3 tons of oil could be purchased with the sale of a ton of sugar. In 1982, only 0·7 tons of oil could be bought with the same amount of sugar;
- in 1960, 37·3 tons of fertilizers could be bought for a ton of coffee. In 1982, only 15·8 tons could be bought;

- in 1959, one ton of copper wire would buy 39 X-ray tubes for medical purposes. By late 1982, only three X-ray tubes could be bought with that same ton.[39]

4.4.1b) The Strategies

In the decade since the 'South' called for a new international economic order, its success at winning concessions from the 'North' has been limited by the worsening recession. Indeed, the 'North's' return to protecting uncompetitive industries in order to arrest rising unemployment has militated against the 'South's' hopes for a greater liberalization of trade. Moreover, depressed demand for commodities and a desire by Western governments to control inflation has contributed to a slump in prices. Prices began to recover only in 1983 with the slight prospect of an upturn in the world economic climate.

(i) The South

The 'South's' main platform for negotiating better terms for their commodities is the UN, especially UNCTAD. In 1974, UNCTAD proposed an Integrated Programme for Commodities (IPC). This would widen the multilateral bargaining between producers and consumers, then confined to a few commodities (coffee, sugar and tin) that had a history of International Commodity Agreements (ICAs) stretching back to the pre-World War II era. In 1976, at UNCTAD *IV* in Nairobi, an IPC programme was adopted, backed up by a Common Fund which would finance buffer stocks, trade on its own account in special circumstances and provide loans or grants to poorer countries needing to diversify their economies. From a range of commodities, ten 'core' products were identified for the initial stage of the programme. These were the traditional commodities already mentioned – sugar, coffee and tin, plus cocoa (its first ICA had been reached in 1973) and cotton, jute, sisal, rubber, tea and copper. The main objective of the IPC proposal was to regulate the short-term fluctuation in supply and demand. This would be achieved through buffer stocking to buy supplies when prices fell below an agreed target and then releasing stocks when prices reached a specific maximum. The cocoa, rubber and tin negotiations have these provisions. Sugar stocks are held nationally under international control. The regulation of the coffee market is operated through a system of export quotas which are tightened or suspended according to predetermined price levels.

The IPC program has been only partly successful. To date, ICAs have been reached only for the five commodities listed above. The Common Fund, when established in June 1981, fell short of the expectations of most 'Southern' producers. Even the ICAs formulated to date have been disappointing to producers in terms of the range of prices negotiated. In the case of sugar, prices have often plummetted below the minimum target price. With the stagnation of demand for raw materials the 'North' has been in a strong bargaining position. These factors have forced the 'South' to review its position, and discussions amongst 'Southern' producers have begun to focus on the creation of associations to further their cause.

Table 4.6: Variables positively influencing a producers' association. *Source:*
Z. Mikdashi, 1976, The International Politics of Natural Resources, Cornell
University Press

Economic variables
 1. A large share of the world market
 2. Low price elasticity of demand
 3. Low price elasticity of supply outside the association
 4. High demand growth
 5. Few producers
 6. Numerous and dispersed buyers
 7. Low disparities in members' fixed-variable cost ratios, reserves, excess capacity
    and social discount rates
 8. High barriers of entry for competitors
 9. Non-recyclable product
10. Absence of major consumer stockpiles

Other variables
 1. Common awareness of vulnerability of members
 2. Common perception of net collective gain
 3. Common perception of effective collective means of action
 4. Cooperation or neutrality of transnational enterprises
 5. Cooperation or neutrality of major industrial powers

Cartelization has not been an effective weapon to date, with the notable exception of OPEC. Oil was a unique commodity, however. It could not be easily substituted. It was in heavy demand by western consumers, and OPEC's membership, especially the Arab nations, achieved cohesion when it mattered in the early 1970s. Nevertheless, the oil cartel has been under pressure in the early 1980s and its position has moved from trying to boost prices to controlling further decreases in prices in 1982/83 through the mechanism of production quotas.

Table 4.6 lists the main variables that dictate the likelihood of success for a producer association. In 1973 OPEC conformed to these positive variables. By 1983 higher prices had depressed demand, encouraged substitution and stockpiling, and parties outside the association had entered the market. Furthermore, the weakening of the cartel had fostered increased disunity among its membership on pricing policy.

The prospects for other commodity groups are not encouraging. The producer associations identified in Table 4.7 were created in the aftermath of the UN's declaration of a New International Economic Order and the immediate success of OPEC.[40] (CIPEC was formed earlier in 1967 in response to weakening copper prices.) Although these cartels control a large share of the world market, mineral commodities can be substituted, regulated and stockpiled, and difficulties have been encountered in achieving membership unity. For example, Chile is a renowned maverick in CIPEC negotiations. Australia, an OECD member, is a prominent producer of bauxite and iron ore and has development objectives different from other members of these cartels. Consequently, transnationals will seek cooperation with OECD members of a group when cartels begin to threaten their position, as occurred with bauxite. When *IBA* became militant along the lines of OPEC in the 1970s, the transnationals diverted production to Australia and to Brazil, which was not a member of the group.

Table 4.7: Major producer associations for commodities (excluding OPEC)

Commodity	Organization	Date of formation	Membership	Extent of Control of the Market
Bauxite	International Bauxite Association (IBA)	1974	Australia, Guinea, Guyana, Jamaica, Sierre Leone, Surinam, Yugoslavia, Dominica, Ghana, Haiti and Indonesia	76% of world production
Bananas	Union de Paises Exportadores del Banano (UPEB)	1974	Columbia, Costa Rica, Ecuador, Guatemala, Honduras, Nicaragua and Panama	78% of world exports
Copper	Counseil Intergouvernmental de Pays Exportateurs de Cuivre (CIPEC)	1967	Chile, Indonesia, Peru, Zaire and Zambia (Australia and Papua New Guinea are Associate Members)	33% of world production, 65% of world exports
Iron Ore	Association of Iron Ore Exporting Countries (AIEC)	1975	Algeria, Australia, Brazil, Chile, Mauritania, Peru, Tunisia, Sierra Leone, Venezuela and Sweden	36% of world production, 75% of non-communist exports

The effectiveness of producer power in soft commodities is even weaker. The problems encountered by UPEB (Table 4.7) are typical of the obstacles confronting many soft commodity producers. Their product is not indispensable. Transnationals dominate the market from the production, distribution to the final processing stage. Hence, attempts at increasing their share of revenue from export taxes have been thwarted by the companies' policy of playing one country off against another and by limiting or stopping shipments from countries adhering to UPEB policy.[41]

(ii) The North

It was shown in 4.2.2 that world commodity development evolved according to the relative military and economic supremacy of 'Northern' countries at any particular moment in time. The British Empire was sustained through its naval power which protected its access to colonial raw materials. By the end of World War II, the US had assumed supremacy in the free world.

US economic power was achieved through its access to mineral wealth at home and overseas. Increased foreign investment by transnationals was encouraged by government, but US-controlled mineral exploitation began to wane by the 1960s. On the one hand, the revival of war-torn economies in Western Europe and Japan witnessed increased competition in the market place. The Japanese in particular became a key negotiator in the 'South' offering technical and financial assistance in return for access to production. On the other hand, nationalistic fervour in the 'South' excluded US companies from areas they had previously controlled and expropriated their assets. Not that the US relinquished control without a political fight. The US government's response to the nationalization of oil refineries and nickel mining operations in Cuba (1959) and Allende's expropriation of Anaconda and Kennecott's assets without compensation (1971) is well known.[41]

The fear of further expropriations by unfriendly 'Southern' governments has made the transnationals ultra cautious about investing in potentially 'unsafe' countries. Industrialized countries now have insurance programmes that guarantee the profitability of foreign investment.[42] Nevertheless, they have tended to play safe by investing in the US, Canada, Australia and South Africa as a short-term measure and exploiting the world's oceans as a medium- or long-term strategy. To this end, they have received full support from their governments, which have refused to sign the Law of the Sea Treaty on this issue.

In the short term, the US, France, Germany and the UK have chosen to stockpile commodities as an insurance against political or economic disruption of supply. The US reserves system was established after World War II. In 1983 it covered ninety-three commodities, with an inventory value of $15 bn.[43] The main aim of the stockpile is to sustain the US through three years of war. Consequently, buying and selling by the General Services Administration to maintain stock can have profoundly disruptive market consequences. For example, 5,000 tonnes of tin were unloaded in early 1982, causing a collapse of tin prices from £9,000 to £7,000 a tonne within a matter of months.[44]

Other countries maintain only a few months' supply of a limited number of key minerals considered to be subject to possible supply contingencies. (Interestingly, the French consider zirconium a key mineral because of its value in its ambitious nuclear programme.) The UK, a recent member of the stockpiling club, took this course of action after assessments made of strategic requirements during the Falklands conflict. Its main priority was to buy four strategic minerals – chromium, cobalt, platinum and manganese – which are essential to defence, aerospace and other modern industrial processes but are difficult to substitute in the short term if supplies are cut off. As the production and reserves of these minerals are concentrated in the USSR, South Africa, Zimbabwe, Zambia and Zaire, continuity of supplies cannot be ensured (Tables 4.4 and 4.6). Indeed, one school of thought believes that the Soviet Union has a master plan to orchestrate trouble in the Middle East and central/southern Africa in order to sever the West's supply of oil and strategic minerals.[45] The prospect of a resource war being initiated in the short term is unlikely considering the poor performance of the Soviet economy and its need to export fuels and minerals to the West in order to gain hard currency to buy imports.

4.5.1 Commodity Futures and the Need for Management

The previous section outlined the forces at play between producers, consumers, transnationals and other institutions which have dictated the pace of commodity development until the present time. In the present period of uncertainty the future is difficult to predict. Will the world economy be restored to health? Will commodity prices pick up again? If so, when? The prospects for soft commodities are easier to foresee because these are less susceptible to changes in the world economy, with the possible exception of 'industrial' commodities such as jute, cotton, hard fibres and rubber. Demand for these 'industrial' commodities is intrinsically tied to the price of synthetic substitutes and thus to the price of oil. With the stabilization of world oil prices these are beginning to lose the competitive edge OPEC gave them in the 1970s. The competitiveness of other soft commodities will be determined by short-term demand/supply considerations and hence the strength of the bargaining position of the protagonists in ICAs.

The mineral commodity situation is more unpredicable. The future of the world mining industry is related to cost/pricing structures, technological change and the political climate within which investment is undertaken. Growth projections formulated in the mid- to late-1970s for the year 2000 envisaged a slow down in annual rates of growth in demand.[46] Nevertheless, a median range of these forecasts would still mean that world productive capacity for minerals would have to increase by between 90 and 190% by 2000.[47] By the early 1980s, even these reduced rates of growth appeared to be optimistic. Depressed demand for minerals (and subsequent low prices and profits for mining companies) has inhibited new exploratory investment for additional productive capacity. Instead, transnationals have been closing high cost mines (albeit temporarily in many cases) and have fallen back on known reserves to meet an expansion in output for the immediate future. Concern has been expressed that if a major economic boom was to occur in the near future this strategy could lead to a minerals crisis because of the long lead times involved in bringing new capacity on line.[48] The situation is dynamic, however. Several of the ailing transnationals have been taken over by profit-rich oil majors seeking to diversify and willing to re-invest gains derived from OPEC price hikes.

The possibilities of mineral crises can be attributed to a lack of investment rather than to any physical shortage of materials. The gloomy picture painted by the Club of Rome in 1972 was somewhat premature. It failed to consider man's constant ingenuity in providing for social needs. Over the last few decades the 'real' price of minerals has remained constant due to the upgrading of technology and the discovery of new reserves at a faster rate than that of production. In addition, impending shortages of a mineral have evoked responses by both users and producers to conserve, recycle or substitute a mineral with better long-term supply prospects.

The ultimate mineral resource base is the total amount of minerals in the earth's crust (virgin materials) plus the quantities of potentially recyclable material present in manufactured goods utilized by the world's population. To give an indication of the long-term future of mineral production, Cook has estimated the 'cut-off' grades in 1975 for a selection of minerals (Table 4.8). For example, the ratio of 56 to 1 for copper is calculated by assessing the 'cut-off' concentration for recovering copper commercially (0·35%) and dividing it by its crustal concentration (63 parts per million). The low ranking of iron and aluminium in Table 4.8 is also a reflection of the relative, higher crustal concentrations of these minerals. In essence, technological advances of a capital intensive nature have enabled 'cut-off' grades to be reduced whilst containing costs. Thus, in the McKelvey Box discussed in Chapter 1, paramarginal identified resources will over time become part of exploitable reserves.

Table 4.8: Ratio of cutoff grade to crustal abundance for selected elements (lowest concentration economically recoverable in 1975). *Source:* E. Cook, 20 February 1976, Limits to Exploitation of Non-renewable Resources, *Science,* 191, p. 678

Element	Ratio
Mercury	11,200-to-1
Tungsten	4,000
Lead	3,300
Chromium	2,100
Tin	2,000
Silver	1,330
Gold	1,000
Molybdenum	770
Zinc	370
Uranium	350
Carbon	310
Lithium	240
Manganese	190
Nickel	100
Cobalt	80
Phosphorus	70
Copper	56
Titanium	16
Iron	3
Aluminium	2

The whole system of mineral resource inventories is a complex one, difficult to measure and constantly dynamic. Costs, prices, exploration intensity, technological know-how and government policies all interweave to keep the stock situation in a state of flux.

In terms of physical supplies, commodity development is guaranteed for the foreseeable future. Whether this development is orderly and stable is another matter. Both producers and consumers have been quick to capitalise on the vagaries of the world market and this short-term approach to international commodity management has led to increasing distrust between 'North' and 'South' in recent years. A modicum of success has been achieved however. A Common Fund has been created to financially support ICA's in the quest for price stabilization at a bilateral level. STABEX, a compensating finance facility, was set up to stabilize the export earnings of African, Caribbean and Pacific (ACP) nations trading with the EEC. These international management initiatives will be discussed in depth in Chapter 11.

Whilst ICAs and STABEX are primarily concerned with soft commodities, it is in the field of mineral resource development that urgent international cooperation is required. Transnationals, despite technological expertise and financial backing, have reduced their exploration investment, especially in 'high risk' developing countries which hold the most lucrative reserves. Producing governments, on the other hand, have sought to increase their 'take' from their own resources by demanding higher prices, better terms of trade and control of their mineral wealth. This stalemate benefits neither 'North' nor 'South' because it is contrary to their mutual interest.

A key management issue, addressed in Chapter 11, is that of achieving a balance between mineral extraction and environmental protection, especially as transnationals have turned their exploration efforts toward countries that have strong environmental lobbies. Consequently, although it may be argued that there is no physical shortage of minerals around the globe, the pace of development may be dictated by the 'trade-offs' among societal goals. Although mining undoubtedly benefits the economy – it is the *raison d'etre* for some communities as a source of employment, it benefits the balance of payments and it fuels our modern economic system – this has been achieved at high cost to the environment. Mining and its associated processing industries create significant environmental damage through land disturbance, air and water pollution and the loss of other, more aesthetically pleasing land uses such as farming, forestry and wilderness recreation. Land disturbance solely from the extractive process is estimated at 1·5 million acres per annum and the land area utilized worldwide from 1976 to 2000 will encompass 94,000 square miles – an area equivalent to that of West Germany.[49] These figures do *not* include the soil erosion, air and water pollution from mine wastes or the pollution from processing activities which affect areas beyond the place of extraction.

The need for good management will become imperative in the years ahead, especially if there is an upturn in the world economy. The pressure on the management system will be greatest in the 'Northern' countries, where the fear of supply disruptions from unfriendly or unstable political régimes may focus attention upon increasing domestic production. Unfortunately, as the mining industry is forced to turn to poorer ores in fragile environments, conflict between the industry and the environmental lobby will necessarily worsen.

5   Food

5.1.1 Introduction

There is no absolute standard or common definition of acceptable food. Food is necessary physiologically. Proteins are necessary for body growth and repair. Twenty-two amino acids in protein are known to be important. More of these are available in fish than in meat, more in meat than in cereals, but because of limiting factors such as digestibility and the low content of particular acids in particular sources, it is generally agreed that a variety of sources is to be preferred.

Besides securing the repair and maintenance of body tissue food is needed as fuel. Energy needs can be met from proteins but are mainly met through consumption of carbohydrates and fats. Proteins can be converted to calories, but carbohydrates and fats cannot be converted to proteins. As one might expect, the body puts its energy needs first. A balanced diet of energy and proteins plus a range of vitamins and minerals with more than a touch of fibre is recommended. In cases of severe malnutrition, a lack of energy means that available proteins are not used to build or repair the body but diverted to the attempt to keep the body going; hence the extreme body wastage and the 'skin and bone' appearance of the victims of famine.[1]

The principal forms of food are cereals and animal products, with a variety of root crops as sources of carbohydrates, pulses and proteins. Fruits and vegetables are sources of fibre and vitamins. Other major components in world food are oilseeds and fish. Oilseeds supplied 68% of total world fat and oil production in 1976, and these are also increasingly important as sources of animal feed, accounting for 33% by volume of the EEC's needs in this respect in the mid-1970s.[2]

In recent decades, marine and freshwater fisheries have been expanded at a similar rate to the production of cereals (see Table 5.1). The energy costs of fish catching and distribution, and the conversion of fish into feed for animals, are increasing. Fish, like meat, can no longer be regarded as a cheap source of protein.[3] So much so, that it is now more economical to think in terms of supplying the market from fish farms. Indeed, projections for the long-term growth of world aquaculture range from 30 million to 50 million tonnes by the end of the century.[4] Several species of fish seem to offer opportunities for the development of factory farming, along similar lines to poultry and pig meat.

5.2.1 Patterns of Consumption

In Figure 5.1 the dietary patterns of developed countries (the 'North') are compared with those of developing countries (the 'South') with respect to proteins and energy. Clearly, the differences between the two revolve around

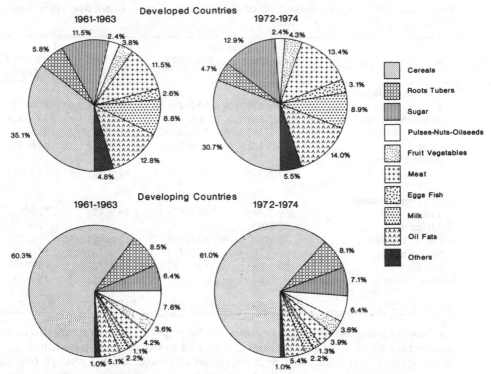

Figure 5.1 Dietary Patterns in Developed and Developing Countries
Source: FAO, 1977 pp.1–25

the much higher proportion of animal products consumed in the 'North'. However, such global averages conceal much. Certain human groups require a different balance, some prefer a different balance, and all consume only what they can afford. Pregnant women, nursing mothers and suckling infants are particularly vulnerable to protein, vitamin, and mineral deficiencies. Hence, a society characterized by a high rate of births and a large population of maturing children (e.g. the 'South') actually requires a higher grade of food than a country with a more mature population profile.

Throughout the world the rich consume more protein and more calories than the poor. Hence a population with rising incomes exerts greater demands

Table 5.1: Increases in food production: comparing 1961–1965 average volumes of production with 1980 levels. *Source:* FAO, 1982, *The State of Food and Agriculture 1981*, p. 182

Cereals	56·05%
Vegetable Oils	69·89%
Meat	67·29%
Fish	55·75%

Table 5.2: Utilization of cereals in food (million tons) *Source: Ceres*, May–June 1981,
p. 23

	Human		Animal	
	1961–1965 (%)	1975–1977 (%)	1961–1965 (%)	1975–1977 (%)
Developed Countries				
Total	159·5(37)	164·1(28)	266·7(63)	413·0(72)
North America	19·2(14)	21·8(14)	122·1(86)	135·7(86)
Western Europe	45·1(38)	43·7(30)	72·3(62)	101·9(70)
Oceania	1·6(43)	1·9(42)	2·1(57)	2·6(58)
Eastern Europe and the USSR	69·5(52)	70·1(31)	63·6(48)	155·4(69)
Developing Countries				
Total	369·7(88)	538·3(87)	48·8(12)	79·8(13)
Africa	28·9(95)	42·4(93)	1·5(5)	1·9(7)
Latin America	28·7(68)	42·8(59)	13·6(32)	29·6(41)
Near East	25·3(78)	39·1(77)	7·3(22)	11·9(23)
Far East	150·6(98)	213·0(98)	2·6(2)	5·0(2)
Asia Centrally Planned	136·0(85)	200·8(87)	24·0(15)	30·3(13)
World Total	529·2(63)	702·4(59)	315·5(37)	492·8(41)

for food. An urbanizing population may be expected to exert an increasing
demand for *cheap* food in a manner not related to the growth in its numbers or
to the type of diet associated with increased affluence. With a change from an
active rural lifestyle to a more sedentary urban one, required calorific intake is
less, but so is the possibility of self-sufficiency and so are the demands on
disposable income for other purposes, such as accommodation, clothes and
transport.

Increasing affluence and urbanization are associated with greater meat consumption. But the production of one pound of meat requires between three
pounds of grain (poultry) and ten pounds (beef).[5] So, as shown in Table 5.2,
significant increases in the quantity of cereals fed to animals are a major characteristic of recent food trends. This in turn has significant implications for
world trade.

There is no clearer illustration of the complexity of the problem of food as
a resource than this. Hunger could be eradicated if only 10% of cereals fed to
animals could somehow be diverted to feed people. But very great problems
exist in matching the market and the institutional mechanisms of food production with every form of consumer demand.

5.2.2 Geography of Food Consumption

As anyone who has attempted to diet will know, it is very difficult to calculate
exactly how much anybody eats. Figures as to variations in world food consumption inevitably contain estimates, assumptions and aggregates that allow
only the most general conclusions to be drawn. Official thinking about what
constitutes adequate food intake has tended to vary over time.[6] For example,
the recommendation of the US National Academy of Sciences in the late 1970s

Table 5.3: Food consumption as a percentage of estimated calorific requirements in selected countries. *Source:* FAO, 1982, *The State of Food and Agriculture 1981*, pp. 172–173

	1966–1968	1969–1971	1975–1977	1978–1980	Estimated Average Requirement (KCal/head/day)
		(% of requirements)			
The 'North'					
North America					
United States	128	131	135	138	2,640
Canada	123	124	126	126	2,660
Western Europe					
United Kingdom	132	133	129	132	2,520
German Federal Republic	121	126	126	132	2,670
Italy	130	139	137	145	2,520
Eastern Europe					
German Democratic Republic	129	132	139	143	2620
Poland	127	129	135	134	2,620
Other OECD Countries					
Japan	114	118	121	118	2,570
Australia	121	124	124	120	2,660
The 'South'					
Central Africa					
Central African Republic	90	96	96	96	2,260
Rwanda	82	88	92	95	2,320
West Africa					
Nigeria	93	94	95	99	2,360
Ghana	94	98	93	88	2,300
East Africa					
Kenya	97	98	93	89	2,320
Tanzania	89	87	91	87	2,320
Central America					
Jamaica	102	110	116	115	2,240
Nicaragua	112	110	109	102	2,250
South America					
Brazil	104	104	104	105	2,390
Chile	112	110	107	112	2,440
Far East					
China	89	90	99	105	2,360
Indonesia	85	91	96	106	2,410
Philippines	84	87	94	102	2,260
Asia					
India	84	90	86	90	2,210
Pakistan	87	95	96	100	2,310
Middle East					
Iraq	90	93	100	110	2,410
Jordan	114	117	120	125	2,340

that an American man in his twenties, moderately active, and in good shape at 154 lbs, needed to consume 2700 calories per day. This is 500 calories less than in the advice issued twenty-five years previously. It is also a similar amount in excess of the daily amounts recommended in the health and fitness handbooks currently enjoying a vogue in the West.

Notwithstanding the confusing nature of the data and the conflicting advice about diet, three points are very clear concerning patterns of food consumption. First, in terms of total consumption, substantial differences exist between countries in the 'North' and those in the 'South'. Second, diets vary in their composition around the world. Finally, great differences exist between the rich and the poor everywhere.

Table 5.3 shows per capita dietary energy supplies in relation to nutritional requirements in selected countries as estimated by the United Nations Food and Agricultural Organisation (FAO). Populations in the 'North' not only achieve their estimated requirements to a much greater extent than elsewhere, but also exceed them significantly. In the 'South' the averaged and estimated calorie consumptions are far from satisfactory in Africa, Asia, and the Far East. Overall, there is a slow improvement in developing countries, but in some areas per capita food production has actually declined in recent years while a lack of foreign exchange has prohibited an increase in food imports.[7]

Added to deficiencies in calories among the poorest peoples and countries, there is the problem of the limited composition of their diet. The proportion of energy derived from cereals and staple foods remains high in many poorly developed countries. For example, in the Sahel these staples account for as much as 85% of calorific intake. In Bangladesh the figure is almost 90%.[8] More generally, cereals provide about 50% of per capita calorific intake and a varying degree of protein (depending on the particular crop: cassava, staple of many tropical countries, contains only 2% protein, as compared with the 12% of durum wheat). Pulses, nuts and seeds in such circumstances provide the protein. But when the protein content of diets are compared, the superiority of conditions in the industrialized countries is clear. Figure 5.1 shows the extent to which the protein content of diets in developing countries differs markedly from those in the 'North' - largely through rates of animal product consumption five or six times less than in Europe or North America.[9]

Everywhere there are large differences in diet according to wealth.[10] For example, a Nutrition Study of Rural Bangladesh (1975/76) indicated that the highest income groups were consuming 16% more calories and 18% more proteins then the lowest income groups of the same sample.[11] In Sri Lanka, higher proportions of vegetables, meats and fish were clearly identifiable among the 20% of the population with the highest incomes. Further, within the poorest groups certain types of people were particularly vulnerable to malnutrition. The Bangladesh nutritional survey, for example, revealed that children (of either sex) between one and three years of age received only 46% of calories and 68% of protein requirements, while adults enjoyed more adequate intakes.[12] More generally, such considerations are reflected in the clear relationship between estimated calorific intake and life expectancy at birth, shown in Table 5.4.

Table 5.4 Calorie consumption and life expectancy in
43 developing countries. *Source: Ceres*
March–April 1982, p. 7

	Calories per person per day 1977/1979	Life expectancy at birth 1979
Ethiopia	1,737	40
Bangladesh	1,787	49
Mozambique	1,906	47
Nepal	1,941	44
Zambia	1,986	49
Ghana	1,996	49
India	1,996	52
Upper Volta	2,024	43
Vietnam	2,033	63
Tanzania	2,040	52
Guatemala	2,062	59
Kenya	2,085	55
Bolivia	2,090	50
Peru	2,106	58
Zaire	2,156	47
Thailand	2,175	62
Sri Lanka	2,200	66
Indonesia	2,203	53
Philippines	2,211	62
Burma	2,223	54
Malawi	2,238	47
Pakistan	2,270	52
Yemen	2,281	42
Nigeria	2,295	49
Sudan	2,339	47
Algeria	2,363	56
Madagascar	2,428	47
Cameroon	2,442	47
Brazil	2,498	63
Ivory Coast	2,528	47
Malaysia	2,562	68
Venezuela	2,625	67
Morocco	2,640	56
Chile	2,662	67
Saudi Arabia	2,669	54
Cuba	2,672	72
Tunisia	2,698	58
Syria	2,765	65
Mexico	2,771	66
Korea Dem. Rep.	2,833	63
Korea Rep.	2,837	63
Turkey	2,931	62
Argentina	3,345	70

HAROLD BRIDGES LIBRARY
S. MARTIN'S COLLEGE
LANCASTER

5.3.1 Patterns of Supply

Food production has expanded significantly in recent decades (see Figure 5.2), and growth of food production is generally in line with growth of population – with the glaring exception of much of Africa. The most important food crops are the grains, particularly wheat. Almost half the production of wheat is in the 'North' (Table 5.5) Two trends have been of recent importance. First, wheat production has exhibited higher rates of yield increase than its principal rivals, maize and rice, indicating investment to sustain per capita production without increasing the area of production. Second, almost all wheat is produced for human consumption (the exception being low-grade production in Europe and the Soviet Union). In countries where wheat is not a traditional food, particularly in South-East Asia and Sub-Saharan Africa, it has become an increasingly important import in connection with urbanization and rising incomes amongst urban élites.[13] The bulk of these imports come from developed countries (the major exception being Argentina). Hence wheat is a major element in the world food trade.

Rice is mainly a Far Eastern crop, although increasing in production around the world especially in North America. The two major producing countries are China and Thailand. These, plus the United States and Pakistan, are also major exporters.

The use of other cereals for livestock feed has increased greatly over the past three decades. Maize and barley account for two-thirds of all cereals fed to livestock. In 1978, some 61% of world maize consumption was for livestock feeding, although it is also the staple food in many developing countries, particularly in Africa and Latin America.[14]

A substantial proportion of the population of developed countries have rich diets – up to 30% in excess of their requirements. At the same time, perhaps 800 million people (nearly 20% of the world's population) do not have an adequate diet because they cannot afford it. The pattern of food production reflects the ability to pay for the food produced. Food problems concern expanding demand, improved marketing and investment. They are not of the 'limits' type, that is, a lack of resources, although there has been some concern over the ability of the environment to sustain expanded production.

5.4 Food Problems

5.4.1 Environmental and Resource Problems

Several authors have expressed concern in recent years over the ability of the environment to sustain food production trends. Eckholm,[15] for example, has tried to draw attention to a set of negative ecological trends: overgrazing, desert encroachment, deforestation, soil erosion, increased flooding, and increased silting of irrigation reservoirs. The United Nations Environmental Programme,[16] on the other hand, reports at least four kinds of influence working towards the sustainable use of land: market forces in the 'North' have encouraged more efficient use of land and other inputs; more appropriate technology, such as trickle irrigation or hybrid seeds, is being disseminated so that it is possible to enhance the production of marginal ecosystems without serious

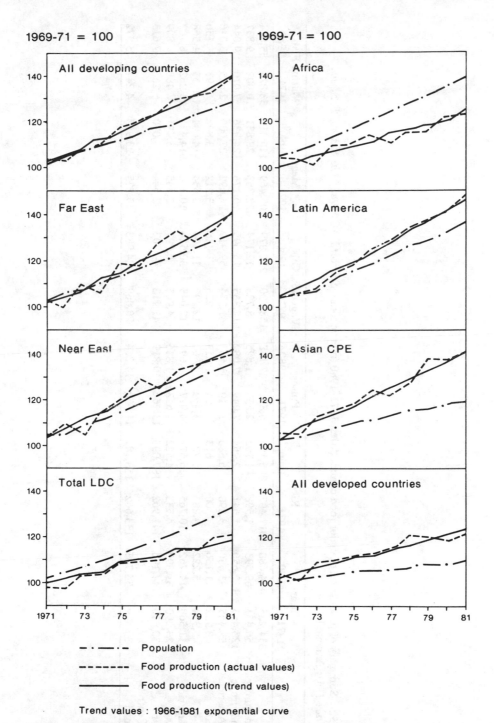

Figure 5.2 Expansion of Food Production in Recent Years
Source: FAO, 1982, *The State of Food and Agriculture 1981*, p. 48

Table 5.5: Summary of production of major food commodities, 1971–1980 (metric tons). *Source:* FAO, 1982, *The State of Food and Agriculture 1981*, Annexe 1

	Wheat		Rice		Pulses		Vegetable Oils		Meat		Marine Fish	
	1971	1980	1971	1980	1971	1980	1971	1980	1971	1980	1971	1980
World	354,285	444,680	317,407	396,155	46,836	47,138	158,620	214,879	108,469	140,418	53,824	55,824
Western Europe	56,464	69,593	1,598	1,702	2,255	1,825	8,728	12,174	22,363	28,831	10,002	9,837
Eastern Europe	123,455	127,650	1,641	2,964	7,949	7,082	14,365	15,695	20,176	24,936	7,010	9,044
North America	58,465	83,650	3,890	6,580	1,119	1,587	41,354	59,919	24,092	27,000	2,673	3,046
Oceania	8,932	11,156	300	613	94	219	226	445	3,212	3,802	93	156
Africa	5,354	5,222	4,883	5,723	3,962	4,568	12,292	11,404	3,654	4,604	1,533	1,568
Latin America	11,568	14,762	10,765	16,571	4,927	4,692	12,045	30,518	10,136	14,421	13,262	8,703
Near East	23,290	31,399	4,535	4,582	1,613	1,856	4,965	6,297	2,445	3,491	488	809
Far East	30,870	44,196	141,962	187,095	13,266	10,819	41,412	49,703	3,664	5,070	5,268	7,613
Asian Centrally Planned	33,579	54,745	133,662	158,101	11,350	14,264	20,069	24,983	15,875	23,963	4,244	5,372

damage; national and international activities in support of agricultural research have been continually strengthened over the last decade; and government measures to counter ecologically unsuitable developments are increasingly apparent.

There is no doubt that much of the earth's surface is unsuitable for food production. An FAO study of the potential of African land resources found approximately 47% of the continent (1·4 billion hectares) to be too dry for rain-fed crop production. The timing of rainfall and the attributes of particular soils and patches of terrain further limit agricultural potential. Nevertheless, the study found that Africa has enough land for food self-sufficiency. Even with the given low levels of inputs (basic labour only), the continent could feed three times its present population.[17]

The area of the globe thought to be cultivable is about 1473 million hectares. This is only 11% of the ice-free land surface. Fifty-five per cent of this area is in the developing countries. A further 23% of the earth's surface will support grazing.[18] Much of this area is ecologically constrained, particularly by drought. Estimates vary, but it is thought that the additional area available to developing countries is approximately 150% of present usage (50% in developed countries).[19] This is, of course, not evenly distributed. Some countries such as Bangladesh and India seem to offer little scope for further expansion of the cultivable area. Where the greatest potential exists, in the tropical rainforests, there are major ecological worries over potential losses to the genetic diversity of flora and fauna, catastrophic soil erosion, and even the global climate.

The costs of extending the cultivable area would be very high. According to some estimates, at 1977 prices it would cost $300/ha for clearing shrub savannah without drainage problems and over $10,000/ha for rainforest areas requiring drainage.[20] For areas requiring irrigation, $1,500/ha for simple sprinkler irrigation schemes under good soil and topographic conditions to well over $10,000/ha for inter-basin transport schemes have been cited. Irrigation does, however, appear to offer the greatest potential for expanding the cultivable area.

5.4.2 Increasing Productivity: The Green Revolution

Increased food production in recent years has been achieved by the application of fertilizer, pesticides, high yielding varieties (HYV) and, sometimes, irrigation. The term 'Green Revolution' has gained currency for such packages of applied science.

Beginning with HYV dwarf Mexican wheat, the Green Revolution spread to India, Pakistan, the Phillipines, parts of the Near East, and North Africa, before expanding across the world in the late 1960s. The FAO Freedom from Hunger Campaign's Fertiliser Programme sponsored some 62,000 trials between 1961 and 1969 on a wide range of soils and in a wide variety of climates, and with a large number of different crops and HYVs. Large increases in production were revealed, further enhanced by irrigation.[21] In addition to providing greater yields, the new seed varieties mature earlier, offering greater opportunities for multiple cropping within the growing season; they also adapt to a wider range of climatic conditions than the traditional varieties.

There was a very significant increase in the HYV wheat acreage – from

23,000 acres in 1965/66 to 24,664,000 acres in 1969/70 – yet many of the countries in the forefront of such trends continue to suffer from food shortages. A number of factors have prevented Green Revolution methods from achieving the status of a panacea. None of them are of a physical or technical nature.

The necessary transfer of technical skill and knowledge is difficult to achieve in countries with low levels of literacy, rapidly expanding population, and imperfectly developed systems of local, regional, and national institutions of the appropriate kind. It requires a well developed infrastructure and good distribution channels to reach the farmer at the right time and place. But, above all, such inputs are expensive. Only the larger and more affluent farmers can afford to adopt such a new approach. As a result, the rich get richer. The poor remain poor. Worse, several analysts report that those who have benefitted from the early adoption of new technology have expanded their holdings, driving the poorer farmers into landlessness, making them so poor that they have no access to the foodstuffs available on the market.

5.4.3 Social, Economic and Political Problems

The evidence seems overwhelming that there is no physically resource-based barrier to adequate food supplies. Instead, as George says:[22]

Hunger is not an unavoidable phenomenon like death and taxes.... Unfortunately for the millions of people who go hungry, the problem is not a technical one ... wherever they live, rich people eat first, they eat a disproportionate amount of the food there is and poor ones rarely rise in revolt against this most basic of oppressions unless told to 'eat cake'. Hunger is not a scourge but a scandal.

Typical of the supporting evidence is Garcia's analysis of food insecurity in Colombia. He analysed trends in food production and availability in Colombia between 1950 and 1975, finding that whilst the proportion of food production going to export remained stable (and small), per capita output and availability had fallen.[23] Given the recommended minimum daily per-capita consumption of 1970 calories per day, there had been no serious aggregate problem in Colombia. But such average figures hide a serious nutritional problem, particularly amongst the poor. Using the historical data available, he identified the probability of shortfalls of varying levels of aggregate food supply for different periods. Using data from a 1972 survey for urban and rural calorie consumption, he derived an estimating equation of the relationship between income and calorie consumption through regression analysis. This allowed the conclusion that whilst 98·5% of individuals' consumption of calories was adequate on an average basis, when income groups were identified, something of the order of 28% to 52% of the Colombian population was undernourished, with clear indications that malnutrition was a more serious problem in rural areas.

Food insecurity in Colombia arises from the fact that the poor spend a high proportion of their income on food (over 50% in the lowest three income groups). A relatively small shortfall in the supply of food that causes an increase in food prices will reduce their real income. This could generate a decrease in food consumption and a deterioration in an already impaired nutritional status.[24]

He observed that a relatively small percentage shortfall in food supply causes substantial increases in prices and larger reductions in the amount of food that the poor can afford to buy. Although the probability of such shortfalls was small (for 1961 to 1975, 0·02 for a 5% shortfall, 0·005 for a 10% shortfall) they had disproportionately disastrous results when they occurred. Shortfalls could and should be compensated for by imports if institutional arrangements for its sensible distribution could be worked out. But:

> The insecurity problem is not caused by absolute poverty for the country as a whole, but rather by poverty for specific groups. If income was equally distributed, people would be consuming calories in excess of the minimum requirements, and the internal production of food would still be larger than the demand.[25]

Land Reform

A principal suggestion for alleviating inequality of income amongst the vulnerable rural poor concerns land ownership. Eckholm[26] points out that in the rural Third World the control of farmland remains the principal key to wealth and power. Perhaps 600 million people live in rural households that are either completely landless or lacking in secure rights to adequate farmland. Yet in Latin America, according to the FAO, 7% of the landowners possessed 93% of arable land in 1975.[27] Eckholm sees a growing tide of landlessness throughout the Third World (hence poverty and deteriorating food access), not only because of population growth but also because of land accumulation by the better-off farmers; emergency sales of land by farmers pushed into insolvency by some crisis; the spread of large commercial farms, sometimes foreign-owned; the eviction of tenants by landowners fearful of tenancy reforms or seeing a chance to profit from the use of new technologies. This he sees as leading to: growing unemployment and underemployment (hence poverty and deteriorating access to available food); soaring rural–urban migration; ecological degradation as unsuitable terrain becomes the scene of futile attempts to sustain farming, sometimes within sight of huge, under-utilized estates on valley floors; and the spectre of political instability and violence.

Even if an adequate landholding is available to him, the peasant farmer may not be in a position to produce surplus food at an appropriate price for distribution elsewhere. It was established earlier that Africa causes most concern as regards trends in food production. Saumoa, Director-General of the FAO, has provided an account of constraints on African food production drawing heavily on the views of Africans themselves.[28] He identifies the crucial vicious circle as: 'Little food because of little strength, little strength because of little food.'[29] Measures are necessary to increase the small peasant's purchasing power and to create a capital capability (to save and borrow) to invest and cover operational expenses. He suggests ways governments may assist, in addition to technical measures such as those of the Green Revolution. They are firstly, the development of credit facilities for farmers, free from the rapacious middlemen, and at reasonable rates of interest. Second, the establishment of a guaranteed minimum price for the purchase of agricultural produce (hence facilitating cash-flow planning and introducing a much needed element of security into agricultural decision making; always providing that prices so determined are reasonably pitched – see below). Finally, the peasant should be able to count on an insurance subsidy against natural disasters. Indeed, agricultural credit agencies, guaranteed prices, and mechanisms of disaster relief figure strongly in the developed world.

But such economic measures are not sufficient in themselves, Saouma argues. There is also a need for an agricultural advisory service that will not only disseminate knowledge of appropriate technology but also communicate in the language and terms of the peasant. The development of rural infrastructure should be given high priority: roads, electricity, schools, and hospitals are necessary to enhance the status of rural living and stem urban migration.

This latter point has more importance than first appears. Nicholson and Esseks roundly declare:[30]

The failure of many countries to manage their food supplies adequately is explained by an urban bias in planning and by the sheer administrative complications and costs of stabilising the food grains market.

In most of the less developed countries rural politics are dominated by factions and are subject of a good deal of patronage. In this situation there is very often little by way of indigenous pressure for a change of system, local élites and the better-off benefitting from the control of patronage. Class conflict between the haves and the have-nots inevitably follows. New technology may even exacerbate the conflict between classes by adding to the numbers of the privileged and creating landlessness and unemployment.

In many countries there are problems of intra-government and inter-regional rivalries, often given an added piquancy through the ethnic identity of ruling parties or favoured areas. Programmes of rural development can have the effect of making traditional leaders redundant. Rural growth can exacerbate regional and hence ethnic differences. Rivalries break out between different ministries. Each of these things is capable of artificially limiting increases in food production.

Note must be taken of the importance of foreign policy and the existence of various degrees of dependence on the existing international economic order. Many less developed countries rely on foreign exchange earned by the sale of cash crops. The cash crop sector may also attract a disproportionate share of land and other inputs, hampering food production. International trade requires servicing from cities. This makes for an urban élite, and those involved in maintaining the apparatus of the state (government, police, army and bankers) tend to have top priority in food policy and hence divert resources such as food and other imports away from the rural sector. It is clear that a wide variety of social, economic, and political constraints conspire to limit food production, quite independently of the agricultural potential of the land or the climate. The agricultural sector needs to be nurtured by government policy.

5.4.4 Food Policies

No government in the world does not, in some way, influence its agricultural sector.[31] Because agriculture is made up of a large number of individual decision makers, there is a tendency to overreact to market signals, leading to too much investment when prices are high, and too large a switch away from particular enterprises when prices are low. The result is a cycle of under- and over-supply, high and low prices, accentuated by weather conditions. An external agent is required to influence the supply of agricultural commodities for the good of consumers as well as the producers.

Agricultural intervention on behalf of the consumer is justifiable on the grounds of controlling domestic inflation and its political repercussions. Some lower limit may be provided for the standard of living of the very poor and, in developing countries, urban élites may be satisfied and government wage bills kept down. Food policy in the United States illustrates the four main methods of intervention in an urban, industrial, and democratic context.[32] The main strategies are guaranteed price support, loans for investment, disposal of surpluses, and selective consumer subsidy. The Agricultural Marketing Act of 1933 established the principles of loans and support prices. The Commodity Credit Corporation (CCC) was established to provide loans to farmers to store suitable products, such as grain, tobacco and cotton at charges related to average prices in previous years. Farmers could then release the stored produce for sale when prices were suitable and pay back the loan in cash, or, if no upturn came, repay the debts in kind, in quantities of the crop. Thus the nonsense of successful harvest leading to a slump in prices leading in turn to the ruin of growers was removed, and some stability was introduced into the production régime. For those commodities difficult to store, such as meat and other animal products, the CCC would provide loans, taking the produce in lieu of payment if it could not be sold at a reasonable price. The CCC then organized the disposal of surpluses, sometimes organizing their destruction but usually sending them overseas; hence the long-standing and prominent role of the US in international food aid.

These measures were spectacularly successful in establishing some stability in agricultural production, but at substantial, and rising costs, and with a growing problem of disposing of mounting surpluses. Public Law 480 of 1954 allowed the shipment of surpluses to developing countries on a variety of concessional terms, but by the 1960s a system of subsidies to take land out of production was necessary in orders to reduce surpluses. The Food and Agriculture Act of 1965 consolidated these measures and broke new ground in introducing the fourth element of policy: selectively subsidised home consumption. The urban food stamp programme was introduced to benefit the poor at home. The guaranteed purchase of surpluses was abandoned in the light of mounting cost, but stability in the production sector was maintained by the offer of direct income supplements when market prices fell below stipulated minima. Since the 1977 Food and Agriculture Act, CCC loans have been available for on-farm storage of produce for between three and five years, and payments may be made to farmers to cover the costs of these loans. If the price of the stored produce rises above 175% of the current support price levels then farmers have to repay the storage costs and loan interest – a necessary measure to combat domestic inflation and the ever-increasing cost of maintaining stability in production.

A similar set of policies has brought prosperity to EEC farmers, albeit with similar growing concern over the cost of support. In the post-war years the UK also adopted policies of support prices, grants and loans for improved production. It also established an elaborate network of agricultural research stations, advisors and marketing boards, all to good effect. In Europe a Common Agricultural Policy (CAP) was established in 1962 as the cornerstone of the EEC.[33] Under the CAP a price is fixed for the main commodities each year.

If market levels fall below this, the European Agricultural Guidance and Guarantee Fund intervenes, buying to the extent necessary to support the price. As in the US, large stocks accumulate which are disposed of by subsidized export (butter to the Soviet Union for example) or as food aid. Some produce, such as skimmed milk, is converted into more saleable forms, cattle food for example. For most commodities EEC prices are normally above world market prices, and, therefore, an elaborate system of import controls and levies is necessary to maintain prices (as are export constraints when EEC levels fall below prevailing world prices). Again, the emphasis is on providing the producer with a certain amount of market security and stability so that investment is more easily contemplated.

Less developed countries cannot afford this level of insurance premium even if conditions allowed. As Tarrant says:[34]

The difficulties for developing countries in enacting effective producer policies should not be overlooked. The creation of a minimum support price as a stabilisation measure alone requires that the government has effective control over the market, has access to all producers, and can control large stocks of grain. Such power is beyond the grasp of many developing countries at present.

There are great difficulties in operating a centralized non-market oriented food policy. This is most clearly seen with respect to the Soviet Union where an entirely collectivized agricultural sector produces, in effect, under contract for centralized planning agencies. The sudden entry of the Soviet Union into the world food market in the early 1970s to make up its own deficiencies was a major cause of the so-called world food crisis discussed below (section 5.5.1) thus drawing attention to the difficulties of centrally planned agricultural production.

Nove[35] had analysed the apparent inability of such a system to function effectively in agriculture. Whilst not underestimating the serious problems of rainfall variability as a handicap to Soviet agriculture, he identifies inefficiencies directly related to centralized planning and party control as directly responsible for poor food production performances. Farms are not sufficiently specialized in production and lack suitable labour incentives and skills; so that for some purposes they are too big, while for others much too small, for some inadequately mechanized, for others totally unmechanized. Machinery is said to be of poor quality, distribution arrangements poor, storage space scarce, and more fertilizer is required. Fertilizers, however, suffer from problems of packaging, transport, and the lack of spreading machines.

Before turning to the world food crisis, however, a further type of food policy should be noted: the consumer-orientated type as operated for example in Bangladesh. Here, since independence in 1972, food policy has been primarily concerned with the maintenance of a ration system.[36] Throughout the 1970s the number and type of people involved in the concessional scheme grew considerably with unfortunate consequences. At first, only one-third or so of those involved were 'priority' public service, military, and industrial employees, the remainder being the urban poor and rural labourers engaged on programmes of public works. In the early 1970s the number of people involved doubled. Clay says:[37]

The ration system has been used by successive regimes to bring influential groups in out of the cold – providing relatively assured supplies of essential foodstuffs at stable, subsidised prices, cushioning them against the effects of hyperinflation and the seasonal and other fluctuations of the open market.

In the early 1970s, most of this subsidized grain was imported, often on concessionary terms (largely wheat), but as the market price of indigenous rice fell, the government has increasingly bought more at 'incentive' prices, effectively supporting market prices. Although such a strategy undoubtedly helped the state to survive a series of disasters ranging from civil war, to floods, cyclones, and famines, there is some evidence that those most in need, the rural landless and labouring classes, did not benefit.[38] The intervention of the state as a major purchaser and dispenser of grain poses several dilemmas. If prices are supported at too high a level, the unassisted poor suffer whilst richer landowners benefit. If the difference between rationed grain prices and market prices widens, black marketing could become a social scourge, discouraging commercial production. If the gap between buying and selling price of government grain rations is too great, a very severe burden is placed on the national budget, perhaps diverting funds away from measures designed to increase overall levels of food production or away from other development projects designed to improve the employment and effective demand for food of those most in need.

Each of the several main varieties of food policy, has its own difficulties and problems. Paradoxically, the most effective type of policy, that of guaranteed minimum prices securing investment, appears to be available only to those least in need of food – the urban, industrial countries of the developed 'North'.

5.4.5 Fisheries: Problems and Policies

Because fishing is a form of hunting, the last of any major importance in global terms, policies are considerably easier to conceive although not necessarily easier to implement. Consistently good catches have to be achieved to warrant fishing on an industrial scale. There must be high levels of primary production in the relevant marine ecosystems and the concentration of fish species so that they may be conveniently caught. Generally the greatest potential for fishing occurs in areas of upwelling currents, areas over continental shelves, and coastal areas.[39]

The problems of fisheries are 'commons problems'. Intensive fishing will tend to reduce stocks and hence the possibilities for achieving a return on investment. But if one owner resists the temptation to reap a great harvest, the benefits of so doing will only go to others who have not. Individuals will therefore continue to invest in the hope that the effects of reduced stocks will fall on others. With everybody scrambling to increase their share of a declining resource, the fisheries finish up being the object of a much greater effort than would be the case if a single, rational decision maker were in charge.

The net result is overfishing, declining catches, destruction of fish stocks and over capitalization and underemployment within the industry. There are two possible solutions: protect the stocks in ways that ensure that the sustainable yield is not exceeded, or regulate entry to fisheries or access to fish stocks by keeping down the number of vessels. Fisheries policies around the world contain elements of both approaches, specifically embodying such measures as:[40]

(1) Limiting the size or nature of fish landed.
(2) Closing certain areas (such as breeding grounds) to fishing vessels.
(3) Closing certain seasons (such as the breeding season) to fishing.
(4) Limiting or restricting the type of fishing gear that may be used (to ensure that appropriate numbers, ages and species escape).
(5) Limiting the size of power of vessels.
(6) Limiting the total size of the catch.
(7) Limiting the total size of the fishing fleet.

The North Sea has seen perhaps the most concentrated and substantial fishing effort in the world. The majority of fish stocks are already fully exploited or overfished. The problem of falling catches was identified as early as the late-19th century, not long after the advent of steam trawling fleets. An International Council for the Exploration of the Sea was established in 1902 to coordinate research into the nature of the problem and propose possible solutions. Little action followed until the 1940s and 1950s. In 1946 the London Overfishing Convention saw agreement reached between the countries of north-west Europe to maximum mesh sizes and to establish minimum landing sizes for the main species, thus developing measures first introduced by the UK in the 1930s. These regulations were gradually applied throughout the 1950s, slowly extending their area of application. Further measures within the comprehensive Fisheries Policy for the EEC have proved extremely difficult to agree upon.

In the Pacific, problems with respect to halibut, tuna and salmon were identified in the 1920s. The International Halibut Commission identified a clear relationship between stock density (catch per unit effort) and fishing effort.[41] A reduction in effort would increase catches. The fishing effort was accordingly limited through the licensing of boats. Stocks were allowed to recover through the declaration in 1936 of a closed season. Consequently, catches in the major grounds off Vancouver Island and Alaska showed the expected improvement. Today, some twenty-two international bodies exist to coordinate research and/or to administer regulatory agreements. Within the coastal waters of the US, however, McHugh reports that most coastal fisheries have:[42]

... no effective management at all, either because they are not important enough locally to command attention by the states, because there is not enough biological information to point clearly to what must be done, or because the subject is so controversial that legislators or state administrators who are supposed to make decisions cannot decide what needs to be done.

To be fair, the 1976 US Fishery Conservation and Management Act took jurisdiction to 200 miles and established a series of eight Regional Management Councils with a view to achieving sustained yields from each fishery, consistent with economic, social, or ecological factors. But it has proved extremely difficult to establish satisfactory fishery management policies around the world because of vested interests.

5.5 Global Perspectives

5.5.1 World Food Crisis 1972/73 and the World Food Conference 1974

In 1973 there was a widely held belief that the coincidence of droughts in several continents and the soaring demand for food spurred by continuous population growth and rising affluence, had brought the world to the oft-predicted food crisis. There were rocketing food prices, declining food reserves and a shortage of fertilizers. The international price of wheat had tripled. Near famine conditions existed in parts of Africa and Asia.[43]

What had happened? Poleman[44] argues that the 'crisis' resulted from the unhappy coincidence of four main influences: an international running down of stocks and a holding down of production in the US (planted acreage was reduced by 10%); unprecedented prosperity and rising demand in Europe and Japan, which led to rapid increases in the use of grain for livestock feed; a general lapse of attention to agriculture in the less developed countries; unfavourable weather in India, the African Sahel and the Soviet Union. The Soviet Union entered the international grain market to an unprecedented extent. Poleman goes on to say that the crisis 'exposed the weaknesses of the international agricultural order' and for this reason it is worth looking at these and other causal factors in greater detail.

As to the role of the US government, Ruttenberg[45] notes the importance of the Nixon Administration's switch 'from aid to trade' as a means of disposing of growing and increasingly expensive stocks of surplus grain. A politically convenient customer (in the interests of 'detente' and global security) appeared in the form of the USSR. It seems likely that a sharp rise in prices would have followed this switch in US policy, regardless of drought. Nevertheless the Soviet purchase of $1155 million dollars worth of grain in two months (July and August 1972)[46] inevitably had its impact on world market prices.

As to rising demand, Tarrant also notes[47] that the world economic boom in the 1960s (the cause of so much anxiety among environmentalists as to the effects of environmental growth recounted in Chapter 2) meant that per capita demand for food was rising at an annual rate of growth of about 1% by 1973. This in itself might explain perhaps 20% of the world food price rise of 1972. Much of this growth in demand came from developed countries and took the form of a demand for meat – which in turn put pressure on supplies of animal feed. At a very unfortunate time, the Peruvian anchoveta industry collapsed in 1972. Fishmeal could be replaced by soya beans, but soya bean acreage, in turn, competes with corn. Prices in all these crops were affected. The imposition of a temporary soya bean export ban by the US government to protect the home cattle industry resulted in a worldwide increase in the prices of animal feed of all sorts.[48]

The exact causes of the anchoveta crisis are not well understood,[49] but it is clear that the resource had been overfished. Between 1955 and 1960, catches had doubled every year. The sustainable yield of the stock, estimated at around 9 million tons, had been achieved by 1964. Regulations concerning closed seasons and other measures were then introduced. But pressure on the resource continued to mount. The fish processing industry of the locality expanded to the point where it was capable of converting the entire world catch into fishmeal. The weekly catch of anchovetas during the short open season was equal to the entire annual US fishing effort in the Pacific. Finally, in the less developed countries, food aid and relatively low world prices had encouraged dependence on imports and in some cases the development of a taste for imported grains, particularly in urban centres.

In the atmosphere of sudden crisis it was hardly surprising that the World Food Conference held in Rome in 1974 concentrated largely on problems of food supply and paid little attention to the lack of effective demand as a major world food problem. A broad range of resolutions were adopted concerning food reserves, food security and food aid. It is sufficient to note here that events in the early 1970s demonstrated the extent to which food was subject to global influences. Crop failures in the Soviet Union, overfishing off Peru and US domestic budgeting considerations conspired to affect people and governments all over the world in a way that suggested, perhaps, that a new international economic order should be established if food insecurity were to be eradicated.

5.5.2 Threats to Food Security

Food security was the dominant theme of the World Food Conference and it is appropriate to end this review of food problems and policies with a more detailed examination of the concept of food security. It may be defined as the ability of food-deficit countries, or regions, or households within these, to meet target levels of consumption on a regular yearly basis – a simple objective which is difficult to achieve in many parts of the world.[50]

Elsewhere, Valdes and Konandreas have attempted to assess the extent of the problem using national aggregate figures for selected countries.[51] They computed the probability of food consumption in any one year falling below 95% of the trend value for individual countries over the period 1961-1976. In 51 out of the 67 countries examined, food shortages (defined as consumption below 95% of the trend value) occurred as often as once every five years; in most Arab countries such a condition could be expected twice every five years.[52] Food imports are an obvious way of mitigating the effects of weather related annual shortfalls. But the ability of countries to afford such imports varies greatly. They calculated a ratio between the value of recorded food imports and the value of total exports between 1965 and 1976 for 24 cases. A high ratio is healthy as it tends to suggest that foreign exchange can be devoted to food imports without cutting back on other imported materials. Except for three of the cases the ratio was less than 15% which, in the opinion of the authors, does not indicate a severe constraint.[53] India and Sri Lanka, on the other hand, were clearly in a difficult position. The desperate position of Bangladesh over the relevant years is also apparent. However, maximum values were also calculated. These indicate that in certain years the position of other countries can sharply deteriorate. This highlights the role of sometimes sharply fluctuating commodity prices in determining the relative strength of certain countries. In conditions of recession or the sudden collapse of commodity trade prices, the extent of food insecurity may be considerably greater than normal.

A factor confusing the examination of food insecurity, however, is the extent to which, as some authors have argued, the food trade recorded in official figures is incomplete. Lele and Candler,[54] for example, hold this view with

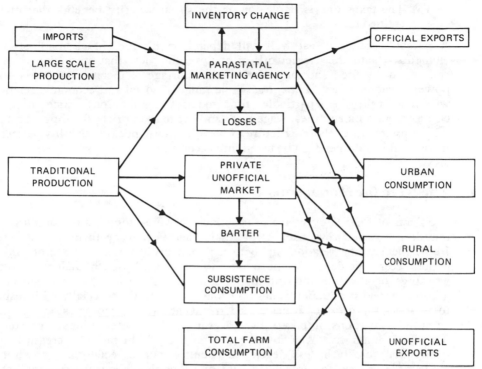

Figure 5.3 Conceptual Model of Food Grain Production and Disposition in East Africa
Source, U. Lele in A. Valdes (ed.), *Food Security for Developing Countries*,
Westview Press, 1981, p. 103

respect to Western Africa. They see the real food system as portrayed in
Figure 5.3. In this context the ability to absorb annual shortfalls is much more
complex. There might be an official national food reserve, and stocks may be
held by official marketing organizations, but there are also private stocks held
by individual farmers and these, except for the period immediately prior to
harvest, will greatly exceed all other stocks. Thus, public stocks largely intended for urban use are by no means the main component of the real food
security system. Instead, the traditional rural sector will hold the greatest
potential, a factor often overlooked in discussions concerning food security
strategies.

This realization leads to a much wider and more fundamental point as to
the nature of food problems. When a number of people have nothing to eat,
they starve. But this does not necessarily mean there is no food. Why do some
people not have enough to eat? Sen argues that it depends on a wide range of
factors such as:[55]

(1) How much the food costs.
(2) Whether employment can be found, for how long and at what rate of
pay.
(3) What can be accrued by selling other assets.
(4) What can be produced applying one's own labour and assets.
(5) The cost of purchasing new materials and services necessary for production (including credit, seed, etc.)

(6) The taxes one is liable for or the social security benefits that one is entitled to.

A person's ability to eat well will depend on his individual 'map' of such elements. Using this framework of analysis the view that starvation may be caused not by food shortage, but by the shortage of income and purchasing power is rudimentary. Thus, the whole range of social and economic relations within a locality at a particular time requires examination – such things as employment opportunities, wage rates and the market prices for inputs and the sale of assets. The whole structure of wealth inheritance, tax liability, access to income and credit needs to be taken into account.

5.6.1 The Need for Management

Problems of food supply and production are wide-ranging and complex, demanding a varied response. A few main themes may be identified however. First, there is the relationship between food problems and the problems of general economic development, including the 'North'-'South' dialogue and the workings of the existing international economic order. Second, sustained growth in food production relies on ecological stability; especially with respect to fisheries there exists a clear need to manage the 'common' stock through suitable regulations imposed by government and international agreement. Third, administrative behavioural problems hamper the task of increasing food production quickly in less developed countries and especially any attempt to subject the process to centralized control rather than allow the free market to reign.

The relationship between food and 'development' is undoubtedly the most pressing task for management. Rural policies to achieve simultaneous advance in both are increasingly being called for. Hitherto, urban and industrial priorities have prevailed. The basic problem appears to be the need to introduce an element of market stability so that further investment in production is made worthwhile and secure. This is the objective of successful food policies in the developed 'North'. In much of the 'South', however, a mature market system does not exist. Traditional peasant practice operates to a large extent outside the national system, which is itself often only a mechanism supporting the needs of urban or other élites. At the international level, food imports may divert investment from other development projects or may have political implications that hamper the aspirations of the mass of the people. The stability of international prices and hence investment is also a major task for management. The efforts of the United Nations and other international forces feature strongly in Chapter 11.

6   Forestry, Wilderness and Protected Landscapes

6.1.1 Introduction

One-third of the world's land area is forest and much forest land is wilderness. Its ultimate survival now depends on man. Other areas of special value to man have been granted 'protected' status as designated parks, monuments and nature reserves. The conservation of the wilderness depends on man's will to preserve what is left of his heritage. Early man made little impact on the wildness of his natural surroundings: he was controlled by his environment. The domestication of plants and animals was only a first step to a controlled environment and man's domination of the wilderness. With the Industrial Revolution, man wreaked havoc on pristine areas. The quest for food, energy, timber and minerals opened up new frontiers, and landscapes were rapidly transformed.

Nowhere is this more apparent than in the US where a 1·9 billion acre wilderness estate was reduced in size by 98% in less than half a century.[1] A wilderness movement, however, emerged in the US by the late 19th century, when prominent conservationists such as John Muir, with political support (Theodore Roosevelt), began to value the wilderness as a recreational resource to be enjoyed by an increasingly urbanized society.

The American definition of wilderness, as stated in the Wilderness Act of 1964, is that 'wilderness, in contrast with those areas where man and his works dominate the landscape, is hereby recognized as an area untrammeled by man, where man himself is a visitor who does not remain'. In a country as young and large as the US, wilderness appreciation is rooted in the nation's culture. By contrast, 'wilderness' is a rarely used term in Western Europe where man has greatly modified the landscape through history. True wilderness, as defined in the US statute books, is rare on the European continent, which is so densely populated that few areas are remote from the impact of 20th century civilization. Protected landscapes have been created for the enjoyment of an urbanized society; but the environment is not conducive to a US wilderness experience. (The term 'wilderness area' was first used in 1973 by pressure groups who wanted a re-designation of Britain's national parks to preserve the wildest areas of the parks from man's intrusion).[2]

Wilderness is therefore a cultural concept. It is dynamic in nature. A culture must it seems lose its wilderness before its value is appreciated and attempts are made to preserve it.[3] Primitive hunter-gatherer societies do not have to differentiate between wilderness and civilization. The Western European can perceive the distinction, though it is too late for preservation. The comparatively wild US has legislated the wilderness into existence.

Wilderness, like forests, is the victim of pressures either for greater recreational facilities or for the exploitation of untapped mineral wealth. Some of the world's most remote regions have succumbed to development; for example, parts of Alaska for oil and gas resources, the Antarctic to tourism. Indeed, the mineral rights of the Antarctic are being negotiated by parties to the 1959 Antarctic Treaty. Preservation versus economic development could be a major flashpoint of the 1980s. Already, the Reagan Administration intends to open up wilderness areas for development, although many of these proposals are unlikely to succeed in environmentally conscious America.

6.2.1 Uses and Demands for Forestry and Wilderness

Crude statistics on average per capita consumption of wood products in nations throughout the world will reveal only minor variations in usage between countries.[4] The figures conceal the major difference between the developed and developing countries in the use of forestry products. Over one-half of the world's forest production is used for firewood or converted to charcoal. However, it is estimated that about 86% of all wood used in developing countries is for fuel[5] and wood accounts for 20% of all fuel consumed in these countries.[6] By contrast, the USA and Canada – two countries well endowed with forestry resources – are mainly dependent upon fossil fuels to meet their energy demands: fuelwood provides only 1% and 4% of US and Canadian fuel needs respectively.[7] Nevertheless, high energy prices have resulted in changing patterns of fuel usage in regions of these countries which contain abundant forest reserves. For example, over one million wood stoves and furnaces were sold annually in the US between 1977 and 1981 as wood resources became competitive with other fuels.[8]

The main demand for forestry products in the developed world comes from industry. Indeed, developed countries monopolize the market, consuming 88% of all industrial wood.[9] Although wood is used in a multitude of products, the construction, furniture and pulp/paper industries are the main market outlets for processed wood products. The demand for these products is largely a function of the nature of the world economy and the changing tastes of a modern Western society. For example, the recession in the US housing sector in the late 1970s dampened demand for sawn wood and wood panel products. In terms of taste, wood-based panels have increasingly replaced sawn timber in the manufacture of furniture and in do-it-yourself home decorating. The use of chipboard and hardboards greatly improves the efficiency of wood production in that a higher proportion of the log can be utilized.

A major use of processsed wood is in the converting of wood to pulp for paper manufacture. The demand for paper and paperboard is heavily concentrated in Western countries, from the extravagant 272 kilograms consumed per head in the US in 1980 to the 122 kilograms per head consumed in the UK. These figures compare with 34 kilograms per head in the USSR and an average of 5 kilograms per head in the countries of the developing world.[10]

Clearly, as the poorer countries of the world develop they will demand an increasing share of the world's forestry products. Indeed, it is estimated that the developing world's demand for industrial wood will rise from 16% in 1976 to 28% in 2000 and 45% in 2025.[11] This could place great strain on supplies both to the developed and the developing world.

Although the world's forests are used mainly in the ways mentioned above, resource managers have actively encouraged multiple use of forest lands in order to minimize ecological disruption. For example, agro-forestry developments in the tropical rainforests can avoid the worst repercussions of shifting cultivation. Water catchment and forestry management can alleviate soil erosion and siltation of rivers. Wildlife and wilderness management can reduce pressure on pristine areas for recreational use.

As Western society has become more affluent, with increased leisure time and greater personal mobility, the demand for resource-based recreation has risen accordingly. Forests, once the hunting grounds of the rich (for example, the royal forests in Britain), were opened up to the public by state forest agencies. Simmons cites the example of the Netherlands where the Forest Service manages most of the country's larger forests for recreation, nature protection and landscape enhancement.[12]

6.3.1 Patterns of Supply

6.3.1a Resource-Based Recreation

Resource-based recreation tends to occur in areas of outstanding scenic beauty, often with unique natural habitats. Around the world, areas have been designated for landscape protection so that future generations will be able to enjoy relatively unspoiled environments. 'National parks', 'areas of outstanding beauty', 'game reserves' and 'wilderness' are only four of the terms which have come to be used to delimit zones for management purposes.

As unspoiled environments have become increasingly accessible to an international market this century, outdoor recreation as a resource has become an exportable commodity. At the other extreme, countries which lack wilderness are willing to 'import' it. Indeed, many international nature protection movements began in Britain with a view to preserving 'wild' environments in the developing world for the pleasure of the neo-colonial rich. Subsidization of wilderness in countries such as Tanzania, Kenya, Zambia and Uganda takes the form of foreign currency revenues from tourism. Without this 'market' for wilderness, it is unlikely that it would survive in the face of the competition to exploit its resources.[13]

These examples show that wilderness appreciation is international. On a more regional scale, a large number of North Americans cross international boundaries to enjoy outdoor recreation. Since 1975 the US has received a net influx of Canadian tourists, bringing in revenue to the tune of $600 million in 1981.[14] Cheap air travel, a lower cost of living and the lure of better weather attracts 'snowbirds' from Canada to the US 'sunbelt', where one half of all Canadian travel spending is registered.[15]

Americans also make the sojourn north. Canadian outdoor resources are the main reason why US citizens travel to Canada.[16] Indeed, some Canadian national and provincial parks are equally accessible to population centres on either side of the 49th Parallel. One million Americans fish in Canadian waters. Fifteen per cent of all visitors to Canadian national parks are US citizens. In some cases, parks in close proximity to the border receive most of their patronage from the US (Ontario's Quetico Provincial Park receives 89% of its visitors from south of the border).[17]

Table 6.1: World forest resources 1978 and estimates to 2000. Closed Forest (millions of hectares) *Source: The Global 2000 Report*, 1982, Penguin Books

	1978	2000
USSR	785	775
Europe	140	150
North America	470	464
Japan, Australia and New Zealand	69	68
Subtotal	1464	1457
Latin America	550	329
Africa	188	150
Asia and Pacific	361	181
Subtotal (LDCs)	1099	660
Total World	2563	2117

6.3.1b Forestry Resources – Patterns of Supply

The world's forests are diverse in composition, ranging from dense tropical rainforests to sparsely wooded savannas. The nature and extent of global forests are the subject of some debate because of problems of classification and the inadequacies of data for many countries. When it was stated earlier that one-third of the world's land surface was covered by forest, this assumption was based upon the 4,030 million hectares that are classed as *forest lands*. Some of this land, however, includes scrub, brushland and areas which have been deforested and where regeneration has not taken place. A more meaningful classification of forests is the dual categorization of *closed forests* and *open woodlands*, the main distinction being in the density of tree canopy. In closed forests, the density is sufficiently high to preclude the growth of grasses whilst in open woodlands this is not the case.

As can be seen from Table 6.1, it is estimated that 2·6 billion hectares of the world are closed forests, with a further 1·2 billion hectares being classified as open woodland. These figures and their regional distribution can give only an indication of the absolute extent of forestry resources. For example, it has been estimated that only about one-half of the global forest area has economic potential and in 1978 about one-third of this economic potential was utilized.[18] Some forests are undeveloped and will remain so because they have been designated for non-production uses such as nature reserves or recreational uses. The commercial justification for logging is a function of demand (discussed in 6.2.1) and the economic potential of forest resources. On the supply side, the resource must be accessible and of the appropriate species mix and quality. The availability of capital, labour and an infrastructure to exploit the resource at a competitive price is also necessary.

The difference between resource base and economic potential is aptly illustrated in the USSR which has the largest forest resource base in the world (30% of the world's closed forest (Table 6.1), 22% of all timber reserves and 66% of all coniferous forests).[19] Around half of the forested area, however, is not worth developing because the wood is either unproductive or inaccessible.[20] Indeed, two-thirds of the forest estates are located in Siberia, and poor infrastructure with which to market the resource has been a contributory factor in the decline in Soviet forestry production, from 395 million m³ in 1975 to 355 million m³ in 1979.[21]

The harvesting of wood is therefore related throughout the world to the balance between supply and demand for forest products. In 1979, 3·02 billion m³ of wood was produced, 58% of which came from the developing countries.[22] It was indicated earlier that most of this was used for fuelwood and charcoal. However, the developing countries' share of the output of *all* forest products has increased markedly since 1965, although their share of the processed wood sector still accounts for under 20% in these industries. Clearly, demand for industrial wood products will increase according to improved economic development status. Until recently, paper production was mainly confined to the developed world because of the unsuitability of hardwoods for pulping. Despite technological breakthroughs that enable mixed hardwoods to be used for paper production, world production of pulp and paper/paperboard is heavily concentrated in the northern hemisphere because of its geographical advantages (a few species within large amounts of boreal forest ideal for pulp manufacture and the proximity of these forests to centres of demand). This is illustrated in Table 6.2 which shows that seven countries, the US, Canada, Japan, USSR, Sweden, Finland and West Germany, not only account for 79% of world pulp production but 68% of paper and paper board production as well.

The developing nations have an abundance of forest resources. They have tropical forests with long growing seasons and high insolation levels giving growth rates three to fives times higher than for forests in temperate lands. A major drawback in their commercial development, however, is the extreme heterogeneity of the rainforests. In Amazonia up to 100 species per hectare are found. In Indonesia only 107 of the 3000 species are utilized commercially.[23] The lumberman has answered this problem by replacing natural forests with plantations of fast-growing commercial species such as teak or eucalyptus. (The ecological implications of this solution are discussed in 6.4.1.) Plantation forests are now estimated to cover 90 million hectares, with reforestation occurring at around 10 million hectares per annum.[24]

Although natural tropical forests are far from ideal for the timber companies, a ready market in the developed world has encouraged development to the extent that between 1950 and 1973 imports of tropical hardwoods rose from

Table 6.2: World production of pulp, paper and paperboard, 1980 (thousand metric tons). *Source: Pulp and Paper*, August 1981

Country	Pulp	Rank	Paper and Paperboard	Rank
United States	45,868	1	56,764	1
Canada	19,944	2	13,471	3
Japan	9,788	3	18,088	2
USSR	9,000	4	8,900	4
Sweden	8,699	5	6,182	6
Finland	7,234	6	5,919	7
West Germany	1,996	9	7,498	5
World	130,341		171,193	

Table 6.3: Major traders of forest products. *Source: The Global 2000 Report*, 1982, Penguin Books

Major Net Exporters	Exports less Imports (*millions $*)	Major Net Importers	Imports less Exports (*millions $*)
Canada	4,921	Japan	4,365
Sweden	3,601	United Kingdom	3,795
Finland	2,273	Italy	1,442
USSR	1,552	West Germany	1,439
Ivory Coast	706	France	1,186
Indonesia	666	Netherlands	1,085
Austria	540	USA	746
Malaysia (Sabah)	373	Belgium–Luxemburg	504
Philippines	237	Spain	479
Romania	218	Denmark	472
Malaysian Peninsula	200	Norway	416
Gabon	133	Australia	295
Chile	115	East Germany	284
Portugal	112	Switzerland	259
New Zealand	94	Argentina	245
		Hungary	244
		Hong Kong	193

5·2 to 52 million m³ a year.[25] This has placed many developing countries high in the league of forest exporters, close behind the 'Big 4' – Canada, Sweden, Finland and the USSR (Table 6.3). Japan and Western European countries, especially the UK, are the main importers of both hardwoods from the developing world and softwoods from Scandanavia and North America. The USA, which is the largest producer of wood (400 million m³ per annum), is such a prolific consumer that it has to import the equivalent of 107 million m³ of forestry products at a cost of $746 million a year.

A major concern, however, is that many of the exporters in the developing world, especially in South-East Asia, are in danger of being 'logged out'. For example, Nigeria has gone from being a major exporter to a net importer in a relatively short period of time.[26] The two large river basins – the Congo and the Amazon – could be next to be exploited by the timber companies for their export potential, although the Amazon may not be economically productive and could be developed to satisfy a domestic, rather than an international market.

Both Grainger and the Council on Environmental Quality have forecast that exports from tropical rainforest areas will decline in the future and that the main importers – Japan and the EEC countries – will become more dependent upon alternative suppliers, the EEC nations for example working in closer collaboration with Scandanavia (for softwoods) and West African nations (for hardwoods).

As can be seen from Table 6.1, the forest resource base in the developed world will remain relatively stable until the year 2000. Indeed, a minor increase is shown for Europe because of present afforestation and reforestation programmes. Throughout the century, developed countries have created an institutional framework to regulate the over-exploitation of forests. This has not occurred to the same extent in the developing world and the amount of closed forest, it is predicted, will shrink to 660 million hectares by the year 2000 (from 1099 million hectares in 1978).

6.4.1 Development Problems: The Ecological Implications of Deforestation, Afforestation and Reforestation

Throughout man's history deforestation has occurred as a result both of climatic changes and human exploitation. It is only in relatively recent times that man has been the most active agent of change. In Europe very little natural forest remains – a reflection of a long history of use and exploitation. Nevertheless, it was shown in previous sections that the area of closed forest in Europe will increase by the year 2000, a reflection of positive management policies throughout the century. While deforestation is only a marginal problem in the 'North', the 'South' is experiencing acute deforestation difficulties. Forests are being removed essentially for fuel purposes, but also to make way for crop production, water regulation, HEP schemes, mining and urban development.

From 1976 to 1980 deforestation in the tropical world occurred at a rate of 0·62% or 7·27 million hectares per annum[27]. The net average lost was expected to increase to 7·5 million hectares per annum until 1985. This use of fuelwood itself accounts for the clearing of 10 to 15 million hectares per year.[28] This rate of usage is so much greater than replacement rates that 'fuelwood crises' are a major socio-economic problem in many countries because of the time and money spent in harvesting a diminishing resource. Uganda, Kenya, Ethiopia and Bangladesh are countries where fuelwood yields have slipped below demand. Even some timber exporters (Ivory Coast and Indonesia) have acute deforestation problems in some areas.[29]

Deforestation – by whatever cause – has had severe ecological implications for landscapes, creating soil erosion and degradation, disruption of water systems and loss of animal and plant species. More importantly, on a global scale, concern has been expressed about the possible changes in world climates that may result from extensive forest clearances.

Much scientific debate has focused upon the possible changes to world climate patterns as a result of increasing CO_2 concentrations in the atmosphere from burning fossil fuels and firewood. The question of carbon balance is more acute in developing countries because the wood is burned, whereas in the developed world a high proportion is used for non-combustible purposes. Sedjo and Clawson[30] argue that US forests have experienced net additions over the past fifty years and that the US can be considered as a net carbon sink. Furthermore, they point out that the world's oceans absorb CO_2, but no one really knows the level of absorption. If the most pessimistic assumptions are made[31] (the present CO_2 level of 330 parts per million doubled), it is possible that average atmospheric temperatures would rise by 2 °C, causing the ice caps to melt and devastating low lying coastal areas with floods.

At a regional level, climatic change could occur if large tropical rainforests, such as those in Amazonia, are removed. In tropical areas, much of the water contained in forests is lost to the atmosphere by evaporation or transpiration but returns to the forest in the form of rain. Forest removal could decrease this evapotranspiration into the atmosphere and lead to drier climatic conditions. Increased desertification would throw more dust into the atmosphere, causing more solar energy to be reflected back into space thus limiting the proportion reaching the earth's surface. According to Olembo,[32] this would lead to greater precipitation in latitudes between 50 and 25° and decreased precipitation between 45° and 85°N and 40° and 60°S. This scenario predicts that the earth would become *cooler*.

As forests are destroyed so is flora and fauna. Tropical forests – those mainly at risk – are rich in biological species, harbouring between two and five million of the world's ten million species of plants and animals.[33] Temperate developed countries such as Britain are limited in biological diversity of species (even the beaver became extinct by the 16th century!). However, deforestation has and will result in a rapid increase in the rate of species extinction. It is estimated that tropical rainforests contain 276 mammals, 345 birds, 136 amphibians and reptiles, 99 freshwater fishes and 20,000 plants that are threatened species. In 1980 one species per day was being lost.[34]

Perhaps the severest impact of deforestation upon man's economic activity has been in soil depletion and erosion and in the subsequent increased run off culminating in siltation, flooding and landslides. Some of these 'natural' hazards are induced by man. Scant regard for watershed management upstream has lead to catastrophic disasters downstream.

In temperate zones, forest lands have been transformed into infertile, peaty heaths and moors. Trees, which retain moisture, were removed and waterlogging ensued. As uplands were denuded of forest cover, soil erosion occurred, giving rise to the silting of rivers and coastal areas. This process was responsible for the demise of two ancient ports in Britain – Bristol and Chester.[35] Tropical zones, however, are much more vulnerable to ecological disruption than temperate areas. The equatorial belt receives half the globe's terrestrial rainfall, and the rain is more erosive than elsewhere in the world.[36] Tropical forests absorb the damaging force of rainstorms. When removed, especially by shifting agriculturalists who quickly deprive the soil and vegetation of its nutrients, leaching could turn some areas into wastelands.

Deforestation in the tropics has profound implications for major river systems and thus for areas which depend upon water regulation for their agriculture. The extent of such river systems means that forest removal in one country could have repercussions in another downstream. The periodic floods experienced in Bangladesh would be aggravated if forested watersheds in Nepal and Assam were removed.[37] The reduction of forest cover in the Himalayan watershed in India has led to recurrent landslides, excessive siltation and catastrophic floods. The most disastrous flood (or more appropriately, series of floods) occurred in the wake of a monsoon in 1978 that turned the Ganges basin into a 'watery grave'.[38] West Bengal was the state that suffered the greatest loss of life. Nearly two thousand people died. Over four hundred thousand cattle were killed, and £130 million of crops damaged. Industrial damage, such as the closure of steelworks and coal mines, cost the country £1·2 billion[39].

India's faith in dam construction to cure deforestation-aggravated flooding problems is proving costly and only partially effective because of soil erosion. Dams are silting up so rapidly that their projected life has been reduced by two-thirds to one-half. The Bhakra reservoir in Punjab, scheduled to last 88 years, is expected to be unusable in only 44 years. The Mirakud reservoir in Orissa is now expected to last 35 years; its original planned life was 110 years[40].

The logical solution is to arrest the rate of deforestation by increasing yields through intensive silviculture and tree farming. Unfortunately, there are negative effects implicit in such forms of forestry management. Intensive silviculture, like intensive agriculture, requires costly inputs of fertilizers, pesticides and herbicides. These can also act as agents of air and water pollution. Intensification also runs the risk of straining the ecosystem and impairing soil quality, especially when natural forests have been replaced by high yield monocultures. Moreover, less biological diversity could jeopardize large sections of forest if pests and pathogens produce epidemics such as Dutch elm disease in Western Europe.

Ecological problems associated with afforestation and reforestation have been encountered in managed forests in temperate zones. For example, in the US the shortening of growth cycles has led to a loss of soil nutrients, whilst the use of particular pesticides to combat disease has met with strong environmental opposition, to the extent that they have been withdrawn from the market.[41] In the tropics intensive silviculture can produce very short growing cycles, but the environmental problems mentioned above tend to be emphasized in environments with such ecological diversity. Indeed, the problems of intensive silviculture parallel those of the Green Revolution in agriculture – high costs, high yields and high environmental risks.

6.4.2a Land Use Competition: Forestry

Land-use competition takes a different form in temperate as compared with tropical zones. In Western Europe, where natural forests have been removed throughout the continent's history, present-day competition occurs mainly during afforestation programmes. In the developing world, forests are being cleared to make way for other land uses. In India between 1951 and 1973, 3·4 million hectares of forest were removed for other uses, primarily farming. This accounted for 2·4 million hectares.[42]

The agriculturalist, from the primitive shifting cultivator to the multinational food corporation, has been principally responsible for the destruction of tropical rainforests. The traditional 'slash and burn' shifting cultivators, who moved within a restricted geographical cycle as exhausted land regenerated itself roughly every twenty years, are now forced to clear more forest because of population pressures. This self-sustained existence was possible when ten or twelve persons per square mile were farming the land. But densities are estimated to be five times greater than this in some tropical areas causing further encroachment into the forest and shorter fallow times.

This population pressure is not induced solely by 'native' farmers but also by immigrant landless peasants who have been forced from their land by incoming logging or agribusiness corporations and by government resettlement projects. For example, transmigration schemes in Indonesia (Java to Kalimantan), Malaysia and the Philippines (Luzon to Mindanao) and in Brazil (from the north east to Amazonia) are attempts to clear land for the landless poor. Ambitious projects of this nature are often seen as political alternatives to the real problem facing the landless peasants, namely the need for land reform of existing farming areas.[43] Serious questions have been raised about the desirability of forest clearing for commercial agricultural purposes when most of the production is geared to the export market.

Cash cropping, introduced during the colonial period to satisfy Western demands, has continued, with exports of rubber, coffee, cocoa and oil palm providing valuable foreign exchange to nations in the tropics. As monocultures, however, they are prone to disease epidemics and they cause degraded environments which impair long-term economic viability. An extreme example of export-led agricultural development was the clearance of 3·9 million hectares of Amazonia rainforest from 1966 to 1975 to accommodate large-scale cattle ranching projects.[44] Most of this poor quality beef ends up in the fast food markets of North America and Western Europe. The removal of Amazonian forest for this purpose has been categorized as one of the most profligate misuses of natural resources in history.[45] Already more than 0·5 million out of 2·5 million hectares converted to pasture in the late 1960s and early 1970s have been abandoned either because of soil exhaustion or poor productivity, which makes the venture uneconomic.[46]

Agriculture has been the main agent of rural change in tropical forests, although mineral exploitation, power and flood regulation projects and infrastructure schemes to support economic development have necessitated extensive forest clearing. In Amazonia alone, 3 million hectares of forest have been removed for highway construction.[47] In the case of mineral exploitation, parallels can be drawn with neo-colonial cash crop development. Tropical areas are rich in mineral resources, and countries such as Zaire (copper), Malaysia and Thailand (tin) became major exporters as a result of Western European colonialism. These countries remain dependent upon the export potential of minerals for a large proportion of their foreign exchange earnings and forest encroachment will be largely a function of commodity markets (see Chapter 4).

In the developed world, pressures on woodland do exist but an institutional framework has been established in most countries to resolve conflicts between users. Most forestry agencies operate with the concept of 'sustained yield' and much of the land-use conflict has focused upon afforestation rather than deforestation. The main exception to this is in lowland forest areas which have been subjected either to urban or agricultural development. In the latter case, the removal of hedgerows in Britain to 'improve' agricultural efficiency has been lamented by conservationists who point out the value of hedgerows as shelter belts and pest eradicators. On being removed, the work of hedgerows has to be done by costly pesticides that may have harmful long-term environmental effects.

The question of afforestation is generally linked to ownership patterns and government policy. In Britain the state forestry agency, the Forestry Commission, has been forced to acquire most areas for planting in economically marginal areas of upland Scotland, Wales and northern England because of the high cost of land in the lowlands. Even then, competition occurs from heavily subsidized hill farmers and from conservation groups who argue that uniform conifer plantations are aesthetically less appealing and accessible than open moorland.

5.4.2b Land Use Competition: Wilderness and Landscape Protection Areas

The prime purpose of creating landscape protection areas is to retain a natural or cultural habitat for the enjoyment of future generations. With the creation in 1872 of the Yellowstone National Park, the US initiated a form of land use which has spread to a hundred nations and over a thousand areas.[48] Wilderness areas (often within national parks), nature reserves, heritage area, sites of scientific interest – all are terms that have been coined to express the need for preservation. Much of the pressure for conservation has been pitched at an international level through the work of bodies such as the World Wildlife Fund and the World Heritage Convention. The former has been instrumental in persuading the Brazilian government to create more national parks in Amazonia and to undertake studies of virgin forest alongside cleared areas to determine the minimum critical size at which a tropical forest reserve can support its wildlife.

A well-publicized example of land-use competition in a World Heritage area occurred in Tasmania where the state government intended to build a dam across the Gordon and Franklin rivers to generate cheap hydro-electric power for the island. The dam would have submerged a natural wilderness area which includes part of the world's remaining temperate rain forests. The issue aroused the feelings not only of Tasmanians but also of international botanists. The political connotations of the international publicity which the proposal has generated committed the incoming Labour Government in March 1983 to abandon the scheme.

The opening up of wilderness areas for energy and mineral development has provoked the greatest criticism from conservationists, especially in the US where the Reagan Administration advocates the release of federal lands for development. This pro-development movement is nicknamed the Sagebrush Rebellion. All the wilderness areas are within the federal public lands, that is in the national parks, forests and wildlife refuges and in lands managed by the Bureau of Land Management (BLM). The Wilderness Act of 1964 established a National Wilderness Preservation System which initially designated 54 areas totalling 9·1 million acres as 'wilderness'.[49] By 1982 the system embraced 23·4 million acres in the lower 48 states and 56·4 million acres in Alaska, with BLM reviewing a further 24 million acres for recommendation to Congress.[50]

One proviso of the 1964 Act was that exploration for minerals or energy development would be allowed until December 1983. Then they would be closed to these uses. In May 1981 the Secretary of the Interior, James Watt, repudiated the policy of previous Interior Secretaries by advising his staff to 'open wilderness areas'. By early 1982 over one thousand applications had been made. Conservationists rallied with a concerted action demanding Watt's resignation.[51] The strong public opposition to the Watt initiative coupled with firm Congressional opposition has prompted the introduction of the Wilderness Protection Act passed by the House in late 1982.[52] This reversed the policy of opening wilderness for development but attached a 'release' clause that would allow development to proceed in the case of national expediency.

Whilst the US is concerned about protecting its wilderness, UK landscape protection areas *are* open to development. Conservationists have to compete for the use of land with water authorities, electricity boards, mining companies, farmers and the Forestry Commission. Mineral working in the national parks is aesthetically the least desirable use allowed in protection areas; yet in certain cases mining activity has increased since designation. The Peak District National Park, for example, has experienced a fourfold increase in limestone production and a threefold increase in fluorspar production during its first twenty years as a national park.[53] Conflict between conservationists and farmers has also arisen because of the so-called 'ploughing problem', especially in moorland areas. Farmers believe that they have the right to do whatever they like with their own land even though this land may be in national parks, sites of special scientific interest or other designated areas. Conservationists argue that reclamation damages the ecology and amenity of the area, negating the purpose of designating it of community value in the first place. Furthermore, they point out that farmers often receive grant aid from the Ministry of Agriculture to undertake such 'improvements'.

6.5.1 The Need for Management

It has been shown that forestry and wilderness are susceptible to pressure for development. In the case of wilderness, development pressure may come from conservationists and recreationists themselves. The problem of over-use is beginning to be a major issue in that the *raison d'être* for these areas becoming designated landscapes is being undermined by human erosion of the features which are supposed to be enjoyed.

In the US popular use of national parks nearly quadrupled between 1961 and 1981.[54] In Britain visits to the countryside, especially national parks, country parks, historic monuments and buildings have trebled since 1945.[55] In both countries, destruction by popularity is taking place necessitating management action. This pressure of demand on recreational resources has been compared to that of tennis players booking a court.[56] The concept of management is accepted by players because of the popularity of the sport. Hence, booking systems, time limits and other rules and regulations are enforced to enhance the enjoyment of tennis for all participants. In the same way, some form of management is required to control the use of landscape protection areas. For example, the 36,000 hikers and 17,000 rafters who experienced the magnificence of the Grand Canyon wilderness in 1981[57] would have had to book well in advance (up to three months) to guarantee a place on the trip. True wilderness proponents would argue that the quality of wilderness experience has declined precipitously regardless of management initiatives: only the least accessible areas such as Northern Canada and Alaska can now give the feeling of wilderness once experienced in areas like the Grand Canyon.

Whilst the management of existing landscape protection areas for recreationists is one problem, another is how to resolve use conflicts in existing and proposed designated areas. The perception of the nature and extent of this problem is manifest in legislative responses to the pressures for change. Chapter 13 will discuss legislation pertaining to wilderness protection, the agencies created to enact it and the classic conflicts which have arisen through the implementation of policy.

In terms of forestry management, deforestation of temperate lands and competition between forestry and other uses for land (invariably marginal land) has promoted institutional responses from as early as the Middle Ages. As forestry moved from the hunting and gathering stage to become a modern, efficient multi-purpose industry in temperate lands, institutions were created to manage this renewable resource. Forests are no longer common property in most of these areas; forests have been turned over to private or government ownership. Forestry management has been fostered through fiscal incentives offered to owners to reforest and conduct R. & D. whilst regulations have been imposed to ensure that an ecological balance of use is sustained.

This may appear to paint a rosy picture of forestry management in the developed world. However, intensive silviculture has produced ecological problems such as those of disease and soil degradation. The use of pesticides has not been particularly successful in arresting disease in certain cases and has resulted in the removal of specific types from the market place. These difficulties have prompted consideration of irregular planting of hardwoods and softwoods, or to change the species in the second rotation.

In the temperate 'North' management problems have centred around afforestation. However, in the tropical zones forestry may still be in the foraging common property stage. The rate of deforestation requires urgent management action. The 'social forestry' concept introduced in several countries is a step in the right direction, encouraging communities to plant and protect their own trees for their long-term development potential. Managed tree plantations, with their rapid growth and even stands, will withstand the pressure of natural forest exploitation although over-intensive silviculture will induce ecological problems of a greater magnitude than in temperate zones.

Although reforestation is a prerequisite for development in 'Southern' countries, more attention needs to be focused upon the causes of deforestation. Much of the pressure on tropical forests is attributable to the need for fuelwood or agricultural land to feed a hungry people. Agro-forestry programs have been established in several countries, for example Kenya, Thailand and the Philippines, to militate against the worst effects of shifting cultivation. Arguably, the pressures on forest lands for agricultural development are related to a lack of institutional reform in many countries. For example, it was shown that Brazil and Indonesia have tended to open up remote parts of their country rather than initiate land reforms within their present agricultural systems.

Firewood crises will become more prevalent if the delicate balance of supply and demand is upset by the loss of forests to other uses. Nevertheless, alternative energy supplies could be considered. More efficient wood-burning appliances could offer the prospect of saving scarce fuel. Small-scale solar energy devices and biogas converters[58] should be encouraged, to ameliorate the worst effects of deforestation in countries where stocks are being replenished at a much lower rate than current usage.

6.5.2 Future Prospects

Of all the resources under investigation, forestry and wilderness are relatively unique in that their development (or lack of development) is intrinsically tied up with multiple use competition. Forestry projects are in competition with more financially lucrative development options, such as mining or agricultural schemes, which may generate a quicker and higher return on capital invested.

Unfortunately, forestry and wilderness have unquantifiable external costs and benefits which must be considered within the cost equation. In the case of wilderness, society must place a value upon a depleting resource. It must weigh up the pros and cons of opening up such areas for development, so as to ensure that *societal* rather than corporate objectives are satisfied. In the case of forestry, environmental costs are already well documented – changes in world climate, the permanent loss of biotic species, degraded environments and increased run off with associated siltation and erosion problems. Indeed, *the Global 2000 Report*[59] argued that changes in the forest environment posed a greater threat to man's environment than any other resource investigated by the study team.

It is not surprising that the Report predicted a gloomy future for world forestry. Net deforestation will reduce the 'closed forest' cover of the world from one-fifth to one-sixth of the land surface by the year 2000.[60] Moreover, the prospects of arresting this decline are not good, especially in the poorer tropical countries where increased population growth coupled with excessive land-use competition will aggravate the deforestation problem.

A more optimistic view is taken by Sedjo and Clawson who feel that the severity of deforestation is overestimated.[61] They point out, for instance, that deforestation of pristine, broadleaf, closed tropical forests is relatively low and that there is little possibility of the world running out of forests *or* of major regions being dramatically denuded of forest cover. They pose questions about what is considered an acceptable rate of deforestation to meet social, environmental and developmental goals. They do agree, however, that excessive deforestation in parts of tropical Africa, Asia and Latin America has created regional, environmental and fuelwood problems. The solutions lie in the hands of political decision makers. It is they who can create the institutional machinery to formulate *long-term* forestry management policies that will maximize developmental objectives.

7   Water

7.1 Introduction

As a resource water has a number of unique characteristics. Not least among
these is its flexibility of use. Table 7.1 lists the major ways in which water may
be exploited. For many uses there is no substitute. Not all uses involve the
withdrawal of water from its source. Some may involve consumption but others
do not affect the quantity available for further use. Because water has been so
basic to the historical development of man, the availability of water has under-
lain the pattern of human activities attempted in any given location. The demands made upon water resources were, for much of history, so small that no
pressure for management of its supply existed and water came to be regarded
as a 'free' good in most places.

With growing concentrations of population, particularly associated with urbanization and industrialization, however, it became increasingly apparent that
intervention in the natural hydrological cycle was necessary. Water has six
useful properties: it is truly vital, in the sense that plant and animal life are
impossible without it; it is a chemical raw material for many useful products
and processes such as paper and ink; it is a medium of movement, providing
navigation or transport facilities for wastes; flowing downhill, it has kinetic
energy which may be harnessed as a source of power, or have to be suffered in
the form of catastrophic floods or erosion; it is an environment in itself, sustaining such ecologically useful forms as fish but also harbouring a wide and
threatening range of diseases and their vectors; and finally, it appears to exert
an aesthetic fascination in itself, many people finding pleasure from swimming
in it, or even from watching it. In short, water is a demand-orientated resource
and these demands may occur simultaneously to exert considerable pressure
for management.

7.2 Uses and Demands for Water

7.2.1 Public Health

The quantity of water required for domestic purposes varies considerably
around the world, according to cultural environment, income and established
standard of living. White[1] has derived the range of daily domestic use per capita
according to the mean of supply (Table 7.2). In developed countries, a considerable amount of water is used for domestic appliances such as automatic
washing machines and dishwashers. Hose pipes may also be used to keep lawns
green and wash cars. In general, affluent districts commonly require between
100 and 300 litres per day per capita, whereas at the other end of the scale,
people using stand-pipes might be expected to use only 10-25 litres daily.

Table 7.1: Components and impacts of water use. *Source:* UN Water conference, 1978, *Proceedings*, Pergamon Press, p. 20, after G.F. White

Components	Common Substitutes	Types of use			Potential Environmental Impact	Potential consumption use (%)
		Withdrawal	In-stream	On-site		
Drinking	none	yes				1–15
Other domestic	none	yes				1–15
Public, urban*	none	yes				1–15
Livestock	none	yes	yes		Organic	1–15
Soil moisture conservation	none			yes	Sediment	0–100
Irrigation	none	yes			Salt	10–80
Drainage	none			yes	Salt	0
Wetland habitat	none					0–10
Aquatic habitat	none		yes			0
Navigation	land transport		yes			0–10
Hydropower	other energy forms		yes			0
Mining		yes	yes			1–5
Manufacturing (cooling)	air	yes			Thermal	0–3
Manufacturing (processing)	mechanical	yes			Organic/toxic	0–10
Waste disposal	air and mechanical means	yes			Organic	0
Recreation			yes			0
Aesthetic			yes			0
Flood reduction	land-use controls		yes			0

* for use in fire-fighting, street washing, fountains, etc.

Table 7.2: Range of domestic water use (per capita).
Source: A.K. Biswas, 1978, *United Nations Water Conference*, Pergamon
Press, p. 48, after A.U. White

Urban dwellers, multiple taps	40–300 litres/head/day
Single tap dwellers	18–140 litres/head/day
Stand pipe users	18– 74 litres/head/day
Rural	5– 38 litres/head/day

Above all, water for drinking and the preparation of food should be free of
organisms injurious to health. In developed countries, this had been nearly
universally achieved by the mid-20th century. In developing countries, however, considerable room for progress remains.

In 1976 the World Health Organisation (WHO) conducted a survey revealing the extent to which communities in developing countries were receiving
safe water supplies.[2] It was found that 76% of the urban population could be
thought of as adequately served, although 20% continued to rely on stand-
pipes rather than house connections. In rural areas, on the other hand, only
22% of the population had access to safe water, leaving a total of 65% of the
population of developing countries vulnerable to the hazards of improper
supply. In addition, it should not be forgotten that to collect water from non-
piped sources such as rivers and wells might well take up to five hours per day,
an effort accounting for 12% of calorific needs (25% in mountainous areas).[3]

Water having been used, it then has to be disposed of safely. In developed
countries a major use of water is flushing toilets. The WHO survey found that
less than one-third of the population of developing countries had access
to adequate sewage disposal facilities, again with a heavy bias against rural
dwellers (only 14% with adequate facilities).[4]

The importance of a sufficient and safe supply of water for meeting basic
needs was a major theme of the United Nations Water Conference, held at Mar
del Plata, Argentina in March 1977. The resulting 'Mar del Plata Action Plan'
contained the recommendation that the 1980s be designated the international
drinking water supply and sanitation decade. Since the early 1960s the World
Health Organisation, the World Bank, UNICEF and other United Nations
agencies have been urgently tackling the problem. Progress has been slow
because of the high cost. In 1976 WHO estimates that the funds required to
raise the availability of potable water in urban areas to 91% of the population
and to achieve reasonable sewage disposal would be 25 billion dollars, whereas
the more modest rural targets of 36% of the population having access to safe
water and 24% access to proper sewage disposal would be 3·5 billion dollars.[5]
Clearly, at this level of cost there is no alternative to limited step-by-step
improvement.

In attempting to assess progress over the 1970s, great difficulties were encountered by the United Nations Environmental Programme (UNEP) in gathering uniform statistics. Nevertheless, it seems that in developing countries the
pace of urbanization outstripped the ability of governments to extend safe
supplies. UNEP reports that the proportion of the urban population in developing countries with access to safe urban water supplies rose from 67% in 1970
to 77% in 1975 but then declined to 75% in 1980.[6] Meanwhile, the proportion
of the rural population with such access is thought to have improved from 14%
to 29% between 1970 and 1980. The position with regard to waste-water

disposal is thought to be even more disappointing. The proportion of the urban population with access to appropriate sanitation is thought to have risen from 71% in 1970 to 75% in 1975, but fallen dramatically to 53% in 1980. In rural areas, the equivalent figures are thought to be 11% in 1970 and 13% in 1980.

According to Fano and Brewster, the World Bank has recently warned that expenditure on improving water supplies and sewerage is likely to run to an unacceptably high rate of $600 billion by 1990 unless some re-evaluation of the technologies being applied occurs.[7] Costs could be halved by adopting simpler methods and less lavish standards than hitherto. For example, simple community stand-pipes could replace individual house connections, so that a minimum level of service could be extended to the whole population at a reasonable cost.

7.2.2 Irrigation

After human health, agriculture is the most important aspect of water use. Agriculture is the largest user of water, accounting for some 80% of world consumption, mainly through irrigation.[8] The potential contribution of water management to increased food production is very high and is illustrated by data in Table 7.3. Clearly, the greatest gains are to be made through a 'Green Revolution' combination of irrigation, pesticides and fertilizer application. Most irrigated land is in developed countries. FAO has published estimates showing that only 92 million of the 223 million hectares of irrigated land in 1975 is in developing countries (see Table 7.4), but it is hoped that this will grow to 119 million hectares by 1990. Considerable cost barriers exist to any expansion of the irrigated area.

In 1980 the FAO study *Agriculture: Toward 2000* contained the estimate that investment of over $430 billion (at 1980 prices) was necessary if progress in world food supplies was to be made between 1980 and 2000. Desirable schemes of flood control and drainage would cost a further $18 billion over the

Table 7.3: Rice yields,* related to water control measures and other inputs (Paddy Rice, 1971–1974). *Source:* UN Water Conference, 1978, *Proceedings*, Pergamon Press, p. 910

Water Control Measures	Additional Inputs	Country	Maximum Yield† (*tons/ha*)
None	None	Laos	1·3
Flood control	None	Kampuchea	1·5
Elimination of drought and flood control	Low amounts fertilizer	Burma	1·7
		India	1·7
		Thailand	2·0
Irrigation and drainage	low to medium fertilizer	Pakistan	2·4
		Vietnam	2·5
		Sri Lanka	2·9
		Malaysia (West)	3·0
Sophisticated water management	high fertilizer – improved seeds, pest control	Rep. of Korea	4·9
		Japan	5·9

* Paddy rice.
† 1971–1974 figures.

Table 7.4: FAO irrigation improvement targets, 1975–1990. *Source:* UN Water
Conference, 1978, *Proceedings*, Pergamon Press, p. 913

	Existing Irrigated Areas 1975 ('000 ha)	Minor Improve-ment Area ('000 ha)	Cost (US$m)	Major Improve-ment Area ('000 ha)	Cost (US$m)	Totals Area ('000 ha)	Cost (US$m)
Africa	2,610	522	209	261	235	783	444
Latin America	11,749	2,349	566	2,349	1,540	4,698	2,106
Near East	17,105	6,368	3,184	3,421	3,079	9,789	6,263
Asia	60,522	17,614	5,284	12,104	8,472	29,718	13,756
Totals	91,986	26,853	9,243	18,135	12,556	44,988	22,569

same period. The cost of developing new works is high, at an average of $4,500
per hectare. Hence improvements on existing main and on-farm systems, covering 45 million hectares in developing countries, are to receive top priority. In
this light, Fano and Brewster[9] report that rising costs of development as well
as improvement of existing schemes give rise for concern:

However, many countries still have a large potential for lower cost irrigation. Consideration must thus be given to the possibility of decreasing costs by developing national
facilities, skills and materials, and by introducing phased development, proceeding with
initial small scale low cost schemes which can be later integrated into major schemes as
national capabilities are developed.

In this light, it would seem that the days of high-technology schemes, involving
sophisticated dams and concrete conduits supplied in a total package by European or North American contractors may be over.

Over the period 1968–1979 all regions of the world reported an increase in
irrigated area of at least 15%, with the largest extended area in Asia, principally
in China and India and the greatest increase in the USSR (63%).[10] Most
encouragingly, there is a trend towards deep wells and distribution systems
that do not involve an extensive network of channels, thus cutting down on
water losses through evaporation and reducing overall costs. In the western
United States, however, extensive development of pump and spray systems has
reduced the water table because rates of extraction exceeded the natural re-
charge of aquifers.[11]

7.2.3 Hydro-electricity

Table 7.5 shows estimates of the hydro-electric power potential that exists
around the world and the extent to which it has been developed. Clearly,
development has occurred to the greatest extent in North America and Europe.
Considerable potential appears to remain elsewhere. Of course, not every site
can be developed. Some river sections will lack geological conditions suitable
for dam construction or feasible topography for the formation of a reservoir.
Many reasonable sites are too far from any centre of demand to make the
transmission of the resulting electricity worthwhile. Nevertheless the competitive position of water-resource development in relation to other sources of

Table 7.5: Hydraulic energy resources and current use (millions of kilowatt-hours per year). *Source:* UN Water Conference, 1978, *Proceedings*, Pergamon Press, p. 36

	Potential Output	Current Annual Production 1974	Realized %
Africa	1,161,741	30,168	2·6
Asia	1,114,305	198,433	17·8
Europe (inc. USSR)	827,676	505,317	61·1
North America	577,086	453,334	78·6
South America	649,763	91,415	14·1
Oceania	103,897	28,897	27·8
World	4,434,468	1,307,564	

power, particularly fossil fuels in the 'South', would seem to be improving and there seems scope for considerable further development. The construction cost per unit of generating capacity has tended to rise as the most promising sites have been developed.[12]

Approximately half of the world's hydropower potential is in the developing countries, of which only 10% has been developed.[13] In its report *Energy and the Developing Countries* (1980) the World Bank estimated that a total investment of $176 million (in 1980 prices) will be required in developing countries during the 1980s, the large increases in oil prices of recent years having made many hydro possibilities into attractive propositions. Because of the long lead time required to bring hydro projects into production (ten to fifteen years, actual construction accounting for a third of this time), investments are being expanded as fast as possible to avoid a crisis in the cost of energy in the late 1980s. In 1980 alone the World Bank financed nearly 5000 MW of new capacity. In most cases, costs can be offset through multiple use of the reservoir – for irrigation, navigation or water supply.

7.2.4 Waste Disposal

Waste disposal is probably the most extensive use made of world water resources, although specific data on sewage and domestic wastes are hard to come by. Industrial waste disposal has been a major problem in many parts of the world. A few industries account for two-thirds or more of all industrial use of water, namely, metal processing, chemical production, petroleum refining, pulp and paper production and food processing.[14] Water used in industry may be combined or included in the product, used in the process and returned as waste or used for cooling purposes and returned unchanged in quality although at a higher temperature. There is often scope for the recycling of cooling and process water, in some cases to retrieve valuable elements in the waste, but the cost of water rarely represents more than a small fraction of production costs. Historically, as production expanded in the developed countries of the 'North' and as economic development increases in the 'South', more wastes are created for disposal and increasing pressure on the quality of water resources is experienced. This in turn threatens the usefulness of water for other purposes such as domestic supply, or even for use by other industrial establishments whose processes require water of a certain quality.

Reporting to the UN Water Conference of 1977, the UN Economic Commission for Europe (which includes in its membership the United States, Canada and the Soviet Union, as well as the countries of Eastern and Western Europe) the following appeared:[15]

No ECE country is without a water pollution problem and, in view of the adverse effect that it can have on all species of life and the deterioration it causes to the quality of environmental and social systems, the urgency of dealing adequately with this problem is intense.

As might be expected, the greatest problems are in areas of dense population and extensive industrial development. Plants most often associated with significant pollution of water are pulp and paper mills, chemical works, oil refineries, textile factories, mining establishments, metallurgical works and various branches of the food industry. The report goes on to draw attention to increasing problems relating to the use and transportation of fuel and, more worryingly, of 'toxic pollutants', substances which even in very low concentrations can seriously damage living tissue. At least in the 'North' polluted water is the subject of a great deal of monitoring and considerable efforts at amelioration. Elsewhere, the following quotation from the regional report of ESCAP[16] appears typical:[17]

Until recently, little or no control has been placed on the use of streams, lakes and the atmosphere as 'sinks' for the disposal of wastes. This has affected the quality and hence the availability of water for many purposes. Furthermore, adequate assessment of water quality is complicated by the increasing use and disposal of new chemicals for domestic, industrial and agricultural purposes. Except in special cases, collection of basic data on water quality has to be limited to a relatively small number of parameters, such as domestic and stock water supply and irrigation.

7.2.5 Recreational Use

An increasingly important objective in water-resource management is the preservation of quality so that recreational fishing may thrive or various water sports can take place without risk to health. This, plus the aesthetic desire to avoid the condition of water bodies causing offence through unnatural colouring or smell, has provided the rationale for much of the pollution control work being carried on in developed countries. Some water resource developments, such as those for hydro-electric power, actually create major new recreational resources.

7.3 Patterns of Supply

7.3.1 The Global Distribution of Water Resources

It is estimated that the total value of water on earth is about 1·4 billion cubic kilometres, distributed in accord with Table 7.6. Water circulates through a hydrological cycle powered by energy from the sun. Water evaporated from the oceans moves with atmospheric patterns of circulation and falls as precipitation. Precipitation evaporates from land surfaces and plants back to the atmosphere

Table 7.6: Total volume of water on earth. *Source:* UN
Water Conference, 1978, *Proceedings*,
Pergamon Press, p. 5, After Baumgestnes
and Reichel

Ocean water	97·3%
Fresh water	2·7%
Location of fresh water:	
Ice caps and glaciers	77·2%
Ground water and soil moisture	22·4%
Lakes and swamps	0·35%
Atmosphere	0·04%
Streams	0·01%

or infiltrates the soil. From there water may be drawn through the roots of
plants, to be transpired through leaf pores, or percolate through the ground,
feeding streams, and hence back to the ocean. Clearly, only accessible water is
of use to man and then only when remaining relatively pure. This means, in
effect, precipitation falling on land or non-contaminated ground water, some of
which may be a fossil reserve built up slowly over a long period of time or in
relation to a past pattern of prevailing precipitation. The amount of water
available at any given location depends largely on the balance between arrivals
(precipitation) and departures (evaporation) and infiltration known as 'run-off'.
Of course, this may be supplemented through the arrival of surface water
flowing from elsewhere, it having fallen in a catchment upstream in the relatively recent past, or, as already mentioned, the arrival of ground water at
economically feasible depths.

Various estimates of available run-off were quoted at the United Nations
Water Conference. These are reproduced in Table 7.7. To this may be added
the total volume of fresh water stored in lakes and man-made reservoirs. Lakes
are thought to hold approximately four times the average yearly run-off from
global lands, whilst man-made storage stands at approximately 11% of yearly

Table 7.7: Estimates of world annual water balance *Source:* UN Water Conference,
1978, *Proceedings*, Pergamon Press, p. 38

	Baumgestnes 1975			USSR Monograph 1974			Lvovich 1974		
	P	E	R	P	E	R	P	E	R
				(thousand cubic kilometres)					
Europe	6·6	3·8	2·8	8·3	5·3	3·0	7·2	4·1	3·1
Asia	30·7	18·5	12·2	32·2	18·1	14·1	32·7	19·5	13·2
Africa	20·7	17·3	3·4	22·3	17·7	4·6	20·8	16·6	4·2
Australia	7·1	4·7	2·4	7·1	4·6	2·5	6·4	4·4	2·0
North America	15·6	9·7	5·9	18·3	10·1	8·2	13·9	7·9	6·0
South America	28·0	16·9	11·1	28·4	16·2	12·2	29·4	19·0	10·4
Antarctic	2·4	0·4	2·0	2·3	0	2·3	—	—	—
Land Areas	111	71	40	119	72	47	113	72	41
Oceans	385	425	−40	458	505	−47	412	453	−41
World	496	496	0	577	577	0	525	525	0

P = Precipitation   E = Evaporation   R = Run-Off.

run-off.[18] What is important with regard to the availability of water at any particular place is the extent to which man is prepared to store supplies and/or transport supplies to the point of use. Generally, there would appear to be an economic limit of 400 miles to the construction of artificial aquaducts but, of course, stored water can be transferred over long distances using natural river channels, providing water quality controls prevent losses through pollution.

In this light the adequacy of water resources in any particular locality depends on four factors: the availability of local sources, the demands to be met, the extent to which sources are rendered unusable through previous use, and the extent to which investment in water engineering structures is thought worthwhile. Because water is ubiquitous (practically nowhere exists where there is absolutely no water available) and usually available in considerable quantities, because it is a renewable resource and because it very often has no specific owner (although the ground on which it falls or the land through which it flows may have an owner), water tends to be very inexpensive. The point-of-use cost of water in the United States is seldom more than $0·30 per metric ton for municipally supplied water, and may be as low as $0·03 per metric ton for irrigation water.[19] Great economies of scale produce the relatively low unit price to which most people are accustomed. It would seem that there is considerable scope for an increase in the real price of water in many locations and hence the interest in new schemes of development and of management considered in the remainder of this chapter and in Chapter 14.

The authors of *The Global 2000 Report* estimate world water withdrawals for 1975 at an aggregate level of less than 3×10^{12} cubic metres per year while the lowest supply estimate was more than one order of magnitude greater, at 4×10^{13} cubic metres:[20]

Other estimates indicate that nearly 60% of all water withdrawn is returned to the environment, so the actual global total of water consumed may be no more than 3% of the aggregate water supply. Barring substantial climatic change, the supply estimate should remain constant throughout the near future, while water withdrawals climb steadily with population and rising agricultural and industrial output. Even if water withdrawals were to increase by a factor of 7 by the year 2000, only about 50% of aggregate supply would be withdrawn and about 15% actually consumed.

This does not mean, however, that local water shortages will not be a problem. Everything depends on whether investment and skilled manpower can be made available in the right place at the right time. Everything depends on good management, the avoidance of political conflicts in the international development of trans-national water resources and in the selection of particular sites for water resource development within nations, and careful management of the impacts that these may have. The pace of development required will mean, according to the authors of *The Global 2000 Report*:[21]

Water shortages will be more widespread and more severe. The availability of water will become an even more binding constraint on the location of economic development. The notion of water as a free good available in essentially limitless quantities will have disappeared throughout much of the world.

As regards the nature and purpose of water resource developments, Beaumont has provided a very useful overview of the 5600 large dams constructed in the United States over the period 1825 to 1977.[22] Generally, the purposes of water resource development have changed since the turn of the century. Most early developments were for domestic water supply, sometimes for irrigation. The maximum number of dams built for agricultural purposes, however, were built between 1950 and 1970, after US domestic agricultural policy had created a climate of stability (Chapter 5). Hydro-electric projects were the most important purposes between 1910 and 1930. Flood control schemes grew rapidly in number from the 1930s to a peak in the 1960s.

Water resource developments are led by demand, so even the most abundant resources may engender problems of management depending on the pressures of demand put upon them. The water resources of Canada and the western United States provide a good illustration of this point.

7.3.2 The Myth of Super-abundance in Canada and the American West

It is difficult to imagine a country less likely to have difficulty with its water resources than Canada. Yet Foster and Sewell have recently argued that even Canada faces an emerging water crisis. In the 1980s water problems are a sleeping giant.[23] Of Canada's vast territory of 9.97 million square kilometres 7·6% is covered by lakes and is thought to have 9% of the total global river flow. Canada has only 1% of the world's population. The picture looks less satisfactory in detail, however; 60% of the river flow is in the direction of the frozen north while 10% of the population and the bulk of the country's industry is concentrated within 300 kms of its southern border. Canadians use about 450 litres per capita per day; these figures are among the highest in the world. An additional 2250 litres per capita per day is taken for agriculture, mining and manufacturing. In all, 120 billion litres per day is taken, of which 9% or 11 billion litres per day is consumed and not returned to its source.

Foster and Sewell identify four trends in modern Canadian society that will put increasing pressure on water resources. Firstly, energy developments of all types will require massive quantities of water for cooling purposes. A (small) 600,000 kilowatt CANDU nuclear reactor, it is claimed, has a water intake approximately equal to the combined water withdrawals of all municipalities in Western Canada. Secondly, mounting demands from the United States may be expected (see below). Thirdly, there is a growing demand for water based recreation in many areas of Canada. Fourthly, there is a growing recognition and appreciation of water based ecosystems (not least salmon spawning beds), making water resource developments very sensitive to public opinion. In the light of these trends and recent per capita growth in consumption greatly exceeding the rate of population growth, Foster and Sewell identify six river basins where scarcities have already appeared and where crisis is certain to appear in the years ahead. These are depicted in Figure 7.1a. This situation:[24]

will force a rethinking in the conventional approach to the satisfaction of water demands, which has been the provision of additional supplies.... Much more attention will be paid to the gains to be derived from such alternatives as waste reduction, recycling and the renovation of waste water. At the same time, proposals for large scale water diversion or for the construction of dams in environmentally sensitive areas are certain to meet with growing resistance.

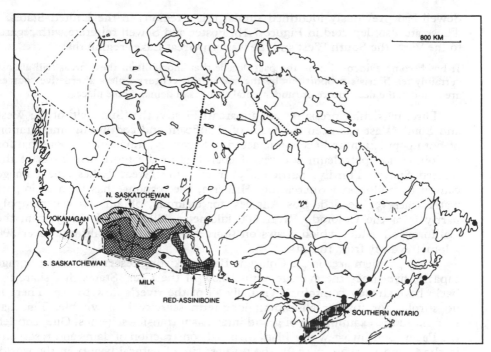

Figure 7.1a Potential Water Deficit Regions in Canada
Source: H.D. Foster & W.R.D. Sewell, *Water: The Emerging Crisis in Canada*, Loromer & Co., Toronto, 1981, p. 18

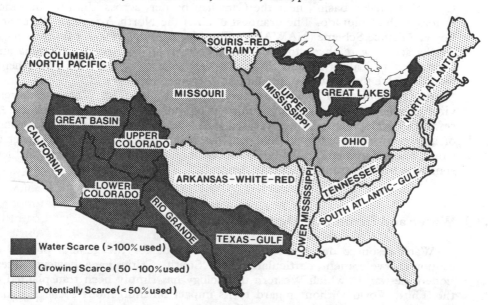

Figure 7.1b Emerging water Scarcities in the US
Source: W.R.D. Sewell, Water Across the American Continent, *Geographical Magazine*, June 1974, pp. 472–479

Sewell had previously identified similar crisis regions in the United States.[25] These are also depicted in Figure 7.1b. Foster and Sewell reiterate with regard to the West, the South West and the western Great Lakes region that:[26]

It has become evident during the past decade that shortfalls in these areas will almost certainly reach crisis proportions by the end of this century unless alternative sources are found in the near future or fundamental changes in demand take place.

Three particular pressures are apparent. Firstly, the 'Sun Belt' of the West and South West has been the focus of significant and continuing immigration of both population and economic activity. Secondly, much of the potential for exploiting non-petroleum sources of energy is in the more arid parts of the United States. Thirdly, particularly around the Great Lakes, the damage caused by pollution is increasing. Hitherto, the response has been to import water wherever needed. Los Angeles, for example, obtains its water supply partly from the Colorado River 600 kilometres distant and partly from the California aqueduct which draws on sources in Northern California over 800 kilometres away from the city.

A key problem area is the Colorado Basin. Existing reservoirs have a storage capacity five times the average annual flow of the river. States that share the basin have already committed virtually all of the river's flow to use. There is no surplus for further allocation; long-term scarcity is inevitable. This has stimulated the examination of grand inter-basin transfer schemes. One, entitled the Pacific Southwest Water Plan, involved construction of dams and reservoirs in the Grand Canyon, perhaps the greatest site of natural beauty in the world. Another involved the construction of an under-séa aqueduct to Los Angeles from north-west California. Yet another planned to divert the waters of the Columbia–Snake 'basin', near the Canadian border, across Utah to the head-waters of the Colorado. The grandest of all is the North American Water and Power Alliance Scheme (NAWAPA). The idea is to divert water from rivers in Alaska across watersheds to the Yukon, from there to British Columbia and from there to California and the south-west states (Figure 7.2). The scheme would involve the creation of the largest reservoirs in the world.[27]

A major objection to such schemes concerns planning. What are the environmental, economic and social impacts of water resource developments? As resource developments have increased in size and complexity, the importance of answering such questions in detail has been realized. Even the impact of single reservoir schemes may be considerable. Unfortunately, several hard lessons have been learnt through experience.

7.3.3 Water and Economic Development

Water resource development has implications for the general process of economic development, particularly in the 'South'. Critics have, however, questioned the way in which Western technology has simply been transplanted to the Third World without regard to its impact on indigenous social systems. Howe has argued that the preconditions for large scale water resource development are that water is a bottleneck to growth, that capital is available, that managers capable of running the technology properly are available and that the technology can be accommodated by the social structure of the relevant

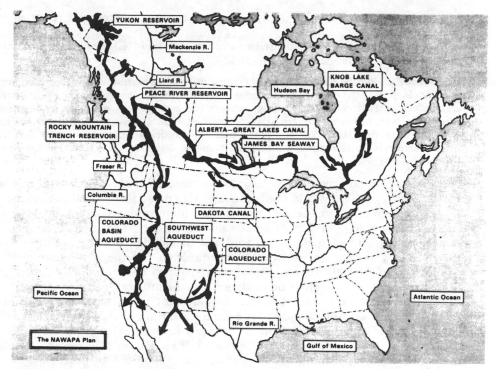

Figure 7.2 The North American Water and Power Alliance
Source: W.R.D. Sewell, Water Across the American Continent, *Geographical Magazine*, June 1974, pp. 472–479

region.[28] But all too often, he claims, these preconditions have not existed and complex, high-technology schemes of water resource development have appeared as major disruptive intrusions into the orderly life of the host region.

The Volta River project provides a good example of the difficulties encountered in technological transplant. It also shows the complex weave of interests involved in major water resource developments in the 'South'. The originators of the idea of building a dam across the Volta to provide power for processing bauxite into aluminium were West Africa Aluminium Ltd, which included major multinational companies such as Alcan, British Aluminium and Unilever amongst its shareholders, although the Kaiser Corporation obtained a 90% stake later.

Hart has traced the development of the project from the first serious feasibility studies undertaken in the early 1950s.[29] By this time the Gold Coast colony had become the newly independent state of Ghana and the new administration was expressing interest in the wider implications of such a scheme – power for economic development generally, irrigation and improved communications through navigation.

Ghana's aims were clearly long term. The short-term benefits were limited, even negative. The construction of the dam would employ a peak number of 5000, and this labour force would require services to the extent of £7 million pounds worth of investment in infrastructure. Meanwhile 62,500 people living in the area to be flooded by the lake were to be compensated and resettled at a cost of only £4 million.[30]

Critics, such as the West African economist David Carney, were not impressed with the scheme. He said in 1952:[31]

The scheme cannot be expected to make any substantial contribution to the secondary industrialisation of the country in the sense of a shift of resources away from agricultural and mining activity to manufacturing industry. In essence it is just another of these enterprises which have characterised and continue to characterise the economy of West Africa as a raw materials economy. It is a plan for winning aluminium, in most part by private enterprise, and exporting it to other countries which will use it in the manufacture of useful articles.

Most of the capital expended on the project returned to the donor countries or their close allies. The World Bank and US AID made this a condition of their grant. The contribution of the export of aluminium to the economy is substantial, amounting to 5 or 6% of total value of export trade (the others being largely cocoa, timber, manganese, gold and diamonds), but the usefulness of this is offset by the need to import chemicals to run the aluminium plant; production of 150,000 tonnes per annum requires about 100,000 tonnes of imported chemicals. There is no evidence that the project has had a substantial multiplier effect (developing other employment opportunities), probably because such a large proportion of the electrical output is used by the smelter[32] (67%). Rather than adding value to Ghana's own resources, the aluminium processed at the Tempa plant is imported from Kaiser's Jamaican bauxite mines. Meanwhile, Ghana's bauxite production is exported for processing elsewhere. Ghana's requirements for aluminium sheet are met by imports.[33]

It is true that the Volta Dam is the country's principal source of electricity. Indeed, some is exported to neighbouring countries. But it is equally true that the original plan to base a major irrigation scheme for the Accra Plains on waters from Lake Volta is now in abeyance, being considered too large and too costly for Ghana's internal economic climate.[34]

It seems that this scheme of water resource development has not achieved its main objective of promoting major advances in economic development. Meanwhile, serious environmental and social consequences have occurred. Hart claims that the situation whereby major schemes have utilized the water resources of Third World countries to someone else's benefit are not unusual:[35]

It is often said about hydro electric projects such as the Volta River Project that a few people may have to suffer for the good of the majority. But one has also to say that the already underprivileged have suffered for the sake of the privileged. That this is not a case of 'development' is clear.

7.3.4   The Environmental Effects of Large Dams

The side effects of the Volta Dam on the displaced population may be examined under four headings:[36] the failure of the resettlement scheme; the failure to improve agricultural production; impact on fisheries; and effects on public health.

The Akosombo dam created a lake of 8,500 km². It affected more than 1% of Ghana's population, some 80,000 people living in 739 villages, although only about 6% of the land covered by the lake was suitable for agriculture or habitation. 67,500 people were placed in fifty-two specially constructed resettlement villages. The remainder drifted to the towns or made their own arrangements elsewhere. The authorities began to plan the scheme only two years before the lake was due to start filling. Problems with the design and style of dwellings, shortage of materials, and serious difficulties encountered in trying to farm the land around the new settlements, meant that something like 40,000 of the original settlers moved away within a period of four years.

The new settlements were to have harvested 41,600 hectares of agricultural land. Their way of life was to have changed from one of traditional peasant subsistence to one of commercial production on small-scale plots of about 5 hectares. These would allow the adoption of modern farming methods using machinery owned and worked cooperatively. By 1967 it was obvious that the scheme had failed. Only 3060 hectares had been cleared and prepared for farming. By 1972 this had increased to 6680 hectares, but holdings averaged less than 1 hectare in size – insufficient land for subsistence. Food aid from the UN/FAO World Food Programme, largely donated by the United States, was needed.

The development of a fishing industry on the lake, however, *was* successful. Production from the lake reached a peak of 60,000 tonnes in 1969 before settling down to the more ecologically stable level of 38,000 tonnes. In 1973, 12,000 fishermen supporting a further 48,000 or so people made their living from this new resource. But many of the fishermen who moved from the lower Volta to the lake were infected with schistomiasis. Conditions on the lake shore for the snails that transmit the disease were near ideal. The lake's use for water supply and waste disposal meant that infection rates rose steeply. In some lakeside villages a 100% infection rate was recorded. Similarly, the incidence of onchocerciasis, a disease involving parasite worms lodging in skin tissue leading to eventual blindness, has dramatically increased.

Such problems are not uncommon in schemes like the Volta. In a report to the United Nations Water Conference, Hafez[37] described the impact made by the Aswan High Dam and Lake Nasser on the River Nile: siltation, alteration of local weather patterns and shoreline ecology, deteriorating water quality in the lake and the river, and harmful social, public health and agricultural effects. Elsewhere irrigation channels have extended the habitat of bilharzia transmitting snails. Malaria is also a potential danger: the spraying of DDT around both the Volta and Kariba schemes has serious implications.[38]

There are of course substantial benefits. In the case of the Aswan dam the list is quite formidable: flood control, water for industrial and agricultural expansion; the doubling of power supplies; and a vast new fishery. Navigation has been improved and the tourist potential of the area extended. But the negative impact must not be forgotten.

7.4 Problems and Policies

With such a broad range of patterns of supply, expressing so many different aims, it is hardly surprising that the problems of water resource development are legion. What are the principal strategies of management in each of the major fields of water development?

7.4.1 Domestic Water Services and Irrigation

It has already been established that the cost of extending services is the major problem in this sphere of water resource development. What is the appropriate level of technology that should be applied? Is it feasible to try to replicate practice in the urban industrial 'North' when seeking to extend water services in the 'South'?

Because of the health implications of a good water supply the United Nations Childrens Fund (UNICEF) plays a leading role in the extension of rural water supplies, the aim being to establish coordinated basic services at the village level in the interrelated fields of food and nutrition, clean water, health, family planning and basic education as well as supporting services for mothers.[39]

Around $1·5 million was spent in 1975 assisting water supply and sanitation projects. The small-scale rural water supply installations on which UNICEF concentrates, are, to a great extent, dependent on ground water resources, normally by means of dug and drilled wells. In the case of dug wells, demonstration wells are funded. In the case of drilled wells a whole network may be provided. In India, for example, 30,000 wells, with hand pumps, were drilled in hard rock areas between 1972 and 1980. From the sanitary point of view deep drilled wells are preferable. A major problem in the spread of safe drilled wells has been the inadequate availability of hand pumps sufficiently robust to withstand rough handling for extended periods by villagers lacking in the knowledge and means to maintain and repair them properly. In certain regions, such as the Himalayas or parts of the Rift valleys of Africa, springs can be capped to ensure a constant flow of safe water in near maintenance-free conditions.

To keep pace with population growth, technologies are required that make the maximum use of local resources and require only intermediate or low capital investment. According to the Intermediate Technology Group Ltd (ITG), the emphasis in water supply should be on low-cost systems available to everyone, using self-help and voluntary labour wherever possible to reduce the investment required; and since the majority of the world's people live in rural communities, not towns, it is suggested that this should be a technology capable of small-scale application, suitable for village use and local control.[40]

ITG has expressed concern over the extent to which prevailing designs of water supply equipment are more suited to the needs of water supply in Europe than to villages in the tropics. Most industrial countries are in temperate lands, a fact that has profound implications for water engineering in hot climates as microbiological and chemical processes operate differently and different organisms are present. In developing countries, evaporation is a major source of water loss, so storage may best take place in bodies of sand, access to the water being gained by wells as for natural ground water. There exist a wide variety of alternatives to the traditional Western concrete or stone impoundment; these assist in water treatment and cut down evaporation losses. Many of them are suitable for construction with local teams of labour. Another important aspect of water supply for Third World areas is whether a scheme is socially appropriate. It is not necessary to install a fully-fledged system of distribution with all the concomitant costs. Large-scale schemes on the European or North American model require tanks, pumps and piping which probably have to be imported, making demands on foreign exchange. Small-scale localized systems of supply can make use of local materials and local labour. Overall, ITG concluded that the most appropriate schemes of supply have an upper limit of service to 3000 people whilst 1000 would be quite satisfactory.

There is considerable evidence that smaller-scale technology may be more appropriate to water development projects in the Third World, particularly in the construction of irrigation schemes. Such techniques offer savings with respect to scarce capital; and they utilize plenty of underemployed labour.[41]

Of necessity, the development programmes of many developing countries involve consultants and contractors from the industrialized countries of the 'North' who are familiar with, and biased towards, equipment and capital-intensive methods. Alternative technologies are rarely considered. Aid is often tied to the allocation of contracts to large companies operating from the donor countries and supports the domestic economy as much as helping development in recipient countries. The multilateral organs of aid, such as the World Bank, often support and reinforce this trend. For example, they often insist that large contracts are put out to international tender and generally offer to finance the foreign exchange costs that result.

7.4.2 Controlling Pollution and Allocating Resources Between Conflicting Uses

A second key issue concerning water resources the world over is that of pollution. Bearing in mind the limited extent to which water is actually consumed in use, the return of contaminated water is a major, and in developing countries, a growing, barrier to the efficient allocation of existing water resources. The historical development of water use has normally been such that existing levels of pollution follow from a web of established industrial and municipal interests. Political intervention is necessary to overrule vested interest. A consistent theme of attempts to resolve problems of pollution is the conflict of interest between industrialists and the state authority seeking the improvement; the former are anxious to avoid pressure on profits from a withdrawal of the right to use water resources as a free resource for waste disposal (and they influence local and central governments anxious to conserve local prosperity). This had led many to define water pollution as an inevitable evil of the capitalist system, although Marx himself had little to say on water pollution confining himself to remarks on the failure of the capitalist system to utilize the waste products of industry, agriculture and human consumption.[42]

Although some Marxists note that capitalism creates pollution and hence argue that to solve the problem of pollution one must remove capitalism, there is mounting evidence that problems of water pollution are and have been equally serious in so-called Marxist states such as the Soviet Union and the countries of Eastern Europe. For example, Fullenbach reports that the most heavily polluted rivers of Czechoslovakia are in Bohemia, notably the Elbe, the Moldan, the Eger, the Belina and the Berounka, around which the most important industries are concentrated.[43] The chemical industry, local authorities and the food processing industry are the major contributors to river pollution, just as in the West. In the German Democratic Republic only 17% of the main waterways are economically viable sources of drinking water supply.[44] Similarly:[45]

Water pollution is environmental problem number one in Poland. In terms of water stocks per head of population, Poland is only in twenty-fourth place in Europe, 'but we often deal with this raw material as if we were in first place!' For a long time water was treated as if it were a free good, and thus available at no cost – i.e. in the terms of classical economics. More recently it has become a commodity and a very expensive one at that.

It seems that in both capitalist and socialist systems there is a positive correlation between the level of industrialization, population density and consumption, on the one hand, and environmental damage on the other. Since the technology used in both cases is more or less identical, the ecological pressures on both sides are similar. If neither economic (profit) nor technological factors explain pollution there remain only philosophical and political factors. At the heart of many water problems lies the notion that water is free, leading to behaviour irresponsible in the long term. The tendency for users to 'do their own thing' can be overcome by comprehensive planning. The major barriers to comprehensive planning, however, are political, as it inevitably defines winners and losers.

In capitalist countries profits are threatened by measures of control often opposed by both owners and employees. In socialist states 'the primacy of production' means that in the central plan the continued and expanded production of goods takes priority over all other claims. In both economic systems, material considerations (ultimately consumer goods) prevail over aesthetic considerations (such as a respect for natural living systems), a situation that reflects the universal attitude of mankind until the idea of 'limits' emerged recently. (Chapter 2).

7.4.3 International Boundary Problems

A further global issue concerns the fact that many of the major rivers in the world are international. As pressures of population, economic development and pollution have mounted, arrangements for coordinating policies and settling disputes across international boundaries have become increasingly important for the solution of water resource problems. Agreements have been reached between two or more countries as and when problems over water use have arisen. Nevertheless no less than twenty-five international disputes could be identified in Europe in 1969.[46]

At 6400 km the boundary between Canada and the United States is an obvious area of pressure. A Boundary Water Treaty was signed as early as 1909. The treaty established an International Joint Commission (IJC), with six commissioners, three from each country, and a small expert staff. The job of the commission is to investigate matters in dispute and make recommendations, which are rarely rejected by either government. Among the achievements of the commission is the St Lawrence Seaway. Completed in 1959, seven locks allow the passage of ships 225 metres long and 20 metres wide up a gradient of 70 metres over 300 km from Montreal to Lake Ontario. A 1·8 million kilowatt capacity of hydro-electrical power installations operates in close association with navigation. This project would not have been possible without an orderly mechanism for joint investigation and action.

The complexity of achieving cooperative water resource development, even among friends, may be illustrated by the Columbia River Basin scheme.[47] The basin is over a quarter of a million square miles in extent. The agreed boundary – following territorial conflict between the United States and the British in North America in the 1860s – follows the 49th parallel. This cuts right through the complex headwaters of the main river, not only leaving 39,500 square miles of the basin in Canada but also creating a situation whereby two major tributaries flow through American territory before joining the main river in Canada. This vast river basin had the greatest hydro-electric power potential in North America. In the 1930s a series of projects were developed in the lower (American) part of the basin, including the Grand Coulee Dam. By 1959 six major projects were using 780 of the 1280 ft of head (gradient of fall of the river, the kinetic energy from which gave the power) on the US side.

In Canada, the distance from the main market of Vancouver, at over 400 miles, limited the potential for development. But several small, 'run of the river' developments satisfied the needs of local mining and timber communities. The use of the river could be improved by storing the snow melt waters for release through the turbines at times of low natural flow but high demand for power. Uncontrolled melt flows represented a considerable flood hazard. Storage could also relieve constraints on downstream land use. In short, upstream storage could greatly benefit the United States in increased power output and flood control. But studies showed that the greatest scope for a suitable scale of storage lay in constructing dams and large reservoirs in the Canadian land-waters or at sites where the storage and reservoir would extend back upstream across the border. Such developments would create water supplies for industrial and domestic purposes and recreational use in Canada but would equally disrupt Canadian land use.

Under the auspices of the IJC studies of various options for the further development of the basin and their implications, followed by negotiations as to how the costs and benefits might be distributed between Canadian and American interests, began in 1944. Each of these had its own environmental and social impact on Canadian land use and benefits in power and flood control in the United States. The investigation and negotiation procedures were further considerably complicated by two factors. First, it was recognized that the sequence of development would make a considerable difference to the value of the benefits of each project and hence to the compensation negotiated for Canada.[48] A second complicating factor lay in the desire of authorities in British Columbia to try to ensure that the pattern of water resources development was in line with the long-term economic and social interests of the province. Argument raged as to whether Canadian potential should be ceded to United States use. Suggestions were made that a wider agreement on hydro-electric power might be more advantageous, encouraging developments further north on the Peace River. A difference of view on the desirability of the Columbia schemes emerged from time to time between Canadian federal interests and the province of British Columbia.

In this context it is hardly surprising that investigations and negotiations lasted for nearly twenty years. The United States–Canada Columbia River Treaty was finally signed in 1961 setting out the operating pattern for the

Arrow Lakes, Micra Creek and Duncan Lake projects in Canada and covering the trans-boundary Libby project. The monetary value of half the downstream flood benefits was to pass to Canada, as was half the additional power. Further wrangling continued. The treaty was not ratified until 1964, at which time the Canadians agreed to accept a cash payment instead of the power.

The importance of this example is threefold. Firstly, even when reduced to its bare bones, the extent to which the full development of a major river basin involves a complex array of different projects and a range of different costs and benefits should be noted. Secondly, even with a well-established procedure, the IJC, note how long it took to achieve an agreed format for action. Thirdly, the reader is invited to consider whether the realization of the full water resource potential of the basin would have been possible if there had been more than two countries involved, or if their culture and political ideologies had not been as close as those of Canada and the United States.

The United States, for all its determination to manage its own water resources to its own advantage, seems to be a good neighbour, relatively speaking. On the other side of the country, over two-thirds of the United States–Mexico border is a river frontier. An international boundary commission was established in 1889 to consider the question of sovereignty over lands affected by the tendency of the Rio Grande and Colorado rivers to shift course. In 1944 the United States–Mexico Rio Grande, Colorado and Tijuana Treaty on water resources allocation between the two countries ended nearly fifty years of negotiations. Not only was Mexico anxious about the share of Colorado waters reaching it, but there were problems of quality because of the intensive use of the waters. In 1962 the remit of the International Commission was extended to carry out studies and propose solutions for problems caused in Mexico by the increased salinity of the Colorado River due to drainage of farmlands in the United States.[49]

The United States is unusual in tackling problems of international water use seriously. Bangladesh is a country on the delta lands of two great international rivers, the Ganges and the Brahmaputra. Monsoon season flooding (June–October) is severe; it can be very damaging. At other times of the year water may be scarce. Clearly, upstream storage could be the solution. But lack of appropriate institutional arrangements as well as of capital, plus the usual difficulty of choosing the exact combination of the most appropriate development projects, combine to prevent any real progress.

Deeply conscious of the fundamental importance of water for economic and social development, the United Nations Water Conference requested the Economic and Social Council of the UN to tackle the problem of achieving greater international cooperation in water resource development and urged the Secretary-General to prepare a study of the most effective and flexible mechanisms to increase the flow of financial resources for such cooperative development.[50]

7.5 The Need for Management

7.5.1 Comprehensive Administration

From this chapter it should be clear that the variety of sources of water, the variety of uses to which it may be put and the widespread implications of water use and development, demand a high degree of management – especially when pressures of population, economic and social development are taken into account. Several authors have pointed out[51] that as pressures on its use build up, responsibility for the functions of water management are progressively transferred from private hands to government agencies, local, regional, national or even international. The basic trend has been to 'internalize the externalities': that is to say, to bring all decisons under the control of a single authority. It is easier to secure new supplies of water for consumption if waste disposal and pollution are also under the control of the same agency. The tendency for all functions of water management to be allocated to a single agency has been reinforced by the growing scale of water resource developments and the extent to which several aims are being served simultaneously, for example power supply and flood control in the Columbia basin, and irrigation, water supply and power supply in the Colorado basin.

Following White, Sewell has ascribed these trends to the adoption of five major concepts of water management: (1) the adoption of a broader perspective on the role of water management in human affairs; (2) a recognition of the need to expand the range of options considered in planning and policy making; (3) the recognition of water as an economic good; (4) the provision of more opportunities for public participation in the politics of water resource development; and (5) the acceptance of environmental protection as a major goal of public policy.[52] These may be dealt with by the creation of appropriate administrative agencies, an institutional structure that will improve efficiency, specifically take into account the external or spill-over effects of water use, and integrate water development into overall economic and social planning. In Chapter 14 the evolution of multi-purpose regional water authorities in England and Wales is considered. Such agencies allow a broader range of policy options to be considered. For example, there are several ways to tackle the despoilation of water by pollution. First, one might establish regulations that define the maximum strength of effluent that may be discharged from any source, industrial or domestic. Because the ability of water to cope with effluent varies according to the volume of clean water available at the point of reception (and this varies according to location in the basin and the time of year), this system might lead to too strict a requirement for pre-treatment in places where plenty of dilution is available and too lax a requirement where dilution is limited. If the controlling agency has powers extending over the whole basin, however, the system of regulations may be a different one in which the degree of pre-treatment required is tailored to conditions at the receiving point which will include the effects of non-point sources of pollution such as agricultural run-off. If the controlling agency has powers over the extraction of water from the basin it may restrict the practice in the interest of maintaining lower treatment costs in an effort to stem pollution downstream; alternatively, it may arrange for extra dilution water to be transferred from storage or from another basin to compensate for the loss of dilution water.

These few examples serve to illustrate the relationship between the powers of the agency as defined and the resulting range of policies available to the agency to tackle a single problem. There are many other approaches to the pollution problem, and, of course, many other problems of water management. Not least amongst these, at least in Europe and North America, are the environmental and social effects of water development. There should be provision for the local politics of water resource development to be conducted in an appropriate forum, such as a public hearing, public inquiry or public participation in planning. But why wait until opposition has arisen? Increasingly, water managers find it prudent to build into their planning and assessment procedures programmes of public participation and environmental impact assessment. These issues are further discussed in Chapter 14.

7.5.2 Water as an Economic Good

Generally, water has been regarded as 'free', available to anybody prepared to invest in its use. This position has become increasingly untenable. Administrative regulation of increasing scope and sophistication is one response. Another, favoured by economists, is to treat water as a commodity, albeit one that occurs naturally in the same way as forests, fisheries and minerals. This implies charging for the use of water according to the demand for its sources rather than the cost of providing the service. Such a change in approach has significant implications. The point may be illustrated by the problem of pollution control. Several countries have introduced policies whereby a charge is made according to the volume and strength of effluents discharged, the revenue being used to subsidize treatment plants or simply added to general tax income. The effect of such a charge is to encourage the installation of pre-treatment. Also, perhaps more importantly, it encourages the development of new production processes producing less waste or the recycling of waste products. This is necessary if the costs to consumers are not to increase. If extra costs are incurred, they pass to the general public, who, after all, are the ultimate beneficiaries of pollution free rivers. A problem arises, however, when an adjacent region or country engages in the same production but without the effluent charge, or with charges set at a lower level. Production may be switched to the area of reduced costs, causing serious economic and social distress. Hence there are strong political pressures operating to keep such a policy off the agenda or at least to restrict charges to a trivial level. Alternatively, varying levels of pollution charge may be seen as unfair competition. Hence the tendency for such schemes to be operated by federal governments and the interest of the supra-national European Economic Community in seeking a common policy amongst its members.

Similarly with regard to irrigation, it may be argued that if charges are set at a high enough level to encourage the maximum productive use of the water provided, either the cost of the product will be too high for the market to bear or the only people able to meet the cost will be the large-scale, agricultural entrepreneurs. This undermines hopes of widespread economic and social benefit reaching the region. The 'economic' approach is likely to be resisted or confined to a trivially tokenistic form, so that its original purpose of providing real incentives towards improved efficiency is lost.

Nevertheless, there is evidence from some countries that consumers do respond to water price changes in a positive and useful way, especially in the domestic sector of the affluent countries. Sewell says that except for that volume of consumption covering basic needs (drinking, cooking and personal hygiene) water demand is fairly elastic: that is, a price increase will result in a more than proportionate reduction in consumption. This is especially so in large-scale uses such as watering lawns or filling swimming pools; in some municipalities in the American western states these account for a considerable proportion of total capacity of the water supply system.[53]

Unfortunately, price schedules do not reflect the fact that these are luxury water uses and are highly elastic. Instead, charges are similar to those imposed on basic uses or, in some instances, even lower. The price per unit may actually go down as more water is consumed. This anomaly is compounded where there is no recognition that luxury uses are generally summer uses: that is, no penalty is levied to the peak demand in summer.

One solution to pressure on water resources in the western states, then, would be to introduce a more appropriate pricing system, so that peak demands were reduced. But the extent to which such a solution would be politically feasible is questionable.

7.6 The Future of Water Resources

Notwithstanding the array of pressures and problems associated with water resources, the future availability of water seems generally assured. The United Nations Water Conference identified four major problems:[54]

1. The extent to which safe water supplies for human consumption were not available to the world's rural poor.
2. The extent to which extended and improved schemes of irrigation could make a contribution to problems of food production, especially in poorer countries.
3. The extent to which a water pollution problem exists now, and the extent to which it might expand in line with economic growth in developing countries.
4. The need for better water management, particularly where resources are shared internationally.

All these problems are capable of solution. But in many countries, the key problems are the prevailing socio-economic organization and the bottlenecks of capital and manpower. Water resource problems are problems of management.

Summary of Part One

In the 1960s and 1970s environmentalists and neo-Malthusians highlighted anew the resource problem facing mankind. In the first half of the 1970s global recognition of resource issues brought together international delegates to conferences on the subject of the environment, world population and world food, heralding a new awareness of the threat of environmental degradation, over-population and food insecurity.

UNCTAD *IV* initiated the demand for a New International Economic Order, with the poorer nations seeking a new approach to the control, pricing and trading of commodities. The 'North–South' dialogue took on new meaning, especially in the wake of OPEC's success in raising oil prices. By 1983, this new promise had faded. With the 1973/74 energy crisis came world recession. Demand for commodities stagnated. 'Real' prices reached all time lows. Development plans for 'Southern' nations were jeopardized; their debts mounted, precipitating an international banking crisis. Among the debtors were even several oil producers.

Most of the world's debtors are newly industrialized countries which have followed a capitalist development model, utilizing the expertise (both techno-logical and financial) of the West for export-led growth. The whole resource issue is intimately connected with corporate imperialism. The non-participants are those who have alienated multinationals and by implication their host governments. The losers who do not participate are the world's poor who do not enjoy the spin-off new 'development' which favours the rich urban élites.

In each of the resources under discussion, their use and development is connected with societal values and technological progress. For the world's masses living in poverty, basic resources such as food, water, firewood and biomass are needed for daily survival. Secondary, value-added resources – processed food, pulp/paper, manufactured commodities and nuclear energy – are the prerogatives of the rich.

The resource needs of the world's people *can* be met from the earth's resources. With the possible exception of forestry resources in parts of the Tropics, no significant crisis of a *physical* nature exists. People need not suffer hunger, poor sanitation, inadequate drinking water and insufficient shelter or heat. The solutions to all these fundamental resource problems are *institutional* in nature. They demand political will and financial support. Nothing illustrates this more dramatically than the case of food. The European Community pro-duces a surplus of food. In the poorest countries of the world, agriculture is either starved of funds or land is given over to growing cash crops for export rather than food for home consumption.

Meanwhile the gap between the 'haves' and the 'have-nots' widens. The 'North–South' dialogue flounders. Conservative and reactionary politics begin to dominate the international scene. The 'Northern' nations, having survived the oil shock of the 1970s by their ability to pay high prices, continue to dictate the pace of world resource development. The oil crisis of 1973/74 was the key resource issue. It challenged the balance of power in resource politics. Since then, the West's main priority has been to secure supplies through stockpiling, increasing domestic production and by harvesting the resources of the 'no man's land' on the ocean floor.

To some extent, these events have reduced the power of the environment movement. The quest for cleaner air and water, for protection of the wilderness and other such issues began to be reviewed in the 1980s in a climate of high unemployment and low economic growth. Environmental pressure groups are fighting a rearguard action to maintain what they achieved a decade before. Is environmentalism a luxury which can be afforded only in more prosperous times? Clearly, most OECD nations are more preoccupied with national security, unemployment and rising public expenditure than environmental issues. In the 'Southern' nations, institutional frameworks are poorly developed and environmental management is given low priority in resource planning especially when confronted with corporate imperialism, as the deforestation of Amazonia and parts of South-East Asia attest.

PART TWO:
RESOURCE MANAGEMENT

8   Resource Management

8.1 Introduction

Resource managers have a difficult job resolving conflicts of view and varying demands on resources. Resource management requires the skill and expertise of many disciplines. Above all, it is a political activity in that management involves the over-ruling of the interests of some in favour of those of others. In this chapter, the major concepts of management and decision making that feature in the succeeding chapters are introduced.

8.2.1 Ideas of Management

The pattern of agencies, laws and policies that pertain to particular resource or environmental issues is termed the institutional structure. The institutional structure is the vehicle through which action can be taken. It consists of agencies, public and private, actors and laws. Actors need to be marshalled within an agency if anything is to be done on a permanent and professional basis. Agencies need legal authority to act. They need legal authority to spend taxes or shareholders' money. And the law defines what courses of action they may take. Agencies are not impersonal, robotic organizations. They are made up of people of different backgrounds in various positions of responsibility and authority. These actors administer, make and enforce policies within the law.

The web of laws, officials and agencies involved in specific problems of resource management form a system of interrelated actions and interests. In the 1960s this 'system' was often blamed for the ills of society, especially by the young. It followed that if these ills were to be tackled, the 'system' should itself be the object of criticism and study as part of the search for the solution to environmental problems. The extent to which institutional structures support modern societies has been steadily growing this century. Governments have taken responsibility for all manner of aspects of social life in response to public demand and political desires. Not least in importance have been, in varying degrees, commitment to welfare, education and health and a concern with the standard of living and the level of employment. To some extent the management of the great economies during World War II proved that government intervention could work to good effect. In the post-war era an unparalleled rise in standards of living and the quality of life for the majority of people, especially in the West, was accompanied by a steady increase in intervention on behalf of the national interest and the growth of bureaucracies of all sorts.[1] In the private sector too, companies expanded, both horizontally (into a variety of products and markets rather than depending on the vagaries of just one or two) and vertically (into the whole span of production, distribution, transport and marketing, thus gaining greater control of inputs and cash flow). Over the post-war period the large corporation increasingly flourished as did the multi-national company and the transnational conglomerate.[2] Both business and government have become characterized by large and complex organizational structures, adding to the impetus to study 'the system'.

The major problem with any organization is that as well as being an agency to effect some task (such as sell oil or manage national parks) it also provides the workplace of its staff. There they act out a major part of their lives at work. This means that all organizations are characterized by jealousies, friendships, competitive relationships and antipathies that interfere with its rationality and efficiency. There are great difficulties in establishing efficient and effective lines of communication so that everybody knows what they are supposed to be doing and everybody is aware of every piece of information that might help them in the performance of their allotted task. There is scope for a great deal of mis-understanding and error by default or omission as messages flow around a complex organization. There is also the 'Peter Principle':[3] that there is a tendency for people to be promoted in a hierarchy beyond their capabilities (because it is only after promotion that it becomes clear when that level of work is beyond them). The human complexity of organizations means that many people spend as much time maintaining or trying to improve their position within the organization as they do in helping to achieve its goals. The 'system' is human to a greater or lesser degree, and the abilities and attitudes of the people who live their lives within it are a focus of legitimate interest.[4]

8.2.2 Studies of Attitudes and Perceptions

Because agencies are also communities, and because officials and managers as well as analysts have often found it difficult to identify exactly who originated what and who decided what in the complex of transactions that occurs within organizations, it has not been possible to develop a science of how organizations behave, although a considerable body of empirical literature exists.[5] There have been several useful attempts to define concepts for use in organizational design and in the improvement of their performance;[6] with specific regard to resources White,[7] Craine,[8] Okun[9] and Mitchell[10] have all considered the organization of water management. A particularly interesting vein of enquiry within resource management concerns the attitudes of groups of professionals. Each resource agency tends to be dominated by a certain type of professional, and several analysts have investigated the consequences of this.[11] Sewell, for example, studied the attitudes of public health officials and engineers in British Columbia and found that engineers tended to favour solutions to problems of the environment which involve building things whilst public health officials favour the application of regulatory measures.[12] Kaufman found that the US Forest Service was remarkably successful in engendering a common perception of forestry problems[13]. The net effect or importance of this phenomenon lies in what White[14] has called the range of choice of potential solutions considered by resource managers.

White distinguished between three kinds of potential strategy—the theoretical, the practical and the actual – and noted the extent to which the actual was smaller than the practical or the theoretical. The latter would include every possibility. It is rare – perhaps unreasonable – to expect any individual or group to be all knowing. But the number of alternatives which are considered may always be thought of as smaller than those which are theoretically possible. The constraints of any particular situation further reduce the possible courses of action to be considered. Finally, this number is further reduced by institutional constraints such as the professional background and training of the actors involved: faced with the problem of water pollution, the engineer will favour the construction of treatment plants, the economist the introduction of tax incentives to encourage the pretreatment of effluents, whilst the planner might well suggest the zoning of activities creating pollution. Thus, it is rare for more than two or three alternative courses of action to be considered. This insight is useful in accounting for the behaviour of actors in the resource–management system. It helps to explain why this or that decision is made. But the complexity of policy making is such that no greater precision can be obtained; scientific laws to explain decision making are out of the question.

Once a resource agency has defined a problem, the next stage is to evaluate each solution, perhaps with respect to agreed goals or political acceptability or more rational criteria such as cost effectiveness, safety and feasibility (Figure 8.1). Resource problems often involve large areas of uncertainty. Resource strategies often involve a degree of risk and so there is often scope for a great deal of debate as to what tests are fairly applicable, how limited data should be interpreted and how environmental futures can be reasonably predicted. Evaluation of alternatives is a major task of resource management; it is considered at length in the following chapter. When made public, evaluation of alternatives is often highly controversial. This makes the stage of evaluation perhaps the most difficult of all. It is at this point that the conflicting perceptions and goals of developers and protesters, politicians and planners are revealed and have to

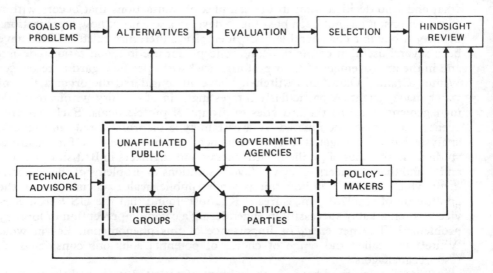

Figure 8.1 A Simple Model of Environmental Policy Making
        Source: J.T. Coppock and W.R.D. Sewell (eds), *Public Participation in Planning*, John Wiley, 1977, p. 9

be reconciled. If no agreement can be reached, the process becomes a political one – that is, the application of power is required. He who can win, does. Some commentators have seen the whole policy-making process as less rational than behavioural, and it is to the major models of policy making that attention is now turned.

8.2.4 Models of Policy Making

Classically, there are two views as to how policy is made in democracies. Each is worth considering in outline. There is the rationalist or normative view of policy making, and there is the behavioural view, a principal variant of which is known as disjointed incrementalism. The rationalist view, already outlined in the previous section, holds that goals are first defined, alternative strategies are then derived, then evaluated in terms of the extent to which they realize the goals, and finally chosen for their effectiveness. Braybrooke and Lindblom have pointed out, however, that in the real world things are not nearly so simple.[16]

It is, in fact, very rare for goals to be either clearly articulated or agreed upon; perhaps the only exception is that of a multinational corporation where the maximization of profit may take precedence over all other considerations in shaping the company's actions. Most situations, however, involve a high degree of uncertainty which makes the evaluation of different courses of action difficult not only to undertake but also to agree upon. In few situations are the money, time and expertise available to actually practise the rational mode of decision making. Instead, Lindblom has suggested, decision makers see problems in terms of something wrong with the status quo; further, that they then see potential solutions in terms of incremental adjustments or marginal changes to the status quo. The status quo is the one thing that an organization has a lot of information about. Therefore, by concentrating on small-scale changes and limited amendments to present practice, the best use of present knowledge can be made and the time and money spent on looking for solutions kept within reasonable bounds. The problem of evaluation is also eased: alternatives can be compared in terms of how they improve on the present situation rather than how they compared to any absolute set of values. This is the behavioural view of policy making. Incrementalists believe that changes in policy occur through a series of small steps, each of which are minor adjustments to the status quo and each of which makes as much use of existing resources as possible. This explains the noticeable tendency towards institutional inertia, with policies usually heralding only limited changes whilst the major part of existing institutional structures remain stable with a relative absence of major, dramatic changes in policy. Disjoints occur when a series of steps changes into a new direction, perhaps because new personnel bring new perceptions of the most appropriate marginal adjustments to be made to existing activities or when external events, such as the outbreak of war or the emergence of a powerful environmental movement, demand that more radical changes of direction occur. The behavioural view explains why it is so difficult to achieve radical changes in the 'system' of decision making and why in tracing the history of policies or organizations one very often finds a series of steps in their evolution rather than isolated and dramatic changes of policy or instances of innovation.

Nevertheless, such things do occur. The incremental view of decision making provides no mechanism to explain the milestone events of radical re-thinking that happen from time to time, not least in the late 1960s and early 1970s with respect to environmental issues. The rationalist view of decision making, on the other hand, does not seem to accord with the facts either. A solution to the dilemma has been proposed by Etzioni who speaks of the normal process of policy making as including forms of 'mixed scanning'.[17] This view holds that normal policy matters are dealt with incrementally, but at the same time, and for a few top priority issues, a wider, more rational scanning of problems and possible solutions is taking place. When environmental issues of pollution came to the forefront of public attention in the early 1970s it was recognized that major changes were required, not just a recourse to the usual incremental adjustments; hence a process of rational search produced the major pieces of new legislation that characterized policy in the United States and to a lesser extent also in the United Kingdom.

Policy making, then, is not the rational activity that it might first appear to be. The situation becomes further complicated when the decisions of organizations move into the public domain.

8.3.1 The Role of Political Culture in Resource Management

Having made their policy, incrementally or otherwise, managements then usually require the political and legal approval of government and people. It makes a great deal of difference what type of political culture exists. As with models of policy making there are two major types of political culture – pluralist and élitist. Broadly, the former refers to the United States whereas the latter is more a feature of the United Kingdom, with other countries such as Canada coming somewhere in between.[18] In a pluralist culture power is held by a variety of groups; business people, farmers etc. Groups form coalitions over one issue, disaggregate and re-form into different clusters over the next issue. In such a society, free communication and compromise are important. Emphasis is placed on the role of the media and the power of many individuals to influence events. A pluralist society is characterized by open government, public discussion of issues and freely available information. Politicians need to keep their ear close to the ground to detect changes in the majority view. In an élitist society, on the other hand, power is said to rest permanently in the hands of an élite which either overtly or subtlely influence and shape all decisions. To get things done it is necessary to identify the right people and then persuade them to your point of view. In such a culture things are unlikely to happen without the approval of the 'establishment'. Policy making tends to take place behind closed doors in a confidential and informal manner, the views of a wider set of people only being sought by invitation. In such a society politicians need not pay much heed to popular concerns or mass protests unless or until the 'establishment' of their own party are sympathetic to the issue.

Identifying the prevailing political culture tells us how things get done and who has to be influenced in order to initiate or abrogate a change in policy. The United States and the United Kingdom differ significantly in their respective political cultures. Many of the tasks that North American resource managers must undertake either do not appear on the agenda of their British counterparts or do so in a much amended form. Conversely, the style of British administration differs markedly from that of North America. Here there is a cosy atmosphere of confidentiality, close personal relations are built up with important people in the relevant field, thus avoiding the glare of publicity and the threat of intervention by the courts. The most noticeable difference between the United Kingdom and the United States in this respect lies in the former's lack of a written constitution. This has the significant advantage of flexibility and has led to a markedly less prominent role for the judiciary and courts, there being no written constitution to which any aggrieved citizen can appeal in cases of dispute or objection to government action. This to all intents and purposes removes debate over environmental policy matters from the courts and into Parliament and the civil service.

At one time the role of resource agencies was relatively simple: faced with a need for water or timber or coal, the appropriate arrangements were made and the desired commodity provided. There was little to distinguish the public agency from the private. The arrival of public interest in the environment changed all that. Resource management became a balancing act: providing a commodity, in the traditional sense of oil, or in the newer sense of something more aesthetic like wilderness or wildlife, whilst at the same time placating a variety of interests over the impact or implications of the process. Since many of the demands for reassurance over the consequences of resource development come from the public at large, the public agencies have had to make arrangements to deal with environmental pressure groups and vocal members of the public. Such mechanisms include public hearings, commissions of inquiry or, perhaps, formal procedures of consultation so that the public may be allowed to participate in the process of choosing the final form of the proposals. A principal mechanism of public participation in North America is Environmental Impact Assessment, considered in detail in the following chapter.

Even private concerns are not immune to demands for public participation in environmental matters, particularly in North America. There is the possibility of pressure from shareholders. More importantly, most corporations find it opportune to adopt a benign profile. Many companies indulge in advertising campaigns to project a favourable image. The Esso tiger proclaims the extent to which the company is fiercely working on behalf of the nation whilst combining strength with beauty and grace. The corollary of this point is perhaps more important: many corporations will go to considerable lengths to avoid creating a bad impression or incurring widespread public criticism. It is possible to embarrass private interests out of an intended course of action.

During the 1960s and early 1970s the number and membership of environmental pressure groups grew enormously.[19] The theme of public participation came to dominate a large part of resource management. Wengert has suggested a number of reasons for the upsurge in concern over this issue.[20] Rapid economic and social change during a period of unprecedented growth in the 1960s made many people feel uneasy. A desire to question 'progress' gradually grew, particularly as national or even multinational considerations appeared to be taking precedence over local knowledge and understanding. This might not have mattered had it not been for a simultaneous disaffection with existing institutions of representative government and a growing distrust of politicians and their motives. The apparent influence of lobby groups, appointed civil servants and party machines over and above the ordinary citizen led many to feel that there was no alternative but to speak up for themselves.

A useful perspective on forms of public participation comes from Arnstein[21] who sees a ladder of possibilities ranging from 'citizen power' through 'token-ism' to 'non-participation'. Citizen power, in her view, involves citizen control, or delegated power in a partnership between citizens and project developers. There would appear to be no examples of this in resource management. More common are degrees of tokenism – the placation of objections through mech-anisms such as environmental impact assessment or public hearings. Non-par-ticipation, the manipulation of the public view, appears most common, how-ever, and instances of small towns being unwilling to tackle problems of air pollution lest the major employing chemical manufacturer be offended, con-tinue to occur.

Apart from any moral feeling that it is the right thing to do in a democratic society, resource management should involve the public, argues Wengert, as a means of gaining political support for agency plans. The agency which can say that 68% of people interviewed supported its plans is more likely to succeed than a rival who has no survey data. Participation can also serve as a form of communication so that valuable local insights can pass to decision makers at little or no cost. By the same token, a hostile reaction can often be defused through participation procedures which tend to neutralize misunderstandings.

The form that participation may take is determined by the nature of the project, its location and by the political culture prevailing. A particular prob-lem, therefore, applies to those countries with élitist tendencies, such as the United Kingdom. Here, considerable controversy has raged in recent years over the role of the public enquiry in resource management and environmental planning. The problem arises, in essence, because modern demands are being made of a system originally devised in the 19th century to deal with other issues.[22] The British Parliament, faced with growing government involvement in all sorts of aspects of national life, could no longer afford the time to consider detailed objections to railway, harbour and water resource developments throughout the country. Instead, a system of local public inquiries was estab-lished. This worked well so long as the disputed aspects of the project involved entirely local interests and the Minister of the Crown responsible for the run-ning of the enquiry had no vested interest. A real conflict of interest arises, however, in modern times when the planned project under consideration might be the latest stage of a government-backed nuclear power programme or the latest augmentation of the national motorway network.[23]

The latter issue seems to have provided a focus for growing discontent during the 1960s.[23] Public enquiries in the context of a growing demand for public participation, are seen by many to be unfair. The public works with which they now deal are much more complex and much larger than the water works and the like for which the quasi-judicial format of evidence and cross-examination was devised.

The quasi-judicial format imposes heavy legal costs on the participants, costs which are easily borne by the promoters but represent great hardship for objectors. The promoter, if a government agency, may have the use of public funds. Inequality of financial resources leads to inequality of access to infor-mation. Major projects are often supported by powerful and well-connected business interests, such as the boiler making and turbine manufacture industries.[24] These lobbies can spend a great deal of time and money marshalling an expert presentation of their case. The promoter also has control of the timing and extent to which advance information is released, reducing the objectors effectiveness even where they can afford equal expertise. Finally, objectors are barred from calling evidence on the wider impact of a project, being confined to cross-examination of the promoter's case. The problems facing protestors are legion. The commonest solution, however, is to organize together into pressure groups.

8.3.2 The Nature and Role of Pressure Groups

The lower half of Figure 8.1 features the actors in decision making. The most important element of these, apart from resource managers themselves, have been pressure groups. Not only have pressure groups triggered action on a wide range of issues, they have also been the principal force arguing at many public hearings for environmental values, for the future, and for a higher quality of life. Many groups have been invited to comment on proposals at the evaluation stage. Others have established a state of anticipatory perception on the part of developers so that proposals known to provoke opposition are not put forward.

Dahl has suggested that the success of such groups lies in their access to a variety of 'bases of influence'.[25] These, he suggests, are such things as money or credit, control over information, social standing, expertise, charisma or popularity. A group has the advantage over an individual. Lowe and Goyder, who have examined environmental groups in politics in Britain, conclude that the necessary resources for a successful pressure group are money, organizational and leadership ability, expertise and 'power of veto'.[26] The latter means the ability to make trouble, to delay by initiating procedures of formal objection, and to stimulate public opposition. Clearly, these qualities are in general accord with Dahl's American-based view.

Lowe and Goyder provide a further set of insights by listing the channels of communication through which, in their view, British groups achieve results. These are: links with administrative agencies, access to senior policy makers, access to Parliament, access to the media as well as direct action. They are in line with what has already been said concerning the UK political culture. As regards direct action, they warn:

the general receptivity of the British system to the group activity, pervasive cultural pressures and fear of disrupting established relationships operate strongly to discourage militant and unorthodox approaches.[27]

There seems a consensus in North America and Britain that political culture is a key variable in determining how action on the part of resource managers is triggered, who is involved in the emergence of a policy, and to what extent proposed solutions for problems are offered to a wider circle than the official policy makers for evaluation. In the chapters that follow instances of the role of pressure groups setting the agenda for action, or conditioning the acceptability of management responses, feature in the context of specific issues and problems.

8.4 Hindsight Review

Figure 8.1 includes a final stage in the decision-making process: a review to check that what was expected to happen as a result of management action, did in fact happen. Lessons for the future might thus be learned. This assumes, however, that the process of decision making is a rational one and not of a more *ad hoc* nature as suggested by incrementalists. In practice, such reviews are rare, partly because it is not in the interest of decision makers to make public their mistakes, but also partly because the incrementalists may be right in suggesting that decision making starts with the status quo. If this is so, there is little point in conducting retrospective reviews because by the time the results become available circumstances will have changed, the status quo will have moved on, and the lessons will not be seen as applicable. Anyway, it is doubtful whether staff, time and money to review policy performance regularly could be made available. The individuals involved absorb the lessons of experience themselves, to be used for their own benefit as they are promoted or to the benefit of their professional association. Academics have attempted retrospective reviews but generally there are strong pressures to leave skeletons in the cupboard, difficulties of obtaining relevant information and problems concerning reliance on the recall of others or with the naming of sources in published literature. These difficulties serve to hinder the development of theory in resource management and produce an over-emphasis on case studies.

A further set of generalizations may be considered useful. These concern the results of decision making. Generally speaking, the most characteristic type of problem encountered by resource managers may be described as a 'commons problem'. Because of this, the most common output of management deliberation is a regulatory solution (although there is the alternative of fiscal policy).

8.5 The Tragedy of the Freedom of the Commons

Perhaps one of the most widely known essays in the field of environmentalism is Garret Hardin's on the tragedy of the common lands.[28] Hardin distilled the essence of the 'commons problem' into a form that has much wider significance than the population and resources debate. He sees no scientific solution to many problems of resources and the environment, only moral reforms and the introduction of new codes of conduct, and he summed up the dilemma with the example of the medieval herder who, with his neighbours, had free access and equal rights to graze cattle on commonly owned pasture. The common has a sustainable yield: the herbage will support a certain number of cattle. Thereafter, the addition of just one extra grazing animal will produce diminishing returns. Each member of the community's herd will receive less feed. But the herder reasons that if he adds that animal most of the benefits accrue to him personally; most of the costs will be spread over all the other herders. There is no law to stop him adding another animal, and there is always the possibility that one of his neighbours will do so. So, the 'rational' decision is to add one. Every herder comes to the same view. Result: the common grazing is hopelessly overgrazed.

The common might stand for any feature of the environment in which everybody has an interest: the oceans, fisheries, the atmosphere, good scenery. The issue is one of selfishness versus public spiritedness, short-term gain over long-term loss. The tragedy of the freedom of access to the common is that each man is locked into a system (of free enterprise or personal greed depending on one's political point of view) that compels him to increase his use of the common without limit in a situation that is limited. This ultimately brings ruin to all. To avoid the tragedy, Hardin contends, there must be mutual coercion to limit individual freedom. Free enterprise must be regulated. Therefore, state intervention, in the form of laws restricting the activities of individuals, is an obvious strategy for dealing with such problems. Such regulations are indeed to be found with respect to fisheries, as noted in Chapter 5, to water and air pollution, as discussed in following chapters. Hardin used his analysis to justify rigorous birth control and argues for an élite class to manage 'Planet Earth' in the best interests of all, despite serious implications for the liberty of the many. Some might say that such an élite has already emerged in the form of multinational corporations.[29] But the importance of Hardin's essay lies in its explanation of why demands for state intervention and state monopoly have become persistent themes in resource management.

A second strategy for dealing with commons type situations comes from Kenneth Boulding.[30] Having described unbridled free enterprise as a 'cowboy' economy, in which the private entrepreneur is seen as riding over the range using and discarding resources as he moves on to the next frontier, Boulding pointed out that there may come a time when there are no new resources over the horizon to be squandered. In a world of limited resources it would seem more sensible to switch to a 'space-ship' economy. In this, the final measure of success would not be growth in production or consumption, but the extent of stock resources. There should be clear financial incentives to conserve resources and the environment. This might be done by state intervention in the form of imposition of taxes on pollutants and wastage of resources. Specifically, a depletion tax might be imposed to encourage conservation of resource stocks. A residuals tax might be imposed on all waste producers to reduce the scale of waste production and to compensate those affected by its disposal. A through-put tax would encourage product durability and reduce product obsolescence. The manipulation of such taxes, he thought, might bring population growth into balance with the use being made of resources and with the environmental effects of economic growth. Instead of imposing external restrictions on economic activity, the suggestion is that the behaviour of individual entrepreneurs should be moulded through tax incentives.

Suggestions for the use of financial incentives as measures in resource management and environmental control have stimulated much academic discussion. Environmental economics is now a recognized branch of the parent discipline.[31] Some countries have imposed pollution taxes (see Chapter 14), but the strategy is not a common one, largely because of the great practical difficulty of calculating the most appropriate level of tax for different purposes, and such taxes might cost more to administer than the cost of damage that they might reduce.

Like regulation, the taxation strategy involves government intervention against the individual. But it represents, perhaps, a form of state intervention more acceptable to those committed to free enterprise as an economic and political system. Both strategies, regulation and fiscal, involve the limitation of free enterprise. For this reason resource management is inherently political. In such situations, some people lose and some people gain. The difficult question is deciding who should lose what and how much.

9   Techniques of Resource Management

9.1.1 Introduction

In Chapter 8 we presented a linear representation of steps in the processs of policy making. In this chapter, two of these are discussed further: first, problem recognition and goal definition, and, second, evaluation. Each has attracted considerable attention from legislators, professional practitioners and academic commentators. Clearly, if a problem is incorrectly defined, impartially recognized or perceived differently by the different groups involved in the policy-making process, then the range of alternatives devised to deal with it will be similarly flawed, evaluation will be incomplete and the ultimate choice of a policy inappropriate. Problems of resources and resource management will persist despite the efforts of professionals, the politicians and the public. Accordingly, the ways in which resource management issues come to be recognized are thought to comprise an important area of study. Similarly, the methods used to evaluate alternative solutions are also thought capable of influencing the final choice of policy and for this reason considerable attention has been paid to the development of standard techniques in the evaluation of the merits of alternative policies or projects.

In defining any problem for resource management there are two themes of particular importance: how concerns about an aspect of the environment or about resources get on to the agenda for action, or how environmental and resource situations become issues; and secondly, techniques of survey and inventory which help define the situation with regard to resources or the environment and hence help define the exact extent of the issue. In terms of deciding what to do about a problem, there are two sets of techniques: first there are those that help the process of choice between two or more policies or projects; and secondly, those that help set the context for the evaluation of policies or projects.

9.2.1 Problem Identification

Many aspects of resource management are highly political. None more so than the processes of problem definition and getting environmental issues on to the agenda for policy making. In Chapter 8 reference was made to the belief that Europe and North America do not share the same political culture, the latter tending towards the pluralistic model, the former, towards the élitist model. Such differences are significant for problem definition.

In North America the pluralistic model demands that a relatively large number of groups and individuals be involved in the policy-making process, and that the media, newspapers, radio and television, should express and broadcast the views of each group to the others thus setting political processes in motion. In this context, researchers have devised the concept of 'environmental stress' to explain how and why issues emerge for the attention of policy makers.[1] The suggestion is that public discussion, or expressions of concern and criticism over a particular aspect of the environment or resource-use, builds up to the point at which responsible officials and representatives feel obliged to act. An example is provided by Colin Wood's analysis of the Goldstream controversy in Victoria, British Columbia.[2]

In 1970, after several years of expanding demand for water, the normal practice of the city's water management in relatively dry years suddenly became the focus of public controversy, forcing a change of policy. To protect supplies of water destined largely for watering lawns, Victoria's reservoir managers proposed to cut back on the water released from reservoirs, thus jeopardizing the salmon's chance of successfully returning upstream to spawn. There had previously been some concern expressed over the situation by conservationists. But the issue did not 'take off' until the fall of 1970 when progressively more and more interested parties became involved. Ultimately a new policy emerged, one that accommodated both traditional concerns over the availability of water and the new issue of concern over the salmon runs.

Anthony Downs has put the idea of 'stress' as a trigger for action into a broader, longer term perspective by defining the concept of an 'issue attention cycle'[3] (see Figure 9.1). This has five stages. In the pre-problem phase, only a few people are concerned about any particular situation. Little or no response is evident on the part of resource managers and environmental policy makers. Many situations remain in this state of limbo. Those who are concerned may succeed in activating a much wider recognition of their views, however, perhaps through the publication of books or by making effective media appearances or with the aid of some 'crisis' that dramatically illustrates the reason for their fears. Faced with widespread concern and agitation, or, in short, signs of general 'stress' over the issue, policy makers are forced to act. If no action *is* forthcoming, the stress continues. When action is considered, and new or amended policies are proposed, Downs suggests that public concern gradually switches to the consequences of new policies, their costs and their efficacy. This involves the calculation by major interest groups of costs and losses in addition to the gains. Either significant progress is too expensive or there is general acceptance of the measures proposed. The 'stress' is relieved. The issue gradually drifts out of the forefront of public interest to eventually arrive at a 'post problem' stage, again with only professionals and a few special interest people continuing to monitor the situation.

How problems become problems helps to explain what sort of issue attracts attention and triggers action and what sort will have less chance of doing so. Largely because of the crucial role of the media, issues with obvious symptoms tend to prevail. Environmental damage that appears to be caused by a clear culprit (such as a specific industry or agency) will tend to catch public attention. And those issues that affect everyone (such as smog) will tend to prevail over those that only strike the few.

In a more élitist political culture, such as exists in Britain, the process is more complex. An environmental situation, such as water quality, still has to become an 'issue' attracting media interest and concern on the part of more than a few interested individuals. But, even if widely recognized, it does not necessarily follow that the issue will be placed on the agenda for action. A

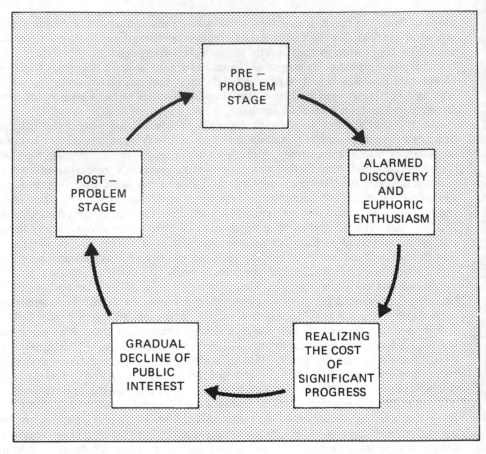

Figure 9.1 The Issue-Attention Cycle
Source: A.J. Downs, Up and Down with Ecology: The Issue-Attention Cycle, *The Public Interest*, 29, Summer 1972, pp. 38–50

further hurdle has to be overcome. It must be established that it is 'legitimate' to act. Whilst 'crises' and waves of popular concern may be sufficient to give an issue the status of an 'issue', a public inquiry or Royal Commission is needed to establish that existing arrangements and policy are definitely deficient. Once the issue has been set into the context of existing practice it must then be evaluated in general terms to see if action is appropriate. Solesbury suggests that issues that run contrary to prevailing policies are unlikely to be adopted.[4] For example, it seems unlikely that any issues involving more public expenditure or more state intervention would find a place on the agenda of the Thatcher Government in Britain; similarly, an issue apparently capable of being resolved through the sale of public assets or a relaxation of existing state controls seems unlikely to gain support from or be adopted by the Labour opposition.

O'Riordan adds the view that the discretion exercised by civil servants and other major figures to consult whom they please in a context of confidentiality and even secrecy, encourages only limited participation in policy making.[5] This in turn influences the type of issues which are normally reviewed for serious consideration. Hence in order to draw attention to their cause greater reliance is placed upon organized pressure groups which can manage their activities in a way that matches the official agencies, government departments or state utilities with whom they deal. By creating an appropriate lobby, certain causes can gain access to the routine circuit of consultation whilst others remain outside it.

Public inquiries, Royal Commissions of Inquiry and the administrative structure of pressure groups are relevant factors in getting the policy process underway and, to some extent, influential causal factors in the way in which an issue is perceived and subsequently dealt with. An important part of resource-management study, then, is a detailed analysis of how an issue was originally reviewed. In order to participate in resource management, an awareness of the administrative and political processes that condition the agenda for action is necessary. Furthermore, as discussed in Chapter 8, the institutional constraints on the derivation of alternative solutions to problems and their evaluation must also be considered. Hence O'Riordan can rightly claim:[6]

One of the least touched upon, but possibly one of the most fundamental research needs in resource management is the analysis of how institutional arrangements are formed, and how they evolve in response to changing needs and the existence of internal and external stress. There is growing evidence to suggest that the form, structure and operational guidelines by which resource management institutions are formed and evolve clearly affect the implementation of resource policy, both as to the range of choice adopted and the decision attitudes of the personnel involved.

The remainder of this chapter is concerned with operational guidelines for resource management – standing procedures for handling particular problems within resource management. Many such procedures have the objective of relieving 'stress', of moving away from subjective conflicts of opinion over the relative merits of alternative policies or projects. Their purpose, in short, is to attempt objective evaluations. Because the issues they address are implicitly value laden, however, standing procedures cannot be truly successful. If the reason an issue has become a problem demanding action lies in dissatisfaction, or fears over present practice, no technique of analysis or evaluation can completely remove policy making from the political sphere or exempt it from controversy or the scorn of those whose interest it does not serve.

9.3.1 Resource Inventories and Resource Management

The compilation of resource inventories is a prerequisite for effective resource management. In order to assess the availability of resources, their carrying capacity and suitability for development, the resource analyst requires adequate information to explain the existing resource situation. Since Dudley Stamp conducted the first major land-use survey using field techniques in the early 1930s, the tools available to the analyst for collecting and mapping data have become increasingly sophisticated. Until the 1960s, vertical aerial photography, augmented by field surveys, formed the basis for manually drawn land-use maps. The art of remote sensing – the observation and measurement of the earth's surface without coming into physical contact with the objects viewed – has experienced major advances in the past two decades. Non-photographic imagery – thermal infrared scanning, radar and satellite imagery - coupled with developments in computer information systems and cartography has facilitated the collection and presentation of data concerning the earth's resources.

At present, resource analysts are persuading their government agencies to add instrumentation to new generation satellites to perfect the data available from LANDSAT imagery. It must be remembered that the first satellite launched specifically to provide earth resource data in 1972 was an experimental satellite. This, and two further LANDSATS have been invaluable to researchers monitoring natural hazards, pollution and changing patterns of land use. However, in areas such as mineral exploration, where extensive use is already being made of satellite imagery, oil and mining companies are working with the National Aeronautics and Space Administration (NASA) to design sensing devices that will be twice as effective in the discrimination of rocks, soils and clay substances.[7] LANDSAT 4 and a new generation of satellites, for example the French SPOT, will raise the level of resolution of the images received and thus the quality of the information to be analysed.

In essence, satellite imagery has revolutionized the field of remote sensing because of its cheapness, frequency of coverage and ability to produce data in computer readable form. Our knowledge of the world's resources has been greatly enhanced since the days of *Limits to Growth* when forecasts were made without the benefit of LANDSAT. Nevertheless, accuracy of prediction is restricted by the nature of image produced, which is of a regional scale (185 kilometres by 185 kilometres). In most instances, satellite imagery is complementary to traditional inventory compilation methods, in that LANDSAT is used as an exploratory phase prior to more detailed analysis in the field or by aerial photography.

This is indeed the case in the mineral business, and LANDSAT has been a boon to the transnationals because it has enabled them to update their inventories, especially in politically 'safe' countries such as Canada, US and Australia. By contrast, some of the developing nations are not in a position to benefit from LANDSAT because they lack the institutions to utilize even conventional technology. It is not surprising therefore that the UN has channelled most of its efforts in the mineral sector towards building institutions for the training of personnel and the provision of an information base to facilitate the exploration effort (see 11.2.4a).

9.4.1 Classification and Capability (Suitability) Analysis

Resource inventories are only the first stage in a process which involves analysis for specific policy objectives. The classification of resource data provides a foundation for ground rules for land-use planning prior to detailed appraisal of more specific projects. The zoning of land parcels into 'use categories' is invaluable to the resource manager in view of the pressure on traditional agricultural and forested landscapes for energy, mineral and industrial uses.

A classic example of this inventory–classification–suitability process was Dudley Stamp's First Land Utilization Survey and his subsequent classification of agricultural land quality.[8] When the land-use inventory was being compiled, the British government required a more meaningful definition of the quality of agricultural land because of the increasing pressure on farming land for other uses at that time. Clearly 'good' agricultural land would require most protection. With a brief to produce a land-use suitability classification, Stamp used his inventory to identify ten classes of agricultural land which were graded by quality from I to III, a system which was to be of value to land-use planners in post-war Britain.

During the 1960s, the Canadians attempted an ambitious Land Inventory which not only monitored existing land uses but classified them according to their capacity for agricultural, forestry and recreational use and their ability to support wildlife. As with Stamp's survey, it enabled decision makers to assess the productivity of existing uses before determining the suitability of a change of use in particular areas.

The difficulty with both land inventories is the strong element of subjectivity involved in the process of classification. In the Canadian case in particular, local information was collected using *national* standards and guidelines to give system comparability. However, in such a vast country, with varying physical and cultural landscapes, local or regional interpretations of resource capability may deviate widely from the national norm.

Assumptions made for any classification process are subject to personal, professional and political judgement. In Chapter 13 it will be shown how a professional agency (the US Forest Service) inventoried its roadless areas as early as 1926 in order to establish 'primitive areas' as the first step towards legalizing wilderness areas. In 1964 when Congress gave legal protection to those 'primitive areas', it also obliged the Forestry Service and other agencies to review all their roadless areas over 5,000 acres for possible designation as wilderness. Here, the political brief was to inventory roadless areas according to the subjective guidelines outlined in the 1964 Act. Objective assessment methods such as cost benefit analysis (9.7.2) and landscape evaluation techniques (9.5.1) are used by the Forest Service to classify wilderness study areas but the final boundary delimitation is a political decision through an Act of Congress.

The compatibility of new developments with existing land uses is normally decided by regional or local land-use planning agencies. The state of North Dakota, for example, has exclusion and avoidance areas so as to guide prospective applicants for the development of energy conversion and transmission facilities (Table 10.2). In Scotland, the Scottish Development Department produced coastal planning guidelines indicating preferred development and preferred conservation zones so as to channel oil-related development away from remote rural areas to those with a sizeable population, thereby minimizing the socio-economic and environmental impact.

In the case of route planning (highways, pipelines, powerlines, etc.), inter-agency and inter-governmental coordination is often needed to determine the suitability of alternative routes, according to physical, socio-economic and political criteria. This takes us beyond resource inventory and land suitability to questions of project appraisal and public participation in the decision-making process.

9.5.1 Landscape Evaluation

Landscape evaluation is another important method of classification and project appraisal. Landscape appraisal is not new: national parks and other protected landscapes bear witness to policy makers' acknowledgement of the value of preserving environments for the use of future generations. The designation of such areas was, however, an *ad hoc* process. Legislative action was an expression of society's concern that certain landscapes would lose their intrinsic appeal if 'undesirable' developments were allowed. Landscape appraisal is a changing concept. An environment valued by one generation may not have the same aesthetic qualities for subsequent generations. It is interesting to note that many of the areas which have protected status in the US were regarded by 19th century frontiersmen as hostile environments. Now they offer peace, tranquillity and solitude – escapism from modern Western society.

Although the 'jewels' of our environment received protected status, the pace of development in the post-war period resulted in the loss of agricultural and forested lands to energy, industrial and urban development. In many parts of the world, traditional landscapes were being transformed. Environmentalists who stood against such developments could not match the sophisticated quantification of the developer who outlined the costs and benefits of projects. By the 1960s and early 1970s, however, government agencies, developers and land-use planners came under legislative pressure to include aesthetic considerations in the planning process. For example, in the UK, 'regional' planning authorities had to produce structure plans as strategic policy and land-use guidelines for lower-tier authorities. Policies pertaining to potential land-use conflict required a method of appraising landscape quality in order to facilitate development-control decisions.

During the last fifteen to twenty years, a plethora of techniques has been devised to evaluate landscape quality. Many of these emanate from the UK as part of structure plan preparation. Two approaches can be identified: a descriptive approach in which specific landscapes are evaluated and ranked according to established criteria, and a preference approach which attempts to evaluate personal tastes in landscape appreciation. The latter, behavioural approach has made use of historical data to monitor society's changing perception of landscape.

The descriptive approach has its roots in three classic studies undertaken in the late 1960s by Leopold, a geologist, Fines, a planner, and Linton, a geographer.[9] Leopold[10] maintained that a more 'objective' approach to landscape evaluation was necessary if aesthetic arguments were to be considered in planning decisions. Similarly, Fines and Linton hoped that their research would facilitate the 'right' decision when a project was being appraised, with all factors being reduced to numbers in order that trade-offs could be made.

Leopold's work was stimulated by an application to the Federal Power Commission to build a hydro-electric power dam in the Hell's Canyon region of Snake River in Idaho. How could the aesthetic value of Hell's Canyon be measured? Much of the research on landscape evaluation in the US at this time was centred on visual impacts, primarily through the work of landscape architects such as Litton and Zube.[11] These intuitive approaches acted as the catalyst for a proliferation of landscape evaluation techniques. Indeed, several studies used the work of the pioneers as a foundation for their own research.[12]

Throughout the 1970s, much effort was spent on trying to establish a consensus on landscape evaluation. For example, both in a Manchester University report and in work by Briggs and France, 'wild' evaluations were screened out or could be explained by respondents' initial response to a reference landscape or set of landscapes.[13] From survey work, landscape types were identified and with the use of multi-variate techniques landscapes of differing quality could be identified.

In essence, the quantification of Linton and Fines had been considerably refined. But the use of such techniques has had limited practical application. Why? Powell argues that

The failure of evaluation techniques to live up to expectations that they would provide facts about landscape quality arose because the whole enterprise started off on the wrong foot. Instead of investigating directly the question of how people perceive quality in landscapes, efforts were engaged in obtaining information which fitted in with pre-conceived ideas about the requirements of the planning process. The a priori position entailed assumptions that provided an unsuitable basis for studying this particular phenomenon.[14]

In her view, the scientific method, which was very successful in measuring scientific phenomena, could not be applied to a subjective subject such as landscape quality. The question of subjectivity poses a challenge to the validity of the variables chosen by those designing the technique and to whom it was applied. Linton, Leopold and others stressed scenic attractiveness, diversity, uniqueness and 'naturalness'. They omitted the historical or user value of landscapes from their variable checklists. In addition, most studies used 'experts', from highly qualified designers to students being trained in environmental-related courses. The underlying philosophy was that some training or experience was a prerequisite for appreciating landscapes.[15]

A final difficulty with the descriptive approach is that of scale. Most techniques are devised for large areas. Indices for these areas are produced by aggregating variables. But as Penning-Rowsell points out, most concern for landscape change occurs at a local level and powers to control change rest with local planning authorities.[16]

In view of the criticisms directed at the a priori descriptive approach, it is not surprising that the research emphasis in recent years has shifted to monitoring public preferences. This has had added significance because of the statutory requirements in many countries to involve the public in the decision-making process. Evaluating public preferences for landscape quality is not an easy task. Perceptions of landscapes are conditioned by the culture of a society at any moment in time. Literary tastes, art forms and the media all present images of idealized landscapes which can be representative of culture through history. Much of the formative research in this field by Lowenthal and Prince sought to identify changing landscape tastes of the public through time.[17]

A more recent direct approach is to solicit landscape preferences from respondents through the use of photographs or site visits. As with descriptive studies, much emphasis was placed upon achieving a consensus view from a predetermined checklist of variables ranked in a conventional or bipolar semantic differential scale (the latter, common to psychology and environmental studies, uses a scale (usually of seven points) with opposing catchwords such as dislike/like, colourful/colourless). Regression techniques were also employed to calibrate evaluation indices for particular population sub-groups. In the UK, two government commissioned reports[18] did identify small differences in landscape preferences by certain groups. The most notable divergence recorded was that between urban and rural respondents in the Department of Transport research. However, this objective scientific method of determining consensus from public preferences suffered from the pitfalls identified in descriptive studies. In order to eliminate personal bias and to be as objective as possible, the technique devised for the Department of Transport was calibrated on landscape evaluations undertaken by people who were *non-resident* in the areas they appraised. It can be argued that this methodology is unacceptable because local landscapes have a social value and their familiarity leads locals to rank them higher than an 'outsider' such as a tourist. For example, migrants have invariably chosen to settle in places that have some association with their past or homeland.

Much ground has still to be covered in producing an adequate technique for evaluating landscape. Consensus in landscape taste is not as readily arrived at as in other social survey analyses. Whereas shopping patterns and other forms of economic activity can be predicted from standard determinants – socio-economic group, sex, age, education and car ownership – these cannot be readily applied to landscape preferences. Other determinants such as childhood experiences, length of residence in parts of the country and observers' familiarity with the landscape to be appraised, are of greater utility. The validity of many of the factors used in predictive landscape evaluation methods can be questioned because of their bias towards appearance. To Penning-Rowsell, the only way ahead for landscape evaluation methodology is not only to ask the public their appearance preferences but to ascertain the use and historical associations of particular landscape typologies.[19]

9.6.1 Carrying Capacity

'Carrying capacity is a product of management judgement rather than a precisely defined measure – it is a decision-making concept rather than a scientific concept.'[20] The carrying capacity of a resource is its ability to support consumption to specified limits. If these limits are exceeded, diminishing returns begin to operate so that overgrazing, overfishing and species extinction, among other things, become features of the environmental system.

What appears to be a fairly straightforward concept is much more complex when applied in practice. Capacity limits change. Physical capacities are constantly revised according to technological advances and management regulation whilst consumers re-value their resource priorities in relation to their cultural milieu. The most general application of the notion of 'carrying capacity' is associated with the 'Limits to Growth' philosophy. This neo-Malthusian approach to the issue of population–resource imbalance has drawn the attention of governments to the dangers of over-exploitation of the global resource base; however, the international response to carrying capacity arguments tends to be of a 'technical fix' nature.

Effective management action relating to carrying capacity is mainly confined to specific resource problems. For example, the depletion of fish stocks, such as the North Sea herring, has resulted in the EEC nations agreeing to ban fishing in certain areas at certain times of the year to allow replenishment of stock.

Most research into carrying capacity has centred upon agriculture, forestry and recreational planning. Researchers have measured the ability of a resource to sustain levels of use and studied how consumers perceive carrying capacity. Much early work was concerned with range and wildlife management.[21] In the

US in the 1930s, government range-management officials used carrying capacity analysis as a means for allocating animal grazing rights on public lands in the western states.[22] It was possible to determine from experience how many animals could be grazed per acre per month without exhausting the land. About the same time, the US Soil Service recommended stock reduction on Indian lands. The harsh Navajo environment in northern Arizona was displaying the signs of overgrazing in the 1920s, aggravated by the great droughts of the 1930s. As the tribal range became less productive, the Soil Service recommended stock reduction and the introduction of new farming practices. The Navajo, however, did not see the problem in the same way. The culling of herds was unacceptable to them. A sizeable flock was a status symbol to the Indian, an indication of wealth and security. In essence, this and other measures to remedy the overgrazing problem were unsuccessful because the reserve managers and the Indians had divergent cultural values and could not see the carrying capacity issue in the same light.[23] At the present time, similar problems are encountered in parts of the tropical forest where peasants cannot understand Forest Service management policies which forbid them to fell trees, encourage them to grow trees rather than crops and advise them to reduce their herds to facilitate forest regeneration. To a peasant suffering a food and fuel shortage, such long term objectives are meaningless (see 13.3.3).

In the post-war period, carrying capacity research has been dominated by studies on the use of areas for recreational purposes. On the one hand, ecological research has been carried out to monitor the human impact on ecosystems, especially the effects of trampling upon vegetation and soil, in order to facilitate trail and campsite management decisions.[24] On the other hand, studies have focused upon the recreational experiences enjoyed by the public and how these could be enhanced through management action. Nevertheless, the achievement of a public consensus about overcrowding and carrying capacity limits presents similar problems to those experienced in landscape evaluation research. In many ways, however, this problem can be resolved in carrying capacity research because it is much easier to define. For example, recreational resource managers are normally planning for a specific area and are trying to reconcile the conflicts of their customers who have differing recreational aspirations – a car-borne 'industrial tourist' will perceive carrying capacity objectives in a different way from a wilderness back-packer. Indeed, two classic studies, by O'Riordan of the English Fens and by Lucas of the Boundary Waters Canoe Area in Minnesota,[25] show how various types of recreationalist used these areas and how they perceived a recreational experience in light of environmental capacity. Some spatial segregation of users was offered as a management suggestion in both studies (see 13.2.2 for a detailed discussion on recreation/ wilderness carrying capacity research).

9.7.1 Techniques of Project Assessment

The techniques discussed in previous sections sought to identify the extent of the resource base, its suitability for particular uses and the limits to which exploitation can be allowed to go before the law of diminishing returns takes effect. The use of resource inventories, land use capability studies and landscape evaluations are invaluable to the resource manager in establishing a framework for subsequent project appraisal and policy review. At this stage, however, alternative proposals are evaluated and techniques have evolved – cost-benefit analysis, environmental impact assessment and risk assessment – to aid the resource manager in reviewing specific projects and/or policies.

Although these project appraisal techniques had their roots in the informal development planning of large-scale projects – mainly water management schemes – in the 1930s and 1940s, it was not until the late 1960s that a more formal, rigorous method of project assessment was introduced in the US and was subsequently adopted by other Western, industrialized nations. Table 9.1 charts the evolution of project assessment techniques, from the informal, limited review method to the sophisticated two-tier environmental impact assessment (EIA) process mooted for the future.[26] The importance of EIA and risk assessment techniques during the 1970s can be attributed to the increased number of large-scale projects, including those of a 'hazardous' nature such as

Table 9.1: The evolution of project assessment techniques. *Source:* T. O'Riordan and W.R.D. Sewell (eds), 1981, Project Appraisal and Policy Review, Wiley, New York, p. 9

	Project assessment technique	National examples
1.	No formal accounting: decisions made on basis of interest group lobbying; little political review of resource agency budgets	Most developing countries; possibly most totalitarian
2.	Conventional cost-benefit analysis: emphasis on efficiency criterion and engineering feasibility	Some developing countries; most West European countries
3.	Conventional risk assessment with emphasis on the perception of and adjustment to natural hazards	US since the 1940s
4.	Innovative cost-benefit analysis: use of multiple objectives and discount rates, imaginative proxy-pricing mechanisms	US in early 1970s; some West European countries
5.	Environmental impact assessment with prime emphasis on description of repercussions of proposals on biophysical processes	US in early 1970s
6.	Environmental impact assessment with wider emphasis on description and evaluation of repercussions of proposals on both social processes and cultural norms and biophysical systems	US in late 1970s; British Columbia
7.	Environmental risk assessment with emphasis on the estimation and evaluation of hazardous technologies	US and UK in the 1970s and 1980s
8.	Environmental impact assessment made at a two-tier level – first, to look at generic issues associated with big projects as a class; second, to investigate how an 'approved' scheme can best be designed with minimal net social and biophysical disruption. EIA visualized as a creative participatory environmental management activity	

chemical and nuclear power plants; these began to proliferate during the 1960s. The physical and social impact of these developments quickly exposed the inadequacies of existing administrative review procedures and techniques of evaluation. Moreover, opposition to some of these projects became more organized, and public policy makers were obliged to create mechanisms for more meaningful public participation than hitherto.

From Table 9.1 it can be seen that the most modern, innovative techniques of project appraisal have been applied in the US. Here, the views of environmental pressure groups have received political expression in a constitutional system which both encourages 'issue orientated' politics and resort to the courts to question inadequate environmental impact statements. By contrast, most developing countries are almost half a century behind the US in the use of project assessment techniques; most have yet to move from Phase 1 identified in Table 9.1. The role of political culture is therefore of prime significance in the acceptance of innovative techniques in the decision-making process. O'Riordan and Sewell, writing about reticence among European governments in accepting EIA, state that

'many governments claim that adequate procedures already exist for implementing a form of EIA for big schemes (a claim disputed by environmentalists) and above all are anxious that particular interests, regarded by them still very much as minority interests, neither accountable for their actions nor representative of broad constituencies, are not provided with a new weapon with which to attack the fortresses of policy formulation'.[27]

9.7.2 Benefit–Cost Analysis

One of the earliest procedures adopted as a tool of objective choice in resource management was benefit–cost analysis (BCA).[28] The calculation of a ratio by dividing estimated benefits by costs to get a unit benefit per unit of cost can be extremely useful in answering three types of question: Is the project worth considering at all?; Has the project an optimum size beyond which there are increasing diseconomies of scale?; and, Which of several projects should be chosen? Thus benefit–cost analysis can be of considerable assistance in either establishing the feasibility of schemes or choosing between them. The major advantage of the technique is the simplicity of comparison between BCA ratios. The major disadvantages lie in the choice of variables included in the BCA and in the calculating procedures adopted to convert these into monetary units. Some variables, such as lives saved as the result of flood protection measures, may be intangible. And what monetary values should be put on lives?

In practice, water resource developments, both in the United States and in the Third World (because of World Bank lending criteria), have been the principal area of application of BCA. But BCA and other techniques of national decision making are successful if the goals of the policies being evaluated are simple, such as the maximization of profit to the promoter. As soon as social welfare and external profits and losses are added as an objective, the calculations become considerably more complicated. Appropriate external benefits and costs have to be agreed upon: for example, a new hydro scheme may stimulate regional economic development and employment, and the costs and benefits of this might be included in the BCA. Nevertheless, some of that economic growth may be the result of transfers from other regions, to the latter's detriment.

Some of the secondary development might have occurred elsewhere had the scheme not proceeded, again to the loss of other regions. Should these costs or negative benefits not also be included, and if so, how?

Where there may be several sets of vested interests in both the projects under consideration and in others elsewhere, the scope for dissatisfaction and disagreement is enormous. BCA works as a useful tool of resource management only if ground rules and procedures are recognized as fair by all those involved in the political process. As part of the growth of environmentalism, pressure groups increasingly pointed to the extent to which intangible aesthetic values and effects on cultural and social life, were not, and indeed could not, adequately be contained in BCA. Hence in the United States, the National Environmental Policy Act of 1969 brought a new and much more comprehensive procedure of project appraisal: environmental impact assessment.

9.7.3 National Environmental Policy Act (NEPA) and Environmental Impact Assessment (EIA)

Concern over the effects of economic growth and the domination of materialistic values grew steadily throughout the 1960s, especially in the United States. This was accompanied by a growing environmental movement which achieved a major victory in 1969 with the National Environmental Policy Act (NEPA). The Act embodied a cautious approach towards the environmental effects of major new developments, the principle of 'look before you leap'. Specifically, the law required the preparation of comprehensive Environnmental Impact Statements (EIS) on any projects which were likely to have environmental implications and were earmarked for Federal lands or proposed by Federal agencies or that were in receipt of Federal assistance. The statements were to be the result of procedures of Environmental Impact Assessment (EIA) subsequently specified during the 1970s by the issue of codes of practice by a US Council on Environmental Quality (CEQ) created by the Act and a series of interpretive court decisions. Assessments would identify the detrimental consequences of particular plans. The idea was to guarantee an interdisciplinary approach to decision making by all agencies of the Federal Government concerned with the management of the nation's environment. The effect of the Act was to give legal authority to interest and pressure groups to participate in cases where they felt irreparable harm to the land, air or water resources of the US was being proposed. A draft EIS circulates for 120 days of public examination and discussion and a final version must include public reaction. Section 102(C) of the Act obligates the agency responsible for an EIS to include[29]

  (i) the environmental impact of the proposed action;
 (ii) any adverse environmental effects which cannot be avoided should the proposal be implemented;
(iii) alternatives to the proposed action;
(iv) the relationship between local short-term uses of man's environment and the maintenance and enhancement of long-term productivity, and
 (v) any irreversible and irretrievable commitments of resources which would be involved in the proposed action should it be implemented.

The availability of impact assessment reports and statements allows members of the public to be informed of the scope of the proposed action and the possible effects of various alternatives. After the initial EIS has been reviewed by the public and other Federal agencies the initiating agency can prepare answers to points raised and incorporate comments into the final version. Action can still proceed regardless of unfavourable comment and opposing views, although a right of appeal to the CEQ exists. This body can advise the President to stop a project. The President need not heed this advice but at least the issue is exposed to the full glare of public opinion.

Because NEPA applies to Federal projects, about half the state legislatives have passed codes of practice involving a requirement for EIA for state-sponsored projects. Some of the 'mini-NEPAs', such as that in California, even extend the requirement for an EIS to major projects sponsored by the private sector.[30]

Sewell and O'Riordan have identified four factors leading to the introduction of EIA.[31] Firstly, the growing scale and associated repercussions of resource development schemes demands a much more systematic and comprehensive review of their possible impact. Projects such as the Trans-Alaska Pipeline open a Pandora's box of potential consequences for the fragile ecosystem of the far north. The security and vetting of personnel that must surround the processing of nuclear fuels and wastes raise far-reaching questions as to the impact of technologies on ordinary civil rights. Secondly, the upsurge of vociferous and perhaps more importantly, informed and intelligent criticism and protest by well organized groups such as Friends of the Earth and Greenpeace demands a similarly professional, informative and detailed response. Thirdly, prevailing assessment techniques were widely perceived to be failing to recognize and incorporate environmental and social dislocation. Finally, the various regulatory agencies, at least in the US, appeared to lack any focal point for harmonizing and co-ordinating their separate perspectives.

It emerged that EIA, as introduced by NEPA, was to bring a systematic comprehensiveness to project appraisal, and several methods have evolved to accomplish this. Five types of method can be identified.[32] Firstly, and most basically, a simple *checklist* may itemize likely consequences. *Overlays* may be prepared, each identifying the intensity and extent of a particular type of impact, an overall impression of total impact being achieved when all are superimposed onto each other. *Networks* (see Figure 9.2) have been used to identify the full range of repercussions in an orderly and systematic fashion. Complex *indices* have been developed to quantify the multiple impact of alternative plans. The most common format, however, has been the *matrix* and, in particular, derivatives and adaptations of the schema proposed by Leopold *et al.* of the US Geological Survey.[33]

Leopold provides an example: the impact of phosphate mining in Los Padres National Forest, California (in Figure 9.3). Aspects of the mining operation are marshalled in columns while aspects of the environment likely to incur damage are listed in rows. Each cell is subdivided and an index number on a scale of 1 to 10 allocated in the upper left division to denote magnitude of the possible impact, 10 representing the greatest, 1 the least order of magnitude. In the lower right division is a similarly scaled order of importance of the likely impact. The difference between the two scales may be seen in the case of an archaeological site lying in the path of a proposed reservoir project. Clearly,

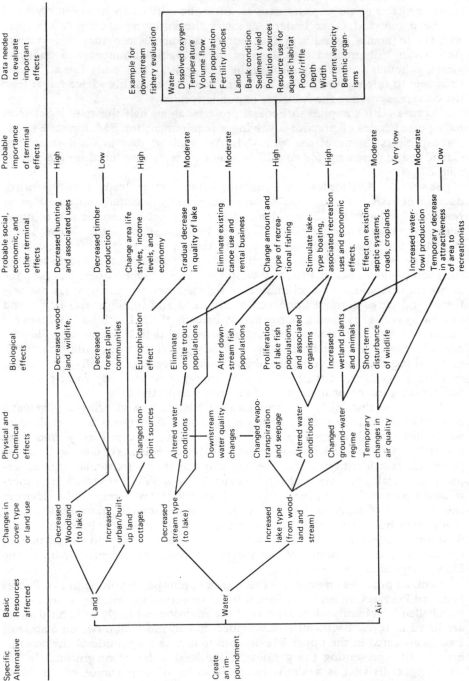

Figure 9.2 An Example of a Network Diagramme for Environmental Impact Assessment
Source: L.D. Canter, *Water Resources Assessment*, Ann Arbor Science, 1979, p. 463

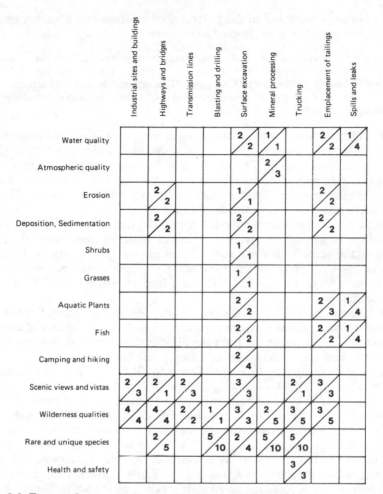

	Industrial sites and buildings	Highways and bridges	Transmission lines	Blasting and drilling	Surface excavation	Mineral processing	Trucking	Emplacement of tailings	Spills and leaks
Water quality					2/2	1/1		2/2	1/4
Atmospheric quality						2/3			
Erosion	2/2				1/1			2/2	
Deposition, Sedimentation	2/2				2/2			2/2	
Shrubs					1/1				
Grasses					1/1				
Aquatic Plants					2/2			2/3	1/4
Fish					2/2			2/2	1/4
Camping and hiking					2/4				
Scenic views and vistas	2/3	2/1	2/3		3/3		2/1	3/3	
Wilderness qualities	4/4	4/4	2/2	1/1	3/3	2/5	3/5	3/5	
Rare and unique species		2/5		5/10	2/4	5/10	5/10		
Health and safety							3/3		

Figure 9.3 Extract from a 'Leopold' Matrix for Environmental Impact Assessment *Source:* US Geological Survey Circular 645, 1971, p. 10

the creation of a reservoir will destroy the site. So the order of magnitude of impact would be 10. The importance of this, however, depends on the context of the archaeological site. If it were to be the only known Viking remnant in North America, the importance of its loss would be of the greatest order, also 10. If it was one of a hundred or more native American sites, all of which had been intensively surveyed and documented, the loss of one would be of the least order of importance and hence scaled 1.

Returning to Figure 9.3, if there is no likely impact on the environment, no entry is made. In the case of phosphate mining in California the most important impact is upon the unique species of the area. The surviving condors of California are awe-inspiring birds of prey, held in considerable regard by naturalists. Their nesting sites were some miles away, but it was thought that the blast from surface mining and the noise of trucks, coupled with sulphur fumes from the processing plant, would reduce the habitat available to surviving birds. The benefit of the matrix lies in the portrayal of information, allowing the following summary statement of the impact to be made easily and quickly:

... the proposed actions which have the most environmental impacts are the construction of 'highways and bridges', the 'blasting', 'surface excavation', 'mineral processing', 'trucking', and 'emplacement of railings'. The environmental characteristics most frequently impacted are those of 'scenic views and vista', 'wilderness qualities', and 'rare and uniques species'.

In all, Leopold suggests 100 project actions of possible relevance and 88 environmental characteristics or conditions, only a few of which might be relevant to particular cases. The condor having been identified as in most danger, the next stage would be to approach the mining company to see if changes in the proposed methods of blasting, processing and trucking could reduce the impact, to an order of magnitude of 1 or 2.

A problem immediately apparent with the matrix, and, indeed, with all uses of indices of impact or quality, is that of ensuring that assessors consistently allocate the same index measure of magnitude or importance to identical or similar cases of environmental impact. Or to put it another way: how bad do things have to be to gain the maximum impact rating of ten? How can consistent scaling be ensured?

Batelle Laboratories and others have developed rational systems for the estimation of environmental impact indices covering most of the major types of damage.[34] For example, in the case of water quality, a consistent approach to impact estimation could be achieved by using something like Figure 9.4. Clean water has a Biochemical Oxygen Demand (BOD) of less than 2 mg per litre. An increase in BOD of 2 mg per litre will either move the body of water concerned out of the cleanest category, remaining only slightly polluted, *or*, if already quite badly polluted, will make little difference. An impact index of a low order of 1 or 2 seems appropriate. Seriously polluted water has a BOD of 12 or more. An increase in the BOD of 12 or so is a very serious deterioration, capable of rendering a clean watercourse incapable of supporting fish. Such an impact, of course, warrants a score of 10. These indices, and others in between, may be read off a standard relationship curve as shown in Figure 9.4 (and the relationship need not be a straight line as shown in this case). Such a curve may be derived through the 'delphi' method of estimation. Several experts in the field may be asked independently to draw their view of the shape of such a curve. If all replies are in accord with each other, the unanimously suggested relationship may be accepted immediately. If not, the alternative views may be circulated and re-circulated until a clear majority view or a universally accepted compromise emerges. This becomes the standard.

Such a procedure can only be undertaken, of course, if knowledge or informed opinion concerning the particular aspect of the environment is available. A major problem with EIA has been the extent to which questions have arisen concerning the working of environmental systems. Many sub-disciplines have received something of a boost since the advent of EIA. For example, few people saw permafrost studies of the Arctic and sub-Arctic environment as of immediate 'relevance' until proposals to transport oil and gas across such terrain raised the question of the impact of permafrost forces on pipelines. In many disciplines, particularly zoology, new questions have arisen as to the normal behaviour, patterns of migration and territoriality of species.

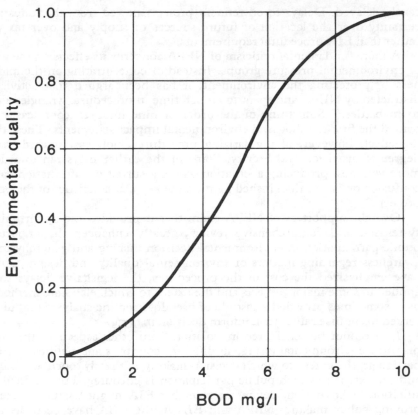

Figure 9.4 An Example Environmental Impact Function

In this light it is not surprising that in some of the few retrospective reviews of environmental impact statements, the ecological basis of predicted damage has been disproved or shown to be incorrect.[35] The most frequent criticisms of EIA, however, concern extra costs and delays incurred while an EIS is prepared. Unfortunately, the EIA system in the United States was just being established when the oil crisis of the early 1970s seemed to demand a rapid deployment of resources in the energy field. It was therefore claimed that EIA was unnecessarily delaying vital energy projects such as the Trans-Alaska Pipeline and nuclear power stations, to the detriment of the nation. Accordingly, Congress was persuaded to pass special exemption legislation, giving the Atomic Energy Commission authority to accelerate the licensing of nuclear stations, then delayed by court wrangles covering the EIA procedure, and to exempt the Trans-Alaska Pipeline from further review of its environmental impact.

Subsequent events surrounding nuclear power stations (Chapter 10) seem to justify the view that EIA, a delaying mechanism, was a valuable aid to decision making because it made marginal projects unviable, and it was the marginally economic projects that tended to pose the most difficult questions of environmental impact. Subsequent study of the period 1970-1975 shows that only 6% of new electricity generating proposals in the USA were significantly delayed. Delays to oil refinery projects flowed from the industry's uncertainty over the location of future sources of supply and over tax changes rather than EIA procedural requirements.[36]

A more fundamental criticism of NEPA concerns its effects on the workings of environmental pressure groups. Instead of concentrating on the main business of protecting the environment, it has been argued that activists were distracted by NEPA and spent too much time in procedural wrangles and court room battles.[37] Something of the order of nine hundred court cases accompanied the first ten thousand environmental impact statements. These did have the effect, however, of regularizing procedures, not least towards a greater degree of provision and brevity. Some of the earlier EIAs ran to a dozen or more volumes, producing a situation where a surfeit of information cast more confusion on issues than it shed light on the key characteristics of the particular project.

Overall, supporters of NEPA claim that it provided the opportunity for a systematic and comprehensive review, greatly enhanced the importance of public participation in environmental decision making and generally increased awareness regarding matters of environmental quality and design. Opponents have emphasized the cost of the procedures, the legislative delays that have applied to some major projects and the extent to which elaborate methodologies have sometimes provided a cascade of pseudo-scientific analyses that ultimately served to confuse rather than inform decision making.

EIA cannot be considered in isolation from other aspects of the system of planning environmental change in different countries and political cultures. In particular, the extent to which decision making is already 'open' or confidential and the extent to which public participation is encouraged or confined to consultation by invitation, define the role that EIA might usefully make in improving policy making. NEPA and EIA in the USA have been discussed at particular length because of its open form of political culture. In Canada, a cabinet directive of 1973 established an Environmental Assessment and Review Process (EARP) for projects involving the Federal government or its agencies, but no full equivalent to NEPA was forthcoming. Several provincial governments, however, have legislated for EIA procedures, notably Alberta.[38] In Australia, specific legislation exists at all levels of government although the question of which major development proposals require an EIS to be prepared is left to the discretion of the relevant ministers.[39]

In Europe, the Council of Ministers of the European Communities initiated a series of studies in 1977 to assess the feasibility of a common EEC approach to EIA. France and Eire have introduced laws requiring EISs for certain proposals. The Federal Republic of Germany has administrative procedures along Canadian lines. The Swedish government, on the other hand, has taken the view that additional procedures to existing planning practice are unnecessary.[40]

In Britain a system of comprehensive planning control over major developments has existed since 1947. Opportunities for a forward review of the consequences of large-scale projects and for widespread public participation are, however, distinctly limited. The limited usefulness of the public inquiry as a focus of debate on the impact of a project or policy has on several occasions given rise to considerable public disquiet. Added to this has been a certain dissatisfaction with existing methods of project appraisal.[41]

The public inquiry in Britain was originally established as an institutional mechanism to substitute for full Parliamentary debate on local laws, to consider 'Private Bills' designed to authorize certain specific actions, such as the enclosure of common agricultural land or the construction of water mains or gas works. To spare Parliament the burden of dealing with objections from affected parties, the public inquiry was established so that opposing points of view could be heard, assessed and passed on to the relevant government minister who had previously been authorized, by specific enabling legislation, to reach a decision in the national interest.[42]

Such a system worked reasonably well until recent times when the scale and complexity of projects had expanded so that many local siting decisions in fact had national policy underpinnings (such as the siting of the nation's nuclear fuels reprocessing plant at Windscale, subsequently renamed Sellafield). Further, there is usually some sort of direct involvement on the part of government so that any minister's claim to be an independent national voice over the local battle is treated with cynicism by opponents of the scheme. For example, a great deal of public disquiet surrounded the motorway construction programme of the 1960s and 1970s, where government ministers were both the promoters of individual projects and final arbiters on objections to them.

People are no longer prepared to accept the view that something is right just because a government minister says so. Nor do they accept that the combined opinion of government administrators and technical advisors can be allowed to pass unchallenged or be accepted without critical review. After all, have not the mistakes of ministers and their scientific advisors led to unnecessary environmental hazards or environmental despoilation? A major part of the groundswell of opinion in the 1960s and 1970s which came to be known as the environmental movement has been a growing disenchantment with technology. The implications of new technical processes once seen only in terms of monetary costs and returns are now to be evaluated in terms of *non-monetary costs*. For example, is the cost to the public of a fully armed nuclear installations police force a fair price to pay for nuclear generation in a country that prides itself on normally unarmed community policing?[43] Then there are the costs to our descendants. Can the safe management of growing quantities of nuclear waste be sustained over thousands of years? And what about the costs to other living things? Should the genetic diversity of an upland assemblage of Arctic flora be sacrificed in the interests of a water supply for expanding chemical plants nearby?[44] There are costs to the landscape. Should an oil platform construction yard be allowed to permanently scar one of the last remaining oases of unspoilt countryside?

The public inquiry in Britain has emerged, in the eyes of many, as a totally unsuitable vehicle to answer such questions. Hence there exists a degree of interest in EIA on the part of planners in Britain. There seems no other way. Benefit-cost analysis has been seen to fail. For example, in 1968 a special commission was appointed, with twenty-three research staff, to evaluate seventy-eight alternative sites for a third London Airport after a public outcry concerning an original proposal to expand an existing airfield at Stansted, Essex. A majority of the commission eventually found in favour of a site near Cublington in Buckinghamshire on the basis of a Benefit–Costs Analysis highly biased towards the rather nebulous concept of the value of businessmen's time saved through proximity to London.[45] Such a conclusion ignored the establishment-based power of the upper middle class of Buckinghamshire, and the government of the day favoured the minority recommendation of Foulness, a raw estuarial site in Essex. Eventually, this suggestion was also withdrawn. Currently Stansted is again the subject of evaluation as a possible third London Airport, the Benefit–Cost Analysis having been little more than an expensive fiasco.

The patent failure of existing techniques and institutions to deal with really big questions of project development encouraged interest in EIA in Britain. Nowhere was this more clearly recognized than amongst promoting agencies themselves. Major oil companies, such as British Petroleum, by now familiar with the NEPA requirements of the US, commissioned on their own initiative environmental impact assessments for their projected expansion in North Sea Oil development (at Sullom Voe, Shetland). The British National Coal Board prepared an EIS for its major new coalfield development in Leicestershire at Belvoir where significant environmental opposition was anticipated. In Scotland, the electricity authority foresaw similar difficulties with regard to a pumped-storage scheme of hydro-electricity generation immediately adjacent to the world famous 'bonnie banks of Loch Lomond' at Craigroyston. In short, promoting agencies, especially those in touch with the international scene, such as the energy authorities and those concerned with water, took the view that EIA would be advantageous. A notable exception to this is the Central Electricity Generating Board (CEGB) which has not produced an EIA for its proposed PWR at Sizewell. Indeed, the CEGB has resisted the use of EIA, primarily because it would have to evaluate all reasonable alternatives to their proposed actions (section 102, Ciii of NEPA).[46] Although time-consuming and expensive (although not in comparison to the contemplated investment or the costs of unforeseen delay), EIA did lead to better-designed and sited installations with long-term financial advantages. Above all, anything that could help avoid the morass of poor publicity and arbitrary political will that follow a British public inquiry would be worth it.

Not everybody was convinced. The Confederation of British Industry took the view that the wholesale import of the American system would introduce an undesirable rigidity in procedure, an undesirable element of pseudo-academic comment, and duplication of effort on the part of the new agency – whatever that might be – responsible for the EIA and the existing pollution control and planning authorities. In any case, without a significant expansion of public expenditure or bureaucratic control, few, if any, existing local authorities would tackle the task competently.

Nevertheless, government Royal Commissions and working parties in the tradition of Solesbury's 'legitimising' agencies (Chapter 8) continued to consider EIA as a real option for the improvement of environmental management in Britain.[47] The Dobry Committee,[48] set up in 1975 to examine possible paths of improvement with regard to general development planning, concluded that there was a case for EIA for major projects and this endorsement was quickly reinforced by the standing Royal Commission on Environmental Pollution (5th Report) the following year.

But the official view was by no means unanimous. The Stevens Committee, established also in 1976 to review planning procedures with regard to mineral workings, saw no need to apply the elaborate methodological superstructure of EIA.[49] The Leitch Committee,[50] however, further supported the concept in its report on the highly contentious issue of how to adequately allow public participation in the planning of motorways. The Labour Government (1974–1979) seemed in 1977 on the point of devising some mandatory requirement for systematic and comprehensive review of the social and environmental consequences of major developments. Then two things happened. World wide recession began to influence the pattern of development: the whole issue was defused by the absence of significant expansionary investment in Britain. Second, the Thatcher Government was elected with a programme ascribing top priority to the reduction of inflation by curtailing public expenditure and by deflation. This too stemmed the flow of controversial projects. At the same time, it introduced a new bias against additional bureaucracy and 'red tape'. Despite a notional interest on the part of the EEC in extending a system of EIA to all member states, in practice the issue of improved procedures of project appraisal now appears to be in abeyance in the UK.

9.7.2 Risk Assessment

The use of risk assessment in project appraisal tends to straddle conventional benefit-cost analysis (adding the risk dimension) and environmental impact assessment (evaluating alternative sites for safety reasons). Risk assessment techniques have evolved in response to the growth of potentially hazardous installations, such as nuclear power plants, liquid energy gas facilities and chemical works, but this is only one avenue of risk research. A more general approach, is the use of risk estimation and evaluation techniques by transnational corporations to ensure an acceptable rate of return for capital invested (11.2.2). The geographical spread of their operations enables them to spread unproductive expenditure throughout the whole organization and to maximize profits from a range of subsidiaries. Investment strategies incorporate political and environmental risk assessments within the decision-making process in order to filter out areas or countries which could be a 'bad' risk for investment purposes. The concept of risk in this case is that of *investment* risk rather than the *technical* risks associated with hazardous technologies. In fact the two types of risk cannot be disassociated when assessing the safety of hazardous installations. For example, the PWR accident at Three Mile Island (see 10.4.2) has had severe economic repercussions not only for the owner of the plant but other utilities operating similar reactors. This 'knock on' effect is inevitable as plants are closed for inspection and safety legislation is amended.[51]

The methodology of risk assessment has its roots in the natural hazard research developed by Gilbert White and the Chicago School of geographers since the 1940s.[52] This research focused upon the response by man to natural hazards such as floods, droughts, earthquakes and landslides. Perception of, and adjustment to, such geophysical events became the research paradigm. Geographers borrowed concepts and techniques from psychology to measure the perceived risks of a hazard. Of course, natural events are only hazards because man has decided to live in zones susceptible to them - earthquake zones, flood plains or arid lands, for example. A hazard - which can be defined as a potential threat to life and property - is often perceived as posing little danger to those at risk because of the infrequency of its occurrence. Resource managers, on the other hand, view the problem in probabilistic terms (see Table 9.2). From the statistical evidence available, estimates of the chances of

Table 9.2: The risk assessment process

Stages	Objectives	Methodology
Hazard Identification	Recognition of the existence of a natural or 'man-induced' hazard	Sensory perception; experience; scientific investigation
Risk Estimation	Measurement of the likelihood of hazard occurrence and its estimated consequences	Probabilistic risk assessment (PRA), delphi techniques; 'wise man' experience or intuitive approaches
Risk Evaluation	Judgement of the acceptability or unacceptability of the risk	Comparative risk analysis; risk-benefit analysis
Decision Making	Acceptance, rejection or modification of the risk	Regulation, enforcement, monitoring through hindsight review, analyses in previous stages

such an event happening can be made. Public policy initiatives can be taken to minimize the dangers of a hazard: for example, building regulations in earthquake areas, 'dry farming' techniques in drought areas and flood control measures in coastal or river flood plain zones.

This research paradigm has been applied to man-induced hazards such as pollution and potentially dangerous technologies.[53] Whereas levels of pollution can be measured and acceptability of risk is a matter of political judgement, estimation of the safety of hazardous installations is fraught with methodological problems. Unlike other hazards, these installations have existed for only a limited number of years and no adequate statistics are available upon which to make an accurate assessment of the risks involved.

The present 'state of the art' in determining the accident probabilities of such technologies is the use of fault-tree and event-tree analysis.[54] Fault trees are used to predict the expected failure of systems when actual experience of failure is low. For the technique to be applicable, the failure rate of the parts which make up the system must be known. Analysis begins by determining the undesired event which has to be assessed. With event-tree analysis, a reversal of this logic is applied. For example, one assumes that an initial event has occurred and the ramifications of this are traced through the system. From analysis of this nature the probabilities of 'events' occurring are calculated together with the consequences. In the case of nuclear power plants and liquid energy gas facilities, the spatial spread of released pollutants is measured by modelling possible weather conditions at different times of the year. The results are normally expressed as a negative log linear relationship between accident frequency and the number of estimated fatalities (Figure 9.5).

Comparative risk analysis and risk-benefit analysis are the main procedures adopted to assess acceptability or unacceptability of a risk (Table 9.2). To date, policy makers have tended to accept that benefits outweigh the low level of risk, drawing comparisons with the risks of everyday life. For example, Figure 9.5 shows that nuclear power offers less risk to the individual in the US than air crashes, fires, explosions or dam failures. Risk comparisons such as these

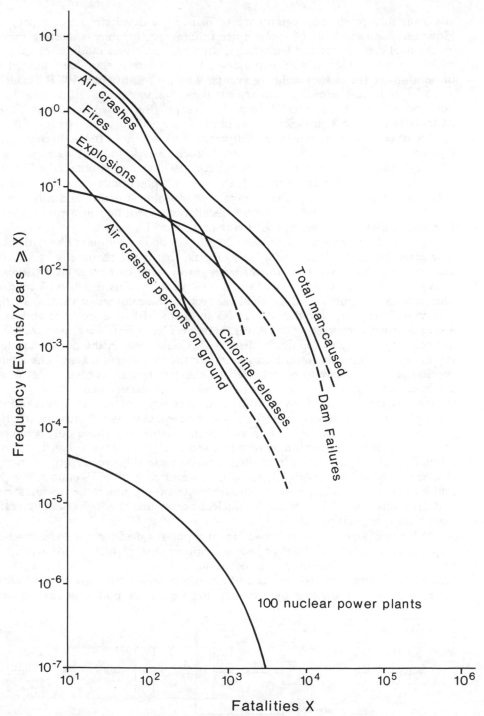

Figure 9.5 Frequency of Man-caused Events Involving Early Fatalities
Source: N.C. Rasmussen, 1981, The Application of Probabilistic Risk Assessment Techniques to Energy Technologies, *Annual Review of Energy,* 6

are invariably produced by industry to justify the development of a project. However, such methods of analysis are fraught with problems, casting doubt on their validity. Event and fault-tree analyses are relatively modern techniques which are being refined with experience. Unfortunately, they have tended to underestimate the risk of unlikely events. The probability of a PWR accident resulting in the release of radioactivity into the containment was estimated at 10^{-7} per reactor year, that is once in 10 million years.[55] But it happened – at Three Mile Island. In this instance, probabilities assigned to errors by operators, maintenance men and computer equipment were too low. It has been argued that other 'unlikely events' – sabotage, terrorist attack and war damage – are often excluded in event-tree analysis.[56] Yet in 1979 terrorists bombed a Texaco depot on Canvey Island in England, the site of a potentially hazardous petrochemical complex. Luckily, the storage tank was almost empty and this installation was not one of the 'high risk' installations identified in a probabilistic risk assessment carried out by the Health and Safety Executive.

Risk comparisons such as those in Figure 9.5 do not compare like with like. The assumptions are based on *individual* risk, that is the chances of an individual being killed based on *national* averages in some cases but on a distance decay function for nuclear power and LNG plants.[57] This is achieved by dividing the total number of individuals at risk by the number of deaths. In the case of nuclear power accidents or LNG spills, the risks are localized and have a spatial effect compared with conventional accidents which are more random in occurrence and geographically dispersed. Consequently, the population living close to potentially hazardous plants are the prime risk takers. Their perception of risk is likely to be coloured by the catastrophic consequences of an accident rather than the quoted low probability of its occurrence.

Ramsay argues that in the formulation of policy, analysis should take into account human preferences as well as scientific evaluations.[58] Consequently the 'maximum credible accident' of an energy installation may have only a remote chance of happening. But it may be perceived as a greater threat than a routine, more identifiable risk. People tend to overestimate the probability of events that are likely to be catastrophic in nature. Research in the US concerning the perceived risks of nuclear power compared with twenty-nine other technologies endorsed this view.[59] For example, nuclear power had the lowest fatality estimate but the highest perceived risk.

At the final stage of the risk assessment process, a decision has to be reached on what is an *acceptable* level of risk and appropriate regulations drawn up to ensure that these objectives can be attained (Table 9.2). Government has tended to accept the risk of hazardous technologies through the belief in 'objective-risk' assessments by industry and regulatory bodies at the expense

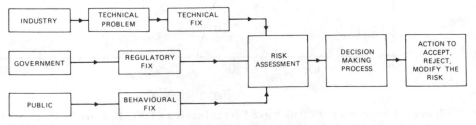

Figure 9.6 Project Appraisal of a Hazardous Technology

of 'perceived risk' evaluation by the general public. For example, during the project appraisal procedure of a hazardous technology industry, the risk generators seek technical fix solutions to any question of risk (Figure 9.6). Regulators (the guardians) seek objective, quantifiable, administrative fix solutions and the public (the risk takers) seek behavioural fix solutions.[60] The arbitrators or assessors of the project (government) favour institutional stability and view human value judgements as 'emotive' or 'irrational' in reaching a decision. This biased approach, which puts faith in 'the experts', is being challenged because[61]

it is not that technical conflict over these questions creates social mistrust in the authorities, but more the latter creates the former.

Hence, if public trust is breached, the credibility of agencies responsible for risk evaluation will be undermined so that the public will no longer believe in 'objective', low probability assessments. The classic example of this is Three Mile Island. Not only did an unlikely event occur, but the institutions responsible for protecting the public were in some disarray in attempting to tackle the problem.

The 'objective' method of assessing the risks of hazardous technologies is an institutional approach in which the guardians of the public at risk are bodies made up largely of personnel who have either worked in the industry to be regulated or in government laboratories/departments undertaking research on the industry. The 'capture' of agencies by hazardous industry specialists is commonplace and any problem becomes institutionalized with 'technical fix' or 'regulatory fix' solutions. In recent years this approach has been seriously questioned. 'Experts' are not always right and the 'uninformed' public are much better equipped to challenge statements from industry and regulatory agencies than in the past. This has been achieved by the increased sophistication of argument presented by public pressure groups which, in some cases, have recruited 'defectors' from the ranks of industry and regulatory bodies.

The process of risk assessment is dynamic, in that changes in each stage identified in Table 9.2 have ramifications for the subsequent stage. Risk assessment is a new technique applied to new technologies. As more experience of their operation is gained the techniques will be refined to produce 'better' decisions. It is to be hoped that past decisions will not lead to an unlikely catastrophic event; the institutional crisis which would follow would almost certainly have serious consequences for the future of hazardous industries.

Summary

Two kinds of techniques are available to the resource manager – general techniques facilitating the compilation of inventories and land use-classifications, and project assessment techniques that evaluate the merits of alternative courses of action. In terms of resource inventories, knowledge of the world's resources has been enhanced by the use of satellite imagery and computer information systems which provide policy makers with a more accurate data base than hitherto.

Resource inventories are, however, only the first stage in a process of project appraisal and policy review. The classification process, assessments of land capability/suitability, landscape evaluations, carrying capacity research and more specific project appraisal techniques are also tools of resource management which aid decision makers in policy formulation and project evaluation.

All these techniques attempt to rationalize choices in an objective manner in order to achieve a consensus view of any particular issue. But, as stressed in 9.2.1, problem recognition and issue identification is intrinsically tied up with the political process. Even when an issue reaches the political agenda, the quest for objectivity is coloured by the relative strengths of the vested interest groups which participate in policy formation or project assessment. In many ways, value-laden 'objective' assessments are made by the 'experts', who are usually government officials or developers. Public preferences running counter to 'expert' opinion are often portrayed by officialdom as misguided, irrational or emotive, thereby utilizing techniques as a mere justification for a 'business as usual' approach.

The US, with its pluralistic political culture, has been more responsive to the use of innovative methods of assessment than other countries which seek to protect their closed system of policy formulation from external interference. As a result, the application of these techniques in the US – with all their imperfections – has allowed a more rigorous review of policy or projects than in the pre-1970 era. All of which has been of benefit to the public interest.

10 Energy Resource Management

10.1.1 Introduction

The main aim of energy resource management is to ensure the long-term availability and security of energy supplies to achieve developmental goals. Although each nation state will pursue its own particular developmental strategy, the forces which shape policy are basically the same, albeit modified according to political cultures. Policy making is a political expression of the collective demands of society and hence is an attempt to reconcile conflicts which occur in the decision-making process. Clearly, major changes in policy direction are more likely to occur in pluralistic democracies with high political accountability and active interest group involvement than in élitist, repressive regimes.

Dramatic increases in the price of oil have caused governments to revise their energy strategies in the post-1973 era of high cost energy. The shift away from over reliance on OPEC oil has altered the geography of world energy production. The development of new oil provinces, the switch to alternative energy sources and a greater emphasis on national self-sufficiency have had important implications for resource management. The achievement of objectives outlined since 1974 has required the creation of a new institutional framework to carry out new policies. In some countries, departments of energy were created to coordinate inter-departmental activity. As new areas were opened up, the 'ground rules' with regard to licensing and environmental standards had to be established. Individual projects would be appraised according to the political system involved. In much of the Western world, this means that the developer has to apply for permits or licences, undertake an environmental impact assessment and have the proposal subjected to a public hearing or inquiry.

Energy resource management involves a complex web of factors. Increasingly, policy makers have tried to secure energy supplies not only at an acceptable but at a politically desirable price. There is a price to pay for security of supplies and minimal political disruption. In the 1960s and early 1970s the price included social and environmental costs as legislation to minimize 'hidden' costs borne by populations living near to polluting energy plants was enacted. Undoubtedly, energy decision making has become a much more 'open' process with inputs from all sectors of society. The transition to new energy forms has provoked much debate, which in itself is in the public interest.

The following sections will look at how management attempts to guarantee future energy supplies; the methods employed to assess technologies and minimize their environmental impact; and the process of decision making within institutional constraints.

10.2.1 Methods to Ensure Long-Term Availability of Energy

The key issue facing resource managers is one of guaranteeing supplies. Physical shortages, which may cause brown outs or black outs, are politically unacceptable. High prices due to forecasting errors or the need to buy more expensive energy from other sources are also contentious issues; they have led to consumer militancy in parts of the US.[1] Thus, energy forecasting lies at the heart of energy resource management in that prudent timing of investments will result in the efficient allocation of resources. Unfortunately, energy forecasting is fraught with difficulties. On the demand side, the forecaster is dealing with unpredictable variables: the relative availability and price of competing fuels, the impact of conservation measures and the performance of an economy which is experiencing major structural changes with the advent of high technology and its applications. On the supply side, the long lead times in commissioning new energy facilities because of construction delays and regulatory obligations have added to the problems of matching supply to demand.

Until the 1970s most forecasts were based largely on trend forecasting; that is, the prediction of future energy use from historical trends in demand. During the 'doom decade', energy consumption was predicted to increase exponentially in much the same way as the consumption of other non-renewable resources. In the 1950s and 1960s a strong correlation existed between the rate of economic and the rate of energy growth. Hence, the energy forecasting was closely tied to forecasts of economic growth. This habit was so firmly entrenched that conservation or reduction in energy use was often perceived as a threat to living standards, on the simple hypothesis that wealth = economic growth = energy growth.[2]

These methods of forecasting have been superseded by the more sophisticated modelling techniques of the 1970s in response to the changing energy situation. The need for more accurate models became apparent as Western societies moved into deeper economic recession and utilities found themselves with overcapacity (a function of optimistic forecasting in better economic times). This is understandable. Economic growth in the first twenty-five years after World War II was unprecedented and was fuelled by unparalleled energy growth. The consumer society demanded more comfort, more leisure and more mobility, resulting in the explosive growth of energy-using appliances – cars, TVs, kitchen gadgetry, etc. Central heating and refrigeration in homes added to material comforts. Indeed, the south-west USA has only witnessed rapid urban growth with the introduction of air-conditioning. The fuel industries responded to this demand by keeping energy cheap through economies of scale. The fall in the 'real' price of energy, coupled with high rates of economic growth, led to a continued rise in consumption.

The oil embargo heralded a new era. Energy was no longer cheap and a reverse cumulative effect has occurred, namely high energy prices, low rates of economic growth and depressed or reduced energy consumption. The idea that the energy–GDP (gross domestic product) linkage was an immutable economic law has now been challenged. Leach, one of the critics of this hypothesis, takes the example of the non-manufacturing sector of the UK economy to highlight his case. Non-manufacturing generates over 50% of the country's GDP but uses only 12% of its total energy.[3] Britain and other industrialized nations are going through a transitory stage as they move to a 'post-industrial' economy.

Increased automation, increased service employment and fewer energy-intensive industries will ultimately slow down the rate of energy growth. Indeed, during the 1970s, when economic growth was sluggish in many European countries, energy consumption continued to fall.[4]

Western governments have been slow to accept that we are living in a new economic era. This partly explains why forecasts of energy demand have been constantly downgraded on the realization that the spectacular growth of the 1960s is unlikely to be repeated.

Two distinct types of model have been developed in the 1970s in response to these changing economic circumstances: the econometric or aggregate model and the end-use model. In practice, most forecasting groups use a blend of both, breaking down and analysing demands by energy sectors.[5] Econometric forecasting is more commonly used by power companies and central government agencies. Econometric or aggregate models rely on relatively few sorts of data, but they can be statistically tested to correlate explanatory variables with demand, and can be easily modified if circumstances change quickly. An added advantage is that data exist over a long time series for each energy-use sector and can therefore be used to project demand forecasts for the future, subject to different scenarios of price levels, economic growth, technical improvements and the impact of conservation measures. The main disadvantage of econometric models is that they simplify the demand situation into too few categories.[6] Consequently, aggregate models can fail to predict changes in specific end-use categories. Furthermore, the 'saturation effect' is not easily monitored. For example, a regression analysis may show that increased wealth has a statistically proven relationship with greater energy use in the home; but at what level does the home become energy efficient, requiring no further increase in heat? Similarly, how many cars, central heating/cooling systems and electrical apparatuses does one require before saturation is reached?

End-use models are designed to detect saturation effects because they are dealing with energy uses, not aggregate variables. Demand is disaggregated by consuming sectors to analyse the final use of energy. In the Leach study this involved four hundred separate categories of demand by end use, type of fuel and appliances utilized. End-use modelling is therefore more complex, in that large amounts of data are required. The models are futuristic by simulating present end-use requirement to estimate need over certain time periods. Whereas aggregate models benefit from historical data, end-use models try to predict from current usage. Because of the level of disaggregation, mandatory conservation measures can be more readily incorporated into the end-use model; indeed, this is a distinctive advantage over trend or econometric models, which are based on historical data. Once projections of sub-sectors have been finalized, these categories are re-aggregated to obtain the amounts of delivered energy required. By working backwards through the energy system, it is then possible to assess which primary fuels could meet demand.

The end-use methodology is exceedingly popular with conservationists in that forecasts of energy demand tend to be significantly lower than other methodologies because of the inherent conservation element built into the model. The question of need is a recurrent theme in public hearings and projects have been abandoned by utilities because of a re-estimation of demand projections.[7]

Whilst demand forecasts have increasingly been under review in the 1970s and 1980s, the appropriate 'energy mix' to meet demand has also been in dispute. The industrialized countries' adoption of a Co-Co-Nuc policy, out-lined in Chapter 3, has been criticized by conservationists because of its em-phasis on coal and nuclear technologies. Leach implies in his research that there is a mismatch between supply and demand in the UK, in that the govern-ment is planning for more electricity generating capacity when low-grade heat is the form of energy required. Not surprisingly, he argues that conservation technologies will limit the need for both new coal mining and nuclear gener-ating capacity. The conventional wisdom concerning an 'energy gap' by 2000 to be met by large-scale capital intensive projects is being seriously reviewed by the protagonists themselves, especially in the US where pressure groups exert a strong influence on policy making. The soft energy pathways advocated by Lovins and others[8] in the mid-1970s are no longer considered to be radical proposals. Conservation and renewable energy resource technologies are given priority in developmental planning over the 'hard' technologies by many federal and state agencies in the Pacific north west and Pacific south west.[9]

10.2.2 Methods to Minimize Conflict

Whilst accurate energy forecasts enable resources to be developed in an orderly, efficient manner, the most contentious management issues arise when forecasts are adopted as policy and become converted into the construction of new energy installations. In the wake of OPEC action in the 1970s, the changing geography of energy supply can be attributed to a new commitment among Western nations to greater self-sufficiency in energy. This single policy objective has expanded the frontiers of energy development into areas previously immune from industrialization. Conflict is inevitable as the public in areas earmarked for development become concerned about changes in their way of life (social and economic dislocation) and the deterioration of water, air and land use quality (environmental dislocation). In many ways, conflict is created because new energy facilities sited in these regions are exporting fuel and power to other parts of the country, as part of national policy objectives, while the people living there are subjected to the unpleasant effects. Increasingly, this local-national friction manifests itself politically. The energy-rich states and prov-inces of western North America have been concerned about federal policy objectives with regard to energy. The Albertan government threatened Ottawa with production cut-backs because of a dispute over oil pricing and natural gas export policy. In the US, Montana, North Dakota and Wyoming have levied severance taxes on coal production to compensate the affected areas. In Louis-iana, Texas and Oklahoma these taxes account for $\frac{1}{3}$ of state taxes (Table 10.1). Similarly, in the UK, the Shetland Islands have charged the oil companies a disturbance allowance on the oil throughput from their Sullom Voe terminal. It is in the field of nuclear power, however, where possible major conflicts will occur in the future. Throughout the Western world, local or state governments have been establishing policies in favour of nuclear development: not only with regard to site selection of mines, mills, enrichment, fabrication, reactor and reprocessing plants, but also in the transportation of nuclear wastes and their disposal. The waste problem is the most difficult to solve. No one wants a waste depository as a neighbour. Yet it is an integral part of nuclear policy.

Table 10.1: State energy severance tax collections, 1979. *Source:* F. Calzonetti (with M. Eckert), 1981, Finding a place for energy: siting coal conversion facilities, Association of American Geographers, Resource Publications in Geography, p. 56

	Revenues ($1000)			Total State Revenues
	Oil/Gas	Coal	Total	(%)
Louisiana	500,666	–	500,666	22·3
Texas	1,021,017	–	1,021,017	17·8
Kentucky	404	153,613	154,017	7·4
Oklahoma	280,982	–	280,982	18·5
West Virginia	245	9,030	9,275	<1
New Mexico	138,511	–	138,511	16·4
Wyoming	308	30,278	30,586	8·9
Montana	8,208	42,049	50,257	12·5
Kansas	1,097	–	1,097	<1
North Dakota	13,533	11,970	25,503	7·9
Utah	6,175	–	6,175	<1

Ultimately, the main issues to be resolved concerning energy development will require politically acceptable solutions whereby satisfactory compromises can be reached among the interest groups involved. In an attempt to resolve conflict, institutional frameworks have been established, regulatory agencies created and guidelines formulated to protect the public from the risks and environmental impact of energy developments. Environmental Impact Assessment (EIA) is the most common technique employed to assess the likely impact of a major, proposed energy project. From its conception in 1969 in the US EIA has become part of project appraisal procedure in one form or another throughout Western industrialized countries (Chapter 9). The use of environmental impact statements (EIS) has promoted greater public participation and inter-agency coordination in planning the 'best' environmental routes for pipelines and transmission lines and minimizing environmental disruption by energy plants.

As EIA originated in the US, it is not surprising that developers have had to produce EISs for a significant number of projects which have been planned as part of America's quest for energy self-sufficiency. NEPA legislation of 1969 mandated that federal agencies, for example the Nuclear Regulatory Commission (then the Atomic Energy Commission), or private developers requiring federal assistance or authorization (leasing of federal lands for example) required an EIS. It is estimated that federal lands, including the Outer Continental Shelf, provide 12% of US production of oil and gas liquids, 28% of natural gas output and 8% of coal production; in addition, they contain much of US resources, with 37% of undiscovered oil resources, 43% of undiscovered natural gas and 40% of the remaining coal resources.[10]

In recent years risk-benefit analysis and comparative risk assessment have been used increasingly in the evaluation of coal, nuclear and liquid energy gas (LEG) technologies. In all cases, policy makers have to identify an acceptable level of risk within financial and political constraints. Much controversy has centred around the siting of nuclear and LEG installations because of the hazardous nature of these technologies. It was shown in the previous chapter that people are more willing to accept established, routine everyday risks over which they feel they have some control rather than the quoted low occurrence high consequence risks associated with relatively new technologies. Nevertheless, even the objective method of Probabilistic Risk Assessment (PRA) has been severely criticized as a means of justifying a nuclear or LEG project. Unlikely events have already occurred. They are just as likely to occur in the future. These 'incidents' have increased public concern and initiated more definitive evacuation procedures in the event of an accident.[11] Although this is a move towards risk minimization, it is difficult to know how people would react in a crisis if a worst-accident scenario was to become a reality. Once again, emergency preparedness schemes are likely to operate much more smoothly when people are familiar with the hazard and have previous experience of it rather than if it is a 'one-off' evacuation. This was highlighted during the Three Mile Island accident when local emergency agencies and the population within the vicinity of the plant reacted in a less positive manner to this crisis than to Hurricane Agnes, a natural hazard, seven years earlier.

All energy technologies carry some risk and some environmental impact. For each technology the level of acceptable risk and its maximum environmental impact must be determined by society. Institutions have been created to oversee the orderly development of energy resources and it is the interactions between developer, regulator and other interested parties that are the subject of the next section.

10.3.1 Decision-making and Institutional Structures

Throughout Part II of this book an underlying theme is the role that actors play in the policy-making process. Although this process is notoriously complex in the energy sector, five main types of actor can be discerned, in a hierarchy running from supranational bodies through to sub-national pressure groups.

At the highest level of the hierarchy, the *supranational* level, management problems are more difficult to resolve because of the need for international cooperation in tackling issues such as 'acid rain', marine pollution and nuclear proliferation. The International Atomic Energy Agency (IAEA) was created in 1956 to be the world's watchdog on the use or abuse of nuclear technology. Along with the Non-Proliferation Treaty (NPT), the IAEA tries to ensure that nuclear technologies are used and exported for peaceful, civilian power. But the present safeguards are far from perfect. Many newly industrialized countries have not signed the NPT, and the IAEA can only detect diversion of nuclear materials; it has no power to prevent their misuse. In terms of gaining access to a nation's facilities the inspectors are governed by the inspected. In Pakistan in 1980 the Agency had to negotiate for eight months to gain entry, during which time Pakistan had sufficient time to cover its tracks if it had been flouting the rules.[12] The question of proliferation is not only associated with relations between 'North' and 'South'. In 1984, much controversy focused upon contradictory statements from the Departments of Energy in the US and the UK in relation to plutonium exported from the UK for the US military programme. Was some of this plutonium reprocessed from the British civilian reactors?

At the *international* level, organizations have been formed to further political or economic objectives. To this extent, they are sub-groups within recognized political and economic blocs. The rise of OPEC was a direct attempt by host governments to achieve a better deal from the transnational corporations. Having successfully realized this objective, OECD members created their own agency, the International Energy Agency, in the wake of the 1973/74 crisis, to counter the power of OPEC. It must be remembered that OPEC is an *economic* organization; the politics of its membership vary considerably even among the Arab states. Nevertheless, the Organization of Arab Petroleum Exporting Countries (OAPEC) was formed in 1968 as a direct result of the Arab defeat at the hands of the Israelis in 1967. Although the constitution of OAPEC is economic in nature, the use of oil as a political weapon has caused much internal disagreement among the pro-US conservative régimes, such as Saudia Arabia and Kuwait, and the anti-US radicals such as Libya and Algeria. With the changing balance of power between the transnationals and the oil producers in the 1970s, especially on the downfall of the Shah of Iran, Western foreign policy has been geared to stabilizing a whole region which constantly threatens to have intra- and inter-state conflict.

The third major actor involved in shaping energy development is the *transnational* corporation. It was shown in Chapter 3 how, with Western government support, the oil majors dominated the oil market until the 1970s through the vertical integration of their operations, from the concessions to the ultimate distribution to the consumer. Loss of control over OPEC reserves and the rise of independent and state-owned oil corporations has re-defined the role of the majors. In the oil business, the transnationals have focused their attention on politically 'safe' areas – the North Sea, Alaska, Canada and, more recently, China. More significantly, however, the transnationals have diversified into other branches of energy, especially coal which is a sound economic and political investment for the future. For example, Gulf's takeover of Kemmerer Coal Company in 1981 added to the reserves of its other operation, Pittsburgh and Midway Coal, whilst Conoco and Occidental control the United States' second and third largest coal combines, Consolidated Coal and Island Creek Coal Co.[13]

The power of the transnational remains strong: Exxon and Royal Dutch/ Shell number one and two respectively in the *Fortune* list of the world's largest industrial corporations. The other five of the 'Seven Sisters' hold places in the top twelve.[14] Throughout the 1970s and 1980s they have been active in the merger market, as rising oil prices and rising profits increased their power at the expense of the vulnerable mining corporations caught in the reverse process of falling commodity prices and reduced profits (see the following chapter). But even the oil giants have experienced a decline in profits in the early 1980s as a result of global recession and falling OPEC prices. In April 1984, the largest merger in American history was approved when two of the 'Seven Sisters' – SOCAL and Gulf – joined forces. A few months earlier Texaco absorbed Getty Oil. These and other proposed mergers are seen as a move by the transnationals to increase their reserves and minimize their exploration expenditure at a time of depressed prices in the oil market.

The problems associated with these corporate strategies over the last ten years are that (a) oil companies are moving away from their traditional areas of expertise through diversification, and (b) they have concentrated on low political but high technical and economic risk areas for oil exploration and development. Even in these areas, state participation and high taxes have acted as a disincentive to exploration and development. Odell and Rosing maintain that a 'real' oil shortage could occur in the future, not because of any physical shortage of oil but through the lack of incentive for the transnationals to develop other virgin petroliferous areas, especially in the Third World.[15] Those countries have neither the technological expertise nor the capital to develop these resources. Furthermore, they are often ideologically opposed to the transnationals, which are viewed as the arm of imperialism. Odell and Rosing claim that an international agency, funded by OECD/OPEC, hiring out the transnationals to explore and develop many of these areas, would promote a more geographically dispersed pattern of oil activity. These institutional initiatives would ensure oil industry growth well into the next century, reactivate a languishing world economy and give a much needed breathing space for the perfection of alternative technologies for our energy future.

It is clear from this discussion that the transnational corporation exerts a strong influence on *national* energy policy objectives. Indeed, in the post-war period, security of oil supplies for Western consuming governments was a common objective of both government and oil corporation. Energy resource management was a routine operation as the price of oil dictated the viability of competing fuel sources. Management problems were more concerned with the accommodation of 'environmentalism' through the enactment of legislation to provide cleaner air and water and to improve or mitigate safety standards and environmental impacts. The 1973/74 oil crisis was to change the direction of national energy policies throughout the world through the influence of the international and transnational actors discussed above. The crises of 1973/74 and 1979 provide a classic example of stress management (see 9.2.1). Energy issues moved high up on the political agenda. Strategic decisions had to be taken advocating new policy directions. New institutions were created to ensure that these objectives were carried out.

As the world economy remains depressed in the early 1980s and the oil shortage has become a glut, politicians have become more concerned with inflation and unemployment than with energy, which has once again slipped out of sight. For example, the Reagan Administration has curtailed funds for energy conservation and renewable energy resources and has even toyed with the idea of abolishing the Department of Energy: a clear indication that the Government feels there is no longer a crisis.

The shaping of national energy policy is complex because of the pressure exerted upon the decision-making process by *transnationals*, *national* and *subnational* actors. As mentioned earlier, the corporate power of the transnational is evident through their oil and mining subsidiaries around the globe and they have considerable political muscle in the corridors of power. The energy industry lobby in all forms wields considerable political influence through associations which represent the fuel and power industries and the industrial combines which act as suppliers to the energy sector. This technocratic power is invariably stronger in state-socialist economies where nationalized energy companies operate as agents of government policy. It has been argued that Britain's poor performance in energy conservation is a reflection of the lack of lobbying power on the part of·small divergent conservation groups when faced with the political clout of the fuel and power industries.[16] To put this into perspective, the National Coal Board is the 38th-largest industrial corporation outside the US. The Central Electricity Generating Board (CEGB) is the 6th-largest company in the UK in terms of turnover and capital employed.[17] In countries such as Britain and France, government is an active agent in energy decision making because in many instances it acts in the capacity of policy maker, developer and regulator.

Ultimately, the direction of policy is a function of the political cultures of the nations involved (Chapter 8). O'Riordan[18] identifies three types:

1. the quasi-dictatorial democracy with low political accountability and low interest-group activism;
2. the representative democracy with medium political accountability and reasonable interest-group activity but moderate political influence;
3. the pluralistic democracy with high political accountability and high interest-group activity which exerts strong political influence.

Totalitarian régimes in the developing world would be an example of the first whilst examples two and three represent the approach of the UK and the US. In the latter country, energy issues can become political issues, pressure groups are active in the policy-making process and decisions can be disputed in the courts. In the UK interest groups are active but have little political influence; once a decision is reached through the public inquiry system, that decision is final. The losers in the debate cannot sue or appeal as in the US.

The internalized decision-making process in the US is thus more complex than elsewhere in the world, in that the site selection procedure has to incorporate the multitude of laws and regulations imposed by government at all levels. None the less, criticism has been levelled at procedures on both sides of the Atlantic because of the relative lateness of public participation in the decision-making process. For example, the public and the regulators are not party to original site selection and only react to the developers' proposals at various stages of project appraisal.[19]

Decision making, however, is much more 'open' than in the past. This is acknowledged by the companies themselves, which have mounted publicity campaigns to win over the public to accept their technologies and chosen sites.[20] Indeed, Dowall argues that local opposition to a particular proposal is based on a no-development option rather than on evaluation of energy alternatives; hence the developer must incorporate into the decision-making model the methods whereby local opposition can be ameliorated.[21] A knowledge of local politics (do they want the revenue spin-offs?) and the participation of local interests to hammer out the best way to mitigate adverse effects and compensate affected parties are seen as prerequisites to a successful outcome at a public hearing. In the UK, an EIS is not mandatory, but BP submitted one to the Shetland Council regarding their application for the oil terminal at Sullom Voe. By doing their 'homework', showing the public that they had worked out the options open to them, and agreeing to pay a disturbance allowance, BP secured approval to proceed with development of the site.[22]

In the US developers are faced with a web of regulation at the federal, state and county/municipal levels. It is estimated that a company wishing to construct a nuclear power plant will have to obtain fifty or more permits in addition to the obligatory licences for construction and operation.[23] The licensing process also involves a lengthy review procedure by the Nuclear Regulatory Commission and further public hearings. Although the federal government has no direct authority over non-nuclear siting, a certificate of need is required from the Federal Power Regulatory Commission before a new facility is constructed. The Department of the Interior is responsible for the management of federal lands, thereby indirectly influencing siting policy. Federal policy has been much more significant in the enactment of environmental legislation in the 1960s and 1970s. Some sites were effectively precluded from consideration. NEPA is the most vaunted piece of legislation because alternative sites had to be considered by the developer and the impact of the proposed development had to be documented for comment by agencies and the general public. In any case, before an EIS would be submitted, sites would be eliminated because of other federal legislation pertaining to air and water pollution, wildlife and historical preservation, and waste management. The Historic Preservation Act of 1966 and the Endangered Species Act of 1973 provide federal protection to both historic landmarks and threatened wildlife respectively. The Resource Conservation and Recovery Act of 1976 does not allow hazardous wastes to be disposed of in floodplains, wetlands, active fault zones or near residences, thereby jeopardizing the consideration of some sites because of the additional costs incurred in ultimate waste disposal. The most restrictive pieces of legislation for power plant operations have been the Clean Air Act and the Federal Water Pollution Control Act amendments of 1977. In both instances, the operator has to install the best available control technology (BACT) to minimize air and water pollution. Power plants constructed in the late 1970s invariably have cooling towers, deemed to be the best available technology to alleviate effluent pollution. The Clean Air Amendments of 1977 and 1979 have had major implications for the geography of coal production because of the implementation of BACT to coal-fired power plants. One study calculated that the Northern Great Plains would produce 388 million tons by 1990 using the 1972 standards but only 200 million tons under BACT.[24] The attraction of western coal to developers was its low sulphur content. Under the old standard, power plants did not require the installation of expensive desulphurization equipment and this coal could therefore be transported economically to regions further east. This cost advantage was negated on implementation of BACT standards which required scrubbers to be fitted to all plants regardless of the quality of coal.

Further regulations pertaining to air quality mitigate against development in parts of the American West, especially areas close to national parks or wilderness areas. Prevention of significant deterioration (PSD) regulations place areas into three classes:

Class i – where almost any air quality deterioration would be considered significant (national parks, for example);

Class ii – where moderate deterioration would be acceptable if appropriately planned;

Class iii – regions where additional pollution would be allowed up to the permitted level.

A developer must obtain a permit from the Environmental Protection Agency (EPA) by showing that its proposed plant will not exceed the PSD limits for the area in question.

Having secured the appropriate federal permits an operator must also comply with state and local legislation. In the aftermath of NEPA and the energy crisis of 1973/74, states produced their own legislation and created new institutions to act as watchdogs over utility forecasting and site selection. Individual states reacted in different ways to federal legislation. Some adopted 'little NEPA's', had strict siting laws and set environmental controls stricter than those proposed by national government, while others only complied with federal authority.[25] The question of need was previously the sole responsibility of Public Utility Commissions (PUCs) which also set rate structures. The Public Utilities Regulatory Policies Act (PURPA) of 1978 authorised the Federal Energy Regulation Commission to require utilities to buy power from small power producers (up to 80 MW) at the marginal cost of additional output. Furthermore, utility commissions began to review their approaches to rate making which had been under a great deal of criticism. Cornell, a top official in the Federal Communications Commission, had argued that traditional rate of return methods slowed down product innovation and locked utilities into obsolete technologies.[26] PURPA goes some way to answering these criticisms in that utilities will be compelled to buy power from small producers if they do not themselves participate in co-generation or small-scale renewable energy projects. Some PUCs are now proposing to reward utilities with higher rates of return by investing in renewable and conservation technologies. These changes have been implemented at varying degrees throughout the country. The General Accounting Office, reporting on electrical development in the south west, illustrates the strong influence which the Californian Energy Commission, in liaison with the Public Utility Commission, exerts upon policy compared with neighbouring Nevada and Arizona.[27] In California, utility forecasts have been challenged by the Energy Commission and utilities have reviewed proposed projects in the light of revised forecasts.

If a certificate of public necessity and convenience is granted, the developer may be restricted in site selection because of legislation that identifies areas not recommended for development. Table 10.2 gives the example of siting policy in North Dakota which excludes energy conversion and transmission facilities from park areas, prime farmland, irrigated land and habitats of rare species, while also discouraging development within city limits, woodlands and wetlands, floodplains and geologically unstable areas. At the local level, municipalities and counties can influence siting through local ordinances, land-use planning and taxation policies, although most criticism of development controls at this level originates from the solar lobby which argues that building codes are not geared to solar energy use. Frank claims that only a handful of the ten thousand municipal building codes throughout the country make provision for solar energy.[28]

Once a site has been chosen, permits have to be obtained from all the relevant agencies. At the state level, this usually involves the health, water resources, transportation and agriculture departments. Public hearings will be held as part of NEPA procedure, state agency procedure or during licensing of nuclear plants. If members of the public feel that they have been unjustly treated, they can resort to the courts. Indeed, common lawsuits have stopped or delayed many large projects. Calzonetti points out that utilities often overstate delays attributed to regulatory or legal procedures (Table 10.3). However, he was directing his comments more specifically to coal-fired plant developments. When compared with the reasons for delay in nuclear plant planning, regulatory lag or modifications, coupled with legal challenges, account for delay in 47% of the cases.

Table 10.2: North Dakota exclusion and avoidance areas. *Source:* North Dakota
Energy Conservation and Transmission Facility Siting Act, 1978, North
Dakota Century Code, in F. Calzonetti (with M. Eckert), 1981, Finding a
place for energy: siting coal conversion facilities, Association of American
Geographers, Resource Publications in Geography, p. 27

Exclusion Areas:
(a) Designated or registered national parks, national historic sites and landmarks,
     national historic districts, national monuments; national wilderness areas, national
     wildlife areas, national wild, scenic or recreational rivers, national wildlife refuges,
     and national grasslands.
(b) Designated or registered state parks, state forests; state forest management lands,
     state historic sites, state monuments, state historical markers, state archaeological
     sites, state grasslands, state wild, scenic, or recreational rivers, state game refuges,
     state game management areas, and state nature preserves.
(c) Country parks and recreational areas, municipal parks, parks owned or
     administered by other governmental subdivisions; hardwood draws, and enrolled
     woodlands.
(d) Areas critical to the lifestages of threatened or endangered animal or plant species.
(e) Areas where animal or plant species unique or rare to this state would be
     irreversibly damaged.
(f) Prime farm land and unique farm land, as defined by the Land Inventory and
     Monitoring Division of the Soil Conservation Service, United States Department
     of Agriculture.
(g) Irrigated land.

Avoidance Areas:
(a) Areas of historical, scenic, recreational, archaeological, or paleontological
     significance which are not designated as exclusion areas.
(b) Areas where surface drainage patterns and groundwater flow patterns will be
     adversely affected.
(c) Within the city limits of a city or the boundaries of a military installation.
(d) Areas within known floodplains as defined by the geographical boundaries of the
     100-year flood.
(e) Areas that are geologically unstable.
(f) Woodlands and wetlands.

Table 10.3: Causes of power plant delay. *Source:* F. Calzonetti (with M. Eckert),
1981, Finding a place for energy: siting coal conversion facilities,
Association of American Geographers, Resource Publications in
Geography, p. 29

Reasons cited	Percentage of Cases Coal-fired	Nuclear
Natural disaster	45·6	23·1
Financial or economic problems	24·6	16·1
Prolonged procedures to obtain necessary certificates from government agencies	12·2	25·2
Legal challenges	6·1	14·7
Equipment problems or late delivery of equipment	4·4	4·9
Re-scheduling of associated facility; e.g. transmission lines	3·5	1·4
Labour problems	1·8	3·5
Changes in regulatory requirement	0·9	7·0
Strikes	0·9	4·2

This overly complicated regulatory process has been criticized by Calzonetti for lack of coordination between regulatory agencies which review developments on a site by site, permit by permit basis.[29] He cites the case of Montana as an exception to this because developers are obliged to list the relationship of their proposed plant to the regional grid system in their siting evaluation. Undoubtedly, the Reagan Administration, which is committed to reducing 'red tape', will streamline regulatory procedures.

In contrast to this overregulation and active public involvement in facility siting in the US, the UK decision-making procedures are relatively straightforward, albeit due to a legacy of 19th century institutional frameworks. Public discussion on energy issues are relegated to the traditional local public inquiry which is only invoked at the Secretary of State's pleasure, or if the developer's application is rejected by the local planning authority. In essence, a project approved by local and regional planning authorities because it conforms to their local and structure plans need not be publicly appraised. Hence the application by British Nuclear Fuels Limited to construct a new Thermal Oxide Reprocessing Plant (THORP) at Windscale in 1976 was supported by the relevant planning authority and technically did not require to be scrutinized at a public inquiry. A project of this nature, which has international significance, could therefore be determined by local agencies. After much lobbying, the Secretary of State announced a public inquiry the following year. Four major public inquiries have been held in Britain to review energy developers' proposals: 1975 Selby (coal); 1977 Windscale (nuclear reprocessing); 1979–80 Belvoir (coal); 1983–85 Sizewell (PWR approval).

Developers in the UK are subjected to limited external constraints by comparison with their US counterparts. Health and safety considerations are monitored or licensed by the Health and Safety Executive and other government bodies whilst environmental questions lie in the domain of land-use planning. The developer is under no obligation to produce an EIS concerning proposed development. The regulators respond to his proposals. The public may be allowed to comment. But by then, the outcome is usually a foregone conclusion. Many commentators[30] have suggested improvements to the present unsatisfactory system, for example, in the form of an Energy Commission with investigatory powers which would in the first instance identify policy issues. The next step would be for this Commission or a sub-group to identify alternative sites for particular projects. In both these stages public input would be encouraged so that the local public inquiry would occur at the end of a lengthy review process and would direct its attention to site and specific details.

To date, the only Energy Commission created by UK government was created by Tony Benn in 1977 to advise him as Secretary of State on a national energy strategy. This body could hardly be classed as impartial. The majority of its membership was drawn from the fuel industries and the trade union movement. The Commission was disbanded in 1979 by the Thatcher government. No new institution has been introduced to replace it. The Planning Inquiry Commission has been on the statute books since the 1960s. It would go some way to meeting the above criticisms. But successive governments have been unwilling to use its powers, namely to review the proposal in principle, conduct research, and hold one or more site specific local inquiries.

10.4.1 Policy Making in Practice

The complex web of interactions between government, developers, regulators and public interest pressure groups is expressed in policy decisions. The US system is more complex than that of most countries because of the larger number of 'actors' involved in the process. As Congressional elections are held every two years, members are continually susceptible to pressure from the electorate. Policy measures invariably produce divisions which cut across party lines, because of alliances created along regional lines: for example, energy consuming states versus energy producing states. Consequently, President Carter, whose advisers had a strong environmental bias, saw his Energy Bill considerably diluted as it went through various House and Senate Committees. Similarly, President Reagan's pro-business approach has met with opposition over gas deregulation and the opening up of wilderness areas to energy development. Energy policy at federal level is therefore the result of a series of compromises between interested parties to arrive at satisfactory political solutions to energy problems. Copulas cites the example of John Dinsell, a Democrat representing Detroit, who chairs the House Commerce Sub-committee on Energy and Power. He was a major force pushing for continued gas regulation and was against stricter pollution control measures on automobiles because he feared it would affect the viability of the automobile industry in his constituency.[31]

The US compromise approach is evident throughout the energy management system, as shown in the previous section on regulation and legislation constraining development. This approach allows for greater public accountability in the decision-making process than in other Western countries. However, the system is far from perfect. A multiplicity of inputs into policy formulation and excessive, overlapping regulatory frameworks result in piecemeal energy planning. In the case of coal mining, the US has weaker health and safety legislation and poorer environmental policies toward land reclamation than has Europe.[32] Why? Because the private coal industry is aggressive toward government and the unions, whereas the public sector industries in Europe, with government support and strong unions, have enacted and enforced stronger legislation. This point has been brought home under the Reagan Administration. Budget cuts have caused reductions in the number of inspectors who enforce health and safety regulations. Overall, European miners enjoy better working conditions from more dangerous mines.[33]

Nuclear power, arguably the most controversial technology of its time, will be the subject of our next case studies, to show the response by power companies to its further implementation in view of government policies and public opposition in a period of sluggish electricity growth.

It has been argued that countries with élitist political cultures and limited public accountability have been pushing ahead with nuclear expansion programmes to a greater extent than more democratic régimes.[34] Whilst the totalitarian régimes in question were the USSR, South Korea and Pakistan, Western countries with strong state-public corporation links have also embarked upon ambitious nuclear programmes. Indeed, France is deemed to be the most authoritarian country in Europe after the USSR.[35] In a study of the French nuclear industry, Sweet draws comparisons with the UK industry and concludes that the French commitment to a nuclear future is unique to France in that a crash programme has been devised without facing the tests of economic feasibility or public accountability.[36] At a conference in 1977 Tony Benn, UK Energy Secretary, commented that the French minister responsible for the nuclear programme had said to him in 1975 that nuclear issues were political issues and France had 'gone nuclear'.[37] Having made the decision not only to embark on an ambitious scheme (half of its energy from nuclear power by the year 2000) but also to adopt PWRs under licence, the French have marshalled their resources and decision-making institutions to implement those objectives. With state support, le Commissariat à l'Energie Atomique (CEA), Electricité de France (EDF), Framatome and Novatome created a nuclear-industrial complex capable of carrying out the planning programme. The role of these decision-making institutions in nuclear policy making explains the difference between the UK and French programmes. Whereas the UKAEA had much internal debate concerning reactor choice, it resisted CEGB pressure to adopt the PWR. In France, the public corporation infighting ended in defeat for CEA and the successful acceptance of PWRs. Commensurate with the aims of building a large number of PWRs, Framatome – a public/private company – was designated as the sole producer of all nuclear components pertaining to the PWR (Novatome is involved in the construction of the FBR). In the UK, the weakness of the nuclear industry has been its inability to fulfil its targets because of construction difficulties. The various consortia in the 1960s only weakened the industrial base and it was not until 1973 that the National Nuclear Corporation (NNC) was established in an effort to move towards the French construction system.

Some of the difficulties associated with a 'crash' programme are only now being realized in France. Framatome took the risk of producing a standard PWR design to cut costs and minimize lead times in construction. However, EDF announced in October 1982 that twenty power stations would have to be closed for repairs over the next two years because of metal fragments discovered in the emergency cooling system.[38] If the US procedure of varying designs with each order had been adhered to, this problem of technical flaws would not have been common to all reactors and would therefore have caused less disruption to the overall programme when the plants were operational.

When compared to the US, the French and UK nuclear industries are similar in institutional structure. Similar commitments exist in both countries to an expansion of nuclear power,[39] and the strong public/private complex of industries are in a position to benefit from such policies. The main difference in the 1980s between the two countries is that Britain is well endowed with energy resources and has not gone as far down the nuclear pathway as the French, whose commitment is almost irreversible. Furthermore, in the UK, the government has hoped that the public will be persuaded to its view on nuclear expansion through the PWR inquiry and public relations campaigns (more money was spent on public relations for nuclear power than for research and development in renewable energy resource development in 1982).[40]

In the US, President Carter's low key approach to nuclear energy has been replaced by a more positive effort by President Reagan to revive the ailing nuclear industry. Nevertheless, neither Congress nor private industry has been persuaded of the merits of pumping finance into fast reactor or reprocessing programmes. In 1981 the Administration had hoped that the amount of electricity generated from nuclear power would increase from 12 to 25% by the early 1990s on the basis of plants under construction.[41] This was an optimistic forecast. In the following year, eighteen reactors were cancelled – the most in any one year – and nuclear power had reached its lowest ebb in terms of confidence, financial credibility and public acceptability. The plight of the industry is shown in Figure 10.1. No order has been placed since 1978 and by

Figure 10.1 The United States Reactor Market 1953–1983

December 1983, 82 reactors were licensed to operate (9 were not in commercial operation at that time), 55 were under construction, 12 were retired and 110 had been cancelled.[42] At the time of writing (May 1984) utilities, with their stock values plummeting, continue to cut their losses by abandoning or deferring projects.[43] Furthermore, two events made nuclear history during this period. Firstly, never before had a utility cancelled a plant when it was almost completed until Cincinnati Gas and Electric announced that its 97%-finished William H Zimmer plant was to be converted to coal. Perhaps the utility feared that problems could have occurred in gaining an operating licence. This in fact was the second piece of history – namely NRC's refusal to grant Commonwealth Edison an operating licence for its Byron facility because of inadequate quality controls during construction.

Utility executives see no improvement in the domestic reactor market in the foreseeable future. Many view nuclear power as a bad risk in both financial and political terms. Indeed, another Three Mile Island accident would almost certainly shelve the nuclear option for generations.

.4.2 Three Mile Island

The gravity of the nuclear industry's problems stems from the accident at Three Mile Island (TMI), Pennsylvania, on 28 March 1979. Already by 1979, sluggish electricity demand and high capital costs had caused utilities to revise their nuclear programmes. It has been shown in Figure 10.1 that the number of new orders began to dwindle by the mid-1970s and previous obligations were reneged. TMI accelerated this process. It showed that after nearly four decades of experience, the nuclear industry had still not perfected an adequate reactor design. A Group 1 accident – a complete meltdown with failure of the back-up safety systems – was calculated a near impossibility: one chance in 200 million reactor years. TMI came within one hour of this unlikely event. The chaotic state of affairs in the wake of the accident did not inspire confidence in the operator of the plant or the regulatory agency (NRC). Conflicting reports on the extent of the accident, media over-reaction and a lack of coordination concerning evacuation plans left the public in a state of confusion.[44] This crisis in institutional confidence has baulked the operator – Metropolitan Edison – from re-starting Unit 1 on TMI, which was down for repairs when difficulties began with Unit 2.

It was not until mid-1982 that the full extent of damage to Unit 2 was ascertained, when a specially designed camera was used to investigate the core of the reactor. Around 90% of 37,000 fuel rods were damaged when temperatures had reached 5,000 degrees fahrenheit in the core.[45] This news meant that the clean up will take five years, longer than expected, and will cost 1 billion dollars. General Public Utilities Corporation (GPU), the parent company operating the plant, sued the reactor suppliers and builders Babcock & Wilcox (B&W) for this amount, plus billions in economic losses because of the cost of alternative supplies of power. But this dispute was eventually settled out of court to avoid any further embarrassment to the US nuclear industry.

The history of events leading up to the accident is revealing. Toledo Edison's Davis-Besse station had encountered similar problems eighteen months earlier and investigators for NRC and Babcock & Wilcox had reported the seriousness of the incidents to their superiors but no action was taken.[46] In short, it was proposed that new operating guidelines should be sent to utilities with B&W reactors instructing them not to shut off the Emergency Core Cooling System (ECCS) unless the pressuriser level was increasing and the primary pressure was 1600 pounds per square inch and rising.

When the same fault manifested itself at TMI 2, not only did it take the operators several hours to realize what had happened but their difficulties were compounded by the shut off during routine maintenance a few days earlier of valves carrying water from the emergency feedwater system to the steam generators. What started as a minor fault – clogging of the main feedwater pipes – almost ended in a melt down. The closure of these valves meant that the emergency feedwater system could not cool the steam generators which began to boil dry. This in turn led to an increase in coolant pressure and temperature and the reactor was scrammed. However, the operators were unwilling to activate the ECCS fearing that an over cooling accident might occur!

Slowly the operators began to realize what had happened but much of the damage had already been done. The zirconium alloy cladding around the fuel rods reacted with the steam releasing hydrogen and gaseous fission products.

NRC experts disagreed about the chance of an explosion so evacuation plans were put into force. Eventually the hydrogen was bled out of the coolant and burnt off. Disaster was averted and radiation emitted from the crippled reactor was within the prescribed limits.

This is the context within which GPU had initiated their civil action. However, the Kemeny Commission was critical not only of the suppliers and operators of the reactor but also of the NRC for its inability to resolve small safety problems before they snowballed into major ones. To redeem itself, NRC ordered a moratorium on licensing until August 1980 while it undertook safety reviews and revised standards. All operating plants were studied according to performance (a report card) on matters such as equipment, operating procedures, radiation and environmental protection, emergency planning and fire/security protection in order to focus inspections on plants with below average performance.

Since the accident all operators have taken extra training and federal licensing has been toughened. NRC has required all plants to install safety vents to release hydrogen accumulations and to put in instruments to measure water levels in reactors to prevent further TMI 2 type accidents. These are only the more urgent of over three hundred actions deemed necessary by the agency in response to TMI 2.[47] The industry has also responded to the accident by forming the Institute for Nuclear Power Operations (INPO) to upgrade training of operators; and plant operators must belong to INPO to qualify for insurance to help pay for substitute power if a reactor is put out of action for a long period. Furthermore, the Electric Power Research Institute has created a Nuclear Safety Analysis Center to examine power plant incidents to review design changes to minimize safety problems.[48]

Despite these improvements, TMI 2 is fresh in the memory of public and industry alike. High capital costs and sluggish electricity demand was undermining the need for new nuclear plant; TMI 2 has eroded financial and public confidence in the industry. No new order will be forthcoming until this confidence can be restored.

10.4.3 The Sizewell Public Inquiry

In view of the demise of the nuclear industry in the US, it is ironical that a public inquiry is being held in the UK to scrutinize the Central Electricity Generating Board's (CEGB) proposal to construct a PWR at Sizewell as the first of a series of PWRs to be built. This nationalized utility has always flirted with the light water reactor option, preferring the boiling water reactor (BWR) to the advanced gas cooled reactor (AGR) in 1964 when a successor to the Magnox design was being reviewed, and outwardly advocating a 'crash' programme of PWRs in 1973. In the event, nuclear industry 'infighting' resulted in victory for the Atomic Energy Authority (AEA) and the AGR despite its technical difficulties, cost overruns and an average of an eleven year delay for the 3 plants recently commissioned (see Table 10.4 for a summary of plants commissioned and Figure 10.2 for their locations).

Indecision over reactor choice has been a feature of nuclear power decision making in the 1970s and 1980s. The Labour Government of 1974 opted for the Steam Generating Heavy Water Reactor (SGHWR) - a modified CANDU

Table 10.4: Public supply nuclear power stations in Britain. *Source:* After Central Office of Information, 1981, Nuclear energy in Britain, HMSO

Station	Type	Date first reactor on power	Declared net capability (*MW*)	
In service:				
Berkeley (CEGB)	Magnox	1962	276	
Bradwell (CEGB)	Magnox	1962	245	
Hunterston A (SSEB)	Magnox	1964	300	
Hinkley Point A (CEGB)	Magnox	1965	430	
Trawsfynydd (CEGB)	Magnox	1965	390	
Dungeness A (CEGB)	Magnox	1965	410	
Sizewell A (CEGB)	Magnox	1966	420	
Oldbury (CEGB)	Magnox	1967	416	
Wylfa (CEGB)	Magnox	1971	840	
Hinkley Point B (CEGB)	AGR	1976	1000*	
Hunterston B (SSEB)	AGR	1976	1000*	
Dungeness B (CEGB)	AGR	1983	1200	
Heysham 1 (CEGB)	AGR	1983	1320	
Hartlepool (CEGB)	AGR	1983	1320	Installed MW Capacity
Under construction:				
Heysham 2 (CEGB)	AGR	1987	1320	
Torness (SSEB)	AGR	late 1980s	1320	

* Interim ratings.

design – only to abandon it in 1978. The incoming Conservative Government in 1979 endorsed the CEGB's commitment to build a new nuclear power station every year in the decade from 1982 and gave the green light to PWRs subject to a full public inquiry. By the time the inquiry began (January 1983), a Parliamentary Select Committee had brought the subject of reactor choice back into the debate by advocating a further assessment of the CANDU reactor because of its excellent performance record compared with other reactor systems.[49] Furthermore, during the inquiry a General Election was held in the summer of 1983 and both opposition parties declared that they would abandon the PWR option if brought to power.

The re-election of the Thatcher administration must have been welcomed by the CEGB because under a Conservative government its plans have a much greater chance of coming to fruition. Indeed, since 1979 the incumbent government has made political appointments[50] to ensure that the nuclear industry continues to be at the forefront of Britain's energy strategy at the expense of the other two 'official' future scenarios – coal and conservation. As was shown in 10.4.1, the public inquiry is one of the few vehicles for public participation, but the Government saw this as an inconvenience, delaying the implementation of the nuclear programme. Through 'leaked' Cabinet documents it was revealed that a wide-ranging inquiry would be undesirable to the Government because it would delay the schedule for constructing the first PWR. Perhaps because of this 'leak', the Government overreacted and the Secretary of State announced in 1981 that the inquiry would cover a broad range of subjects to take into

Operated by the UKAEA ●
"   "   " BNF ▲
"   "   " CEGB/ ■
            SSEB
under construction □
Proposed Greenfield Site ◪
for a PWR

N

Dounreay

Torness

Hunterston (A & B)

Druridge Bay

Chapelcross

Hartlepool

Sellafield &
Calder Hall

Heysham (2) □ ■ Heysham (1)

Springfields

Risley

Wylfa

Capenhurst

Trawsfynydd

Sizewell A

Culham
Harwell

Berkeley

Bradwell

Oldbury

Hinkley Point (A & B)

Dungeness (A & B)

Winfrith

0   km   100

Figure 10.2 Nuclear Establishments in Britain

account the need for and economic justification of the project in addition to safety, environmental and planning issues. By April 1984, the inquiry had been in session for over two hundred days with the prospect of it continuing until the following year. As the inspector's report would be submitted in 1985, it is unlikely that the CEGB would be able to commence construction in 1986 even if the recommendations were positive. The remainder of this section will concentrate upon the key issues which have been raised at the inquiry.

As the CEGB believes that it can design a British PWR to satisfy the requirements of the Nuclear Installations Inspectorate (NII) much of the thrust of its case has been based on the economic and strategic arguments for adding a PWR to the generating system.

The strategic argument focuses on the long-term need for this plant and others to replace obsolete capacity, whilst at the same time it will enable the CEGB to diversify its fuel supplies away from UK coal which makes up 80% of its existing fuel needs. Both these strategies have come under attack during the inquiry and the CEGB have conceded that Sizewell B is not required purely on capacity grounds but as the foundation for further plant ordering if and when needed. The extent of the downgrading of CEGB forecasts during the early 1980s has astounded even nuclear opposition groups. For example, in 1979/80 the Board estimated that maximum demand would grow from 44·2 GW to 60·6 GW in 2000; one year later, 53·7 GW was estimated for 2000 and in 1982 the figure was lowered further to 46·9 GW.[51] In a remarkably short period of time, the equivalent of ten, 1300 MW power stations have been deemed unnecessary for future ordering – almost the level quoted in 1979, namely one nuclear power station per annum for a decade.

The other strategic argument, the need to diversify away from domestic coal, has strong political overtones, because of the risk of security of supplies in the event of a miners' strike. Nevertheless, this high dependence upon coal is merely a function of the unfulfilled realization of CEGB planning programmes. In essence, the ordering of AGRs and oil-fired plant in the late 1960s should have given the Board diversity of supplies. Instead, the AGRs were inordinately delayed and newly commissioned oil plants became economically obsolete in the wake of oil price increases in the post-1973 era. Increased coal burn has been necessary to fill this vacuum.

The case for diversification is weak in that the CEGB see diversification solely in terms of nuclear development. With no fossil fuelled plants envisaged in the foreseeable future and renewable technologies making little impact, the UK will become *overdependent* on nuclear-generated electricity by the turn of the century. For example, with nuclear plant under construction and the Department of Energy's estimate of new orders, it is forecast that nuclear power will provide 41% and 66% of UK electricity in 2000 and 2010 respectively on the *least* optimistic estimate of demand.[52]

The relative weakness of the strategic argument meant that much of the time spent at the inquiry in 1983 was devoted to the scrutiny of the CEGB's economic case for ordering a PWR. Clearly, the Board feels that such investment will reduce the 'net effective costs' within the overall electricity system. However, the economic arguments are complex and controversial. The controversy was fuelled by the publication of two reports by the House of Commons Select Committee on Energy (HCSCE) and the Monopolies Commission prior to the public inquiry. Both reports were particularly critical of the investment appraisal methodology adopted by the CEGB. The Monopolies Commission thought that it was 'seriously defective and liable to mislead'.[53] The HCSCE claimed that

'this distorts the effect of inflation on capital costs, thus rendering the resultant figures highly misleading as a guide to past investment decisions and entirely useless for appraising future ones.'[54]

In short, historic cost accounting assumes that capital costs are paid for at the time of construction and fuel costs at current prices. On those assumptions, nuclear plant will tend to benefit over fossil-fuel because capital costs are a higher proportion of total costs. Since this criticism, the Board have moved to current cost accounting and have conceded that coal generated electricity has been cheaper than nuclear generated power. Why should the future be different?

The CEGB maintains that Sizewell B can be built to schedule (90 months) and to cost (£1147 million). To justify the cost of construction, it is assumed that the plant will operate at an average load factor of 64%. All of these predictions have been criticized as over-optimistic in view of the worldwide performance record of PWRs. For example, the annual average load factor of all PWRs (and Westinghouse 3 and 4 loop reactors) is below 60%;[55] the average construction time for US 4 loop Westinghouse PWRs is 102 months;[56] cost overruns are notorious in UK nuclear construction programmes. The CEGB, on the other hand, finds the cause of delay in US financial, legal and labour problems and argue that they can meet stricter schedules more akin to the French programme, with an average construction time of 69 months. Furthermore, the Board have assumed greater control over project management, reflected in the success of current construction projects at Drax B (coal) and Heysham II (AGR). These projects, however, have the benefit of years of experience (some of them unfortunate!) and the CEGB is at the top of the learning curve with schemes of this nature. The PWR is a different matter: the CEGB has no track record with this type of design. Unresolved safety problems identified by the NII can only add to costs and delay the construction schedule.

In the debate over net effective costs, the viability of the PWR is largely dependent upon the relative costs of its main competitor – coal-fired plant. As the CEGB prefers PWRs on strategic grounds, it has always opted for worst case scenarios in coal costs and best case scenarios in nuclear costs. This is implied in both the HCSCE and Monopolies Commission reports[57] and has been further developed by others such as the Town and Country Planning Association[58] and Jeffrey.[59] The gist of the argument is that coal costs are fully represented in the 'net effective costs' exercise but nuclear costs are only partly accounted for because nuclear plants incur substantial costs long after they have produced their electricity. The costs at the back-end of the fuel cycle – reprocessing, decommissioning and waste management costs – are subject to a high degree of uncertainty, and Jeffrey argues that the CEGB grossly underestimates these costs in their economic analysis.

A final point in the coal versus nuclear costs debate relates to the indirect costs and benefits of the PWR option. If world coal and oil prices do not increase at levels assumed by the CEGB, and Sizewell B and other PWRs *are* constructed, the employment implications for the mining and associated industries could be devastating. Sizewell B alone could lead to 8000 job losses and as large a programme as envisaged in 1979 could increase this figure to 70,000.[60] If PWR generated electricity were to prove cheaper, that would boost economic growth and consumer expenditure, but whether this could redress job losses and the social costs of pit closures is debatable. Furthermore, the preference for PWRs over AGRs will hardly benefit the nuclear industry in the UK in the early years of its development as key components and architect-engineering expertise will be imported.

By early 1984 the focus of the inquiry had moved from economic arguments to the safety of PWRs. The safety issue has always figured prominently in

PWR evaluation and was probably the crucial factor behind the Labour government's choice of the aborted SGHWR in 1974 (at this time Sir Alan Cottrell, former Chief Scientist to the Government, had voiced criticism of the danger of crack propagation in the steel pressure vessel). Since then, an AEA report (whose main author is now Chairman of the CEGB) concluded that a PWR could be licensed to British safety standards. It is difficult to know what this means in practice. Safety principles are devised on the ALARA rule, that is, radiological discharges should be as low as reasonably achievable. NII operate under the 'as far as reasonably practicable' dictum in relation to the prevention or minimization of accidents.

The weakness of this philosophy has been exposed by 'events' at the Windscale reprocessing plant in November 1983, when the inquiry was in session. At the Windscale (now Sellafield) plant, an operator error led to radioactive sludge being pumped out to sea. Although the Department of Environment and NII have severely criticised British Nuclear Fuels Ltd.,[61] the inspectorate did not have sufficient evidence to prosecute the company, even though 15 miles of beach was closed to the public because of the contamination.

The role of the NII as an independent watchdog has been challenged at the inquiry; indeed Friends of the Earth sought an adjournment of the inquiry when it became clear that the inspectorate would not have completed its final safety report until after the inquiry was over. Although this state of affairs is unfortunate, the dialogue between the CEGB and NII is continuous and cannot be conveniently slotted into an inquiry schedule. Nevertheless, the work of the NII is largely secretive in nature and the Sizewell safety assessment will be the first time that such a detailed report will have been published. Even then, the dialogue between applicant and licensor remains closed and circular, with little active participation by other bodies. The inspector drew attention to this by criticizing the NII for failing to inform him of the extent of their reservations on the design.

It is clear that many safety issues have still to be resolved to the satisfaction of the NII. Moreover, 'independent' scientific assessments of the CEGB's safety claims show them to be highly optimistic in terms of risk assessment. The Board believe that they can design and operate reactors that are completely safe. In fact, their Chairman implies that the extra £100 million being spent on design safeguards and the reduction of occupational doses of radiation to operators are 'licensing for unlikely events'.[62] History has shown that unlikely events have occurred; incredible but possible accidents could happen in the future. On paper, the Sizewell PWR may be much safer than its US counterpart but its more complex system leaves event-free analysis open to even greater fallibility. In practice, the safety of a plant is dependent upon a multitude of variables – design modifications, the quality of construction work, maintenance and operational efficiency. NII are concerned that the Board have not considered the likelihood of earthquakes or aircraft crashes in their safety assessment (Sizewell A is a turning point for pilots!).[63] Sabotage or terrorist attacks are other, unlikely but possible events which should be assessed in view of the strategic importance of nuclear plants.[64]

In view of these uncertainties over nuclear safety in the UK, it is interesting to draw comparisons between the Nuclear Regulatory Commission, which has the greatest experience of PWR licensing, and that of NII in terms of safety philosophy. In the US, siting and safety goals have been under review in recent years and regulations will be produced shortly to minimize the residual risks of nuclear generation through a more 'remote' siting policy and more stringent safety standards. The NII continues to guide licencees with a 'relaxed' siting policy introduced in 1968.[65] Overall, the differences in siting and safety philosophy can be summarized as follows:

(1) Utilities in the US are guided by the design objective that the frequency of occurrence of a large uncontrolled release of radioactivity is less than 10^{-5} per reactor year; in the UK, the design target is 10^{-7}.

(2) The US has planned to reduce the consequences of Class 9 accidents (those deemed incredible and beyond the design basis); in the UK little attention is paid to accidents outside the 'maximum credible' category. This is reflected in the differences in the size of emergency planning zones. In the US, a 10-mile evacuation zone and a 50-mile food ingestion zone were incorporated into NRC regulations in 1981; in the UK a 2- to 3-kilometre evacuation zone is in force.

(3) NRC are assigning low priority to the use of probabilistic risk assessment (PRA) in licensing decisions during this review period; the CEGB continue to justify PWR safety through the use of PRA.

The safety issues are intrinsically tied up with economic questions. In the US, question marks over PWR safety have made nuclear power a poor financial risk. It must be remembered that since 1982 US utilities have had to bear the full costs of any nuclear accidents (the government indemnity section of the Price-Anderson Act was phased out on the licensing of the 80th power plant); in the UK, the financial liability of the CEGB in an accident is miniscule (£5 million), a legacy from the 1960s. Perhaps this explains the greater complacency in the UK towards using siting as a safety measure. The CEGB, by opting for the PWR because of its internationally proven design, leaves itself open to the criticism that if anything were to go wrong with a similar design anywhere else in the world, costs would be incurred during inspection or backfitting. Indeed, Evans and Hope maintain that a $7\frac{1}{2}\%$ surcharge on capital costs should be added to cover the possibility of such an event.[66]

At the time of writing (May 1984), the safety debate at Sizewell was expected to continue through the summer. The inspector had invited the South of Scotland Electricity Board (SSEB) to give evidence at the inquiry because it is known to favour the AGR over the PWR design. The CEGB have also commenced work on an AGR proposal for the Sizewell site. Perhaps the tide is turning against PWR approval?

Summary

The nuclear case studies outlined in the previous section highlight the complexity of energy resource management. An energy decision is the outcome of a process of review involving a multiplicity of viewpoints. Compromise is the order of the day. Nevertheless, compromise decision making occurs to different degrees according to the political culture of the society involved. It has been shown that the US, with its loose political system, a Freedom of Information

Act, strong environmental legislation and politically active pressure groups, has produced a unique decision-making environment. Few major energy decisions in the US are clear cut. By contrast, the more élitist structures of Britain and France have produced predictable decisions. Government policy is enacted by nationalized fuel industries tied into an established industrial complex that wields a degree of political influence. National policy goals are paramount to local interests and public inquiries are used to persuade public opinion on the merits of government policy. The US system, despite its faults, is still the model towards which countries must strive if they are to secure true public participation.

11 Commodity Management, With Specific Reference to Mineral Resource Management

11.1.1 Introduction

In the previous chapter, much of the discussion on energy resource management centred upon interaction between developers and regulators, and case studies from the UK and North America were used to illustrate the process of policy making. Clearly, mineral companies are subject to constraints on their operations just like their energy counterparts. However, the emphasis here will be upon the *international* nature of the management problem. The transnational corporations were the main agents of mineral development until the 1960s when host governments challenged their domination either by expropriating assets or by demanding a greater share in their own mineral wealth. This conflict will constitute a major theme of this chapter. Issues pertaining to soft commodity management will be discussed in the context of general commodity agreements pertaining to both hard and soft commodities are highlighted in sections on the role of international institutions, UNCTAD and the EEC/ACP Lomé Agreements.

11.2.1 Decision Making and Institutional Structures

Figure 11.1 shows the flow of inventory stocks throughout the mineral supply system. The activation of the system to determine the nature of flow depends on the relative strength of participating institutions which influence the decision-making process. The dominant institutions – nation states, transnationals, producer and consumer associations – play significant roles as owners, regulators and managers of the mineral supply system.

In Figure 11.1, three decision-making points are identified. At Point C, the consumer institution is most influential. As society has become increasingly affluent, it has demanded a wide range of consumer goods, while at the same time becoming discriminatory against particular products containing minerals that could endanger health (mercury and asbestos for example). The consumer's changing needs should be met by the manufacturer, who responds to changes in the market place. In many ways, however, it is impossible to decipher the interdependences within the system. Consumer developments have influenced manufacturing developments, but the transnationals are tightly integrated corporations who influence product choice by their R. & D. and marketing strategies. Hence, corporations have a rolling programme involving substitution and conservation of materials, particularly strategic minerals, in relation to their relative costs and scarcity.

At Stage B in the mineral supply system the design of the final product is crucial in determining whether it can be recycled or disposed of. Technically, all minerals in finished goods can be recycled, but those with high entropy

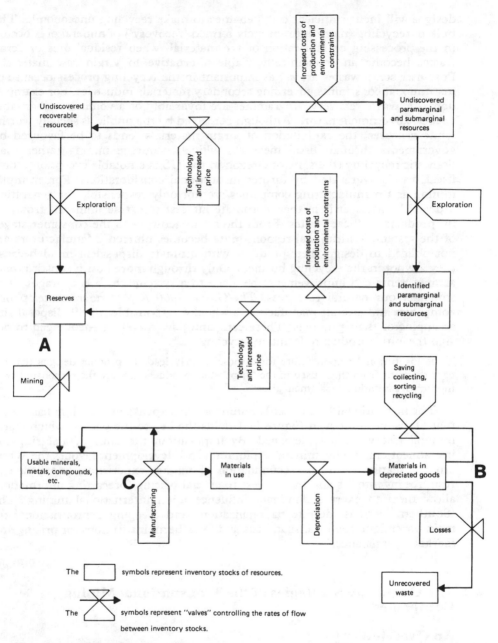

Figure 11.1 The mineral supply system
Source: *The Global 2000 Report*, 1982, Penguin Books

designs will incur sufficient cost penalties to make recycling uneconomic. The bulk of recycling (more appropriately termed 'recovery') of mineral ores occurs in the processing or fabrication of the material, when residual ores or scrap wastes become an economically viable alternative to virgin raw materials. Post-user scrap wastes are *not* as important in the recycling process because of institutional constraints governing secondary materials industries. For example, domestic waste recovery programmes are invariably of a voluntary, charitable or local government nature. Although perceived by the public as socially worthwhile ventures, the exploitation of virgin materials tends to be favoured by governments through fiscal measures which encourage mining rather than domestic recycling (the state of Oregon in the US is a notable exception). This fiscal bias is aggravated by further institutional considerations. For example, mining and manufacturing companies are not only responsible for generating industrial wastes, it is in their corporate interest to extract minerals from the by-products of these wastes. From the manufacturing to the consumer stages of the system, institutional responsibility becomes blurred. Manufacturers are not obliged to design their products with ultimate disposal in mind because they are not in the recycling business. Only through more positive institutional arrangements can improvements be made to a system which encourages us to squander our natural resources. *The Global 2000 Report* refers to telephone companies and aircraft manufacturers who are responsible for the disposal and scrapping of their products. These companies are therefore encouraged to design the initial product to facilitate recycling.

Thus institutional responsibility for disposal clearly leads to product designs that are very different from those used in the 'disposable' products that are the responsibility of municipal sanitation departments.[1]

The institutional bias towards mining at the expense of recycling has meant that Decision Point A in Figure 11.1 holds the key to the pace at which world mineral reserves are replenished. By implication, the onus of assessing the investment climate for mineral exploration and development favours the Western transnationals. Their accumulation of market experience, knowledge of resource inventories and their access to crucial pricing/forecasting information, allow them to exert a dominant influence upon international mining. The 'Southern' nations, despite nationalizations and creeping expropriations, remain dependent upon transnationals and 'Northern' institutions for pricing and marketing assistance.[2]

11.2.2 The Corporate Strategies of the Transnational Mining Companies

An Overview

The world mining industry has been transformed since the one-man-prospector days of the Klondike/Yukon Gold Rush. It is now dominated by corporate entities such as the multinationals listed in Table 11.1. These international companies started as small, single stage firms in the late 19th and early 20th centuries to exploit particular discoveries. For example, the Anaconda Copper Company was launched in 1882 on the discovery of giant copper deposits in a

Table 11.1: The top twenty multinational non fuel mineral companies in 1978 (billion dollar sales). *Source:* The 500 largest industrials, *Fortune*, 7 May, 1979 and the 500 largest corporations outside the US, *Fortune*, 13 August, 1979

Company	Country	Principal Mineral	Sales
Pechiney-Ugine-Kuhlmann	(France)	Aluminium	6·1
Alcoa	(US)	Aluminium	4·1
Rio Tinto-Zinc	(UK)	Diversified	3·8
Alcan	(Canada)	Aluminium	3·7
Metallgesellschaft	(Germany)	Diversified	3·4
Alussuisse	(Switzerland)	Aluminium	2·8
Reynolds	(US)	Aluminium	2·8
De Beers	(South Africa)	Diamonds	2·6
Kaiser	(US)	Aluminium	2·5
Nippon	(Japan)	Diversified	2·2
Inco	(Canada)	Nickel	2·1
Kennecott*	(US)	Copper	1·9
Anaconda†	(US)	Copper and Uranium	1·8
AMAX	(US)	Diversified	1·8
Consolidated Gold Fields	(US)	Diversified	1·7
Noranda	(Canada)	Diversified	1·6
IMETAL	(France)	Diversified	1·5
Asarco	(US)	Diversified	1·2
Phelps Dodge	(US)	Copper	1·0
Mitsui	(Japan)	Diversified	1·0

* A subsidiary of Standard Oil of Ohio (SOHIO).
† A subsidiary of Atlantic Richfield.

silver mine in Butte, Montana, by an Irish immigrant, Marcus Daly. The transition to an integrated company was short.

With his corporate profits, Daly bought a smelter, a refinery, a railroad to carry the ore, timberlands to provide material for mine supports, a sawmill to cut the wood, and a water company to supply the copper settlement of Butte. Competitors and partners were bought out, copper-fabricating plants were begun, and by the 1920s, Anaconda had secured a huge share of the world copper market by controlling every phase of copper production 'from mine to consumer'.[3]

Most mineral companies, especially those involved in base metal mining, followed the Anaconda model. The increased demand for minerals to fuel the economic, military and political aspirations of Western powers led to a commensurate growth of the major mining companies. To meet demand, exploration moved into new areas and technology was constantly upgraded to mine, refine, process and transport minerals as efficiently as possible. All of this needed capital well beyond the capabilities of small firms. Hence, the process of integration, coupled with partnerships between the companies and the great finance houses (for example, Kennecott-Guggenheim, Rio Tinto-Rothschilds), led to the wholesale institutionalization of the industry on classical capitalist lines.

Undoubtedly, high risks and costs of the mining industry have created a form of economic organization strongly oligopolistic and integrated in nature.

The multinationals in Table 11.1 have carved out empires through horizontal and vertical expansion, often at the expense of weaker competitors. Paradoxically, this process continues so that several of the big companies have themselves become weak and vulnerable to takeover bids.

The early phase of horizontal integration was illustrated in the case of Anaconda. By the inter-war period expansion was sought through the creation of foreign subsidiaries – the US multinationals concentrated on the Caribbean and Latin America, the European corporations on southern and central Africa and Australasia. At the same time, a high degree of vertical integration was taking place, especially in companies dealing in minerals such as aluminium, in which the mineral accounts for a large proportion of the total cost of the product. All the aluminium companies in Table 11.1 are totally integrated through ownership of bauxite mines, alumina plants, smelters and fabrication factories; at one time they were specialists in particular stages. Alusuisse was initially established to exploit cheap hydro-electric power for smelting French bauxite. Reynolds was essentially a fabrication company until it integrated backwards into smelting and mining in the 1940s to safeguard supplies.

Although the copper industry shows less overall integration than aluminium, the 'majors' in Table 11.1 have been integrated corporations for several decades. Indeed, the copper majors – fearing competition from aluminium products – diversified into aluminium (and other industries) to widen their product base and spread their risks rather than concentrate them on one industry. Some of the other mining multinationals have tended to follow this diversified strategy by becoming involved in different processes and products (RTZ and AMAX). On the other hand, many of the German and Japanese companies are primarily trading organizations offering financial and technical assistance to develop projects in return for long-term contracts to fuel their smelters and refineries at home.

In essence, the world mining industry is oligopolistic and strongly integrated, giving the transnationals a dominant role in the world market place. This dominance has been challenged in the last twenty years by Third World governments which have nationalized the assets of the transnationals and created an insecure investment climate for corporate expansion. Moreover, the early 1980s has been a disastrous period for the mining industry, with low prices and continued rising costs impairing profitability. In 1982, only one copper mine was profitable – RTZ's Palabara mine in South Africa.[4] Copper prices have been particularly vulnerable in world markets since the mid-1970s, and the poor performance of the copper 'majors' has undermined their stock value making them ripe for takeover by the successful and very profitable oil corporations. For example, the two companies that were the target of the Chilean expropriations – Anaconda and Kennecott – have since been acquired by Atlantic Richfield and SOHIO respectively. AMAX, which has major copper interests, narrowly avoided being taken over by Standard Oil of California (SOCAL) in 1981. (SOCAL already has a 20% share in the company.)

The Risk Business

The ultimate corporate strategy of the transnationals is to maximize profits and minimize risks. Risks, whether technical, economic, political or environmental,

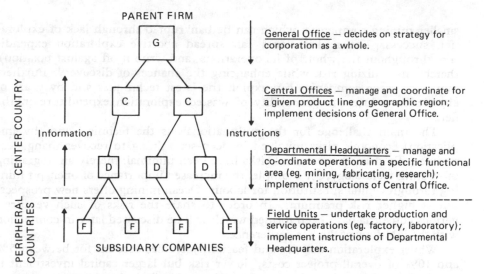

PARENT FIRM

G

General Office — decides on strategy for corporation as a whole.

C   C

Central Offices — manage and coordinate for a given product line or geographic region; implement decisions of General Office.

Information   Instructions

D   D   D

Departmental Headquarters — manage and co-ordinate operations in a specific functional area (eg. mining, fabricating, research); implement instructions of Central Office.

CENTER COUNTRY

PERIPHERAL COUNTRIES

F   F   F   F

SUBSIDIARY COMPANIES

Field Units — undertake production and service operations (eg. factory, laboratory); implement instructions of Departmental Headquarters.

Figure 11.2 Administrative Levels and Associated Power Relations in the Transnational Corporation. *Source:* Girvan, 1977, *Corporate Imperialism: Conflict and Expropriation*, Monthly Review Press

are built into the decision-making process. The previous section on horizontal and vertical integration showed how companies spread the geographical risks of their operations by creating foreign subsidiaries controlled by the parent company. Figure 11.2 highlights this process. Corporate strategy is dynamic, with foreign subsidiaries supplying sister processing and manufacturing affiliates according to a fluid plan which seeks to maximize profits from this mix of facilities. A contingency plan for unfortunate events such as labour disputes, government policy changes and wars is drawn up to tackle any foreseeable supply disruption. Clearly, the larger the scale of the whole operation, the greater degree of flexibility in bringing the product to market.

While this deals with the economic organization of *existing* facilities, the transnational operates a long-term development strategy to replace existing production facilities with new investment opportunities. Historically, an incremental approach was adopted and production moved away from domestic to foreign subsidiary development. The uncertain political and economic environment has not only reversed this trend but has put a brake upon new investment expenditure.

Regardless of where investment is intended, the same phases of decision making are encountered: large scale exploration programmes are conducted, feasibility reports assess the best sites, projects are selected, debt financing is acquired and the project is brought to fruition. However, the company will first have to ensure that target profit levels can be achieved. This is a difficult and risky task because of the numerous assumptions which have to be made about the future. In particular, in order to determine the rate of exploration expenditure, forecasts of costs and prices in an uncertain business environment have to be projected ten to twenty years ahead. This phase in the development process carries the greatest risk because much risk capital is involved with varying degrees of probability that the investment will not be recovered. The sheer size of the multinational corporation gives it a competitive advantage over smaller mining companies, which can be bankrupted through lack of exploration success. The multinational can spread abortive exploration expenditure throughout the whole of its operations (and write it off against taxation), thereby minimizing risk while enhancing the chances of discovery. Furthermore, the large companies can exploit the latest techniques and by years of experience reduce the probability of wasted exploration expenditure in the field.

The main challenge for the multinationals is the technical and (by implication) economic risks involved in deep-sea mining to recover manganese nodules. To date, the technical risks have been minimal: merely an upgrading of existing technology, for example, the increased importance of open-pit mining through capital substitution for labour. Ocean mining offers new prospects but at higher risk premiums. In order to share the risks of such ventures, various consortia have been formed which will be discussed later in connection with the UN Law of the Sea conferences.

Whilst exploration activity and feasibility studies account for between 5% and 10% of overall project costs,[5] lower risk but larger capital investment is required in the project development phase. Unlike oil companies, mineral multinationals do not have large cash flows to finance these projects. They have to secure debt financing from bank consortia, international lending agencies and companies potentially involved in the project. In order for these agencies to commit large sums of money, they must anticipate a good rate of return from the project. The standard procedure for investment appraisal is the Discounted Cash Flow (DCF) method in which target rates are assumed for different parts of the world, allowing for non-economic factors such as political risk.

The DCF profit rate calculations are based on the expected per annum cash flows generated from an initial capital investment until the end of the working life of the mine.[6] In reality, investment is phased from clearing the site to infrastructural development to constructing the mine. The initial capital invested will not yield a return for several years until the mine comes into production. What this amounts to is that the DCF rate reflects the opportunity cost of investing in one project rather than in others. The corporation assesses a range of potential projects and assigns them in order of investment priority. The crude DCF is not the sole criterion for deciding project suitability. Some projects may have a quicker pay-back period than others, an important factor in a country deemed politically risky. Indeed, political risk is probably the most significant factor in project assessment: financiers will only back such projects at appropriate, high DCF rates. Although high political risks may be incurred in Third World countries, high profits have been a feature of the great majority of projects. The average rate of return on foreign investments by US multinationals from 1953 to 1977 was 7·4% in Canada, 13·9% in Latin America and the Caribbean and 30·4% in South Africa.[7]

Political risk assessment has been elevated to a key role in corporate decision making. The increase in bargaining power of Third World countries, leading to nationalization, creeping expropriation and renegotiation of contracts, has meant that transnationals assess countries on their 'riskiness' for investment, and incorporate into their management strategies methods to ameliorate this risk.[8] In general terms, the transnationals rank political instability as the main deterrent to overseas investment, above administrative and legislative requirements such as profit remittance and exchange controls, expropriation and taxation policy.[9]

In order to keep abreast of the changing political and economic climate in potential investment areas, companies monitor the situation through advice from their local subsidiaries, field personnel, embassies and consultants. Risk assessment methodologies vary from the subjective, qualitative approach of experience in the field to the more objective, quantitative approach of political analysts who model variables deemed to be appropriate to inducing political change. Whichever method is employed (usually a multiple approach is adopted), the transnational has to base a strategy on the assessment of potential mining areas. Once a decision to invest has been made, there are seven identifiable strategies of risk management:[10]

(1) risk premiums;
(2) political risk insurance;
(3) mobilizing international support;
(4) engaging home government support;
(5) courting of local population patronage;
(6) minimization of equity exposure;
(7) accelerated pay back periods.

The last strategy (7) and the first two (1,2) – higher DCF rates, and insuring of risks through bodies such as the Overseas Private Investment Corporation in the US – have already been discussed (the latter in 4.4.1). Of the other approaches, the minimization of equity exposure (6) is probably the most effective strategy. When a project is broad based in its financing, international support will be forthcoming if a government reneges on its contractual or other legal obligations. This international condemnation approach is more popular than the traditional method of political brinkmanship by national governments in support of their transnationals, although the termination of foreign aid to 'naughty' governments has been an effective weapon in the past.

Alignment with a particular government (4), especially if this involves bribes, corruption and possible scandals, incurs heavy political risks. A change of government with a different philosophy could jeopardize existing projects. A more sensible arrangement is to enter into joint agreements with host governments, local investors and firms willing to participate in the project to secure a better local public image, thereby minimizing the possibility of political action against the corporation (5).

Parallel to the problems of political risk in foreign investments are the difficulties presented by environmental risks at home. This is particularly relevant in the US. Concern has been expressed about land disturbance and air and water pollution by the mining industry. As a result of public pressure, legislation has been enacted against the worst effects of mining and processing industries. Standards vary from country to country; the UK has been mainly concerned with land disturbance and the reclamation of a proposed site whereas in the US, air and water standards are of prime importance. Indeed, the regulations discussed in the previous chapter pertaining to coal mining and power plant siting are equally relevant to the non-fuel mineral industry.

Environmental costs can add substantially to total costs. The average cost of copper production in US mines in the late 1970s was 62 to 65 cents a lb, of which 6 to 8 cents were accounted for by the national pollution abatement requirements stipulated by EPA.[11] Furthermore, at the forward integration stages of the non-ferrous metal industry, additional costs are incurred. These companies spend 24% of their total investment in plant and equipment on pollution control, most of it (77%) to comply with air quality standards.[12]

The corporate response to environmental legislation throughout the 1970s was one of reluctant compliance. The main procedures for minimizing environmental risk are:

(a) avoiding areas of high environmental sensitivity;
(b) anticipating adverse reaction to a mining proposal and preparing a master plan to deal with this contingency (good public relations is a prerequisite for this action);
(c) lobbying decision-making agencies to secure support for proposals.

The world's minerals are found in some of the more inaccessible yet beautiful parts of the earth's surface. Corporations have argued that ores can only be mined where you find them. However, mining entails more environmental risks in some areas than others. Transnationals have to take this into consideration when appraising possible sites for project development. The economic risks and costs attached to exploration activity and feasibility reports have already been stressed. Additional abortive expenditure may be incurred if an environmentally sensitive site is chosen and the project is delayed or abandoned because of 'regulatory lag', especially protracted public hearings.

The transnational can gauge public response to a proposal for given areas and then set the public relations machinery into motion to bolster its case. An image of corporate responsibility for the environment must be portrayed, usually by referring to specific 'environmental mines' currently in operation. For example, AMAX has gained much mileage from its 'Experiment in Ecology' at the Henderson molybdenum mine in Colorado. After consultation with local amenity groups, the company spent $100 million on constructing a pipeline to divert molybdenum waste from the main river systems.[13]

A well-tried strategy is to play upon the job creation aspects of the proposal by arguing that environmental impact will be minimized and employment opportunities created. Local government officials, faced with rural depopulation and a weakening tax base, are often convinced by these arguments. In the UK these issues have been raised when proposals have been made for mining in National Park areas. Unlike their US counterparts, the UK National Parks are socio-economic entities dependent upon extractive industries and tourism for their economic well being. Trade offs between loss of amenity and employment generation have tended to dominate public inquiries in these areas. In one particular case, RTZ tried a novel tactic in trying to secure approval for open-cast copper mining in Snowdonia National Park. Anticipating environmental opposition to any proposal in the Park, the company applied to drill at two sites – a copper area in the southern part of the Park and a nearby estuary – where it hoped to mine gold. Mining in the estuary, a well-known beauty spot, was bound to meet with hostile reaction and would concentrate the opposition's case on an unlikely prospect while RTZ substantiated their case for the less environmentally sensitive copper mine.[14] The scheme backfired. Environmental groups plagued RTZ through the media, tarnishing its image. The company eventually withdrew its proposal.

One long-term strategy of the mineral companies is to maintain strong pressure on decision makers to change or modify legislation. As they are generally based in countries with high import dependence on minerals, especially strategic minerals, arguments are raised concerning the vulnerability of supplies. In the US, an amendment to the Defense Production Act of 1950 is passing through Congress which would create a $5 billion fund for price supports to strategic minerals.[15] At the same time, US corporations point to the difficulty in developing domestic resources because many potentially rich mineral areas in the western USA are public lands withdrawn from mining development. Hence, on the one hand, it is argued that they are being deprived of new exploration opportunities whilst, on the other, profitability is being impaired because of low prices and increased costs, much of which can be attributed to compliance with air quality standards.

The views of the transnationals have received much sympathy from the Reagan Administration and steps have been taken to create a more favourable business environment for the mineral industry. Clean air legislation is being weakened. Deadlines for attaining air quality standards have been extended by several years. Enforcement actions have declined in the wake of Environment Protection Agency (EPA) budget cuts.[16] Concurrently, the Sagebrush rebels[17] have found allies in the Reagan Administration, which is opening up public lands for mineral development and accelerating wilderness review procedures on lands administered by the Bureau of Land Management (see Chapter 13).

At a regional level corporations maintain that mining activity acts as a catalyst to economic development. Jobs versus amenities is a well-rehearsed argument among local government officials, and with unemployment rates reaching unprecedented heights, environmentalism becomes a luxury that they cannot afford. In recent years, however, mines have been closed in the US because of low prices; this has had devastating local impacts for communities which are 'company towns'. The plight of the copper industry has led to wholesale closures of mines and smelters, especially in Arizona where unemployment rates in some communities were reaching 50%.[18] In 1983 two Arizona representatives, Udall and McNulty, were attempting to pilot two bills through Congress: one that would guarantee copper purchases for the national stockpile and a second proposing the imposition of an environmental equalization tax on imported copper.[19] The latter bill is aimed at equalizing the unfair advantage gained by foreign producers because of weaker environmental standards.

1.2.3 State Corporations, Developing Countries and Mineral Development

It was shown in the previous section that political risk had become a key factor in the corporate strategies of transnationals since the 1960s in response to changing patterns of mine ownership in the developing countries. By the late 1970s, around 60% of primary copper output was produced by majority-owned government companies, 50% of iron ore production was controlled by state mining enterprises and the bauxite industry had been subjected to nationalization or part nationalization in Guyana and Jamaica.[20]

The state corporations[21] that have been created in the wake of nationalization vary in size, technical and marketing expertise and may have different corporate goals. Their *raison d'être* was to give host governments greater control over their own resources in order that profits from mines could be re-invested at home instead of being taken out of the country. For example, it has been calculated that US companies expatriated $10·8 billion from Chile between 1910 and 1970 but invested only $103·5 million.[22] As a result of the political undertones in state mining company philosophy, corporate objectives differ from those of the transnationals. The multinational sees an affiliate in a particular country only as a piece in the jigsaw of overall corporate profits. The state corporation acts as an agent of government; its production levels and investment strategies are integrated within the social and development policy of the nation as a whole.

Regardless of the operating efficiency of state corporations, they are at a competitive disadvantage to the transnationals because of the geographical restriction of their operations. In times of recession and falling prices, transnationals have greater flexibility. They reduce output from their high cost

Table 11.2: Conditions desired by the foreign investor for mineral project development. *Source:* R.F. Mikesell, 1979, New patterns of world mineral development, p. 50, British–North American Committee, London, Toronto and Washington

(1) majority equity ownership;
(2) full control over production, employment, investment, purchases of materials and equipment, marketing and distribution of earnings;
(3) tax provisions that will enable the foreign investor to earn and repatriate the capitalized value of the investment, including the repayment of external indebtedness, within a relatively short period of time, and a corporate tax rate that does not exceed that imposed by the home country of the parent company;
(4) foreign-exchange arrangements that permit the foreign investor to hold sufficient export proceeds abroad to meet all external obligations, including those arising from current foreign purchases, and to remit dividends and authorized capital repatriation;
(5) freedom to make payments to the parent company, or to other foreign firms, for technical services and the use of patented processes and to import equipment and materials from any source so long as the prices and quality are competitive;
(6) exemption from import duties on equipment and materials employed in construction operations;
(7) no export or production taxes or royalties, and guarantees against the imposition of new taxes or other legislation or regulations that would affect the operation and profitability of the investment that did not exist at the time of the investment agreement, or were not specified in it;
(8) guarantees against expropriation or contract renegotiation during the life of the agreement;
(9) negotiation of an agreement covering exploration, production and operations before any substantial exploration outlays;
(10) a minimum tenure of life of the mine, often at least 30 years after the initiation of commercial production;
(11) in the event of expropriation, a guarantee of full compensation based on replacement cost of assets or present value of projected earnings;
(12) arbitration of disputes arising in the implementation of the contract by an independent arbitration agency such as the International Chamber of Commerce Court of Arbitration or the World Bank International Center for the Settlement of Investment Disputes.

mines. State companies, on the other hand, do not have this flexibility and are under pressure from government to maintain employment. Furthermore, for foreign earnings reasons, production may be increased as prices fall to keep development strategies on course.

For nationalization to be truly successful, the state corporation has to

(1) attract experienced, trained personnel to manage the company;
(2) acquire and develop technological 'know how';
(3) be able to market their products to consumers independently;
(4) control prices;
(5) have access to capital markets.

Some of the larger state corporations such as CODELCO in Chile and Vale de Rio Doce in Brazil had a tradition of mineral development which allows them to satisfy the first two conditions but, as with smaller, less experienced state corporations, they remain dependent upon transnationals for financial and marketing services. Although marketing institutions have been established in state concerns, these continue to use private companies as agents to sell their minerals. The relative failure of producer associations, except OPEC, has also meant a dependence upon transnational-controlled 'producer' prices or the 'Northern' based metal exchanges.

The main obstacle to an independent approach by state corporations is the large capital requirements necessary for modern mine projects if additional capacity is deemed a national priority. Before foreign investment and World Bank involvement in projects of this nature can be secured, equity participation by a transnational is normally required. Moreover, in some cases, majority

Table 11.3: Conditions demanded by host governments for mineral project development. *Source:* R.F. Mikesell, 1980, New patterns of world mineral development, p. 51, British–North American Committee, London, Toronto and Washington

---

(1) majority government ownership, or the option to acquire a majority of the equity at some time following the exploration period; and in some cases, the option to acquire 100% of the equity after a certain number of years of operation with compensation to be made at book value and often in long-term bonds;
(2) gradual replacement of all expatriate personnel by nationals, and the establishment of training programmes designed to achieve localization targets in accordance with rigid timetables;
(3) high excess-profits tax on acccounting profits in any year resulting from higher than anticipated market prices, with no carry forward and no accelerated depreciation;
(4) repatriation of all export earnings to the central bank and the application of existing foreign-exchange regulations to the foreign investor;
(5) government control over marketing of the products;
(6) domestic processing of minerals and gradual expansion to downstream operations;
(7) the right to demand contract renegotiation whenever the government decides that changes in the contract are in the national interest;
(8) full application of all national laws to foreign investors with no guarantee against changes in the legislative framework in contracts with foreign investors;
(9) the settlement of all disputes between the government and the foreign investor through national judicial procedures and the rejection of any form of international arbitration.

---

ownership by foreign firms of specific projects has occurred in countries with a well-developed nationalized industry, for example Chile and Zaire.

Whichever method of foreign investment is employed, similar lengthy negotiations ensue between investor and host government over contractual details. Tables 11.2 and 11.3 illustrate the ideal bargaining position for the antagonists. Ultimately, a compromise solution is reached which is broadly satisfactory to both parties. Joint ventures and phase-out agreements are the most common solutions to contract conflict. Transnationals tend to accept greater government participation in their concessions if they can secure long-term supplies to their affiliates and maintain control of downstream activities. Some examples of transnational-government negotiations will be discussed later in this chapter.

11.2.4 The Role of the United Nations in Commodity Development

Through its numerous agencies, the United Nations (UN) has been the main vehicle for promoting mineral and general commodity development in the developing countries. The quest for a New International Economic Order was instigated through UNCTAD in the drive for better trading terms and more remunerative prices. The Integrated Programme for Commodities (IPC) and the Common Fund are attempts to achieve a better deal for the 'South'. The UN Law of the Sea Conferences (UNCLOS) tried to secure the 'no man's' seas as the common heritage of mankind and the various UN agencies have been active in encouraging the poorest countries to explore for their own mineral resources.

a The UN and Mineral Development

UN assistance is mainly directed at training a country's manpower so that it can explore and evaluate its own mineral sector. Indeed, the Special Fund in 1958 (superceded by United Nations Development Programme (UNDP) in the early 1960s) was formed to strengthen institutions in former colonies which had experienced an exodus of trained personnel on independence. Between 1958 and 1979, the Special Fund and UNDP had spent $170 million on 200 projects in 75 countries.[23] To place this sum in perspective, however, it is worth bearing in mind that the mineral sector secures only about 6% of UNDP's budget.[24] With the transnationals turning their backs on developing nations for exploration, it appears that recipients of UNDP funds also perceive the mineral sector as too risky and of less priority than other areas for investment purposes.

The need for increased exploration in developing countries is not in question. A World Bank study of 70 developing countries in 1978 showed that of the 23 nations with mineral potential only 7 had been adequately explored.[25] It is not surprising therefore that most UN activity is geared towards institution building (strengthening government departments and universities in the geology/mineral sector) and mineral exploration projects.[26] Within the UN system the organizations mainly responsible for this assistance are the Department of Technical Cooperation for Development (TCD), UN Educational, Scientific and Cultural Organization (UNESCO) and the World Bank.

Emphasis on increased exploration activity in the developing countries led to the establishment of the UN Revolving Fund for Natural Resources Exploration in 1973. The purpose of the Fund, which is limited to exploration activity, is to spread risks among developing countries. For example, a recipient government which has no success in locating an economically viable ore has the cost of the project absorbed by the Fund; if a viable deposit *is* discovered the government is obliged to 'top up' the fund through a contribution of 2% of the annual value of mine output for 15 years.

As most monies pledged to the Fund became available only in the late 1970s, it is too soon to monitor the success of this UN initiative. However, UN-supported projects have resulted in the discovery of minerals valued at $26 billion at 1977 market prices. Those which have attracted finance for development include the porphyry copper deposits at Petaquilla (Panama), La Coridad (Mexico) and Los Pelambres (Chile), gold at Buck Reef (Tanzania) and tin at Heinze Basin (Burma).

When projects – UN supported or otherwise – reach the post-evaluation and implementation stage, the World Bank[27] becomes an active agent in the financing of mineral resource developments. From 1957 to mid-1977, the World Bank had made 34 commitments totalling $850 million to developing countries.[28] Furthermore, the Bank is increasing its lending in the hope that its international presence in mining projects will act as a stimulant to investment from other private sources in the developing world. The Bank hopes to bridge the gap between host governments' demands and those of the foreign investor (see 11.2.3) by contributing around 15% of total project costs.[29]

b UN Law of the Sea Conferences (UNCLOS)

After a quarter of a century of negotiations, a Treaty of 320 articles covering all aspects of human activity upon and beneath the ocean floor was formulated in the spring of 1982.[30] The text contained codes for navigation, overflight, mineral exploitation, pollution, fishing and shipping. Heralded as a landmark in international relations and a step towards the New International Economic Order, the Treaty has nevertheless run into trouble. Of the 151 countries involved in the negotiations, 130 have signed the Treaty, 4 voted against (the US, Israel, Turkey and Venezuela) and 17 abstained (mainly European nations).[31]

The main cause of contention is Part 11 of the treaty which relates to ocean mining outside the agreed exclusive economic zones (200-mile limits) or continental-shelf jurisdiction areas (out to 350 miles in places). Ironically, the US has been the chief opponent of deep mining resolutions despite its earlier enthusiasm for UNCLOS and Henry Kissinger's proposal for an International Seabed Authority in the mid-1970s. Why the volte face? The US's enthusiasm for UNCLOS was initially motivated by its desire for transit passage through the world's straits to maintain its military presence around the globe. On the development of long-range missiles, her attention has turned to the $3,000 million[32] bonanza on the ocean's floor in the form of nodules rich in manganese, cobalt, copper and nickel. It is conservatively estimated (although only 3% of the ocean floor has been surveyed in any detail)[33] that 54 million square kilometres of the sea floor is covered with nodules and one of the areas of high potential lies in the Pacific between Hawaii and California.[34]

The importance of these strategic minerals to the US's economic and military development has been stressed in Chapter 4. It has been estimated that if a US ocean mining industry could produce 16 million tonnes of nodules by the year 2000, the US could reduce its net imports of manganese from 98% to zero, cobalt from 97% to zero, nickel from 77 to 42% and copper from 19 to 15%.[35] As can be seen from Table 11.4, US transnationals have formed consortia with other 'Northern' companies to explore and develop the ocean floor for its mineral wealth. Consequently, many of the UN deep-mining proposals will infringe upon the *laissez faire*, free enterprise approach advocated by the transnationals. Powerful lobbying by the mining industry in Washington over these issues has received sympathetic support from the Reagan Administration, which has refused to back the treaty unless amendments are made to the deep-mining sections. The main points of divergence concern the role of the International Seabed Authority, the transfer of technology and the imposition of production ceilings to regulate prices on the world market.

The general philosophy of securing the open seas for the common heritage of mankind was embodied in Kissinger's proposal for an International Seabed Authority. Indeed, the principles enshrined in the Kissinger formula had been accepted by all nations until the Reagan renege of 1981/82. The Kissinger scheme envisaged that the Seabed Authority would conduct its own mining on behalf of developing nations through an operational arm entitled 'Enterprise', whilst at the same time the Authority would have the power to license other companies to mine on their own behalf. This parallel system of development should in theory benefit the consortia and the Authority equally, operating for the benefit of the poorer countries.

In reality, detailed aspects of the legislation are not acceptable to the transnationals, who have found political expression through their own government's support. The US maintains that there should not be undue interference with the operations of private companies and that Enterprise's role should be reduced. For example, the Treaty proposes that a private company should propose *two* sites of comparable value to the Authority for permission to mine; Enterprise would choose one site to mine or hold in trust whilst the company was free to develop the other site subject to royalties and taxes in production. In addition to opposing this proposal, the US is unhappy about the conditions pertaining to technological transfer. In the event of a company receiving a licence, it is obliged to transfer to the Authority the requisite technology for an agreed commercial settlement. The companies claim that this part of the Treaty negates their competitive edge. Rose finds this point debatable in that the enterprise would not have the expertise to go it alone and would have to entertain joint ventures with private consortia.[36] A final issue causing debate is that of production ceilings once a concession is being developed. Countries such as Zaire, Zambia and Chile from the developing world and Canada from the industrialized nations have been concerned that ocean-based mining could have serious implications for their land-based resources, from which they derive much export revenue. Proposals for production ceilings to regulate prices and give greater market stability have been opposed by the consortia because they would undermine the potential for attracting the large amounts of capital needed to win these nodules.

By 1983, the situation was in stalemate. The opponents and abstainers had already produced their own national legislation giving them rights to license

Table 11.4: Consortia involved in ocean mining. *Source: South*, November 1982

Consortia/Companies	Investment (% share)	Nationality	Estimated Cost to Date
Ocean Mining Associates:			Total spending
US Steel Corp.	25	US	US$80 million
Union Minière	25	Belgium*	
Sun Co.	25	US	
Samin	25	Italy*	
Kennecott Consortium			US$50–60 million
Kennecott Copper Corp.	40	US	
Rio Tinto-Zinc	12	UK	
Consolidated Gold Fields	12	UK	
Noranda Mines	12	Canada*	
Mitsubishi Corp.	12	Japan	
British Petroleum	12	UK	
Ocean Management Inc.:			estimated US$45–50
International Nickel	25	Canada	million jointly
Arbeitsgemeinschaft Meeres Technische Gewinnbare Rohstoffe Metallgesellschaft, Preussag, Salzgitter			
Deep Ocean Mining Co.	25	West Germany	
Sumitomo etc.	25	Japan	
Sedco, Inc.	25	US	
Ocean Minerals Co.:			US$120 million
Lockheed Missiles and Space	30	US	
Standard Oil of Indiana (Amoco Minerals)	30	US	
Royal Dutch Shell	30	Netherlands	
Royal Bos Kalis Westminster	10	Netherlands	
French Association for Nodule Exploration:	Unavailable	France	US$45 million to 1980; US$38 million between 1980 and 1982
Centre National Pour L'Exploitation Des Océans Commissariat L'Energie Atomique	–	France	
Bureau De Recherche Géologiques et Miniéres			
Société Métallurgique	–	France	
Nouvelle/Société le Nickel	–	France	
Chantiers de France Dunkerque	–	France	
Continuous Line Bucket Group:			
Approximately 20 companies from six countries: Australia, Canada, France, West Germany, Japan and the US			US$1·5 million

* Participation through subsidiaries incorporated in the US.

and regulate companies operating in ocean areas.[37] Indeed, the US has been trying to win support for a rival 'mini-treaty' from Western countries who did not sign the UN treaty.[38] The Soviet Union, an initial abstainer, has agreed to sign the UN treaty. However, this is the only route open to Moscow to participate in sea-bed mining. The multinational character of several of the consortia in Table 11.4 allows Western companies to operate under the sponsorship of one state so that the Kennecott Consortium could use Japan or Canada as sponsors and non-signatories – Britain and the US – could still reap the benefits.

c The Integrated Programme for Commodities and the Common Fund

The 'South's' disappointment over UNCLOS is matched by the failure of another 'New International Economic Order' initiative, that of the IPC programme and the Common Fund. It was shown in 4.4.1 that the UNCTAD *IV* proposal for ten core commodities (of which only tin and copper are 'hard' commodities) to be backed by a Fund of $6 billion has not been realized.

The Common Fund was originally envisaged as a new financial force in international lending with a strong 'Southern' bias in contrast to the 'Northern' dominated management of the World Bank and IMF. The $6 billion fund would be divided into two parts: one ($5 billion) to finance buffer stocks through international commodity organizations (ICOs), the other ($1 billion) to support long-term development objectives such as R. & D., productivity improvements and diversification schemes. The latter form of financing was regarded as a significant breakthrough in development assistance because the aid channelled through ICOs would be earmarked for specific *commodity* projects viewed in a holistic framework rather than the present *ad hoc* nature of aid from conventional channels to *countries*.

Unfortunately, the Fund has been reduced to $650 million, with $400 earmarked for buffer stocking and $250 for other development purposes.[39] For the fund to be larger and more successful, it required the cooperation of producers and consumers to create ICOs and formulate International Commodity Agreements (ICAs). This has not been forthcoming. Indeed, two of the ICAs in force prior to UNCTAD *IV* – cocoa and tin – have suffered difficulties over renegotiations, with the US not being party to either ICA.[40] With the exception of the international rubber agreement, no commodity agreement is making progress along the lines envisaged by UNCTAD. Hence, there has been little enthusiasm for the Common Fund Agreement of October 1980. By March 1982 only 77 countries had signed and 22 ratified it.[41]

Fortin suggests that the failure of current negotiations lies in structural changes occurring in commodity trading.[42] The stabilization of demand in industrialized nations could be a more permanent trend than is often accepted; he advocates a greater degree of trading amongst 'Southern' partners themselves. 'South–South' cooperation could also be enhanced by long-term supply management using OPEC as a model for other commodity producers. For example, to maintain prices and depress production the richer OPEC nations were willing to finance Nigeria's deficit in export earnings rather than allow it to increase production to further flood the market.[43]

.3.1 Policies in Practice

We now provide a more detailed analysis of some of the concepts introduced earlier through case studies of particular organizations. In terms of international negotiations pertaining to commodity management, the Lomé Agreements between the EEC and African, Caribbean and Pacific (ACP) countries were hailed as a model for 'North–South' relations, mainly because of a novel compensatory finance scheme, STABEX. After discussing the Lomé Agreements, attention will centre upon corporate level decision making through assessing the policies of two transnationals, Kennecott and RTZ, to build upon the points raised in 11.2.2.

3.1a The Lomé Agreements

Lomé I (1976–1980) and Lomé II (1980–1984) were fashioned out of the original Yaoundé Conventions of the 1960s which gave preferential trading agreements and financial/technical assistance to former colonies of the original six members of the EEC. Upon the admission of Britain to the EEC in 1973 the strong francophone, African bias to these conventions was widened to include her Commonwealth in Africa, the Caribbean and the Pacific (ACP).

After extensive negotiations, Lomé I came into being in 1976 at a time of increasing antagonism in 'North–South' relations. The agreement gave free access to ACP exports and the $4·4 billion package covered soft loans and grants to finance development projects, most of which were in rural areas.[44] However, the most progressive element of the agreement was the $470 million fund (STABEX) designed to compensate ACP countries for a loss of export earnings due to adverse weather or market conditions. STABEX 1 covered 12 product groups and 29 individual products. With the exception of iron ore, all products are 'soft' commodities (Table 11.5).[45] To qualify for STABEX assistance, two conditions had to be met. Firstly, the product for which a transfer of funds was requested must account for 7·5% of total exports in the year preceding the shortfall (in the case of 34 countries classified as least-developed or otherwise disadvantaged, this threshold was lowered to 2·5%). The second condition relates to the extent of loss of earnings: to be able to draw upon these funds a fall of 7·5% on export earnings had to be experienced over an average of the four preceding years (once again, this was lowered to 2·5% for the poorest nations). Transfers made under STABEX had to be repaid within one year of export earnings reaching this reference level, although poorer countries received their aid in the form of grants rather than loans. This scheme was initially welcomed by ACP as a more favourable arrangement of compensatory financing than the IMF's Compensatory Financing Facility (CFF). The CFF was linked to the total export earnings of a *country* requesting a transfer rather than STABEX's focus on export earnings of a particular *product*. Furthermore, CFF financing was in the form of loans, and stringent conditions were often imposed on countries receiving aid compared to the free discretion of use by recipients of STABEX funds.

On the implementation of Lomé I, the ACP nations had hoped that STABEX would be the start of a new relationship with the EEC over the transfer of resources. As renegotiations began for Lomé II, ACP countries requested a broadening of product coverage to include non-agricultural commodities and services. Moreover, they wanted the size of the STABEX fund to be increased, transfers to be index-linked to account for inflation and the threshold levels to be significantly lowered. ACP had argued that the imposition of rigid threshold levels does not take into account the *absolute* shortfalls in export earnings. For example, a country specializing in two commodities, could have one with a 6·5% fall from the reference level and the other at 8·5%. The latter commodity may account for only a small proportion of export earnings compared to the other commodity, yet it would qualify for a transfer of funds because it had broken the 7·5% threshold.

When Lomé II came into existence in 1980, the EEC had conceded only minor concessions to the ACP countries. The new agreement was an updated consolidation of its predecessor. Of the new $6 billion fund, STABEX's allocation was increased to $731 million. But this had to cover the accession of all eleven new countries and a range of new products which were added to the scheme (Table 11.5). Other minor amendments to STABEX I were the lowering of thresholds to 6·5% and more relaxed payment conditions.

Important omissions from the list of new products in STABEX II are minerals or service industries, such as tourism. Indeed, iron ore – the only mineral included in STABEX I – was to be phased out by 1984. Instead of adding key minerals to STABEX, a new scheme, SYSMIN, with a $390 million budget, was incorporated into Lomé II to help maintain mineral production capacity in ACP countries.[46]

The EEC had been concerned about the lack of exploration expenditure in ACP countries, especially Africa, and were aware of their dependency upon these nations for several key minerals. For example, ACP countries supply 51% of the EEC's bauxite and alumina, 29% of its copper, 31% of its manganese and 16% of both phosphates and iron ore.[47] However, the EEC was unwilling to include minerals in the STABEX scheme because much needed aid could be diverted away from the agricultural sector. Cheysson, a former EEC Commissioner for development policy, also had reservations about the role of transnationals in that they could manipulate STABEX knowing that reduced output would be compensated for from the EEC budget.[48]

SYSMIN imposed more severe conditions on the transfer of funds than STABEX. To qualify for SYSMIN, an ACP country must satisfy three conditions:

(a) a dependency threshold in which a particular mineral accounted for not less than 15% of its exports for the previous 4 years (10% for the poorest countries);
(b) a capacity shortfall of at least 10% which would impede a country's development strategy;
(c) that (a) and (b) are beyond the control of the ACP state.

Unlike STABEX, mere compliance with the preconditions does not automatically secure a transfer of funds. With STABEX, governments could use this aid for any project, not necessarily agricultural schemes, but aid granted under SYSMIN must be allocated to specified projects in the mineral sector. Although the aid is in the form of grants or low interest loans with long pay-back periods, stringent conditions along the lines of IMF guidelines are often imposed. For example, the Zaire government which borrowed $41·2

ble 11.5: STABEX I and II in the Lomé agreements. *Source:* South, December
1980

ACP States

Bahamas	Guinea	Rwanda
Barbados	Guinea-Bissau	Senegal
Botswana	Grenada	Sierra Leone
Burundi	Guyana	Somalia
Cameroon	Ivory Coast	Sudan
Central African Rep.	Jamaica	Swaziland
Chad	Kenya	Tanzania
Congo	Lesotho	Togo
Dahomey	Liberia	Tonga
Equatorial Guinea	Madagascar	Trinidad and Tobago
Ethiopia	Malawi	Uganda
Fiji	Mauritania	Upper Volta
Gabon	Mauritius	Western Samoa
Gambia	Niger	Zaire
Ghana	Nigeria	Zambia

New ACP States

Benin	Papua New Guinea
Cape Verde	St Lucia
Comoros	São Tomé and Principe
Djibouti	Seychelles
Dominica	Solomon Islands
Kiribati	Surinam
	Zimbabwe

Products covered by the Lomé Convention: 1

Groundnuts
Groundnut oil
Cocoa beans
Cocoa paste
Cocoa butter
Raw or roasted coffee
Extracts, essence or concentrates of coffee
Cotton, not carded or combed
Cotton linters
Coconuts
Copra
Coconut oil
Palm oil
Palm kernel oil
Palm nuts and kernels
Raw hides and skins
Bovine cattle leather
Sheep and lamb skin leather
Goat and kid skin leather
Wood in the rough
Wood roughly squared or half squared,
    but not further manufactured
Wood sawn lengthwise, but not further prepared
Fresh bananas
Tea
Tow-sisal
Iron ores

Products added

Vanilla
Cloves (whole fruit, cloves and stems)
Sheep's or lamb's wool, not carded or
    combed
Fine animal hair of Angora goats – mohair
Gum arabic
Pyrethrum (flowers, leaves, stems, peel
    and roots; saps and extracts from
    pyrethrum)
Essential oils, not terpeneless, of cloves,
    of niaouli and of yiang-yiang
Sesame seed
Cashew nuts
Pepper
Shrimps and prawns
Squid
Cotton seeds
Oil-cake
Rubber
Peas
Beans
Lentils

Threshold Variation 7·5%

2·5% for least developed landlocked and
    island states remains unchanged

New Threshold Variation
6·5%

million from SYSMIN had to agree to reform its taxation laws in the mining sector.[48]

By late 1982, the Lomé Agreements had formed a watershed in relations between the EEC and ACP to the extent that a Lomé III may not be negotiated. Conflicts have arisen in all areas of the convention but most of the disagreements have centred upon STABEX. Low commodity prices in the early 1980s have placed excessive strain on the STABEX budget and claims for assistance have overshot the annual budgets by a factor of 2.[49] The EEC has been unwilling to vote for additional funds to make up the shortfall and ACP nations have had to accept reductions in their claims. To make matters worse, the EEC has been monitoring the effectiveness of STABEX at solving long-term structural problems in the ACP agricultural sector. EEC officials have argued that STABEX transfers are not being applied to the commodities or sectors for which assistance was requested.[50] As a result of this, agricultural productivity and efficiency within the rural sector is not being enhanced and ACP countries are becoming increasingly uncompetitive with other 'Southern' producers. The likely upshot of this is that the EEC will attempt to impose conditions on transfers similar to those in operation in SYSMIN.

Clearly, the ACP nations will try to block these proposed changes. At the same time they are beginning to promote greater cooperation among themselves, especially in trade to free them from a dependence upon former colonial links. The survival of Lomé could depend upon the fate of STABEX which is considered to be the key element of the agreement. Perhaps, the vagaries of the commodity market will decide the fate of Lomé III?

11.3.1b Kennecott Copper Corporation and Rio-Tinto Zinc Corporations: the role of the Multinational

Having discussed the practical aspects of international agreements between supra-national organizations, we will now focus on the policies of two of the private transnationals which have been actively involved in mineral developments throughout the world. Kennecott, which specializes in copper products with most of its operations in North America, was another copper company to be taken over by an oil major when SOHIO successfully acquired it in June 1981. RTZ, on the other hand, is a diversified mineral company involved in all stages of mineral development, with operations in Australasia, the Americas, South Africa and Europe. In both cases, however, the corporate objectives are the same – profit maximization and risk minimization. The extent to which this has been achieved is a reflection of the management policies of either firm and the investment strategies deployed by them through their history.

The Kennecott Copper Corporation

Kennecott displays the classical format of a multinational corporation which has included risk assessment into its decision-making process. The company's incorporation in 1915 was an attempt by the Guggenheim family to spread the geographical risks of its operations between Alaska, south-west USA and Chile.[51] The original Kennecott Mines Company was formed in 1906 to mine rich copper ores in SW Alaska and secured massive capital backing by the Morgan-Guggenheim group to lay down an extensive infrastructure over this difficult terrain. The partnership between the best mining engineers of the period (Birch and Smith) and a renowned finance house quickly established Kennecott as the world's largest copper company. Already by World War I, it had the distinction of operating the world's largest underground mine (El Teniente, Chile) and the largest open pit mine (Bingham Canyon, Utah). Both mines are still in operation today and the Bingham mine has produced more copper than any mine in history and is the world's largest man-made excavation.[52]

Until the 1930s and the early post-war period, the company had tended to specialize in mining and had not become an integrated company in the same way as its competitors[53] (mainly because the Guggenheim's stake in American Smelting and Refining Company (ASARCO) had ensured markets for its supplies on long-term contracts). This was to change when Kennecott sought to diversify its interests while belatedly moving towards forward integration in the copper industry. The logic of this two pronged strategy was that (a) existing production capacity was deemed sufficient to meet foreseeable demand and (b) copper's future was uncertain because of the possibility of its substitution by aluminium in certain production processes.

To minimize the risks pertaining to the copper industry, Kennecott had to guarantee outlets for its mines *and* diversify into more lucrative ventures. Vertical integration was a success. Diversification was a disaster. Its ventures into oil and aluminium proved disappointing and the acquisition of Peabody Coal in 1968 ended in 1976 with a divestiture order by the Federal Trade Commission. Kennecott was unfortunate in this anti-trust suit which complained that the merger would reduce competition in the coal industry. After all, as we have shown in 10.3.1, the oil majors have been particularly active in diversifying into coal. Ironically, Kennecott eventually sold to Newmont Mining, the US's fourth copper producer with an 8% share in St Joe Minerals, a major coal producer.[54]

Kennecott was more fortunate with management initiatives over the Chileanization of its El Teniente mine. Here is a model example of successful political risk management. The company had anticipated that its holdings in Chile were vulnerable to expropriation and took appropriate steps to minimize this risk. In 1964 Kennecott sold 51% of its El Teniente mine to the state for $80 million. But under its own expansion package, the company agreed to use these proceeds plus an Export–Import loan and government funds to manage a new corporation with assets four times larger than their original subsidiary. In essence, Kennecott's share of profits increased significantly without injecting new capital into the mine.[55]

Furthermore, to protect its 1964 deal, Kennecott worked out intricate financial arrangements with a host of banks and government agencies. These included:

(a) insuring its $80 million share with the US Overseas Private Insurance Corporation (OPIC);
(b) receiving unconditional guarantees from the Chilean government for its contribution and that of the Export–Import Bank, subject to the laws of New York;

(c) entering into long-term contracts (for future protection) with European and Japanese firms;
(d) selling these contracts to a consortium of Japanese and European financial institutions.

According to Girvan, Kennecott's aim was to tie up the Chilean government in a web of contractual agreements which would mobilize international support if its assets were expropriated. This is precisely what happened. When the Allende Government nationalized Kennecott and Anaconda assets without compensation in July 1971, Kennecott quickly mobilized international support. Allende yielded to claims for compensation within seven months. By contrast, Anaconda, despite re-investing more of its profits than Kennecott during its mining history in Chile, could not secure immediate international support because it had not planned for these political risks.[56]

By the mid-1970s, the loss of Kennecott's Chilean subsidiary and the relinquishing of its coal and aluminium assets had narrowed its operational interests largely to the copper industry in the US (copper accounted for around three-quarters of its product sales). This proved to be a weakness. As copper prices slumped after reaching an all-time high in 1974, costs continued to rise and profitability began to suffer. Environmental costs began to absorb much capital investment – the Garfield smelter in Utah required $280 million to comply with EPA and Utah State air quality standards.[57] Not surprisingly, Kennecott's final diversification attempt was the takeover of Carborundum, a pollution control company. However, copper prices remained depressed and Kennecott, like its Chilean competitor before it, became part of an oil conglomerate (11.2.2).

Rio Tinto-Zinc Corporation (RTZ)

RTZ managed to weather the storm of low prices and poor profitability in the late 1970s and early 1980s. It emerged in much better shape than most of its competitors. RTZ's strength was Kennecott's weakness. Since its creation in 1873, it has developed into an internationally diversified mining group with hundreds of subsidiaries and associated companies involved in the mining and manufacture of a range of mineral products throughout the world.[58] Moreover, it was fortunate to discover several 'bonanza' deposits such as the rich copper ores at Bougainville, Papua New Guinea and Palabara in South Africa in addition to the vast uranium reserves at Rossing, Namibia. This has enabled RTZ to make substantial profits in years of good prices and has offset losses and poor profitability in other parts of the corporation.

Table 11.6 illustrates the contribution made by these mineral products to turnover and profitability. The fluctuations in sales and profit by product between years highlights the flexibility with which RTZ can operate to modify its product mix to market conditions and thereby maximize profits. For example, the high contribution of copper to overall profits in 1974 and 1975 is a reflection of the high price of copper and the outstanding profitability of the Bougainville mine. More recently, uranium has been the money spinner – the Rossing mine alone contributed 11% of pre-tax profits from 5·5% of all product sales in 1982.[59]

Table 11.6: Sales and profits of RTZ products (1974–1978). *Source:* J.M. Stopford
et al, 1980, *The World Directory of Multinational Enterprises*, p. 856,
Macmillan

Product sales (%)	1978	1977	1976	1975	1974
Lead and zinc	16	17	15	15	15
Aluminium	14	16	17	15	22
Copper and gold	13	14	16	15	23
Borax and chemicals	13	13	11	12	9
Uranium	10	6	4	4	3
Iron ore	10	12	13	14	10
Steel	8	8	8	9	8
Other	16	14	16	16	10
Total (%)	100	100	100	100	100
Total sales (£ million)	2,116	1,918	1,751	1,262	1,209

Product profits (%)[1]	1978	1977	1976	1975	1974
Lead and zinc	7	9	17	17	15
Aluminium	18	24	17	(11)	8
Copper and gold	15	16	23	38	55
Borax and chemicals	36	22	17	24	16
Uranium	12	9	6	14	5
Iron ore	12	20	18	20	5
Steel	6	5	3	8	7
Other	9	12	15	14	8
Exploration costs etc.	(15)	(17)	(16)	(24)	(19)
Total (%)	100	100	100	100	100
Total profits[1] (£ million)	113	96	95	48	75

[1] Net profit attributable to RTZ shareholders, before miscellaneous interest income
and exploration and research costs.

RTZ is presently organized into five main groups – Conzinc Rio Tinto of
Australia (72·6% group interest), Rio Algom Ltd (51·3% group interest), Rio
Tinto South Africa Ltd, RTZ Industries Ltd and RTZ Borax Ltd. The last
three are wholly owned subsidiaries of RTZ. Although the company is not
organized strictly along either geographical or product lines, it is possible to
identify the sources of RTZ's profits. Table 11.7 stresses the importance of
foreign sales to its overall profitability. Australasia, especially Papua New
Guinea, was by far the most profitable region for RTZ until the early 1980s.
RTZ had negotiated an extremely favourable agreement with the Australian
Government in 1967 for the Bougainville project which included tax exemption on income for the first three years. When the mine came into production
in 1972, RTZ's net profits for 1973 and 1974 were Aus$154·4 million and
Aus$114·6 million, which accounted for 65% and 42% of *total* company profits
in these respective years.[60]

Following the declaration of the 1973 profits, a new agreement was negotiated with the independent Papua New Guinea government. A two-stage

Table 11.7: RTZ net sales and profits by subsidiaries (1974–78) (million pounds). *Source*: J.M. Stopford et al, 1980, *The World Directory of Multinational Enterprises*, p. 858, Macmillan

	1978	%	1977	%	1976	%	1975	%	1974	%
Total net sales	1,954		1,823		1,673		1,184		1,165	
By Foreign Subsidiaries[1]		73		73		76		77		77
Australia and New Zealand		22		25		26		28		34
US		16		16		15		11		}26
Canada		16		16		18		18		N/A
Papua New Guinea		8		7		8		9		7
South Africa		5		5		6		5		10
Other		6		4		3		6		4
Exports										
Net profit[2]	98		82		81		39		63	
Foreign		85		76		78		97		92
Australia and New Zealand		25		37		27		36		54
US		24		10		9		18		}26
Canada		14		14		14		20		N/A
Papua New Guinea		9		9		13		28		14
South Africa		6		4		6		6		
Other		7		2		9		(11)		(2)
Earnings per share[3] (pence)	39·04		32·68		32·34		15·57		27·91	
Profit before tax	284		272		279		154		279	
Foreign trading profit		88		87		88		98		94
Australia and New Zealand		27		44		35		35		55
US		16		6		5		8		}21
Canada		17		18		19		23		N/A
Papua New Guinea		15		11		14		23		17
South Africa		9		7		11		12		1
Other		4		1		3		(1)		

[1] Percentage figures based on sales by source (not destination) including intra-company sales; includes exports; South Africa includes South-West Africa/Namibia for 1976 and earlier.

[2] Attributable to RTZ shareholders after deducting outside shareholders' interests before extraordinary items.

[3] Adjusted for rights issue in 1975.

system of taxation was implemented: a normal rate of corporation tax (36·5%) on income up to 15% of the capitalized value of the investment and an excess profit rate of 70% on taxable income above this amount[61] (provision was made in the tax formula to account for inflation bearing in mind that the capital committed had to be adjusted to current prices). Not surprisingly, the share of Bougainville to RTZ's profits has declined considerably since 1974 (Table 11.7).

Conzinc Rio Tinto of Australia (CRA) has experienced difficulties in recent years. The 1974 agreement, labour disputes, increased costs and stable prices led to a sharp decline in profits in the late 1970s and a subsequent loss in 1982. Furthermore, the 'Australianization' of the subsidiary has caused the parent to look to new pastures for investment opportunities.

The political overtones in RTZ operations are mainly evident in South Africa, especially Namibia. In addition to the low wages and impoverished living conditions which the coloured RTZ labour force endures, the Rossing mine has been operating since 1978 in defiance of UN resolutions. In anticipation of Namibian independence, RTZ has begun a training and educational programme for its employees and improved their wages and living conditions – all in an attempt to foster good relations with a future government.

In a nutshell, RTZ's 'bonanza' mines have been the subject of much political manœuvring in the last decade. It is perhaps indicative of the company's future plans that it acquired a 49% interest in the Cerro Colorado copper project in Panama in 1980.[62] Australasia and South Africa is now off the investment list and the Americas could be the favourite location for new projects in the 1980s.

Summary

These final case studies highlight the dominant role that transnationals continue to play in the world mineral industry. It is true that producing nations have weakened the power of transnationals through nationalizations, fiscal policies and more favourable agreements over new projects. They remain dependent, however, upon transnationals and other 'Northern' based institutions for assistance in the pricing and marketing of their commodities.

The 'Southern' nations' quest for a greater say in their own resource development has received active support from the United Nations, primarily through UNDP, UNCTAD and UNCLOS. Overall, the original optimism that 'North–South' relations would become more harmonious through the creation of a Common Fund for an IPC and an International Seabed Authority for deep-sea mining in UNCLOS has evaporated as the economic recession has created a hardening of attitudes at the negotiating table. The Lomé Agreements typify the problem. Each renegotiated agreement has witnessed a further polarization of views on the future of the Convention. With the 'real' prices of commodities at an all-time low and costs continuing to rise, it is understandable, if regrettable, that an 'every man for himself' approach is becoming a feature of the 1980s – hardly an advertisement for sound international commodity management.

12   Food Management

12.1 Introduction

In Chapter 5 it was argued that the basic problem of food production concerns how secure conditions can be created so that investment in the technologies of increasing yields and improving availability can take place. Food problems are institutional: organized effort is necessary to promote economic growth so that a proper diet may be afforded by all and investment secured in food production and marketing.

12.1.1 Rural Poverty and Rural Development

People are hungry because they are poor. Poverty may be defined in terms of three things – inadequate access to land, leading to insufficient production; inadequate means of exchange (of labour, production, and other assets) through which the shortfall may be recouped; or inadequate public and private transfers of goods and services to meet minimum needs when production and exchange fail. Evidence for the first of these comes from sources such as the 1975/76 Nutrition Survey of Rural Bangladesh, the principal results of which are reproduced in Table 12.1.[1] Clearly, access to land and food intake are directly

Table 12.1: Per capita food consumption and nutrient intake per day in relation to size of land holding. *Source:* FAO, 1982, *The State of Food and Agriculture 1981*, p. 85

Landholding (*acres*)	Food consumption (*grams*)	Nutrient intake Calories (*K cal*)	Protein (*grams*)
Landless	694	1,925	53·9
0·01–0·49	683	1,924	52·6
0·50–0·99	745	2,035	57·7
1·00–2·99	783	2,193	62·5
3·00 +	843	2,375	67·6

related. Further, the FAO point out that not just the quantity of land may be relevant. The quality may be a crucial variable: small farmers on irrigated fertile land with a potential for double or even triple cropping cannot be compared with those lacking access to irrigation. The rents small farmers have to pay may also be of great significance – sometimes a large proportion of production may be diverted to landlords as rent. In Africa, where land is relatively plentiful, a further difficulty exists in the form of limits to food output through lack of labour power. Confined to the hoe and the digging stick, the family may not be able to cultivate sufficient land for its needs and may be too poor to afford to hire labourers. More generally, the ability to sustain draught animals may be crucial.

It is thus possible to find families plunged into poverty by an inadequacy of any of the major factors of production – land, labour, or capital – but the relative importance of each of these may differ between various countries, type of household, and situations, although the crucial factor is land.[2]

If insufficient food is available from one's own efforts, employment and reliance on the local food market is necessary. A major cause of poverty in rural areas is the lack of lucrative employment opportunities, partly because of the prevalence of self-sufficiency as a means of production, and partly because of the lack of other spheres of economic activity such as local manufacturing and government services such as health care, education and water supplies. Such services are most often developed enthusiastically only in urban areas. Thus the relationship between hunger, rural poverty, and rural development is complex and wide ranging, involving land arrangements, land prices, rents, and credit charges; the prices commanded by products and labour; the terms of trade for necessary inputs; and the ability to survive setbacks such as illness or drought.

A failure to appreciate the complexities of poverty has led to a dearth of effective solutions and it calls for a much clearer understanding of poverty processes if cures are to be found in future. Governments will have to give much greater effort to understanding the detailed functioning of the rural economy and the identification of the many people who are suffering from various types of deprivation and poverty.[3]

What is to be done? A world conference on Agrarian Reform and Rural Development in July 1979 authorized the FAO and other UN agencies to 'sensitize' member countries to the problems of rural poverty. Specifically, FAO has called for programmes of action.[4] *Land reform* is a top priority, not only where land ownership is concentrated into the hands of a few:[5]

Even where access to land is not currently a problem, for instance where customary land tenure is practised and/or where shifting agriculture still exists, governments would be well advised to consider introducing policies with respect to the holding and owning of land. This is because with increased pressure, increases in size of holdings by land purchase, appropriation of public lands and 'privatisation' of communal lands by the more economically, socially, or politically powerful families in a locality can rapidly lead to a situation where the least fortunate families in the locality can find themselves deprived of their source of 'livelihood'.

The complexity of causal factors relevant to rural poverty demands urgent attention to *decentralization* and participation by the affluent groups in any scheme of development. Otherwise the scope for alienation, misunderstanding and failure in any scheme of improvement is enormous. Communal self-help can overcome many of the potential bottlenecks:[6]

... groups can share out a bag of fertiliser or seeds or a can of spray materials which may be too large for any single poor household to purchase. Disadvantaged rural groups can also form their own credit institutions to mobilise and pool whatever savings they can generate. ...

The development of *appropriate technology* is also urged:[7]

Even where governments have ensured a good regional coverage of research activities aimed at small farmers, it is still possible to find groups of farmers unable to adopt output-increasing techniques, or unwilling to do so. Very often further investigations show that this is because these households lack the resources required to implement the complete technology package.

In this context, programmes of education designed to improve literacy also have an important role to play. *Simplified delivery systems* for fertilizers and infrastructural development are also required. A truck-based scheme of improvement clearly has little relevance to areas lacking bridges and roads.

The problem may not be production-based, however. Many farming households are in difficulty because the prices received for surplus produce are not sufficient to cover their costs. Similarly, the poor are in a weak bargaining position with respect to the price of essential inputs – fertilizers, water services and machinery. Close *attention to the micro-economics of rural production* is therefore urged, particularly through the formation of local credit unions:[8]

Increasing the access of low income farmers to formal credit institutions in this manner, and hence increasing the competition faced by informal lenders, is probably a much more effective way of lowering the cost of credit than attempting to legislate against high interest rates or introducing subsidised credit schemes.

A principal theme in the financial plight of poor small farmers has been the urban bias of many existing government policies. Whereas it is true that the main beneficiaries of a move away from cheap food policies would be the larger, more commercial farmers, the greatest benefits in terms of quantitative improvements in the standard of living, it is argued, would go to the small farmer. The landless would not benefit, and such a move would have to be closely coordinated with other policies designed to improve their lot.

Increased employment opportunities in rural areas are essential if the cycle of poverty is to be broken down. Legislation designed to discourage the exploitation of cheap labour in the cash-crop sector may be useful in this context. 'Food for work' programmes of public works to improve local infrastructure may also have a role to play. Cooperatives may be established to develop and expand traditional craft industries such as furniture making. More fundamentally:[9]

Governments can also encourage the location of industry in rural areas, especially small and medium sized firms, by adopting systems of fiscal incentives and expanding infrastructures for power and water supply, transport, communications, and housing. The development of agro-industry through government promotion of both local production and processing of agricultural raw materials, strengthens agro-industrial linkages.

It is too early to assess the extent to which such advice has been heeded,, but Mabogunje has reviewed programmes of rural development and concluded[10] that whereas it had been recognized that a 'big push' was required, meaning a 'speedy and dramatic, comprehensive and total transformation of the rural areas of a country, accomplished by the people themselves, with their muscles, resources, and organizational talents, and with a minimum of foreign financial assistance', what actually happened was the confusion of a 'big push' with 'big investment' and hence a failure to achieve any extensive impact. He finds[11] that land reform produced marked increases in production and productivity where the necessary infrastructure, credit, advice, and other supports were made available to the new small landowners. He also sees cooperatives as a realistic path to rural development but warns[12] that attempts to develop them in many underdeveloped countries in the past have met more often with failure than with success.

In fact, food policies within developing countries have often exacerbated the maldistribution of wealth. Generally, government payments that subsidize inputs to agriculture go primarily to those farmers already relatively well placed with regard to access to factors of production, for example land and credit. Further, the overall effect of infrastructural improvements such as road schemes (or canals) benefit only those who have vehicles (or boats). More distant markets, perhaps offering better prices, become available to those with the ability to use the new facilities. The small men are left to deal at local markets, perhaps to become increasingly dependent on a reduced number of traders offering poor prices. Government investment, therefore, actually worsens the plight of many.

Perhaps the divisive consequences of élitist economic rural development are most clearly to be seen in Latin America. Barraclough[13] has found a dualism in Latin American agriculture. On the one hand there is a modernizing commercial sector of mostly large farmers who have access to the best land, easier access to national and international markets, to credit, new technology, services, and manufactured goods; on the other hand, the bulk of the rural population, without such access, produces primarily for family consumption and local markets. Successive land reforms have helped to disintegrate former feudal haciendas into large commercial farms and traditional small holdings. The latter account for approximately 70% of the labour force and are characterized by a great deal of unemployment and underdevelopment. The small producers place family subsistence and risk avoidance as top priorities when making decisions. Little security can be offered for loans. Low incomes, high costs of purchased inputs and capital, limited land, low prices and low incentives for surplus production, militate against the traditional peasant producer taking advantage of expanding urban markets.

A further set of limiting factors stems from commercial cash crop production:[14]

The control of sugar, wheat, meat, feed grains, cotton, bananas, dairy products, fruits, etc., that are sold in the large cities or abroad is generally concentrated in the hands of relatively few financial groups. These oligarchies work hand in hand with the multinationals and other foreign investors, and with national and local government officials. They usually have great influence over government bureaucracies, either directly by furthering bureaucrats and politicians self-interests, or indirectly through their own considerable political power.

In short, traditional agriculture has been continually squeezed. It seems that the problem of rural development cannot be left to private enterprise. All the evidence suggests that this, in practice, leads to an exacerbation of differences in opportunity and problems of mass poverty. On the other hand, where is the funding, the expertise, and the organization of Mabogunje's 'big push' going to come from? Food aid from external sources is one answer and is discussed below (section 12.4.2). A new international economic order allocating a larger share of profits from 'North–South' trade to producer countries is another oft-canvassed solution (Chapter 11). The International Fund for Agricultural Development (IFAD) was established in 1977 for this very purpose.

12.2.2   The International Fund for Agricultural Development

IFAD was established to mobilize food production through assistance to small farmers and landless labourers in the form of concessionary grants to the governments of developing countries. Just over a billion dollars was made available, 56% by the OECD countries of the 'North' and 43% by the OPEC countries. Between 1978 and 1980 about 90% of initial resources were committed to food production and rural development projects in 69 countries; subsequently funds have been replenished. Many of the IFAD-supported projects are co-financed with other international financial institutions such as the World Bank. In Pakistan, the Agricultural Development Bank was the partner in a scheme to extend credit to small farmers throughout the country. Rural credit officers on motor cycles were able to service even the remotest villages. Elsewhere, assistance has also improved credit facilities, although irrigation projects have also featured, in Nepal and Bangladesh for example.[15]

Many see rural development as an economic problem capable of solution only through international action and cooperation. For example, Lamond takes the view:[16]

In some countries it would be logical to stop short of full self-sufficiency in food whilst others should become exporters, e.g. Sudan and Brazil, but investment to do so relies on availability of stable prices and assurances that stability of prices would not be undermined by the erection of protection barriers around existing countries involved in production.

As seen in Chapter 4 and further developed in Chapter 11 the notion of stabilized commodity prices is a major theme of UNCTAD's deliberations in recent years.

Valdes[17] points out that agricultural commodities account for a large part of the export earnings of most less developed countries (LDCs). Rural development, as with any economic growth in many countries, depends on export revenues. If agricultural exports are expanded, the increase in the domestic production of LDCs could raise income-earning employment among low-income farm families. But a variety of agricultural trade barriers, including tariffs and non-tariff barriers such as export quotas, exist to frustrate such expansion.

Valdes attempted an exploration of the effects of a 50% reduction in agricultural protectionism on the part of OECD countries. He calculates a resulting increase in the real income of 56 LDCs of 1 billion US dollars per annum, although only 15% of this, he thinks, would accrue to low-income countries, the bulk going to South America's already large commercial producers such as Argentina and Brazil. The higher prices expected to follow trade liberalization, however, could lead to a loss of $605 million for grain importers amongst LDCs including Bangladesh, Egypt, Upper Volta and Venezuela. These countries export few agricultural products while they import foods that are highly protected in the OECD. It would appear, therefore, that there is no panacea to the problem of rural development. No magic wand can be waved, whether in terms of the internal institutional structure and policies of a country, or in terms of the international economic order. There seems to be no alternative to the present patchwork of rural development projects, efforts to increase food security, and attempts to alleviate the situation through food aid.

2.3.1 Decision making and Institutional Structure

Hopkins[18] has defined a 'global food system' in terms of three interrelated functions – production, distribution, and consumption – and in terms of their interconnections via public and private transactions. This indicates the major actors in food policy making. Of course, decisions are the province of many individuals ranging from peasant farmers to bacon packaging plant managers. Indeed, as Paarlberg[19] says, each of us is an actor in the global food system. In policy making, groups tend to be more influential, and organized groups are most effective when backed up by the power of governments. Paarlberg identifies five types of actor in describing the global food hierarchy reproduced as Figure 12.1.[20]

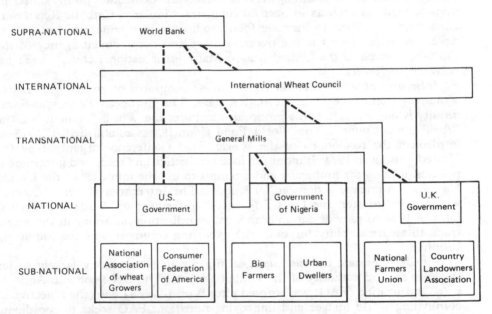

Figure 12.1 Food Actors
Source: Hopkins *et al*, 1982, *Food in the Global Arena*, Holt, Rinehart & Winston, p. 33

Sub-national actors include groups of farmers and commodity producers, such as the National Farmers Union in the UK and the National Farmers Organization or the National Association of Wheat Growers in the US. Consumer groups have become increasingly important as has the advertising industry, with nine of the top fifteen holding companies promoting UK advertising being involved with food or confectionery products and spending a total of over £300 million in 1982.[21]

As outlined in Chapter 5, *national* actors, in the form of government departments of agriculture have been and are of the greatest importance in supporting, encouraging (through research and development) and regulating food production and distribution. Government departments concerned with overseas trade also have an important role to play. Their influence is as complex and varied as the production and distribution of food itself. In the United States in

1979 for example, there were five Senate Committees, six Congressional Committees, and two committees within the executive office of the President as well as the Federal Department of Agriculture, the Department of Commerce, and the Department of State involved with aspects of food policy. The United States Department of Agriculture itself had almost twenty major divisions or agencies with concerns at home or abroad. Food policy is as big a business as food production.

Transnational actors in the form of multinational companies and international aid organizations may be identified as the third level in the hierarchy. Agribusiness is of such importance that it forms the subject of the next section. Transnational aid organizations include Oxfam and Catholic Relief Services. Oxfam was founded in 1942 in Oxford, England, as an international famine relief and rural development agency. It collects and distributes public subscriptions to food aid projects in over 80 countries. Similarly, Catholic Relief Services supports efforts to increase food production in a wide range of underdeveloped countries. It is the overseas relief and development agency of the Catholic Church in the United States. Many other national churches are involved in such work.

International actors include organizations composed of government representatives from more than one nation state. The European Economic Community is one such, but this group also includes the Wheat Council, and the World Food Council. The World Food Council was established in 1975 to implement the resolutions of the World Food Conference organized by the United Nations in 1974. It monitors food production and trade and government policies, looking for problems, and attempts to use the influence of the United Nations to stimulate action on bottlenecks. The International Wheat Council was established after the GATT (General Agreement on Trade and Tariffs) talks of 1948 to provide the international coordination necessary in the wheat trade to assure stability for both the exporting countries and the importing countries.

Finally, there are the *supranational* organizations, operating largely under the auspices and authority of the United Nations. The UN Food and Agriculture Organization (FAO) was formed after World War II with the objective of eliminating world hunger and improving nutrition. FAO seeks to coordinate the efforts of governments and technical agencies in programmes for developing agriculture, forestry and fisheries. It carries out research, provides technical assistance on a project basis to individual countries, and maintains statistics on world production, trade, and consumption. The World Food Programme (WFP) was established in 1961 jointly by FAO and the Economic and Social Council of the General Assembly (ECOSOC). The programme provides food rather than technical assistance towards the production of food. The food so distributed is donated by member countries, the United States, Canada and the European Community having made the largest contributions. The United Nations Development Programme was established in 1965 and is the world's largest channel for international technical advice and cooperation.

The most important supranational organization is the International Bank for Reconstruction and Development, commonly known as the World Bank. Formed in 1945 to provide loans for post-war reconstruction, the bank operates to finance a wide range of projects that further the economic development of member states. Only a proportion of these are agricultural or rural. A subsidiary of the World Bank, the International Development Association (IDA) is organized specifically to provide finance for development projects in less developed countries on concessionary terms. After the World Food Conference of 1974 the needs of rural development were felt to require higher priority and a special institutional structure and, as already considered, the International Fund for Agricultural Development (IFAD) was established in 1977. The growing demands for a 'new international economic order' featured in Chapters 2, 4 and 11, have not been confined to UNCTAD. The World Food Programme has also been seen as a key method by which the least developed countries may be able to establish a better deal for themselves. The problem facing these countries (the group of 77) in achieving a greater influence on policy making on the supranational scene has been succinctly put by Talbot:[22]

... the group of 77 (not including its rich O.P.E.C. members) has the votes, but the O.E.C.D. and wealthy O.P.E.C. member states have the money...

Talbot describes events at supranational meetings as a kind of battle, with the group of 77 trying to achieve full implementation of the resolutions of the World Food Conference, whilst the OECD countries continue to organize things to their own advantage.

The OECD countries have a clear policy that food aid should go to the poorest nations, whilst the group of 77 believe that some of the poorest of the poor are to be found in middle-income developing and newly industrialized countries. They are not such a united group as to allow a disproportionate share of aid to be allocated to one part of the world. Talbot says that the WFP bureaucracy has to balance the allocation of aid on the basis of equal shares for regions as much as need.

All this is to say that, like policy making within national agencies, the policies and decisions of the supranational bodies involved with food are the product of a web of interests and underlying pressures and are by no means solely the end product of rational calculation. By comparison, policy making on the part of the transnational corporations heavily involved in food around the world is straightforward and relatively simple.

2.3.2 Agribusiness

The term agribusiness refers to the whole system of modern industrialized agriculture, including not only the production of food and other soft commodities but also related products such as machinery, pesticides, fertilizers, seeds and animal feeds. In both developed and developing countries the way in which food is presented and produced, and at what price, is being increasingly determined by the investment and trading decisions of transnational corporations. The domination of such companies and the dependence of producing countries with regard to the great traded commodities has already been discussed in Chapters 4 and 11. With particular regard to food, Table 12.2 shows the world's biggest food and beverage processing companies in order of size, as published by the radical magazine *New Internationalist*.[23] Much of the literature on agribusiness has been critical. Burbach and Flynn[24] have scathingly described the impact of transnationals in South America with such chapter headings as 'Canned Imperialism: Del Monte in Mexico', and 'A New 'Banana Republic': Del Monte in Guatemala'. They say:[25]

Today the tentacles of the transnational agribusiness corporations extend deep into Latin America. Old time banana companies such as United Fruit have been joined by an array of modern agribusiness enterprises intent on penetrating the most dynamic of profitable sectors of Latin America's emerging agribusiness system. Food processors such as Pillsburg, Standard Brands and General Foods, agrichemical producers such as Du Pont and W.R. Grace, and farm equipment manufacturers such as International Harvester and John Deere now number among the biggest transnational agribusiness investors in Latin America. And these corporate giants are far more active in Latin America than in any other world region – over three-fourths of all U.S. Agribusiness subsidiaries in the third world are now located in Latin American countries.

And further, they note:[26]

The corporations use their control of technology, financial resources, manufacturing facilities, and marketing to penetrate and dominate key economic sectors in the third world. In terms of sheer size, the big transnationals often overwhelm third word countries. The sales of each of the top ten U.S. Agribusiness corporations exceed the Gross Domestic Product of twenty-one of the twenty-eight republics in Latin America and the Caribbean.

Table 12.2: The world's largest food and beverage processing companies 1976.
    Source: New Internationalist, February 1982, p. 11

Company	Home country	Revenue from Food processing (*million* US dollars)	Total revenue (*million* dollars)	Proportion foreign (%)
Unilever Ltd	UK/Nld	7,900	14,800	71
Nestlé	Swiss	6,248	7,248	95
Kraft	US	4,776	4,977	15
General Foods	US	4,402	4,910	26
Esmark Inc. (Swift)	US	3,955	5,301	16
Beatrice Foods	US	3,943	5,289	21
Coca-Cola	US	2,911	3,033	44
Greyhound Corp.	US	2,385	3,738	–
Ralston Purina	US	2,365	3,394	24
Borden Inc.	US	2,336	3,381	16
United Brands	US	2,130	2,276	26
Iowa Beef Processors	US	2,077	2,077	0
Imperial Group	UK	2,070	5,790	12
Archer-Daniels-Midland	US	2,065	2,118	27
Pepsico	US	2,051	2,728	21
Assoc. British Foods	UK	2,050	3,012	–
Carnation Co.	US	2,004	2,167	15
CPC International	US	1,968	2,696	55
LTV Corp.	US	1,919	4,497	–
Heinz	US	1,882	1,882	41
Seagram	Can	1,874	2,049	94
Rank Hovis & McDougall	UK	1,801	1,861	13
Procter & Gamble	US	1,800	7,349	25
Nabisco	US	1,780	2,027	29
General Mills	US	1,735	2,909	16

The basic issue raised by these transnational investments concerns the social impact they have on the Latin American countryside. The accusation is that nearly all market-oriented investment favours the large landowner. Nearly all agribusiness development, it is argued, drives a deeper wedge between the haves and the have-nots. The beneficiaries, it is said, are urban élites and the already affluent countries of the 'North' who import the resulting produce. Meanwhile, the traditional rural peasantry become poorer.

Not everybody, however, sees the intervention of transnational corporations in negative terms. Harman has argued that the advent of the great food companies has considerably reduced vulnerability to climatic variations and disasters because they have created a buffer of food processing and marketing resources.[27] The companies, it is argued, offer technology to overcome institutional and climatic barriers to agricultural development in three important respects. On the farm, mechanization, water and land management can greatly increase productivity. Post-harvest losses are greatly reduced when production is under the control of the transnational corporations. Food processing, it is argued, often improves the quality of the food, albeit through the addition of artificial nutrients. His basic argument, however, is that through the basic mission of the TNC 'to transfer and commercialise the technologies it creates',[28] the TNCs transfer useful products, provide technical assistance, establish local service facilities, and play an important role in the training of personnel.

As to the organization of the companies themselves, and their procedures of policy making and planning, very little is known. Reference works on international business such as the *World Directory of Multinational Enterprises*, give profiles of the complex web of subsidiary operating companies and brand names that are in the control of particular groups. The Nestlé Company for example operates in ten major market sectors of the food business ranging from infant and diabetic products to restaurants and hotels. In all, the company operates in forty-five countries through over ninety principal subsidiaries. As well as the Nescafé coffee brand, the company promotes Libby fruit juices, Chambourcy yogurts and Findus frozen foods around the world. The company began as a Swiss manufacturer of condensed milk in the 19th century, expanded into chocolate in the early decades of this century, grew significantly in the 1930s due to its involvement with instant drinks such as Nescafé, but really burgeoned as a major world force in the post-war decades.

Morgan has provided some insight into the nature of corporate policy-making and the web of worldwide influence enjoyed by the major grain companies, although his approach is anecdotal.[29] He argues that the five major world grain merchants, Cargill Inc of Minneapolis, the Continental Grain Company of New York, André of Lausanne (Switzerland), Louis Dreyfus of Paris, and the Bunge Corporation (Argentina), enjoy status and influence equal to that of the 'Seven Sisters', the seven major oil companies:[30]

Grain provided the cash flow and capital for the post-war expansion of the five grain giants, just as oil financed the vertical and horizontal integration of the petroleum companies into uranium, coal, chemicals and plastics. Mysterious and obscure as the firms may be, they are near perfect stereotypes of the new global corporations that manage the distribution and processing of basic resources in the late 20th Century.

The grain companies control shipping, storage, communications and processing, and therefore, in effect, are the major pipelines of world grain trade.

Cargill and Continental deal with half of all US exports of grain. The Big Five, according to Morgan,[31] dominate the grain trade of the Common Market, the Canadian barley trade, the South African maize trade, and the Argentinian wheat trade. All five are private companies run by family shareholders. Trends such as the growing importance of American-style diets requiring the import of grain, and the growing diplomatic importance of food aid, have helped the grain companies grow; they have indeed been fostered and encouraged by them in their own interests. Morgan argues that their role in the world food crisis of 1973/74 (Chapter 5) was crucial: they were the agents of unexpectedly large supplies to the Soviet Union.

12.4.1 British Food Policy in the Post-War Years

When the authors of this book were infants, food was rationed in Britain. Today, food of all kinds is freely available in a wide variety of retail outlets. There is no possibility of shortages or queueing for a meal. The food is available at a price, but pensions, welfare payments and incomes are such that no one need experience acute hunger in modern Britain. To this extent, food policy has been spectacularly successful. In this section the policies that have achieved this are first outlined and the changes brought about in British agriculture are discussed. In recent years, three questions have arisen, however, over the desirability of practice. These concern the high cost of the policy, the possibility that the tax payer may be heavily subsidizing the degradation of his environment, and the extent to which world trade in food has been unnecessarily and damagingly disrupted. Each of these is considered in turn. Table 12.3 shows changes in the home production of crops and livestock in the UK over the period 1952–1977.

Whilst the area of agricultural production and the numbers engaged in agriculture have fallen, production has increased in every sector save three (oats, potatoes and milk), in some cases spectacularly (e.g. wheat and barley) and yields show very satisfactory increases. This has been achieved through the intensification of agriculture by capital investment. Capital investment has been made worthwhile, and directly subsidized, as a result of deliberate policy.

The Agriculture Act of 1947 introduced a system of guaranteed prices for the major food commodities (salad and other green vegetables being the major exception). A system of deficiency payments was established to 'top up', if necessary, the difference between market prices and the guaranteed price. The guaranteed price was supposed to provide a secure climate for investment. Tariffs were imposed on food imports so that its price reached the level of the guaranteed price when necessary and hence did not undermine the home producers. A system of marketing boards for major foods such as eggs and potatoes, established in the 1930s in an attempt to ease the deep depression of British agriculture, was continued and extended. Depression followed by war had left an enormous backlog of investment.

The price policy did not at first cause the desired increase in investment[32] so, in 1951, the first of what was to become a formidable array of direct production grants was introduced for the purchase and application of phosphate fertilizers. In succeeding years, grants became available for the re-seeding of pasture, beef cattle breeding, land drainage and permanent investment in a

Table 12.3: Changes in British agriculture. *Source:* Royal Commission on
Environmental Pollution, 7th Report, Agriculture and Pollution, 1979,
HMSO, p. 7

	1952	1977
1 Area of agricultural production ('000 ha) (crops and grass – excluding rough grazing)	12,616	11,989
2 Numbers engaged in agriculture (thousands)	869	373·2
3 Production (thousand tonnes)		
Wheat	2,344	5,274
Barley	2,371	10,531
Oats	2,816	790
Potatoes	7,974	6,621
Sugar	587	949
Beef and veal	606	1,032
Mutton and lamb	168	229
Pork	153	650
Bacon and ham	397	218
Poultry meat	86	678
Butter	18	134
Cheese	64	206
Milk for liquid consumption (million litres)	7,617	7,485
Eggs (million dozen)	688	1,156
4 Yields		
Wheat (tonnes/ha)	2·85	4·90
Barley (tonnes/ha)	2·57	4·39
Oats (tonnes/ha)	2·41	4·06
Sugar (tonnes/ha)	4·35	5·40
Potatoes (tonnes/ha)	19·90	28·50
Liquid milk (litres/dairy cow)	2,734	4,452
Eggs per hen	145	240·5

wide range of new fixed equipment. By 1960/61 such direct grants had reached
a total value of £100 million and accounted for 40% of all payments to farmers.[33] Not only 'technical fixes' were being applied. The National Advisory
Service and research stations produced a torrent of advice on more efficient
practice. A series of higher-rated grants was also developed to cater for the
investment needs of upland farmers. The importance of guaranteed prices for
investment, notwithstanding the availability of grants, led to the annual review
becoming the highlight of the farming year. In 1956 long-term assurances were
given that the government would not reduce the level of support prices by
more than 2·5% in any one year. This secured further investment by helping
forward planning. By the early 1960s surpluses were being produced in the
dairy sector and 'Commodity Agreements' were established limiting food imports (such as New Zealand butter) to acceptably non-competitive levels.

In 1973 the UK joined the European Economic Community and hence
subscribed to the Common Agricultural Policy (CAP). Under CAP the European Council of Ministers guarantee prices as before, but the mechanisms of
assuring farmers' incomes differ. Instead of paying deficiency payments direct
to farmers, the EEC buys commodities to assure that the market price is maintained at the guaranteed level and takes action to prevent imported supplies
reaching the market at lower prices. The purchased commodities are stored for
sale later (a rare event) or for 'denaturalization' (made unfit for human con-

sumption) and sold for industrial purposes or as animal feed. They may also be exported at a cut price. The average level of CAP prices was higher than the British average level and consumers experienced an increase in food prices whilst producers received a greater incentive towards increased production. Direct investment grants from the British Government were replaced by a system of CAP 'Farm Capital Grant Schemes' of similar intent and effect. Bowers and Cheshire calculate that in 1980/81[34] the effect of the CAP in Britain was to award each farmer in Britain an average of £1918 per annum (a total of £567·6 million), and that the total cost of the policy (including the difference between CAP prices and estimates of what might have been world free-market prices, and including all sorts of hidden subsidies such as fuel tax relief and other tax advantages enjoyed by the farming community) at between £9418 and £12,112 per farmer in 1979. Thirty years of investment security and grant-aid have produced the situation shown in Table 12.4, which shows the extent to which British agriculture leads the EEC in economic efficiency. British firms are larger and more intensive than all their continental counterparts.

Table 12.4: The efficiency of British agriculture: agriculture in the major countries of the EEC. *Source:* EEC, 1983, p. 7

	West Germany	France	Italy	United Kingdom
Share of agriculture in GDP (%)	2·0	4·2	7·5	2·1
Employment in primary industry (000s)	1,518	1,871	2,925	637
% Population in agriculture	6·0	8·8	14·2	2·6
Number of farms more than 1 ha (000s)	797	1,135	2,192	249
% Farms less than 10 ha	51·0	35·0	86·0	24·0
Average utilized agricultural area per farm (ha)	15·2	25·4	7·4	68·7
Cattle per owner	27	33	13	75
Dairy cattle per owner	12	14	6	53
Fattening pigs per owner	41	30	9	225

Britain leads the EEC in the performance of its agricultural policy, and the EEC has commented officially that the progress which has been achieved since the commencement of the Common Agricultural Policy 'can only astonish'.[35]

Since the foundation of the common agricultural market, food supplies in Europe have improved unprecedently in terms of both quantity and quality. The community is now self-sufficient in most agricultural products of prime necessity (with the exception of tropical products and protein feeds). Shortages have been avoided and sometimes violent and often speculative fluctuations on world markets absorbed. The food supply for the European consumer is today more plentiful and of higher quality than ever.

In recent years concern has increasingly been expressed over the cost of CAP. The Thatcher government, committed to strict control of public expenditure, finds itself with a significant budget item over which it does not have full control. Thus far, attempts to renegotiate the whole basis of CAP have floundered because of the political importance of small peasant farmers, heavily dependent on its high-price régime, in other member states.

Body estimates that since 1946 a total of £14 billion (40 billion at current values) has been spent on agricultural support. Between 1979 and 1981 the Thatcher administration succeeded in reducing public expenditure in real terms on overseas aid (by 20%), transport (by 4·8%) and education (by 3·5%). Spending on health and personal social services were contained (+0·7%) but the agricultural budget grew by 13·9%.[36] He estimates the total sum of agricultural support at around £3,350 million per annum when all tax and other considerations are included, and says:[37]

As the sum of £3,350,000,000 is being diverted each year away from where it would otherwise be spent, in effect from other industries and services, it may be instructive to compare it with the capital of our greatest companies. It is almost the total capital of our four main clearing banks (£3,546,000,000). It is very much more than the capital of I.C.I. (£1,936,000,000), three times that of Unilever (£1,133,000,000) and thirteen times that of Courtaulds (£245,900,000). To suggest that thirteen new companies, the size of Courtaulds, could be established every year, were a different policy pursued, cannot be entirely unreasonable.

He argues that the level of support given to agriculture represents a misuse of resources, emphasizing the view that the more the resources of Britain are misused, the more the people of Britain are pushed towards a lower standard of living and are deprived of what they could otherwise have.

Further, it might be argued that current fixed policy is socially regressive. If subsidies meant high taxes and low food prices, because a greater proportion of the income of the poor goes on food, then the system would be progessive. The rich, who pay most taxes, would be cross-subsidizing the poor, who would benefit most from cheap food. But present policy involves high tax subsidy *and* high prices. The rich pay taxes *and* the poor pay a lot for their food. Landowners gain. Bowers and Cheshire argue that the result of massive capital subsidy in British agriculture has been to triple land prices.[38] This, they say, demonstrates a normal market reaction to a high level of agricultural subsidies. An acceleration in land prices in the 1970s reflected both the higher levels of support from CAP and the general movement of assets into real property in the face of accelerating inflation.

Body points out that farms that changed hands at £10 per acre in the 1930s are now worth a hundred times more. Modern, intensive and highly capitalized agriculture is so well protected that land ownership is almost a licence to print money. Consequently, insurance companies and banks have poured money into agricultural land. Every pound so used is diverted away from investment in trade and industry elsewhere. Further, the pressure is on to show an adequate return on capital invested. The pressure is on to make investments pay, and this, it is argued, has had disastrous effects on the quality of the British countryside.

All over the country upland areas are being ploughed, fertilized and reseeded. Talking of one beauty spot in Wales, Bowers and Cheshire comment:[39]

Developments such as these are not the result of some inevitable technical progress or pressure of population on resources. They result solely and simply from the economic insanity of agricultural policies and support measures.

Hedgerows and other habitats for wildlife are being ripped up in the search for higher rates of return on capital. British policy with regard to the countryside is considered in the following chapter, but it is appropriate to note Bowers and Cheshire's view here:[40]

In a rich and leisured society, where obesity is a greater health risk than malnutrition – despite unemployment and slow growth this is still the case in Europe in the 1980s – it is absurd to pretend that adding to surplus food production gives clear economic benefit; whilst environmental quality, pure water supplies, pollution or beautiful countryside, are figments of some namby-pamby environmentalist's imagination.

In 1979 a Royal Commission on Environmental Pollution produced a report on agriculture and pollution. They found that since World War II the use of pesticides of all sorts (including herbicides) had grown enormously. They estimate the value of the products applied to have increased from around £40 million to over £140 million (both at 1976 prices) between 1950 and 1976.[41] They received a great deal of evidence of growing concern over the dependence of modern agriculture on pesticides and the risks posed by these chemicals to wildlife and potentially to man.[42] They concluded[43] that tighter controls on pesticide use were desirable, not only on environmental grounds but in the interests of farmers.

There had also been a marked increase in the use of fertilizers, especially of a nitrogenous variety. As well as a major factor in increased yields, especially of cereals, intensive dairying made heavy use of such chemicals to improve pasture. About 1·2 million tonnes of nitrogen are now applied annually.[44] This has caused rising nitrate levels in many sources of water supply. The health implications of prevailing levels require further investigation.[45] A number of trends in livestock farming also gave rise to increased pollution – indoor housing of herds posed problems of liquid slurry disposal, new techniques of silage production had produced a particularly acute form of river pollution where accidental discharge of effluent had occurred.[46] Intensive livestock rearing (factory farming) posed new problems; in the Commission's view, insufficient attention had been given to the pollution they may cause.[47]

If one adds to all these issues those concerning conservation discussed in Chapter 13, and the wider issues such as the depopulation of rural villages and the difficulties of the children of farming families gaining entry to the business on their own account, it is clear that the capitalization that has occurred under recent policies has not by any means always produced beneficial effects on the countryside of Britain. A final criticism of food policy in Britain concerns its impact on the rest of the world.

The arrangements contained in The Lomé Convention for encouraging the import of non-competitive foodstuffs to the EEC from elsewhere in the world were discussed in Chapter 11. It is sometimes argued that the exclusion of one of the best food markets (the EEC) has the effect of discouraging investment in the intensification of agriculture around the world. Perhaps countries of the 'South' would gain significantly if they could negotiate contract sales of their produce in Europe at lower prices than currently prevail. Perhaps even the farmers of North America could benefit from access to this large, easily serviced and relatively affluent market. According to this view, the wild fluctuations in 'basic' food prices which occur from time to time on the world market, happen because it is a residual market. The United States, Eastern Europe, the Soviet Union and the EEC all look inwards and make their own arrangements, leaving no great body of blue chip customers to form a reliable market.

Further, the tendency to dump surpluses on the rest of the world does nothing to help the prospects for investment for production in developing countries. On the other hand the EEC points out:[48]

The proportion of world agricultural exports accounted for by the (enlarged) European Community increased slightly between 1973 and 1980 from 9·5 to 11%; the share of the United States, one of the main critics of the Community's agricultural exports, fell just as slightly, from 19·8 to 19%. This variation can hardly be regarded as a sign of superseding competition. It is not an aim of the common agricultural policy to oust others from the world market, but rather to provide European farmers with a reasonable share of world trade and its growth.

The community also participates in programmes of food aid, either directly or through aid organizations. Food aid is intended to help in emergencies but it can also contribute to the recipient country's economic development.

2.4.2   Food Aid

Although currently only about 8% of the food eaten in developing countries is imported, the extent to which food aid appears necessary is frightening.[49] Several types of food aid exist. First, *investment* is required in land and rural development. Second, *surpluses may be transferred* from one part of the world to another, effectively from 'North' to 'South'. Third, *project aid* may be established whereby food is made available to specific projects in specific countries rather than to governments for distribution and sale: these include *supplementary feeding schemes* for particularly disadvantaged nutritional groups such as nursing mothers and infants; the provision of *free school meals*; and, a variety of *'food for work'* schemes whereby public works (often designed to improve rural infrastructure) are financed, at least in part, through the payment of workers in food. Fourth, within countries, governments may attempt to extend food aid to particular groups of citizens by means of rationing or *selective subsidies*. Finally, *emergency programmes* of food distribution may be mounted in time of famine or as a major aspect of international measures of disaster relief. Each of these types of food aid are now considered briefly in turn.

Investment aid comes from a variety of sources, with multinational agencies such as the World Bank to the fore. Table 12.5 shows the trend of official assistance to agriculture over recent years. The flow of such assistance more than doubled in real terms between 1973 and 1980.[50] The share of agricultural and rural development in the lending of the multinational institutions rose to nearly 30%. Most of this goes to programmes for irrigation, drainage and the development of new agricultural land, although road construction and infrastructural developments have also had an important role to play. As regards the disposal of surpluses it has already been noted that this has a long history with respect to American and European domestic food policy. United States Public Law 480 of 1954 was intended as a mechanism for the removal of surpluses acquired by the Commodity Credit Corporation to be used as 'pump priming' in developing countries so that commercial exports might follow. From time to time, food aid has been closely associated with the United States' foreign policy. In 1974, over half the aid available went to South Vietnam and Cambodia.[51] The greater part of food aid in cereals throughout recent decades has been distributed by the United States, with Canada and Australia trailing. European

Table 12.5: Official assistance to agriculture, 1973–1980 (millions of US dollars at constant 1979 prices). *Source:* World Bank. 1982, *World Development Report*, Oxford University Press, p. 51

	1973	1974	1975	1976	1977	1978	1979	1980
Official Development Assistance								
Development assistance committee of OECD (inc. EEC countries)	1,594	2,819	2,359	2,246	3,279	3,633	4,304	3,773
Multilateral agencies	1,533	1,833	1,530	1,814	2,139	2,761	2,503	2,969
OPEC (bilateral and multilateral)	69	218	640	378	461	307	243	179
Total official assistance	3,196	4,870	4,529	4,438	5,879	6,701	7,050	6,921
Percentage change		+82	−6	−2	+32	+14	+5	−2
Other Official Flows								
Development assistance committee of OECD (inc. EEC countries)	351	275	137	395	159	403	329	222
Multilateral agencies	902	1,610	2,944	2,150	2,816	3,275	2,319	2,621
OPEC (bilateral and multilateral)	63	90	333	221	80	49	99	48
Total other official flows	1,316	1,975	3,414	2,766	3,055	3,727	2,747	2,891
Percentage change		+50	+60	−19	+10	+22	−26	+5
Grand Total	4,512	6,845	7,943	7,204	8,934	10,428	9,797	9,812
Percentage change		+62	+16	−9	+24	+17	−6	

involvement had to wait until the Common Agricultural Policy of the EEC had gone a long way towards achieving its aims of self-sufficiency. This was not until 1968. The Food Aid Convention of 1967 arose as a by-product of general agreements on trade and tariffs (GATT) between the industrialized countries of the 'North'. The Convention allowed for the following minimum availability of food aid:[52]

United States	1.89 m. tonnes
European Economic Community	1.03 m. tonnes
Canada	0.49 m. tonnes
UK, Japan and Australia	0.26 m. tonnes

In addition, the EEC agreed to supply milk fats as part of the World Food Programme operated by the UN and FAO since 1963.

Turning now to project aid the World Food Programme, established as part of the United Nations first development decade (the 1960s), is now the largest source of such aid. According to Tarrrant,[53] this has largely taken the form of school meals and food-for-work schemes. Neither of these approaches are without their problems. School meal programmes may well become available after nutritional damage has been sustained. Many food-for-work schemes are focused on road improvements. This work has to be done during the dry season: the very time that harvesting and other traditional sources of casual employment offer competing opportunities.

A range of food subsidy and ration schemes exist throughout the developing world in an attempt to reach the most vulnerable groups.[54] These often work in close association with schemes of primary education and health care. Gavan, working in Bangladesh,[55] has illustrated the difficulties of raising the food consumption of the world's poorest people by means of food subsidies. He says:

... the essential problem is to make food available at prices which the poor can afford while not reducing prices to producers to such an extent that production falls, making the policy self-defeating.

Five polices to reduce the extent of malnutrition (defined as a daily calorific intake of less than 1870 k. cal.) were identified and costed for Bangladesh:

(1) extend the existing system of subsidized rations;
(2) extend the existing system whilst at the same time trying to confine it to the poor;
(3) divert the grain at present rationed to the free market so that this extra supply reduces prevailing prices by 25%;
(4) adopt a food stamp system whereby purchases by the poor at free market prices are subsidized; and
(5) extend the coverage of the existing system but increase the extent to which supplies are procured from domestic sources.

The costs of these options were calculated as in Table 12.6. These calculations suggest that the cheapest solution, maximizing government revenue, is that of free market manipulation through the release to the market of government supplies (Option 3). Extending the existing system had serious implications for the balance of payments through an increased need to import. Resolving the dilemma by subsidizing consumption, whilst at the same time buying on the domestic market thus increasing production incentives (Option 5), was the most

Table 12.6: Costs of various food policies in Bangladesh. *Source:* J. Gavan, quoted in J.R. Tarrant, 1980, *Food Policies*, John Wiley & Son, New York, p. 169

	Policies				
	1	2	3	4	5
	Extend Rationing	As 1 but to low income households	Government grain sales	Food Stamps	As 1 with domestic procurement
Additional supplies needed (tons)	545,000	430,000	915,000	250,000	300,000
Change in market price	−7·0%	−5·0%	−14·0%	0	0
Government Net Revenue Import Costs Zero (million taka)	580	460	2,500	−750	−2,000
Import Costs at World Prices (million taka)	−914	727	0	−1,439	−2,800

expensive solution of all. The food stamp system (Option 4) also had disastrous implications for government revenue. The budget pressure to continue the existing ration system is clear, but this of course has a simultaneous depressive effect on producer prices. Gavan concludes that policies that lower prices seem destined to increase these countries' reliance on imports and food aid.

More generally, the World Bank takes the view that subsidy schemes are often wasteful in the sense that some of those receiving aid could afford their own food, thus diverting large sums of money away from other uses. The Bank prefers schemes in which strict means-tests or health screening reduce the overall costs of subsidy. In addition:[56]

Targeting by commodity, which involves changing relative prices to encourage consumption of nutritious but unpopular foods, is rarely used, but shows some promise. Sorghum was sold at half the price of wheat and rice in ration shops in Bangladesh in 1979. The poor participants, particularly in rural areas, bought more Sorghum, increasing the calories in their diet. The better-off participants in the capital city, however, preferred to pay double the Sorghum price in order to have rice or wheat.

The effectiveness of food aid has been a matter of some considerable controversy in recent years. Questions have been raised as to the extent to which aid merely replaces normal imports, and even the extent to which domestic production may have been supplanted or discouraged through artificially low prices. Tarrant[57] thinks it unlikely that these effects have occurred on a large-scale; food aid has probably had a neutral effect on levels of domestic production. More serious is the suggestion that the very existence of food aid has allowed governments to sustain policies that inhibit or ignore rural development. It is difficult to say what would have happened without food aid, but it seems unlikely that food aid in itself would create the political circumstances whereby the mass of the population's needs are ignored, or indeed in some cases, undermined.

Particular controversy has grown up around skimmed milk donated as food aid. Milk requires the enzyme lactase for its digestion. Many of the world's peoples do not have this, thus making its consumption dangerous. The use of polluted or contaminated water to reconstitute powdered milk has also caused problems, as has the improper use of skimmed milk as a substitute for breastfeeding, a practice, some say, shamelessly encouraged by multinational food distributors.

12.5 Concluding Comments

Food policy is difficult and characterized by division of opinion. On the one hand, there are the interests of those who already have more than enough food and seek to reduce or dispose of surpluses. On the other hand, there are those who do not benefit from the operation of existing arrangements. Differences of opinion serve to hamper progress in improving food security. The picture is not encouraging.

Attempts to extend programmes of rural economic development suffer from fundamental conflicts of interest between existing landowning élites and those who require greater access to the land, and between the urban middle-classes and the rural poor. Until some non-disruptive method of tackling gross inequalities of wealth and opportunity in the Third World can be found, the hungry will be with us.

If the fundamental problem cannot be tackled, perhaps some progress can be made through better organization of current production. The development of local cooperatives seems the most likely vehicle for progress, but these are vulnerable to corruption by those who are pursuing political ambitions, and are an object of suspicion on the part of existing vested interests. Certainly, the administrative skills, and perhaps even the integrity, required to operate state marketing systems seem lacking. Monolithic structures appear not to work; hence decentralization.

Turning to policies in practice, the affluent countries can afford to offer a total and all-embracing system of support to food producers. But is the cost too high? The current British situation, in which the poor pay high prices so that the highly capitalized farming community continue to increase their investment and enhance the value of their land, and in which the ordinary citizen is directly subsidizing the biggest threat to the landscape since the Industrial Revolution, certainly seems bizarre. Elsewhere, the interests of transnational corporations dealing in the disposal of United States surpluses resulting from a similarly successful system of support, has retarded progress towards food security around the world. The need to dispose of such surpluses may well have allowed governments to sustain policies that inhibit or ignore rural development; although to be fair, an appalling list of internal political difficulties act equally as barriers to achieving self-sufficiency in many countries. This is the unacceptable face of élitist political cultures. The United Nations and its sponsored and inspired organizations are trying to create a system of world food security, but these fall foul of the agribusiness corporations and the apparently close association between United States commercial and diplomatic interests. Food policy seems to be another example of the corporate imperialism discussed in the previous chapter.

The institutional structure of food appears heavily biased towards geopolitical considerations and provides a good example of the need to engage in 'North–South' dialogue. Overall, food policy touches on fundamental political interests 'North' and 'South'. The alleviation of the food problem seems a long way off, because of poor administration in the 'South' and vested interests in the 'North'. People are what they eat. They eat what they can afford, and what is available. Availability is conditioned by a web of global economic and political interests that involve some of the most difficult questions facing mankind – poverty, injustice and social conflict. Food for thought indeed.

13   Forestry and Wilderness Management

3.1.1 Introduction

It was noted in Chapter 6 that forestry and wilderness resources are developed and managed according to the value society is willing to place on them. With these resources, more so than with any others in this textbook, 'management' is synonymous with 'conservation' in that policy objectives should be framed with *long-term* equilibrium of resource-use being a top priority. The ideal is far from being realized, as issues of national security, land ownership and conflicts over the use of forest and wilderness areas lead to inevitable 'trade offs' between development and preservation.

The designation of areas as protected landscapes requires some form of subjective assessment of the resource base. Resource managers become part of an inherent political process in that they have to allocate and classify areas according to techniques of evaluation prior to the political scheduling of management zones. On establishing priority areas, management of the resource is conducted according to the institutional philosophy prevailing at the time.

Ultimately the responsibility of forestry and wilderness resources rests with government because of the control government exerts through managing its own property (most of the world's forests and protected landscapes are publicly owned). Government is therefore the main agent of change. Policy will be shaped according to the pressure exerted by interest groups who wish to develop or preserve national resources. An excellent example of such a fluid system is that of the US, where the former Secretary of the Interior from 1980 to 1983, James Watt, epitomized the pro-development approach of the Reagan Administration in contrast to the more preservationist stance adopted by previous Secretaries, such as Mo Udall, the main instigator of legislation to designate wilderness in Alaska. Much of this chapter will focus on the US experience because invariably it has been used as the development model for other countries. Furthermore, the recent change in policy direction and the opposition to it is worthy of detailed investigation. Finally, classic land use conflicts and the inability of government to provide a satisfactory solution will be illustrated by the UK example, where problems of land ownership and the development of natural resources within designated areas make it a contrasting case when compared to the US.

3.2.1 Resource Inventories and the Allocation Process

It was shown in Chapter 9 that the resource manager's task in completing resource inventories had been facilitated in recent years through the use of remote sensing techniques and computer-assisted cartography. These techniques highlighted our lack of knowledge of the nature and extent of the world's forests. For example, until LANDSAT pictures were used in the Philippines, the country had assumed that 57% of its land area was covered by forests, when the true figure was in fact 33%. The concern expressed at the lack of a reliable data base upon which to make meaningful management decisions has prompted a resolution from the World Forestry Congress that FAO produce an accurate report of the world forest area by 1984.[1]

The advantages of remote sensing at this scale are its cheapness compared with aerial photography, its ready manipulation for computer handling and the frequency of coverage (once every 18 days). Of course, this is dependent on cloud free days; many parts of the world, including the tropical rainforests, cannot guarantee a large number of useful images. None the less, this data can provide information which would show the extent of forest cover, type of species and, more significantly, because LANDSAT is repetitive, rates of de-forestation and afforestation. At a smaller, more detailed level, conventional methods of aerial photography and land-use surveys are undertaken. Parry claims that high-altitude photography, implemented by the US Land Use and Land Cover Mapping Program, is an invaluable tool in identifying and moni-toring land use in rural areas.[2]

Although our knowledge of the availability of resources has improved, the use to which it is put is invariably a matter of subjective evaluation. Landscape evaluation techniques have been subject to a great deal of criticism because of the difficulties in quantifying scenery, landscape and wilderness (see Chapter 9). Consensus on such issues is rare and numerous lawsuits in the US have accompanied agencies' attempts to classify wilderness to comply with US legislation.

Attempts at using Linton's and other methodologies in identifying National Scenic Areas in Scotland were considered by the Countryside Com-mission for Scotland to be of limited value. Cripps argues that there is no substitute for the 'wise men' approach, whereby experts in rural land-use issues would be instrumental in landscape appraisal.[3] In practice this amounts to pressure for protected landscape status for certain areas by environmental groups and the testing of the practicality of these proposals. After twenty years of mounting pressure for the creation of national parks in Britain, John Dower, a research officer in the Ministry of Town and Country Planning, produced his influential report which ranked areas as 'suggested' parks, 'possible' parks and 'other amenity areas'. His ranking was based upon his definition of a park which was:

an external area of beautiful and relatively wild country in which, for the nation's benefit and by appropriate national decisions and action (a) the characteristic landscape beauty is strictly preserved (b) access and facilities for public open-air enjoyment are amply provided (c) wildlife and buildings and places of architectural and historic interest are suitably protected while (d) established farming use is effectively maintained.[4]

In practical terms, 'wild landscape' and 'access to the public' excluded much of lowland Britain because it was only in upland areas that a greater freedom of access could be achieved. Furthermore, one of his 'suggested areas' – the Cornish coast – was eliminated on the grounds of the administrative difficulties in managing a geographically elongated area. Overall, the national park concept in the U.K. differs from that of most countries because lands are not designated as museum pieces but reflect the socio-economic character of communities in scenic areas (see point (d) above, in Dower's definition in relation to farming activity).

The international guidelines for the definition of a national park say it is a relatively extensive area in which:

(a) one or more ecosystems have not been physically altered by exploitation and occupation, where plant and animal species, geomorphic sites and habitats are of special scientific, educational and recreational interest, or where the natural scenery is of great beauty; and in which

(b) the country's highest competent authority has adopted measures to prevent or eliminate exploitation or occupation of the entire area in the briefest possible time and to effectively compel respect for the ecological, geomorphic or aesthetic features which have led to its establishment; and in which

(c) visitors are allowed entry under special conditions for inspirational, educational, cultural and recreational purposes.[5]

Such a definition is more appropriate to Britain's National Nature Reserves than its National Park system because of the emphasis on protection of flora and fauna in nature reserve designation. The criteria for site selection are open to wide interpretations. For example, in 1977 the Nature Conservancy Council reviewed its reserve acquisitions programme and produced a list of criteria which included vague terms such as naturalness, potential value and intrinsic appeal.[6] The whole aim of the exercise was to provide guidelines for planning in the countryside.[7]

US agencies have experienced classification problems because of the general instructions mandated through legislation, for example, the Wilderness Act 1964. 'Primitive areas' within the domain of the Forest Service plus all roadless areas of over 5,000 acres were designated as wilderness study areas (WSAs) for agency review prior to their acceptance or rejection into the National Wilderness Preservation System.

In Section 2 of the Wilderness Act, wilderness was defined in general terms, but two parts are important to our current discussion, namely, 'an area where the earth and its community of life are untrammelled by man, where man himself is a visitor who does not remain' and is characterized by 'outstanding opportunities for solitude or a primitive and unconfined type of recreation'.[8] This latter, unquantifiable and subjective guideline has caused bitter disputes between the Bureau of Land Management and conservationists over the omission of large tracts of desert terrain in the south west.[9]

The Forest Service did attempt to quantify their roadless lands according to the costs and benefits of designating areas as wilderness. The procedure developed by the Service was called the Roadless Area Review and Evaluation (RARE). After identifying WSAs, they were evaluated according to:

(a) size of roadless area;

(b) a quality index rated by field personnel on a scale of 0–20 for three factors: $QI = 4(S) + 3(I) + 3(V)$, where $QI =$ quality index, $S =$ scenic quality, $I =$ isolation and likely dispersion of visitors, and $V =$ variety of wilderness experiences and activities available; maximum $Ql = 200$;

(c) an effective index $(EI) =$ gross area $\times Ql$;

(d) and an opportunity cost index based on acquisition costs, running costs and the costs incurred through the loss of value of timber output, mineral development or water acquisition.[10]

The RARE methodology has serious deficiencies, the most obvious being the calculation of the QI and EI. Hendee et al[11] point out that the three factors used in the QI measure recreational potential rather than the ecological condition of areas and therefore cast doubt on the basis upon which wilderness quality is measured. Even if these factors are considered appropriate indicators, judgements are subjective and inconsistent.

The EI index compounds the problems outlined with the QI index. In the first place, EI is almost totally related to size yet I in the QI index had already quantified isolation and dispersion of visitors – surely a function of the size of an area?

The opportunity cost analysis has also been criticized from both a philosophical and a specific viewpoint. Hendee et al[12] claim that wilderness cannot be costed according to its intrinsic value compared with the readily measurable timber output, mineral reserves and so on. However, they question the values attributed to timber output because stumpage prices were particularly high at the time of evaluation whilst much of the timber in question was of marginal value being low density and of low commercial value.

The RARE procedure will be referred to later in the chapter in the sections on institutional structures and policy making. Meanwhile, other concepts of resource management will be discussed.

13.2.2 Resource Management Concepts Pertinent to Forestry and Wilderness

All forests are and must be managed for the production of any output of the forest; the management may be intensive or extensive, skilful or inept, economically efficient or wasteful, successful in terms of achieving desired results or not, and in other ways variable. But there is no such thing as a totally unmanaged forest in the United States today – if indeed there ever was. Even a wilderness area, where the emphasis is upon light use and individual privacy, may be managed; for instance, the number of parties, their time and distance spacing, and other aspects of use may be controlled; or the number or location of trails might serve as a means of accommodating more people with less confrontation between groups.[13]

The management of forestry and wilderness revolves around the concepts of sustained yield and carrying capacity in that both resources need to be maintained for perpetuity, maintaining harvest yields and visitor enjoyment.

The principles of sustained yield were established in European forestry circles and were incorporated into management objectives in North America. The concept ensures that forestry production is maintained by ensuring reafforestation after harvesting. But it has been subjected to criticism from economists (and even ecologists!) in a North American context.[14] The concept of carrying capacity, when applied to wilderness management, is dependent upon management goals for an area and is subject to continued reviews in order to minimize their effect upon the physical and human environment.

Much of the work on biophysical and behavioural carrying capacities was devoted to recreation or wilderness studies (see Chapter 9). Ecological studies have been undertaken to measure the effects of increased recreational use on natural environments. The effects of trampling on soil and vegetation have received most attention, providing useful data for decisions on trail and campsite management. Two separate studies by Frissel and Duncan[15] and Merrion and Smith[16] produced similar results on campsite deterioration, showing that most ecological impact occurred in the early years of use prior to stabilization of a hardier, more resistant vegetation cover. If it is thought desirable to maintain the original climax vegetation, restrictions would have to be placed on use. Merrion and Smith recommended that continued usage of campsites in the Boundary Waters Canoe Area was acceptable if the alternative was opening up new areas for use. Their logic relates to recovery time exceeding impact time by four years, making more areas subject to similar levels of deterioration than could be contained at present sites.

Clearly, the effects upon the physical environment are a function of the type of recreational user and the equipment used (hiker, boater, horseback rider). In some instances, the resource manager can use biophysical studies to reroute, close or open trails according to the severity of damage attributed to certain users.

Behavioural carrying capacity research has become a key ingredient in visitor management. Different users perceive wilderness in varying ways, and an understanding of their interpersonal contact and how it enhances or detracts from the wilderness experience is invaluable in the planning for a wilderness area.

The classic study by Lucas[17] of the Boundary Waters Canoe Area showed that canoeists preferred greater solitude than motorboaters; indeed, the canoeists preferred no contact whatsoever with motorboaters. From this information, Lucas suggested that canoeists' experience could be enhanced without affecting other users' enjoyment through modifications in campsite and access point location within each user's perceived wilderness. Other research by Stankey[18] and Stankey and Badger[19] at four western wilderness areas in the US indicate that while backpackers prefer some, if only minimal, contact with other hikers, their tolerance for horseback riders was less. Carrying capacity will vary with area. Overcrowding has not, in fact, proved an obstacle to user satisfaction along the Colorado River in the Grand Canyon, although this could be an exceptional case. The commercialization of river rafting also brings into question whether this is a 'true' wilderness experience.

The use of the wilderness and travel behaviour of the participants are monitored by resource managers to enable them to draw up strategies to satisfy the wishes of these users whilst at the same time enhancing their wilderness experience. Simulation models have been used by managers to assess their current management initiatives and to allow them to amend their management policy.

Data are required on the area and its use by various groups. Travel behaviour within the wilderness – entry points, routes taken, time spent and exit points – can be collated from permit information (Figure 13.1) and other survey methods such as questionnaires, diaries or log book records. This information can then be used to simulate the likely behaviour of particular groups who enter the wilderness at given points. If existing patterns were not realizing management goals, if for example certain routes were being overused, action could be taken to directly or indirectly influence visitor behaviour. In the work undertaken by McCool and Lime[20] at Dinosaur National Monument several simulation scenarios were tested according to varying degrees of usage and the

WILDERNESS PERMIT
U.S. Department of Agriculture-Forest Service

. . . . .Wilderness or Primitive Area

1 – 2
(code)

When signed below, this Permit authorizes

. . . .

(Name)

. . . .

(Address)

. . . .

3 – 7

(City)   (State)   (Zip Code)

to visit this Wilderness or Primitive Area
and to build campfires in accordance with
applicable regulations.   from

8 – 9	10 – 11	to	12 – 13	14 – 15
(Mo.)	(Day)		(Mo.)	(Day)

The number of people in the group will be . . . .

16 – 17

The number of pack or saddle stock used will be . . . .

18 – 19

The place of entry will be . . . .

(Location)

20 – 21

The trip will end at . . . .

(Location)

22 – 23

I agree to abide by all laws, rules, and regulations which apply to this area, and to follow the rules of behaviour listed on, or attached to this permit. I will do my best to see that everyone in my group does likewise.

. . . .

(Date)   (Visitor's Signature)

. . . .

(Date)   (Issuing Officer's Signature)

**The visitor must have this permit in his
possession during his visit to the Wilderness**

This section for optional use of issuing officer.

Planned travel route, duration, and location of camps.

Travel Zone (see map)	24–25	26–27	28–29	30–31	32–33	34–35	36–37	38–39	40–41	42–43
Nights of use by zone	44–45	46–47	48–49	50–51	52–53	54–55	56–57	58–59	60–61	62–63

Visitor receives white copy.
Send yellow copy to the Forest Service Regional Office in San Francisco.
Send pink copy to the Ranger District where the trip starts.

Figure 13.1 An example of A Wilderness Permit *Source:* US Department of Agriculture-Forest Service

modification of access points. A more straightforward simulation model was used at Boundary Waters Canoe Area and Quetico Provincial Park (Ontario)[21] to predict campsite occupancy levels, given numbers entering at various points. This was used to establish limits on entry so as to prevent overcrowding at campsite locations.

The last example illustrates a *direct* management response to a potential problem of exceeding carrying capacity. Gilbert *et al*[22] have identified *direct* and *indirect* techniques for controlling visitor behaviour. It is generally agreed that indirect management methods are more desirable in that the visitor retains the freedom to chose, albeit within the realm of management manipulation (Table 13.1). This management option has several alternatives, from trail site and camp planning through providing information and advice to manipulating costs. On the other hand, direct management measures are more necessary in heavily used areas where carrying capacity is being stretched. Visitor behaviour is strictly controlled and enforced. The use of wilderness may be zoned, precluding some uses in particular areas. The most common option is to make

Table 13.1: Direct and indirect techniques for managing the character and intensity of wilderness use. *Source:* J.C. Hendee *et al*, 1978, Wilderness Management, p. 324, Forest Service, US Department of Agriculture

Type of Management	Method	Specific Techniques
Indirect (Emphasis on influencing or modifying behaviour. Individual retains freedom to choose. Control less complete, more variation in use possible)	Physical alternatives	Improve, maintain or neglect access roads. Improve, maintain or neglect campsites. Make trails more or less difficult. Build trails or leave areas trailless. Improve fish or wildlife populations or take no action (stock, or allow depletion or elimination).
	Information dispersal	Advertise specific attributes of the wilderness. Identify range of recreation opportunities in surrounding area. Educate users to basic concepts of ecology and care of ecosystems. Advertise underused areas and general patterns of use.
	Eligibility requirements	Charge constant entrance fee. Charge differential fees by trail zones, season, etc. Require proof of camping and ecological knowledge and/or skills.

Table 13.1—*contd*

Type of Management	Method	Specific Techniques
Direct (Emphasis on regulation of behaviour. Individual choice restricted. High degree of control).	Increased enforcement Zoning	Impose fines. Increase surveillance of area. Separate incompatible uses (hiker-only zones in areas with horse use). Prohibit uses at times of high damage potential (no horse use in high meadows until soil moisture declines, say 1 July). Limit camping in some campsites to one night, or some other limit.
	Rationing use intensity	Rotate use (open or close access points, trails, campsites). Require reservations Assign campsites and/or travel routes to each camper group. Limit usage via access point. Limit size of groups, number of horses. Limit camping to designated campsites only. Limit length of stay in area (min/max).
	Restrictions on activities	Restrict building campfires. Restrict horse use, hunting or fishing.

visitors book in advance and limit the numbers visiting the wilderness and their length of stay. Because of the pressure on an area, restrictions will be imposed on certain activities such as off-trail travel, making camp fires and the type of food and drink containers allowed.

13.3.1 Decision Making and Institutional Structures

The preceding section has discussed the techniques used in decision making. The purpose of this section is to evaluate the role of the actors involved in decision making and the policy background to forestry and wilderness management. The role of government is paramount in dictating the use of wilderness and forested areas of the world. Official designation of protected status, the use of public lands and the guidelines given to agencies administering these lands are matters of government responsibility. The ultimate destiny of these lands is a political issue, and policy is shaped by the pressures exerted by business and environmental lobbies.

.3.2 Forestry in the Developed World

The institutionalization of forestry management has long existed in parts of Europe where the landscape was stripped of forests as the European economy grew and diversified away from its agrarian base. Throughout Europe the main forestry crises occurred in the 19th and early parts of the 20th century. Exceptional growth in population, uncontrolled growth of industry and urban development, and the demands of a war economy, depleted forestry stocks to critical levels. In the UK the Forestry Commission was created in 1919 primarily for strategic reasons, to build up a reserve for use in case of further war. The forestry schools of Europe were training foresters in the principles of selective logging, sustained yield management and careful 'housekeeping' measures to minimize erosion and encourage natural regeneration. One European scholar was to have a profound influence on US forestry - Gifford Pinchot, the first Chief of the US Forest Service on the transfer of the Department of Interior's Forestry Division to the Department of Agriculture in 1905.

During the push to the west in the US, vast tracks of forest had been cleared. But the carefree 'cut and run' methods of the frontiersman left a legacy of a spoilt environment - soil erosion, ruined watersheds, overgrazing on poorly regenerated secondary forest growth and the loss of wildlife habitats. Public concern over the devastation of forest lands promoted the creation of forest reserves in 1891, which evolved into a national forest system; its main impetus was during the years when Pinchot was forestry chief and T R Roosevelt was President.

The management of national forest systems in the US and the rest of the developed world has followed a similar path. The philosophy has changed from purely sustaining forest yields to multiple-use management, whereby timber production is only one aspect. Where governments are the landlords, the utility of forests must be maximized for the benefit of the public which it represents through licensing procedures.

Government plays an indirect role in the management of private forests, essentially through the medium of fiscal policy. As investment in forestry incurs a long payback period, Tax concessions and other financial inducements have been used to persuade landowners to plant trees on their land. In the UK a system of dedication agreements has existed since 1947. Here, private owners could dedicate their forests to being managed by the Forestry Commission in return for grant aid amounting to £300 per hectare for plots of ¼ hectare to 3 hectares and £250 per hectare for plots of 3 hectares to 10 hectares for broadleaf planting.

.3.3 Forestry Management in the Developing World

In the developing world the situation is more complex. Forestry management and associated institutionalization are poorly developed compared with industrialized countries. Indeed, the common property nature of the forest in many regions has led to overgrazing, shifting cultivation and premature fuelwood gathering, which has reduced the ability of the forest to sustain itself - a classic example of the tragedy of the 'freedom of the commons'. Although parallels can be drawn with the situation in Europe several centuries ago, the problems to be solved are greater because of population pressures, land-use competition and a colonial legacy which still leaves much control of forest development in the hands of external powers. Simmons claims that one of the better legacies of the colonialist era was a technically competent forest service.[23] Nevertheless, these richly endowed forest states have been subjected to the ravishes of 'cultural imperialism'. In South-East Asia, former colonies have trodden the classical development model of export-led growth, dependent upon capital intensive projects funded by foreign investment. The winners in this strategy have been the multinational corporations and the ruling urban élite, which benefits from foreign earnings; the losers are the rural people whose lifestyle and habitat have been destroyed in the wake of lumber exploitation. Growing local opposition to this process has been evident in Papua New Guinea where local landowners have refused to allow logging at existing royalty rates and have thus jeopardized timber projects.[24]

Muthoo criticizes Third World forestry planners for their narrow view of forestry's role in the economy.[25] He argues that no country has a timber mining policy. The institutions responsible for forestry policy see the negotiations with timber companies as their primary preoccupation at the expense of other forest resource-management initiatives. The granting of licences and concessions to log forest areas is open to bribery and corruption with the licensees paying lip service to long-term forestry management.[26] Plumwood and Routley[27] discuss the 'joint ventures' between transnationals and the military and governing élite of Indonesia which is effectively a 'pay off' partnership. Other studies of timber company operations in Indonesia show that the terms of concessions are flouted, especially with regard to selective logging.[28] To be fair, in Indonesia, as in other parts of the Tropics, road clearing for timber extraction has opened the way for shifting agriculturalists and other exploiters of the forest, which makes reafforestation a meaningless investment for a logging company.

Clearly, forestry management in tropical areas is a matter of international concern, but the international agencies – FAO, UNEP, UNDP and the World Bank – have supported these grandiose projects, although the emphasis has changed in recent years towards environmental rather than purely industrial projects.[29] Conservation programmes and fiscal initiatives for reafforestation by well-intentioned state agencies are often difficult to implement in practice. Peasants fighting for survival find it hard to believe that growing trees is more rational than growing crops, that trees should not be felled for firewood during a fuel shortage and that their herds need to be reduced because of overgrazing in the forest. Enforcement of legislation is difficult, it not impossible. For much of the developing world's population, the concepts of sustained yield and 'untouchable' forest reserves are management ideals of the rich. For them it is the management of survival.

13.3.4 Wilderness and Protected Area Management

The designation and management of protected landscapes and habitats is a government responsibility. Hence, a commitment by government to conservation measures is a function of the political pressure which can be exerted by lobbyists to create an institutional framework for preserving landscapes from excessive development.

At the present time, international agencies such as the UN and its Environment Programme, the World Wildlife Fund and the International Union for the Conservation of Nature and Natural Resources (IUCN) attempt to promote conservation and coordinate the management strategies of the nations of the world. Bodies such as these draw international attention to the depletion of species and the loss or potential loss of heritage areas to modern development. In 1980, a worldwide perspective on conservation was unveiled, *The World Conservation Strategy*.[30] Nation states have responded to this document through publications by their own conservation agencies.[31] Ultimately, the success or failure of well-intentioned strategies will depend upon the political clout of environmental pressure groups. To some extent this explains the relative success of the well-organized, politically motivated groups in the US compared to those in Canada, the UK and other industrialized nations (notwithstanding the political success of the 'Greens' in West Germany).

In many ways the US system is unique and therefore worthy of detailed investigation in the next section. However, the environmental philosophy rooted in the 19th century has found expression throughout the world. The concept of conservation is not new. Medieval kings and European aristocrats imposed Game Laws to preserve their hunting stock. But the US philosophers, Catlin, Thoreau, Marsh and Muir, created popular support for species and landscape protection, having witnessed the near extinction of the buffalo and the devastation of primitive cultures and landscapes in the name of progress. The catalyst for realizing their ideals arrived in the form of T.R. Roosevelt, propelled into power in 1901 on the assassination of William McKinley. Roosevelt was a great believer in the outdoors. He was friend and hiking companion of John Muir, founder of the Sierra Club in 1892, John Burroughs, the naturalist and Gifford Pinchot, the forester. He was strongly influenced by their views and was committed to halting the exploitation of the nation's natural resources through federal protection policies. During his term of office, which lasted from 1901 to 1909, he created the first federal wildlife refuge and added fifty more, introduced the national monument system, establishing 18 sites, added 5 new national parks and enlarged the nation's forest reserves to 194 million acres.[32] These protected lands provided the basis for the National Park Service Act of 1916 which created the administrative framework to manage the increasing number of units in the national park system.

Although institutionalization of the national park concept had begun at Yellowstone forty-four years earlier, the philosophy enshrined in the 1916 legislation influenced politicians in other countries. To some extent, the words 'promote and regulate the use' and 'conserve the scenery and the natural and historic objects and the wildlife therein'[33] identify the basic conflict which exists at the present time concerning the dual aims of conservation and recreation. At the 1983 World Congress on National Parks, the theme was 'parks for sustained development' and much debate centred on the meaning of 'development'. It became apparent that the spirit of the concept was shared by all nations, although the interpretation of national park objectives varied considerably according to local circumstances. If success can be measured by statistics, 124 countries have national parks and protected areas accounting for 2611 units and covering 5% of the earth's surface.[34]

Variations in interpretation of protected area philosophy worldwide are related to a multiplicity of factors, the most important of which are the pressures for development, ownership patterns, and public and government support for conservation. The US model is difficult to achieve in many industrialized countries because of the problem of land ownership. Whereas federal agencies in the US were custodians of *public* land, countries such as New Zealand, the UK and Japan had to designate protected areas on *privately* owned land (the 1949 UK Act is entitled 'the National Parks and *Access to the Countryside Act*'). Management of private lands by government agencies is a recipe for conflict and voluntary negotiation. Indeed, in the case of the UK and Japan, the problems are compounded by high population-to-area densities so that developmental pressure by recreationalists aggravate existing land-use conflicts pertaining to agriculture, forestry, mining and water management.

The development versus conservation debate will be enacted within agencies responsible for nature conservation and landscape protection. Abbey – a wilderness protagonist – laments that the 'developers' have exerted more influence than the 'preservers' in National Park policy, which has led in the US to industrial tourism and despoilation of pristine areas.[35] Probably more significant at the present time is the Reagan administration's appointment of officials who are well known for their pro-business, anti-environmental views in key environmental agencies. The influence of vested interest groups in agency policy making has been cited by Hendee in New Zealand[36] and Lowe in the UK.[37] In the latter case, argues Lowe, the independence and authority of the key statutory agencies responsible for conservation have been undermined by the Thatcher government's bias of appointing pro-development personnel to represent farming and forestry interests.

The US has moved towards a more 'untouched' nature and landscape preservation system. The early designation of national parks in North America served the needs of the recreational rich. Spectacular scenery at Yosemite, California and Banff and Lake Louise, Alberta attracted quality hotels and catered for the whims of a newly formed urban society. Wilderness was experienced at a distance. Bearing in mind that the frontiersmen had only recently conquered the wilderness, it was not until the 1920s that the term 'wilderness' was associated with peace and tranquility. Even then, it was not the National Park Service which designated wilderness reserves within their areas but the Forest Service. Foresters such as Leopold and Marshall – founder members of the Wilderness Society in 1935 – did much to promote the establiishment of primitive areas within the Forest Service in the inter-war period. The first allocation of public land for wilderness recreation was designated by the Forest Service in 1924 with the creation of the Gila Wilderness Reserve in New Mexico.

In time, the American public wished to share the wilderness experiences treasured by Muir, Leopold and Marshall. To this end these men founded two of the most active and politically persuasive environment pressure groups in the US – the Sierra Club and the Wilderness Society. Both of these groups were the chief instigators of the draft bill in 1955 which became the legally sanctioned Wilderness Act of 1964.

'Wilderness preservation has evolved from a holding strategy for minimizing unplanned development until more carefully thought-out plans could be formulated to a carefully defined and legally sanctioned national system for protecting the ecological integrity of selected areas.'[38]

It must be stressed that statutorily defined wilderness on this scale is unique to the US. Countries, states and provinces may have wilderness legislation and zoning policies within protected areas to minimize recreational impact, but permanent preservation such as that mentioned by the US Wilderness Act is uncommon. This has caused several US commentators to despair at the immaturity of the Canadian management system.[39] Whereas the Wilderness Act in the US is a commentary on dissatisfaction regarding National Park management by those who wanted more than industrial tourism, the traditional 'visitor attraction' policy is generally accepted among Canadians. There was hardly any public opposition to the construction of the dams that damaged wilderness areas in two parks in British Columbia in the 1950s. At about the same time, pro-wilderness groups in the US actively blocked the proposal to build the Echo Park Dam in Dinosaur National Monument.

3.4.1 Policies in Practice

The aim of this section is to give a more detailed insight into the policy-making process at work by referring to specific examples of forestry and wilderness management practices in both the developed and developing world. Initially, forestry management in the tropical world will be discussed with a view to illustrating the agro-forestry and social forestry programmes seen by many as the panacea for the ills of deforestation. By contrast, attention will then be focused upon the management of the US National Forest System, which is an important prerequisite of wilderness management in the US. Finally, the classic example of conflict between developer and preservationist will be portrayed through analysing the management planning of UK designated areas.

3.4.2 Agro-Forestry and Social Forestry in the Tropics

Social and agro-forestry programmes are based on the same philosophy. It is to attempt to encourage individuals, such as farmers, or communities, to plant and preserve their own trees in order to arrest further depletion of forest stocks and to minimize environmental degradation. In the well-known case of the Chipko Andolan 'tree hugger' movement, these North Indian villagers were the main instigators of a change in state forestry policy.[40] The Chipko had become aware of the relationship between cause (deforestation) and effect (floods, landslides) and linked arms to protect their trees from advancing lumberjacks.

The new social forestry approach is intended to be a part of a rural development strategy in which the Forestry Service's role moves from a regulatory responsibility to an advisory agency. Instead of purely prohibiting forest removal, a tree planting scheme is initiated. In India, the social forestry programme has been acclaimed as a success story.[41] Shiva, Sharatchandra and Bandyopadhyay, however, deem it a failure.[42] The gist of their criticism is that in the state of Karnataka, most reforestation occurs in private, not in village woodlots. Consequently, high value timber (usually eucalyptus) is grown for pulp or rayon production *not* for local firewood needs. They argue that eucalyptus would be useless for cooking. It harms the fertility of the land and has a minimal affect on employment because timber contractors tend to use labour drawn from the cities. The net result is woodlots for distant markets. This fails to meet the objectives of a social forestry programme in which local communities are supposed to determine their own destiny.

The advantage of agro-forestry is that the peasant sedentary farmer or shifting agriculturalist can receive an additional income from timber production whilst maintaining soil fertility for *long-term* agricultural productivity. This is of particular relevance to the shifting agriculturalist because increased population pressure on the forest has given it less fallow time for renewal, leading to soil deterioration. Throughout the tropical environment much experimentation is taking place on the type of trees to mix with crops. Leguminous trees offer most potential because of their fast-growing nature and their ability to produce nitrogen in their foliage which acts as excellent fertilizer for the soil.[43] This is an important consideration for peasant farmers who cannot afford chemical fertilizers.

In Thailand, much of the country's teak output, jeopardized by shifting agriculture encroachment into the forest, is managed by the Forest Industry Organisation (FIO). The solution was to integrate the farmers into the forestry system by encouraging them to settle in villages to practise sedentary agriculture in the best areas and to replant trees in previously cleared stretches of forest. The FIO offers each farmer a plot of land in the village and pays them to cultivate and tend taungya[44] areas. Consequently, the farmer is no longer dependent upon crop growing for a livelihood. At the same time the FIO can carry out a reforestation programme which is more cost effective *and* eradicates the possibility of widespread forest destruction. The programme has experienced difficulties. It is hard to persuade shifting agriculturalists to give up their traditional way of life and to convince them to plant crops with a production cycle *greater* than the normal fallow period. But more than 19,000 hectares had been reforested between 1968 and 1978, with villagers planting a variety of trees as their interest in the project heightened.[45]

13.4.3   The US National Forest System

In contrast to the problems faced by forest services in the tropics, the US Forest Service has developed into a sophisticated agency undertaking scientific research in its experimental stations and attempting to strike a balance between the various claims being made on national forests. Although multiple-use management was implicit in the establishment of forest reserves, it was not until the 1960 Multiple Use–Sustained Yield Act that legislation was enacted to embody this philosophy. The main reason for the legislation was the increased attention being paid by the lumber industry to national forests as demand for pulp, paper and timber products placed pressure on private forest stocks.

Since the 1960 Act, the pressures for policy changes have intensified. The sustained yield concept was criticized and the Reagan administration has been quick to adopt the view of the National Forest Product Association that many old western forests need to be cleared to make way for new, productive forests. To enable him to carry out this policy, Reagan appointed John B. Crowell as Chief of the Forest Service, much to the chagrin of environmentalists who saw his stewardship role in the same light as James Watt's. It was a case of putting the wolf in charge of the sheepfold. Crowell had been the chief counsel to the Louisiana Pacific Corporation, one of the largest holders of timber rights in the national forests.

Two acts of the 1970s – the Forest and Rangeland Renewable Resources Planning Act (1974) and the National Forest Management Act (1976) – advocate a long-term management programme for the National Forests based on traditional philosophy. The Reagan administration has weakened the regulations in these Acts by allowing cutting of old virgin forests and opening up virgin areas, thereby removing them from possible designation as wilderness.

The move from a balanced approach to forestry management to a bias towards timber production is reflected in the 1983 budget proposals for the Forest Service. Whilst timber sales, mineral development and livestock grazing are allocated adequate funding, funds for recreation, fish and wildlife and watershed protection have been slashed.[46] Environmentalists have been particularly concerned about the Reagan administration's proposals to increase timber sales at a time when the housing market is depressed and a backlog of stocks exists equal to the equivalent of three years supply.[47] Furthermore, Crowell believes that current production levels could be tripled making the US a net exporter of wood and the 'wood basket of the world'.[48] A future scenario of such proportions clearly has ramifications for other forest uses, for example, the use of wilderness for outdoor recreation.

As the Forest Service has been in the vanguard of wilderness management since the days of Leopold and Marshall, the next section identifies the role of the Service in evaluating and recommending wilderness areas for congressional approval.

The Forest Service's commitment to designating wilderness areas goes back to 1926 when the Chief Forester, W.F. Greeley, instructed his assistant L.F. Kneipp to inventory all roadless lands for which the L-20 Regulations were established in 1929. The L-20 Regulations authorized the Chief of the Forestry Service to establish 'primitive areas', and field staff had to submit management plans for each area. This amounted to a list of permitted and prohibited activities within such areas, and an interim measure to slow down haphazard development until more detailed proposals were forthcoming. More definitive proposals were embodied in the U-Regulations in 1939 which allowed three types of area to be designated: wilderness areas (those in excess of 100,000 acres), wild areas (between 5000 and 10,000 acres) and roadless areas. In the first two, cars were not allowed, and timber production or any commercial activity was forbidden. This was, in effect, a considerable tightening up of the L-20 Regulations. Nevertheless, the new regulations did not guarantee protection of the wilderness, for they were implemented at the discretion of the Forestry Service. It was not until 1964, after years of lobbying and Congress deliberations, that the Wilderness Act gave legal protection to these roadless areas.

Table 13.2 shows how the Forest Service 'primitive' areas were reclassified on the introduction of the U-Regulations. By the time the Wilderness Act became law, the fifty-four areas already classified as wilderness by the Forest

Table 13.2: Forest service primitive, wilderness, wild and roadless areas, 1939 to 1964. *Source:* After J.C. Hendee *et al*, 1978, Wilderness Management, Forestry Service US Department of Agriculture

	Primitive Areas	Acres (million)	Wilderness Areas	Acres (million)	Wild Areas	Acres (million)	Roadless Areas	Acres (million)
	Number		Number		Number		Number	
1939	75	14·2	–	–	–	–	–	–
1949	58	11·2	4	1·4	12	0·5	3	0·8
1959	42	8·2	12	3·9	26	0·9	1*	0·8
1964	34	5·4	54	9·1	–	–	–	–

* The three previous roadless areas were classified into one.

Service were the first areas to be included in the National Wilderness Preservation System. The remaining thirty-four primitive areas had to be reviewed within the decade for possible inclusion into the system. Other undeveloped and roadless areas were also to be subject to review.

In the case of National Forest primitive areas, the wilderness classification process is illustrated in Figure 13.2. As can be seen from the diagram, the Forest Service's review procedure was further complicated by the obligation to submit an EIS after NEPA in 1979. In the early stages of the classification process, the Forestry Service reviews an area, produces a draft EIS and a wilderness proposal. After appropriate public review procedures, the final proposal is submitted to the Secretary of Agriculture who can also make amendments. From there the Office of Management and Budget (OMB) holds a sixty-day review during which other federal agencies can comment upon the impact of the proposal on their programmes. Assuming this is approved, legislative procedures are set into motion. Draft legislation is submitted to the President for signature and then Congressional action is taken when the legislation is sponsored by a Senator or Representative who endorses the Presidential recommendation. Invariably, alternative schemes are proposed by other Congressmen. These legislative drafts then have to go through the committee stage where major amendments can take place after public hearings are held to gauge response to the final proposal. Finally, both House and Senate debate and vote on the legislation. Even then major differences may still occur and compromises will have to be reached before the legislation is signed into law by the President.[49]

The above process highlights the complexity of wilderness designation and the lengthy review procedures involved in re-classifying the primitive areas of the redundant U-Regulations. In the case of undeveloped roadless areas, much controversy centred around the interpretation of the Wilderness Act, from a rigid approach of only identifying wilderness in existing primitive areas to one of extending Forest Service reviews to other roadless areas. The Forest Service interpreted the Act liberally. Hence, a total of 1449 areas containing 56 million acres were inventoried by 1972, and the RARE process discussed in section 13.2.1 was used as a tool to identify wilderness study areas for possible inclusion in the national system.[50]

As there was some concern about the adequacy of the RARE methodology, further initiatives were advocated by the Department of Agriculture in 1977 to produce yet another review of the undeveloped roadless lands. Generally known

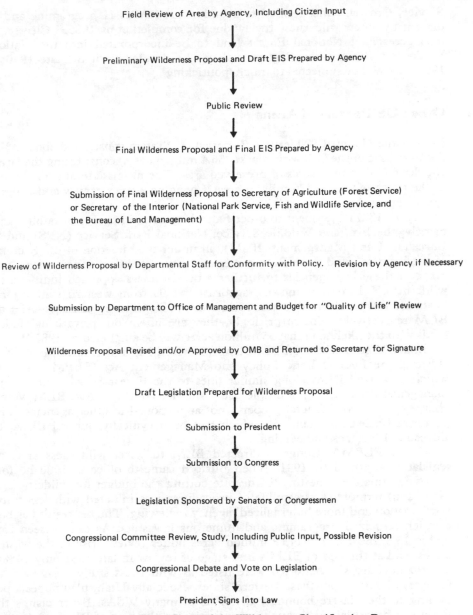

Field Review of Area by Agency, Including Citizen Input

Preliminary Wilderness Proposal and Draft EIS Prepared by Agency

Public Review

Final Wilderness Proposal and Final EIS Prepared by Agency

Submission of Final Wilderness Proposal to Secretary of Agriculture (Forest Service) or Secretary of the Interior (National Park Service, Fish and Wildlife Service, and the Bureau of Land Management)

Review of Wilderness Proposal by Departmental Staff for Conformity with Policy. Revision by Agency if Necessary

Submission by Department to Office of Management and Budget for "Quality of Life" Review

Wilderness Proposal Revised and/or Approved by OMB and Returned to Secretary for Signature

Draft Legislation Prepared for Wilderness Proposal

Submission to President

Submission to Congress

Legislation Sponsored by Senators or Congressmen

Congressional Committee Review, Study, Including Public Input, Possible Revision

Congressional Debate and Vote on Legislation

President Signs Into Law

Figure 13.2 Generalized Flow Chart of the Wilderness Classification Process
Source: Hendee *et al*, 1978, Wilderness Management, US Department of Agriculture–Forest Service, Miscellaneous Publications, No. 1365, p. 96

as RARE II, the purpose of this directive was that the Forestry Service should build upon its existing data base to place these lands into three categories: (1) immediately proposed as wilderness; (2) those which require further study before Congressional action could be taken; and (3) non-wilderness designation. Unfortunately, this process was once again changed by the head of the Forest

Service, Crowell, who decided to abandon the RARE II programme and replace it by a new wilderness review due for completion by 1985.[51] Clearly, the final acreage of National Forest land to be incorporated into the National Wilderness Preservation System will not be decided until the late 1980s or 1990s and will be subjected to much 'politicking'.

13.4.4 Other US Protected Areas

In 1982 the National Wilderness Preservation System constituted about 3% of the land-base of the US, with Alaska (56·4 million acres) constituting the largest chunk of 79·8 million acres of preserved area. The ultimate total is likely to be in the range of 115 to 135 million areas[52] pending agency review and congressional approval.

Figure 13.2 is pertinent to other federal agencies in charge of public lands, namely, the Fish and Wildlife Service, National Park Service (NPS) and the Bureau of Land Management (BLM), all under the direction of the Secretary of the Interior. Under the Reagan administration, political appointments were made in these key agencies to further a pro-business approach indifferent to wilderness.[53] Two well-known Sagebrush rebels from western states, James Watt and Robert Burford, became heads of the Department of the Interior and BLM respectively. Not surprisingly, they are intent on 'privatizing' federal lands with the likelihood that 35 million acres will be auctioned by 1987.[54]

In addition to selling off BLM lands, Burford has undermined much of the spirit of the Federal Land Policy and Management Act (FLPMA) of 1976 which organized BLM along similar lines to the Forest Service with similar management objectives - multiple-use planning. Until this Act, BLM were in charge of 'left over' federal property not apportioned to other agencies. They performed a leasing agent role which had been cynically dubbed BLM, the Bureau of Livestock and Mining.[55]

Under FLPMA, Congress directed BLM to select wilderness areas for legislative approval by 1991. When Burford came to office in 1980 he foreshortened this deadline to 1984 despite cutting the budget for wilderness review. Furthermore, a streamline of procedures was initiated with less public participation and more 'internalized' agency reviewing. The net result has been a much criticized programme and numerous law suits. As can be seen from Table 13.3, most of the 173·8 million acres under review arise in the western states, and at the end of BLM's first stage of review in late 1981 only 14% of the roadless areas inventoried were listed as wilderness study areas (WSAs). Conservationists from these western states, especially Utah, filed appeals pertaining to the bizarre boundary divisions of many WSAs. Baker claims that these can be explained through irregularities on the part of BLM when compiling its inventory.[56] Instead of reviewing *solely* the wilderness potential of areas, BLM were incorporating development plan material into their decision-making process, thus eliminating areas from WSA designation, if energy or mineral claims had been filed with the agency.

As BLM has to undertake a 'crash' review of WSAs before final designation, and conservationists see these potential wilderness areas as their last chance to save roadless areas for posterity, much conflict is in prospect as BLM's less than thorough proposals are attacked by opponents.

Table 13.3: BLM wilderness inventory results. *Source: Sierra*, March/April 1983

State	Acreage Subject to Inventory	Number of WSAs	WSA Acreage	Percentage of Total
Arizona	12,663,000	132	3,038,000	24
California	16,585,000	243	6,777,000	41
Colorado	7,996,000	64	808,000	10
Idaho	11,949,000	69	1,732,000	14
Montana	8,140,000	46	468,000	6
Nevada	49,118,000	100	4,593,000	9
New Mexico	12,847,000	52	999,000	8
Oregon	13,965,000	94	2,652,000	19
Utah	22,076,000	87	2,705,000	12
Washington	310,000	1	5,000	2
Wyoming	17,793,000	46	582,000	3
Subtotal	173,442,000	934	24,359,000	14
Michigan	1,200	0	0	0
Wisconsin	3,500	0	0	0
Minnesota	45,000	0	0	0
North Dakota	68,000	0	0	0
South Dakota	277,000	0	0	0
Oklahoma	7,000	0	0	0
Total	173,843,700	934	24,359,000	14

Note: Figures do not include appeals pending before the Interior Board of Land Appeals or reflect areas later withdrawn by Interior Secretary Watt.

In contrast to BLM, the other agencies responsible to James Watt have finalized their wilderness reviews. Their main concern is the lack of funds with which to buy new land to protect wildlife or scenic areas. For example, Watt has been unwilling to use monies from the Land and Water Conservation Fund (LWCF) to acquire priority areas for wildlife refuges in order to protect them from development and habitat destruction.[57] LWCF was established by Congress in 1965 so that taxes from oil and gas exploitation would be used to acquire public lands for the use of all Americans. From 1965 to 1981, 1·7 million acres were purchased for use by the National Parks Service, the Forest Service, the Fish and Wildlife Service and State Departments responsible for outdoor recreation.[58] Watt slapped a moratorium on new parkland acquisition on the grounds that the monies would be better spent to improve existing facilities rather than adding to the financial burden through further area designation. Congress blocked his plan to divert money from the Fund. Watt's opponents argue that the underlying logic behind the proposal was his ideological opposition to purchasing private lands for public use. Indeed, he has suggested that he may 'privatize' the Park Service by encouraging private capital for renovations and waiving the franchise fees of concessionaires in return for investment in park improvements.[59]

Watt's proposals are no more than refurbishment schemes to upgrade roads, sewer systems and so on at existing parks. Many conservationists view this approach as a retrogressive step in Park Service philosophy, a back to the cater-to-tourists approach of the pre-1970s era. In 1968 Abbey wrote that the Park Service's idea of resource management is to cater for industrial tourism rather than preserving natural resources from increased numbers of recreationalists.[60]

Clawson has identified a 5-stage life cycle through which the park system has evolved, from the initial stage of reservation, to minimal management, rising public interest, excess capacity and management restrictions.[61] In the early years of the Park Service, directors such as Mather and Albright stressed the 'provide-for-enjoyment' rather than 'leave-them-unimpaired' aspects of the 1916 Act. The resort image, heavy PR campaigns, 'come-and-feed-the-bears' attitudes, did stimulate public interest. In the early post-war years, this philosophy continued. Investment was poured into infrastructure improvements. Even more visitors were encouraged by programmes such as 'Mission 66' and by the use of slogans such as 'Parks for the People'. The people responded to the extent that by the late 1960s carrying capacity was stretched in the most popular parks and park policy had to change direction.

In the 1970s and 1980s a shift to a preservationist philosophy has been evident. No longer are people encouraged to feed the bears, but to keep a clean camp to discourage garbage bears, the 'Yogis' created by 'Mr Ranger's' earlier marketing strategy. The NPS identifies three types of area within its system – natural, historical and recreational. Its 334 units have a variety of nomenclatures from National Parks, Monuments and Seashores to National Historic Sites, National Battlefields, National Parkways and Recreation Areas. The creation of 'recreation' parks, most notably National Recreation Areas, is an attempt to reduce pressure on the National Parks. The designation of urban parks within this system offers a chance for the socially disadvantaged to enjoy the pleasures of more remote park facilities.

'De-development' has been the recent motto of the Park Service for its main National Parks. Restrictive measures and more active management initiatives have been used to stop people loving their parks to death and spoiling them for future generations. For example, at Yosemite and the Grand Canyon, minibus shuttle services convey tourists to the sights, minimizing pollution and congestion.

Park policy is at a crossroads under the Reagan administration. Parks are popular: one in four Americans visit part of the system each year. In 1980, there were 300 million visitors, 10 times the number of 1950.[62] Whilst the current debate revolves around the restoration/acquisition issue, it must also be noted that Park Service units are being threatened by pollution. In 1980 the Park Service listed 4345 specific threats to park natural resources. Half the problems were generated by developments adjacent to park boundaries creating air and water pollution within the park. The situation can only deteriorate if any relaxation of the Clean Air Act occurs. Clearly, the first priority of any administration committed to restoring national parks, is to tackle those issues reported by the Park Service itself. Otherwise, the raison d'être of National Park philosophy will be placed in jeopardy.

13.4.5 Conflict in the Countryside: The Case of the UK

Unlike the US, where much of the current controversy centres on the use of *public* lands for scientific, aesthetic or economic purposes, the conservation movement in the UK has always faced immense problems because most designated, protected areas are in *private* ownership and economic activity there is *not* discouraged. By the time the appropriate legislation was enacted the economies of these areas were heavily dependent upon primary industries and the development-conservation trade off became inevitable. In 1979/80, it was estimated that rural resource development accounted for £18·5 billion or 10% of GDP.[63]

The question of protected landscapes has tended to divide conservation groups in their quest for government action. Throughout the first half of the 20th century, the Ramblers Associations fought to gain access to private land in the countryside. But bills were blocked by powerful landowning interests in and outside Parliament. The Royal Society and other scientific preservation groups pressed for a state system of nature reserves. Indeed, this dual approach was reflected in the Addison Committee's recommendation of 1931 that there should be two kinds of national park - one, to cater for regional outdoor recreation, the other to preserve landscapes and wildlife for the nation.

After a series of other reports,[64] the National Parks and Access to the Countryside Act was passed in 1949. It created a National Parks Commission to prepare a programme for the establishment of National Parks and to advise local authorities on the management of these and Areas of Outstanding Natural Beauty (AONB).[65] The Nature Conservancy was established at the same time, with a scientific research and advisory brief to identify and manage nature reserves and other sites of scientific interest. By the early 1980s, National Parks, Areas of Outstanding Beauty, Heritage Coasts, National Nature Reserves, Sites of Special Scientific Interest and Country Parks encompassed a large proportion of the UK land area (Table 13.4). But land ownership did not change upon designation. This has inevitably proved a recipe for conflict between owners and conservation agencies. Of the National Nature Reserves, only 14% are owned by the Nature Conservancy Council. The National Park authorities own less than 1% of the land they manage, except on Exmoor and Dartmoor (see Table 13.5). The Countryside Commission owns no land and has no powers of compulsory purchase to preserve valued landscapes. As can be seen from Table 13.5, the jewels of the British landscape, the National Parks, are mainly in private ownership. Much of the land in public ownership is not put to use for conservation purposes (Ministry of Defence activities, for example). The Forestry Act of 1967 and Water Act of 1973 do, however, oblige the Forestry Commission and water authorities to consider the needs of conservation and recreation in land-use decisions. Furthermore, the National Trust owns around 10% of National Park lands and owns 229,000 hectares throughout the UK. It is Britain's largest private landowner. The Trust's half a million members endorse the society's attempts to preserve landscapes and historic buildings for future generations.

The Trust is a unique body in that it has special powers to declare its land inalienable, which prevents its sale. But whilst the National Trust is sympathetic to the aims of the Nature Conservancy Council (NCC) and the Countryside Commission, this is not necessarily the case with other private landlords. It has been estimated that 85% of the rural landscape in the UK is in the hands of landowners and occupiers who have no legal responsibility to practise the conservation measures suggested by these various agencies.[66]

Governments have never been willing to use compulsory, positive measures to further conservation practices. They have always preferred voluntary solu-

Table 13.4: Landscape and nature conservation designation in the UK. *Source*: Adapted from TRRU, 1981, The Economy of Rural Communities in the National Parks of England and Wales, p. 67 and T. O'Riordan, 1983, Putting Trust in the Countryside, *in* I. Pollard, *The Conservation and Development Programme for the UK*, Kogan Page, p. 193

Type of Designation	Agency Responsible	Number	Area	Land surface (%)
National Park (England and Wales only)	Countryside Commission (National Parks Authorities)	10	1,362,000 ha	9·0
Areas of Outstanding Natural Beauty (England and Wales only)	Countryside Commission	33	1,449,000 ha	9·6
Area of Great Landscape* (England and Wales only)	Countryside Commission	–	2,860,000 ha	19·0
Heritage Coast* (England and Wales only)	Countryside Commission	–	1,084 km in length	24·7 (of coastal frontage)
National Scenic Area (Scotland only)	Countryside Commission	40	1,002 sq km	12·1
National Nature Reserves (Excluding N. Ireland)	Nature Conservancy Council	195	150,000 ha	0·54
National Nature Reserves (N. Ireland only)	Department of the Environment, Northern Ireland	36	3,000 ha	N/A
Sites of Special Scientific Interest (Excluding N. Ireland)	Nature Conservancy Council	4,150	1,471,000 ha	6·4
Areas of Scientific Interest (N. Ireland only)	Department of the Environment, Northern Ireland	47	74,000 ha	N/A
Country Parks	Countryside Commission (local authorities)	164	21,000 ha	N/A

* Not statutory designations.

tions to land-use conflict in the countryside. This is a legacy of the 1949 Act and the thinking behind its formulation. The prevailing philosophy of the 1940s was that farming, and to a lesser extent forestry, should be maintained. Indeed, the Scott Committee heralded farmers and foresters as the nation's landscape gardeners.[67] As a result, forestry and farming were exempt from planning controls embodied in the 1947 Town and Country Planning Act. In the same year, however, the government of the day committed Britain to a support policy for farming with the Agriculture Act and thus stimulated the era of modern farming. Price supports, subsidies, improvement grants and tax concessions created a revival in agriculture as it became efficient and capital intensive at the expense of countryside conservation. (See 12.4.1) Hedgerows were uprooted, moorland and wetland were 'improved' and chemical fertilizers created run-off pollution problems.

As agricultural change led to landscape change, the 1949 legislation also failed to envisage the growth and extent of outdoor recreation. As most of the vocal pressure group for access to the countryside had been members of the Ramblers Association, it was generally thought that walkers, hikers and cyclists would form the majority of outdoor recreationists. With rising affluence, longer vacations and increased mobility through car transportation, the countryside quickly became subjected to vehicle-based recreational pressure. The policy makers of the 1940s would not have believed that by 1980, ten million people would visit the countryside in England and Wales on an average summer Sunday.[68]

The early pressures for change and competition for land in the countryside prompted the introduction of the Countryside Act of 1968. Under this Act, the Countryside Commission was formed, with a general and rather contradictory brief to provide and improve facilities for recreation in the countryside and to conserve its natural beauty and amenity. One of its main tasks has been to advise and financially assist (through grant aid schemes) local authorities and private owners to establish Country Parks and picnic sites in intermediate accessible areas. This attempt at relieving recreational pressure on the established, designated areas is a similar strategy to that behind the creation of National Recreation Areas and State Parks in the US.

The 1968 Act strengthened, albeit marginally, the Nature Conservancy Council's powers to prevent development of Sites of Special Scientific Interest (SSSI) under the Section 15 clause in which the Council could make agreements with landowners with SSSI on their land. Statutorily, the powers of the NCC, the Countryside Commission and the local authorities are weak and they lack an adequate budget to compensate landowners to conserve rather than develop. Direct annual expenditure by central government on conservation and recreation amounts to £10 million compared with agricultural support of £400 million.[69] (The direct/indirect subsidy by government has been calculated at £3·35 billion).[70]

Throughout the 1970s and early 1980s, further conflict ensued (mainly between farmers and conservationists), with the SSSI in danger being given much media attention. A plethora of reports, most notably the Sandford report on the National Parks and a series of reports by the Countryside Review Committee,[71] discussed new landscape classifications/designations and the possibility of imposing stricter planning controls. All the reports recognized that the current system of landscape and wildlife protection was inadequate.

Table 13.5: Land ownership in the National Parks, 1979. *Source:* TRRU, August 1981, The Economy of Rural Communities in the National Parks of England and Wales, p. 53

Land Ownership	National Parks 1979									
	Brecon Beacons[1]	Dartmoor	Exmoor	Lake District	Northumberland	North Yorks Moors	Peak District	Pembrokeshire Coast	Snowdonia	Yorkshire Dales
			Hectares							
Total area of National Park (thousands of hectares)	134	95	69	224	103	143	140	58	217	176
Land owned and managed by National Park Authority	50	1,175	1,533	2,259	131	865	805	38	770	84
Land leased to and managed by National Park Authority	2	8	10	876	0	0	81	46	5	0
Land managed by National Park Authority through agreement with landowner	5[2]	801	0	0	0	0	NA	15	0	0

Table 13.5—*contd*

National Parks 1979

Hectares

Land Ownership — Land held by:	Yorkshire Dales	Snowdonia	Pembrokeshire Coast	Peak District	North Yorks Moors	Northumberland	Lake District	Exmoor	Dartmoor	Brecon Beacons[1]
Other local authority	0	19	155	NA	190[3]	0	c2,000	142	469	20
National Trust	1,721	19,130	1,741	14,200	1,200	767	37,833	6,605	1,882	4,733[4]
Forestry Commission	424	26,330	720	2,600	23,690	22,298	11,646	1,344	1,907	11,078[5]
Water Authority	221	2,400	0	19,940	271	1,202	15,560	332	4,710	NA
Ministry of Defence	716	300	2,710	1,200[8]	768	22,700	461[7]	0	13,987	1,006[6]
Nature Conservancy Council	11	1,140	313	139	0[3]	36	216	0	302	779
Other public ownership	NA	7,759	NA[11]	NA	0	0	NA	2,422	27,952[10]	798[9]

[1] 1978.
[2] Plus 57 ha managed jointly with owner.
[3] 63 ha managed as national nature reserve.
[4] Including 283 ha leased by Ministry of Defence to National Trust.
[5] Including land leased from Welsh Water Authority.
[6] 64 ha managed by Nature Conservancy Council.
[7] Land and foreshore; clearance and firing rights held over a further 484 ha mostly foreshore.
[8] Held under licence.
[9] 57 ha British Waterways Board; 741 ha National Coal Board.
[10] Duchy of Cornwall.
[11] Foreshore (Crown ownership).
NA Not available

Note: There may be overlap in the statistics presented. For example, where one body owns an area and leases it to another the area of land will be recorded twice.

The Wildlife and Countryside Act of 1981 was the Conservative government's response to a decade of criticism of the existing management system. Unfortunately, no strategic changes in policy have been made. A classic example of 'incrementalism' prevails, in which irreconcilable conflicts are meant to be resolved through consultation and cooperation. Figures 13.3 and 13.4 outline the changes introduced by the Act pertaining to agricultural change in SSSI and landscape protection areas. The main improvement in protecting SSSI is a statutory obligation for both parties to notify each other of the perceived value of the SSSI, but the same weaknesses are still evident: those farmers who do not require grant aid[72] could legally defy NCC objectives as cooperation is voluntary and the cost of compensation or compulsory purchase is prohibitively high for the NCC. Since NCC received in 1982/83 only

Figure 13.3 The Likely Pathway of Action to Safeguard SSSIs under Sections 28 and 29 of the Wildlife and Countryside Act, 1981
Note: All proposed land use changes regarded as notifiable by the NCC must be registered even if grant aid is not sought.
Source: T. O'Riordan, Putting trust in the Countryside, *in* I. Pollard, *The Conservation and Development Programme for the UK*, Kogan Page 1983

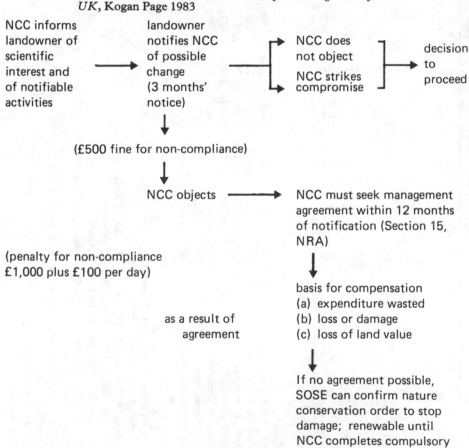

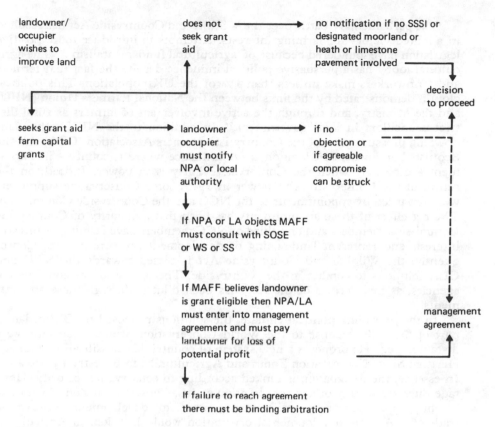

landowner/ occupier wishes to improve land → does not seek grant aid → no notification if no SSSI or designated moorland or heath or limestone pavement involved

decision to proceed

seeks grant aid farm capital grants → landowner occupier must notify NPA or local authority → if no objection or if agreeable compromise can be struck

If NPA or LA objects MAFF must consult with SOSE or WS or SS

If MAFF believes landowner is grant eligible then NPA/LA must enter into management agreement and must pay landowner for loss of potential profit

management agreement

If failure to reach agreement there must be binding arbitration

SOSE: Secretary of State for the Environment
WS: Secretary of State for Wales
SS: Secretary of State for Scotland
NPA: National Park Authority
MAFF: Ministry of Agriculture, Fisheries and Food

Figure 13.4 The Likely Pathway to Safeguard Parts of National Parks and other Specially Designated Areas Likely to be Subject to Official Grant Aid but where Conservation/Ammenity interests are believed to Predominate (Section 41 Agreements).
Source: T. O'Riordan, Putting trust in the Countryside, *in* I. Pollard, *The Conservation and Development Programme for the UK*, Kogan Page, 1983

£600,000 with which to carry out its responsibilities under the Act (and much of this budget is absorbed by administrative costs), it is nearly an impossible task for the NCC to safeguard all key sites; the cost of doing that is estimated at £20 million over ten years.[73] A similar situation exists with Section 41 agreements pertaining to National Parks and other designated areas (Figure 13.4). Here, the agencies responsible have even less power because they cannot make compulsory purchase of the land and can pay compensation only for loss of potential profit. Once again, the amount of financing is small, with the Countryside Commisssion making only £200,000 available for these management agreements compared with the £4·6 million spent on all their grant aided schemes.[74]

The parliamentary battle over the Wildlife and Countryside Act has resulted in a muted victory for farming interests. Attempts to introduce more positive legislation have foundered because of 'agricultural fundamentalism'.[75] The agricultural lobby has a persuasive political influence despite the fact that farmers and farmworkers make up less than 1% of the UK population. This political clout is demonstrated by the links between the National Farmers Union (NFU) and the Ministry, and through the active involvement of farmers as rural district councillors in local government.[76] In addition to the NFU, other landowning pressure groups, the Country Landowners Association (CLA) and the Scottish Landowners Federation, have influence where it counts - in Parliament - especially when the Conservative Party is in power. Indeed, on the return of the Conservatives to power in 1979, some Conservative supporters were rewarded by appointments to the NCC and the Countryside Commission. The net effect of these appointments has been that a majority of Countryside Commission members and one-third of NCC members have farming or forestry interests and represent landowning or development pressure groups. Consequently, the Wildlife and Countryside Act is biased towards the NFU and CLA solutions to conflict in the countryside. The opposition of conservation agencies, as main critics of the Act, has been diluted through these appointments.

In the prevailing political climate, the solutions proposed by O'Riordan as part of the UK response to the World Conservation Strategy can only be a distant hope.[77] He proposes a new system of countryside classification, namely, Heritage Sites, Conservation Zones and Agricultural and Forestry Landscapes. In essence, the designation is ranked according to conservation priority. Heritage Sites are worthy of key conservation status. Conservation Zones would be amenity areas requiring strict management to development/conservation trade-offs. A more developmental orientation would be taken in Agricultural and Forestry landscapes. Even in the latter category, Areas of Local Conservation Interest (ALCI) would be identified, demanding strict management controls by local authorities in their structure plans. In total, these ALCIs, Heritage Sites and Conservation Zones would represent about 30% of the UK countryside. The establishment of a lead agency would be required to prepare a general management plan, which would then be adapted for local use through a system of liaison panels to coordinate the needs of various interest groups.

The main difference between this proposal and the existing system is that government money would be channelled into conservation rather than into development. Management would preach ecological, aesthetic and socioeconomic sustainability. Thus, inappropriate land-use changes would be discouraged and government grants only awarded for 'good management practices'. In a nutshell, the current farming practice of securing profits through government subsidization for the production of food which ends up in EEC stockpiles and endangers soil fertility would be discouraged. In its place, tax incentives, compensation and other fiscal measures would make the farmer no worse off for practising conservation.

Summary

Wilderness and forestry management involves complex issues at all levels. Perceptions of management differ markedly from the affluent countries of North America to those of the tropical world, where notions about recreation, wilderness preserves and nature conservation are regarded as luxuries for the rich and basic survival is the primary concern.

Two main points emerge from this chapter. In the first place, a high degree of uncertainty exists about the implications of the development of our forest and wilderness resources. Good management decisions can only be taken when an adequate inventory of resources exists. The sophistication of the hardware in recent years has facilitated this goal, although evaluation and classification of wilderness will always feature an element of subjective assessment.

The second point concerns the political will, or lack of it, to conserve these resources. Sustainability was a term used in the last case study to provide good management for UK landscape planning. Forestry and wilderness are renewable resources. The degree of their exploitation determines the level of use for future generations. The strong pro-development lobby and its political influence in the UK is currently mirrored in the US and is an established goal in Third World planning. On the other hand, the conservationists are represented by divergent groups who are politically weak. The notable exception to this is in the US where the present system of wilderness, national forests, parks and nature refuges is the result of the political activism of conservationists. Although diverse in their interests, they are invariably common in their purposes. In 1982 they united to demand the removal of James Watt![78]

14   Water Management

14.1 Introduction

In Chapter 7 it was argued that water is vital to public health, economic and agricultural development in the countries of the 'South'. In the 'North', pollution may be identified as the most important pressure on resources. Above all, water problems are directly related to demand. Even in North America there is a possibility of regional shortages in the not too distant future. Here, at least, money can be found for large-scale and 'extensive' water resource developments. In the 'South', however, there exists a lack of finance for water development and doubt about the appropriateness of technology from the 'North'.

In this chapter, we first consider methods of water management. In the developed countries there is increasingly powerful opposition to solving problems of supply by building bigger and larger reservoirs regardless of their impact. The solution that has emerged involves the adoption of comprehensive and multi-purpose structures of management. Unless the institutional structure can both meet economic needs and protect the quality of water, the full potential of the renewable resource that is a river basin cannot be realized.

14.2 Developing Institutional Structures: England and Wales

Three principal forms of management response to water-resource issues may be identified: the 'technical fix', the 'administrative fix', and the 'behavioural fix'. Each of these may be identified at various stages of increasing pressure on water resources and a general historical trend of development from technical to behavioural policies by way of administrative reform may be identified in several leading countries.

'Technical fix' approaches involve the construction of new facilities, the extension of existing works and the application of technology to problems of water shortage. When more water is required, new reservoirs and aqueducts are built, inter-basic transfers arranged, and water brought from where it is available. Sewell refers to this as the 'extensive' approach and comments on its prevalence in the United States.[1] A 'technical fix' to problems of water quality would involve the construction of treatment plants at all major sources of polluting discharges.

But the cost of building one's way out of water problems may be prohibitive. New sources of supply may be too far away. Effluent treatment on a large scale may be too costly. In such circumstances, the 'administrative fix' might be applied. The existing agencies and authorities might be reorganized so that, for example, surpluses held by an authority adjacent to another in need may be pooled, or more efficient use made of existing facilities by taking a broader view and connecting previously separate operational systems. The existing pattern of laws and regulations might also be broadened to allow control over the location of major effluents. Economies of scale in the treatment of wastes might also be achieved in this way.

More recently, however, it has been recognized that reforming the institutional structure of water management may not do enough to relieve some of the fundamental problems of water management. Instead, what may be required are policies to change the behaviour of water users. 'Behavioural fix' policies seek to curb anti-social behaviour in the use of water resources. The imposition of a tax on the discharge of effluent is likely to encourage re-cycling and a redesign of processes of production to eliminate pollutants. Similarly, conservation of domestic water may be encouraged by tariff schemes which discourage excessive use for non-essential purposes such as lawn watering and car-washing.

The history of water management policies in England[2] and Wales since the 1930s is illustrative of the general trend from technical to behavioural policies by way of administrative reform. The development of an institutional structure for water management in Scotland took place in a different context. Scotland has special features with respect to water management not discussed here.[3]

In the 1930s the principal concern of water management in England was the provision of wholesome water supplies, although these were often destined for industrial as well as for domestic use. A fear of water-borne diseases such as cholera led to the adoption of the 'sanitary idea' and the municipal provision of piped water supplies from the 1840s onwards. This service developed first in the cities, spreading to the larger towns during the second half of the 19th century, and to the rural villages and country districts in the early decades of this century. Water management was the responsibility of local authorities, one of a range of their public health functions, although in a few places private companies continued to supply water under public supervision. Outright adoption of the water services by local authorities had the advantage that developments could be funded by borrowing against the security of income from local rates (property taxes).

The major disadvantage of this structure of administration lay in the fact that boundaries suitable for local democracy were not always those best for water management. Each authority provided water works, each of which required specific authorization by Act of Parliament to override the rights of others to water diverted from catchments and streams. The peak of activity in local schemes of supply came between 1870 and 1900. At first, local sources could always be found, but in time authorities had to go further afield to where unexploited sources could be found. This resulted in a jumbled pattern of large and small resource developments and even overlapping in the routing of water mains. Parliament adjudicated on objections but did not act to rationalize water resources. A great deal of wasteful duplication and underdevelopment occurred.

The first challenge to this largely 'technical' approach with little or no administrative coordination between authorities came in 1934 when severe drought forced a reappraisal. In 1937 the Central Advisory Water Committee was established to consider permanent institutional changes. Its work was overtaken by the outbreak of war in 1939, but by 1943 it was clear that water would be as essential to reconstruction as it was to the war effort.

The Water Act of 1945 introduced a number of administrative reforms.

The Minister of Health and central government officials were given a statutory responsibility for the use of water resources. The Minister was empowered to authorize all new schemes of supply. He could encourage collaborative schemes and reject those that underdeveloped available resources. The Minister was given powers to compulsorily amalgamate water authorities so that surplus reserves could be shared, economies of scale achieved, better planning units created, and the boundaries of water authorities follow the spatial spread expected in the post-war years (suburbanization of housing stock and the development of industrial estates on the outskirts of towns). As one smaller authority after another ran into trouble during the 1950s and 1960s, this power was used to progressively reduce the number of water authorities, from 1030 in 1956 to 260 in 1968 and 187 in 1974.[4] Meanwhile, sewerage remained the responsibility of local authorities despite the fact that the Central Advisory Committee had warned that much more use of rivers as sources of water supply would be necessary in future.

Before rivers could be used as sources of supply or as cheap and efficient aqueducts for inter-basin transfers of water, some sort of effective system of water pollution control had to be established. In 1948 a system of thirty-two river boards was established for England and Wales. These boards were to assess the water available for diluting pollution in advance of a new code of waste water disposal. The latter was established in 1951, when the Rivers (Prevention of Pollution) Act established a temporary system of control over all new discharges into rivers. The consent of river boards was needed before any discharge to a river could be made. It became a criminal offence to dispose of waste waters without this. The consent of the River Board could be made conditional on quality standards appropriate for that point on the river. This flexible system of control meant that the full natural capacity of rivers to absorb polluting material could be utilized. But without control of all existing discharges the system could do no more than ensure that the quality of rivers did not deteriorate further. It was intended that a system of standard rules and regulations governing the quality and quantity of permissible effluents for each river would be devised, and when that work was completed, all discharges would have to comply with it.

However, another drought in 1958 focused public attention once again on the water service, prompting a further report from the Central Advisory Water Committee, which once again drew attention to the need for effective national planning.[5] The controls of central government could stop unwise local proposals, but there was still no administrative structure specifically intended to promote good planning. Accordingly, the Water Resources Act of 1963 introduced a system of river authorities throughout England and Wales. Twenty-eight of these replaced the River Boards in the operation of river pollution control law. The 1961 Rivers (Prevention of Pollution) Act abandoned the idea of a standard code to suit all discharges. Instead it extended the existing system of 'consent' conditions. A start could at last be made on the job of improving river water quality and making resources available for water supply. The power given to the new river authorities concerned the abstraction of water. The river authorities were to assess the water resources of their river basin(s), assess future demand and work out plans to match the two. These river basin plans were to be coordinated into a national picture by a new national agency, the Water Resources Board. The river authorities already had control over discharges into each river and it was logical that they should also control abstractions. This was necessary as part of the pollution control programme, as a major new withdrawal could upset all calculations on which 'consent' conditions had been worked out. There was also the point that unless river authorities had control of withdrawals of water, there was no guarantee that the water supply authorities would follow the river authorities' advice as to the most appropriate further development of the water resources of a basin. During the late 1960s the river authorities busily extended controls over existing sources of water pollution and produced water-resource development assessments for each basin. In this process it became apparent that the major barrier to more effective use of English rivers was the inadequacy of a large number of sewage treatment plans run by local authorities.[6]

Over 1400 separate sewage authorities existed, the majority of which were too small to finance the degree of improvement of treatment that might be required as part of a national water-resources plan. As with water supply ten years before, many of them were recognizably deficient in terms of the number and quality of staff they employed to run sewage works. As the Water Resources Board worked towards the final version of a national plan for water resources, published in 1973,[7] it was increasingly recognized that administrative action would have to be taken to remove the bottleneck of poor sewage treatment. Simultaneously, it was being proposed that the system of local government in England and Wales as a whole was in great need of thorough overhaul. A Royal Commission had produced plans for radical reform,[8] greatly reducing the number of authorities that would remain to run both sewage services and participate in amalgamated water supply authorities. The question arose as to whether, in the light of the national water-resources plan, the water and sewage services should remain under the control of local government. The national water-resources plan showed considerable scope for inter-basin transfers. Would a system of large authorities, controlling all aspects of the hydrological cycle, be better suited to the nation's water needs?[9]

The Water Act 1973 created a system of ten regional water authorities, each being an amalgamation of the river basin areas of the river authorities they replaced (see Figure 14.1). The number of water supply authorities was reduced from 187. Even more dramatically, there would be only ten very large sewage treatment authorities. These would be able to provide the finance and expertise that the removal of the water quality bottleneck required. Thus, it was recognized very early on that a continuation of the strategy of offering 'technical fixes' could not guarantee an end to problems of water supply, particularly in years of drought. By a series of administrative reforms, more and more information was secured, first by the river boards, then the river authorities and the Water Resources Board, all of which indicated the need for a national water plan. This, in turn, required a few very large units of management with control over all aspects of the hydrological cycle.

Ironically, as soon as the 'administrative fix' to implement the national plan had been established, fundamental changes and weaknesses in the British economy became apparent. Recession dramatically reduced the rate of increase in demand for water. Further, a need for significant restraint in public expenditure was identified from the mid-1970s and the new Regional Water Authorities found themselves committed to major plans of expenditure on upgrading sewage treatment works and on new reservoirs, whilst at the same time their

Areas in England within Welsh National
Water Development Authority

Areas in Wales within Severn Trent
Water Authority

Figure 14.1 Regional Water Authorities in England and Wales

revenue base from industrial charges for water was falling and successive governments pressed for reduced public spending. Consequently, the Regional Water Authorities have become highly unpopular with consumers.

Simultaneously, a change of pollution control strategy has occurred. The Control of Pollution Act 1974 re-enacted previous water pollution control powers, with the important addition of the right to charge dischargers to local sewers a sum proportional to the volume and strength of the wastes to be treated at the end of the line. The consent system was extended to industrial discharges to sewers, completing the circle of control. This allows the efficiency of sewage treatment plants to be greatly improved and offers the possibility of changing strategy from a 'technical fix' to the 'behavioural'. Rather than continue to build new sewage treatment plants, it is now possible to guide producers of waste water into a pattern of behaviour more in line with existing capacity through the use of both 'consent' licences and the trade effluent charges which act as an incentive to reduce the use of sewers.

The development of an institutional structure for water management in England and Wales is a good example of progression from extensive, 'technical fix' strategies to a growing use of the 'behavioural'. More generally, the adoption of the river basin as the unit of management is the feature of English water management that has attracted most attention and praise. In developing countries, river basin plans for water management have often been expanded into comprehensive programmes of regional development. For example, there are several examples of river basin commissioners in Mexico, acting as fully fledged regional development agencies responsible for water supply, road construction, rural electrification, industrial development and agriculture. Not all river basins are suitable for such an approach; many are lacking in the regional identity and economic linkages that make the creating of a comprehensive agency worthwhile. Many river basins have no relevance for current patterns of economic activity, particularly in countries formerly colonies of European countries and countries long involved in the export of primary commodities to the urban and industrial nations of the 'North'. Many river basins are simply too large and extend across too many political, cultural and socio-economic divisions for any attempt at comprehensive management, for example, the Rio de la Plata in South America (shared by Argentina, Uruguay, Paraguay and Brazil) and the Senegal river in Western Africa (Senegal, Mauritania, Mali and Guinea).[10]

4.3.1 Principles of Water Management

General principles of water management have been derived by Cunha et al as part of an attempt to work out a new water policy for Portugal.[11] They found the basic goal of water management to be to obtain maximum beneficial use of water resources for society whilst at the same time conserving the ability of water resources to sustain beneficial uses indefinitely. To do this in a situation of mounting demand pressures requires concepts of planning and comprehensive controls.

All water management arrangements have certain tasks to fulfil. These vary with the complexity of available resources and the pressures of demand, but they invariably include building works for water storage, flood control, irrigation, power supply, sewage treatment or whatever. As pressures mount the task of maintaining water quality through pollution control becomes increasingly important, and as pressures mount further there may be a need to work out a framework of charges for water services that does not distort local and regional economies and ensures that wasteful use of an increasingly scarce resource is avoided. A review of practice in developed countries suggests that four principles of water management emerge. These are:[12]

(1) the need to consider the river basin as the basic water-resource unit;
(2) the need for effective state intervention in the form of licences for permitted uses to avoid interference between uses and excessive consumption;
(3) the need to bear in mind overall development trends, particularly those of a land-use planning nature; and
(4) the need to plan the use of water resources.

Water resource management must deal with existing situations and therefore much of the work of water management is integrating established uses with new pressures of demand. This tends to favour the adoption of local units of management whilst the need for planning tends to suggest a broader perspective. Water management tends, therefore, to be a 'tiered' activity with a hierarchy of management agencies undertaking tasks at the most appropriate scale – from the national perspective of planning water resource development, through the river basin scale of water conservation and quality control, to the local level of operating water supplies and irrigation schemes. Most developed countries have a hierarchical series of institutions interested in water management. England and Wales are unusual in lacking the lowest tier of local water undertakings, although it is true that day-to-day operational functions are broken down into more local units of management within the regional water authorities.

14.3.2 The United Nations and Water Management

A commitment to development around the world and the role of water in development for social and economic purposes provide the twin rationales for United Nations involvement in water management. Two resolutions of the Mar del Plata Action Plan, the product of the UN water conference in 1977, indicate the importance attached to good water management and reinforce the trends discussed in the preceeding section.[13]

Institutional arrangements adopted by each country should ensure that the development and management of water resources takes place in the context of national planning and that there is real co-ordination among all bodies responsible for the investigation, development and management of water resources. The problem of creating an adequate institutional infrastructure should be kept constantly under review and consideration should be given to the establishment of efficient water authorities to provide for proper co-ordination.

To this end member states were urged to reform their institutional organization for water management whenever appropriate to secure the most suitable balance between local and centralized authorities and adequate representation and participation in management for all affected parties. Countries were urged to consider 'as a matter of urgency and importance' the establishment and strengthening of river basin authorities to achieve more efficient, integrated planning and development of river basins.

Admittedly this may not be warranted by prevailing administrative and financial circumstances, the UN Administrative Committee on Coordination and the Environmental Coordination Board having reported[14] that in the real world it was virtually impossible to attain the ideal type of management where water policy was an integral part of an overall socio-economic development plan because actual policies tended to be sectoral, (dealing separately with each aspect of the economy), even though such policies could conflict. Water management, rather than being deduced from overall or even sectoral policies, was more often an *ad hoc* response to particular, pressing problems with only a limited number of countries promoting water management at the national level.

Nevertheless, delegates to the UN water conference agreed:[15]

Each country should formulate and keep under review a general statement of policy in relation to the use, management and conservation of water, as a framework for planning and implementing specific programmes and measures for efficient operation of schemes. National development plans and policies should specify the main objectives of water use policy, which should in turn be translated into guidelines and strategies, subdivided, as far as possible, into programmes for an integral management of the resource.

Such national guidelines are relatively rare, the US producing its first in 1968, the UK in 1973; even the Canadian Government has yet to do so.[16] A major reason for this is the extent to which sophisticated investigation is necessary to produce an assessment of water resources. Such inventories are fundamental requirements for any rational water-resource policy and in most developing countries, information, especially with regard to quality, is poor.[17] United Nations agencies are providing assistance and guidance to strengthen national assessment services by preparing guidelines and technical recommendations, improving and standardizing methods of observation and assisting in the planning of hydrological monitoring networks. The United Nations Educational Scientific and Cultural Organization (UNESCO), the World Meteorological Organization (WMO) and the International Association of Hydrological Sciences (IAHS), are all involved in such work. For example, between 1976 and 1978 WMO was involved in hydrological survey and water-resource assessment in Central Africa and Central America.[18] Faced with a general lack of interest or ability in the sphere of multiple-purpose, integrated and comprehensive water management, the bulk of the United Nations effort has been dedicated to creating infrastructure, establishing institutions and organizing manpower training in the individual sectors of water use.

Finally, several UN agencies are actively involved in programmes of environmental conservation in which emphasis is placed on promoting strategies for multiple-use development and sustained utilization of water resources.[19] Of particular note here are programmes concerning the increasing numbers of chemical additives used in agriculture which eventually contaminate water. Not much is known about safe limits for some of these chemicals. The World Health Organisation (WHO), in cooperation with the United Nations Environment Programme, is collecting and evaluating data and has published a series of environmental health criteria. The environmental impact of water-resource developments is also the subject of study sponsored by UNESCO, whilst WHO, the World Bank, the United Nations Development Programme and the

World Food Programme provide direct assistance to countries for controlling water-breeding vectors of disease like malaria and yellow fever.[20]

14.4 Policy Making in Practice

As pressure of demand increases on water resources there is a generally perceived need to advance in two directions: comprehensive planning of integrated and often multi-purpose water works and the control of water quality within the context of river basin management. In the following sections each of these two strategies is looked at in greater detail.

14.4.1 Benefit-Cost Analysis and the Evaluation of Water Resource Projects

A clear, single-purpose goal of providing additional water supply greatly reduces the complexity of evaluating different programmes of water resource development. Generally, however, and particularly in the United States, multiple-purpose planning is more normal, and for the evaluation of such developments sophisticated techniques have commonly been used. Major water-resource projects in the United States must pass on each of five criteria before proceeding: engineering feasibility, political feasibility, social feasibility, financial feasibility and most important, benefit-cost analysis. Clearly it is important that a project should be designed in a manner that ensures it will provide the benefits expected. Clearly a project must be able to accrue the political support necessary for its authorization or support from public funds or grants. It should be reasonably certain that the people the project is intended to benefit will in fact benefit. It should be clear that money is forthcoming to fund the works. Most important of all, in a situation where the potential number of projects exceeds the funds available it should be clear that the benefits gained from the works amount to more than the costs, and if they do not do so directly, it should be clear that some sort of intangible social benefit (such as reduction of threat to life and property through floor control) would follow government subsidy of the project. Because many water resource developments include within their range of multiple purposes intangible benefits such as reduction of flood hazard or enhanced quality of life through the provision of new recreational opportunities the Federal Government has commonly been a major promoter, financier and participant in water resource planning. This then necessitated some guarantee that decisions on the allocation of funds were not being made on an entirely political basis, but rather in some context of objective and intrinsic worth of the project itself. Because of suspicion that federal funds might be allocated in return for political favours, benefit-cost analyses came to play a major role in American water-resource planning and for similar reasons tend to accompany many of the internationally funded river basin developments of the Third World.[21]

Costs may be recognized as being of two kinds: construction costs and the other costs of the project. The former may be relatively easily calculated using established procedures of quantity surveying and engineering design. Similarly, a substantial body of experience is normally available to estimate maintenance, replacement and operating costs. The costs of the project may be regarded as the 'negative benefits'. Most important here is the cost of capital, but such things as the direct costs of the additional investment necessary to take advantage of the project, for example, the equipment necessary to take advantage of irrigation water required by farmers, should also be included. Then there are the indirect costs of the project such as when roads, telephone lines and the like have to be diverted around a new lake or when economic development attracted by a new scheme of water development obliges local authorities to install extra or new facilities to cater for population growth. Clearly there is considerable scope for estimates to vary widely in these kinds of calculations, hence introducing a considerable element of uncertainty.

This problem is greater still for benefits of the tangible and intangible sort. Here too there is considerable scope for judgement as to what may appropriately be included and what might be left out. When the balance between the costs and benefits of a project is marginal, the inclusion or exclusion of benefits such as the value of enhanced ability to fight forest fires following the construction of a new reservoir in a forested area, may make all the difference to the final benefit-cost ratio and hence to decision making.

This is assuming that reasonable estimates of the benefits can be derived. There are significant problems in this. Perhaps these are most clearly seen with regard to projects in developing countries lacking the statistical surveys of more developed economies. Nguyen has reported the procedures adopted when evaluating the development of the Senegal River Basin in West Africa.[22] The scheme in question involves the construction of a salt barrier to facilitate the use of river water for irrigation, the construction of hydro-electric power installations and the improvement of navigation. These facets of the scheme primarily benefited agriculture, the mining industry and river transport (including agricultural produce and minerals). But it was not possible to compute navigational benefits because of a lack of data concerning existing trade flows and it was therefore necessary to substitute estimates of the difference in cost between road, rail and river transport. It was possible to calculate the benefits of electrical power to the mining industry, but not to the wider market of domestic and industrial use, again because of a lack of basic information. Therefore, it was necessary to include within the calculations of benefit, the difference between the cost of supplying the relevant amount of power by hydro methods and by thermal (oil or coal). Only the calculation of the agricultural benefits was relatively straightforward.

The adoption, of necessity, of surrogate methods for calculating benefits must raise doubts as to the validity of the whole exercise. Surely no one in their senses would consider importing oil or coal for purposes of power supply in up-country West Africa. Benefits calculated in this way must be considered rather spurious. By careful examination of the way in which costs and benefits have been calculated, of what discount rate has been chosen, of which tangible or intangible benefits and costs have been included, questions can be raised about the validity of just about any benefit-cost analysis. With the rise of the environmental movement in the late 1960s close examinations of the forest of technical figures that accompanied benefit-cost analyses became more and more common and public confidence in the technique began to wane. In short, the suspicion grew that a benefit analysis could be manipulated to prove the case for almost any scheme according to the elements included and the estimates made within the calculations.

Further, a number of researchers began to point out that the actual costs and benefits of projects did not match the predictions made for the project when hindsight reviews were undertaken. For example, J. Chadwick Day reassessed the Branch Deer Creek Project in Ontario.[23] The tangible benefits of the scheme include improved irrigation and a new road whilst increased recreational opportunity, livestock watering, fire-fighting, domestic water supply, downstream water flow in summer, groundwater table levels, regional economic growth and flood control, had all been cited as intangible benefits in the original assessment of the project in 1967. With a projected cost of nearly 600,000 Canadian dollars the project's benefit-cost ratio had been calculated at 2.2:1 over 50 years, assuming a discount rate of 4%.

Reviewing the situation in 1971, two years after completion, Chadwick Day found the actual cost to have been 89,000 dollars more than the original estimate, although over half this increase related to engineering fees higher than predicted, a factor which could not easily have been foreseen. The cost of land purchase, however, had been seriously underestimated. As regards the primary benefit, that of irrigation, Chadwick Day found that: 'interviews in 1971 with all farmers on the 1900 acres to be benefited by the reservoir indicated that the anticipated cropping pattern is unlikely to develop because of faulty assumptions made in the feasibility study'.[24] Most serious of these was the estimate made of the acreage devoted to high-value tobacco production. He further reports that few of the intangible benefits claimed for the project appear warranted. The area has no history of shortage of water for domestic purposes. The reservoir is too low to make any effective contribution to fire-fighting. The pattern of operation of the dam and reservoir provides few flood control benefits, and there is anyway little to protect in the section of river downstream. New recreational opportunities were created but the dam destroyed one of the best remaining trout streams on the North shore of Lake Erie (an ecological impact not considered in the original feasibility study).

Overall Chadwick Day is able to conclude: 'the social and ecological desirability of this multiple purpose water and land management project was inaccurately and inadequately justified'.[25] As mentioned in Chapter 9, suspicion that this was the case in a large number of cases, the absence of any estimate of ecological and environmental damage in any benefit-cost calculations and the general drive towards greater public participation in resource management stemming out of the growing environmental movement, led to the replacement of benefit-cost analysis as a technique of water resource development evaluation in North America.

14.4.2 Environmental Impact Assessment and the Evaluation of Water Resource Projects

Practice with regard to Environmental Impact Assessment in the United States is based on NEPA, discussed in Chapter 9. During the early 1970s all the major US agencies involved in water management produced guidelines for the application of EIA. In 1972 the US Environmental Protection Agency produced a manual to assist in the effective water quality planning that was required by new water pollution control legislation (see 14.4.3). The following year a more specific manual appeared for the facilities, plans and area-wide plans required in the 1972 Federal Water Pollution Control Amendments Act.[26] In 1973 the US Water Resources Council established principles and standards for water resource plans.

By 1977 the US Army Corps of Engineers had developed the early work of Leopold (Chapter 9) into a fully fledged operational system known as WRAM (Water Resource Assessment Methodology) which included guidance not only on the identification and presentation of impact but also a weighting system to accommodate the scale of impact and an extension to include its social aspects.

In the UK a manual was produced by Clark et al on behalf of the Scottish Development Department and Secretary of State for the Environment in England and Wales. Intended to guide planners in the blending of EIA procedures with normal procedures for major developments, the manual contains a special discussion of the environmental impacts of selected water-related developments. In this, four major categories of potential impact are identified (social, economic, aesthetic and ecological) and the principal focus of wider planning concern is seen as revolving around enhanced recreational opportunities.[27]

Principal social effects discussed include possible disruption following the arrival of an incoming labour force and the effects of relocation on indigenous communities. The main economic impact arises from the effects of a reservoir on loss of agricultural land and on employment opportunities, although the controlled release of water from a reservoir may have benefits for agriculture downstream. The 'extensive zones of visual influence' of large reservoir schemes are the focus of concern from the aesthetic viewpoint. Ecologically the distribution of existing habitats has to be balanced with the creation of new opportunities for water-based wildlife.

The potential loss of salmon spawning beds is a particularly serious loss as is the potential loss of unusual assemblages of plants and animals around upland lakes once water quality is changed by the diversion of water from new sources. The Water Act 1973 required water authorities in England and Wales to take such steps as were reasonably practicable to develop the recreational use of reservoirs and associated land. Clark et al point out[28] that in some cases the provision of recreational facilities and consequent increase in visitors to an area may cause more concern among local people than the scheme itself and so particular care should be taken with regard to recreational planning lest the scheme suffer delay through vehement opposition on this count.

A good example of the use of EIA in water-resources planning comes from central Scotland. As part of consultations over reforming the institutional structure for water management undertaken in the late 1960s, concern was expressed over the extent to which national planning needs would be adequately catered for by the regional structure proposed. This brought a commitment by the Scottish Development Department to undertake a national water-resources assessment subsequently published in 1973.[29] This showed that any problems of planning would occur in the central, most populated part of the country, broadly speaking between the cities of Glasgow and Edinburgh. To ensure supplies for this area the Central Scotland Water Development Board (CSWDB) had already been established to administer inter-regional schemes of water resource development, the first, and only one of which was centred on the internationally famous Loch Lomond. The CSWDB commissioned a study of the future needs of central Scotland and determined that another inter-regional scheme would be required before the end of the century.[30] Because of uncertainty over the extent of increased demands for water, the strategy of development selected for further evaluation was that of river intakes supported where necessary by regulating reservoirs upstream. A wide variety of alternative schemes of development was examined, the choice being finally reduced to three, each based on a single river, the Tay, Forth and Clyde schemes. (See Figure 14.2). The natural minimum flow of the Tay is sufficiently large to sustain water resource development without the construction of regulating

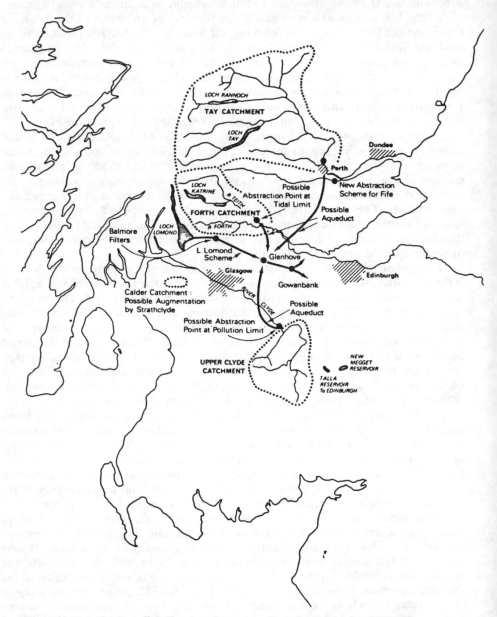

Figure 14.2 Options for Further Resource Developments for Water for Central Scotland

Table 14.1: Water for central Scotland: costs of alternative schemes. *Source:*
CSWDB, 1977, *Water for Central Scotland*, p. 186

		455 Ml/day	Yield Targets Stage 1	910 Ml/day	Stage 2
Tay scheme	Annual cost	£13·4m		£22·1m	
	Unit cost per Ml		£81		£66
Forth scheme	Annual cost	£11·5m		£23·4m	
	Unit cost per Ml		£71		£69
Clyde scheme	Annual cost	£10·8m		£21·6m	
	Unit cost per Ml		£65		£65

storage upstream. Conventional calculation of the engineering costs of each
scheme was undertaken with the results shown in Table 14.1. The Clyde
scheme appeared to be the cheapest.

Although there have been no major public controversies over the development of water resources in Scotland it was then decided to conduct an EIA on
each alternative in the light of the general environmental concerns revealed
whilst undertaking the engineering design and evaluation of the alternative
schemes. The Forth and Tay survive as salmon rivers, and the abstraction of
large volumes of water, it was thought, might have some adverse impact on the
migration of fish. The construction of a regulating reservoir might adversely
affect spawning grounds in the Forth whilst the removal of fresh water from
the industrialized estuary of the Forth might also hinder the passage of fish
through enhanced levels of pollution. On the Clyde fears were also expressed
over the implications of the removal of a large volume of clean water upstream
of one of the most urbanized and industrialized tidal river stretches in the
country.[30]

As elsewhere, a simplified form of the Leopold matrix was adopted for the
presentation of the environmental impact statement.[31] Each section of each
scheme was allocated a row and three major types of impact, concerning visual
amenity, ecology and existing land-use formed columns. In each intersecting
space, impacts if any were briefly described. Figure 14.3 indicates the structure
of the statement and gives extracts illustrative of its content. In these cases
most of the issues raised were relatively trivial. Nevertheless a total of 137
items of potential concern were identified and each allocated a classificatory
letter according to the code listed in Figure 14.4 which distinguishes between
long- and short-term benefits, or long- or short-term damage, the latter being
reversible, the former irreversible. Damaging aspects of the projects were listed
and re-examined to see if by redesign or re-routing or in some other way the
impact could be reduced. Those that could not be modified are marked with
black dots.

To facilitate the easy comparison of the three alternative schemes, simple
bar charts were drawn as shown in Figure 14.4. This procedure has the advantage of encapsulating the range and seriousness of impact in an easily visualized
form, but the disadvantage of allocating each an equal weight, which is questionable. Loss of agricultural land and associated employment is clearly not an
impact on a par with the creation of straight swaithes through woodland. A
second set of bar charts recorded the position after modification to reduce
impact. The greatest scope for so doing lay with the Forth scheme. An inspec-

CHEME	SUB AREA	VISUAL KEY ISSUES	REV. CLAS	C	U
TAY	1 NORTH MUIRTON	1. Visual intrusion of housings at side intakes	●		E.
	2 PIPELINE TO HUNTINGTOWER	1. Visual intrusion of the pumping station (unless located on Industrial Estate)	●		E
	3 HUNTINGTOWER TO FORGANDENNY	1. The distribution of rock and spoil abstracted from the Aberdalgie tunnel	D	●E	
	4 OCHIL TUNNEL	1. The distribution of rock and spoil abstracted from the Ochil tunnel	D	●E	
	5 GARTMORN RESERVOIR	1. The effects of raising the waterlevel on firmly established habitats and on existing landscape 2. Disturbance of rock and spoil abstracted from tunnel	●D / ●	D / ●D	●D
	6 GARTMORN TO OAKBANKWOOD	1. The creation of straight swathes through woodland	D	E	
	7 OAKBANKWOOD	1. Siting of the pumping station	E		●E
	8 OAKBANKWOOD TO GLENHOVE	1. The creation of straight swathes through woodland	D	E	
MIX				1D4E	1D3E
REVISED MIX				4D	1D1E
FORTH	1 LOCH MAHAICK	1. Spoil disposal from tunnel 2. Drawdown effects on reservoir banks and bed	C / ●	D	●E
	2 THE KNAIK	1. Appearance of the site during construction on a tourist route (the B827)		D●	
	3 DOUNE/BRACO CORRIDOR				
	4 RIVER TEITH— INVERARDOCH TO DRIP				
	5 DRIP RESERVOIR INTAKE; PUMPING	1. Visual intrusion in highly visible and historic area 2. Design of intake close to Conservation Area	D		E● / E
	6 DRIP TO OAKBANKWOOD	1. Disposal or landscaping of tunnel residue 2. Creation of straight swathes through woodland	D / D	●E / E	
	7 OAKBANKWOOD	1. Siting of treatment works and pumping station	E		●E
	8 OAKBANKWOOD TO GLENHOVE	1. Disturbance to woodland and the cutting of swathes	D	E	
MIX				2D3E	4E
REVISED MIX				1C4D	1D2E
CLYDE	1 DUNEATON RESERVOIR	1. Establishment of a totally different visual character			●E●
	2 DUNEATON TO BONNINGTON LINN				
	3 BONNINGTON LINN	1. Visual intrusion of new intake 2. Effects of lessened flows on Falls of Clyde - longer periods of reduced flow 3. Downstream effects of changed flows on Clyde Gorge & SSSI	● / ●B/E / E		●E● / ●E● / ●E●
	4 AQUEDUCT TO NEWKAYS	1. Creation of straight swathes through woodland 2. Disposal of tunnel spoil 3. Crossing of SSSI	D / D / D	●D / ●D	
	5 NEWKAYS RESERVOIR AND TREATMENT WORKS	1. Establishment of totally different character 2. High visibility from surrounding areas	●A / ●A		●E
	6 AQUEDUCT TO CLYDE	1. Creation of straight swathes through woodland 2. Crossing of the Nethan Gorge SSSI and AGLV	D / D	●D	
	7 CLYDE CROSSING				
	8 AQUEDUCT TO DALMACOULTER	1. Creation of straight swathes through woodland - Jock's Burn SSSI	D	E	
MIX				3D3E	6E
REVISED MIX				6D	2A3E

Figure 14.3 Extract from the EIA of Alternative Schemes of Development for Water for Central Scotland.
Source: CSWDB, 1979, *Water for Central Scotland; The Way Ahead,* prepared by Percy Johnson-Marshall & Associates Ltd. This material is included merely to demonstrate the lay-out of the Environmental Impact Statement.

ECOLOGICAL KEY ISSUES

ECOLOGICAL KEY ISSUES	REV CLAS.	C	t'	
Trapping of smolt and parr on intake screens			E	1. Ef
Effects on fishing during construction		Do+		
Change of fish movement patterns of Tay/Almond junction	E		mE	
Double disturbance of phased pipelines		Do		1. Do 2. Di
The distribution of rock and spoil abstracted from the Aberdalgie tunnel	D	mE		1. Te 2. De
Construction of the Earn crossing		Do+		
Crossing of wooded areas		E		
The distribution of rock and spoil abstracted from the Ochil tunnel	D	E		1. Th 2. Th
The effects of raising the water level on firmly established habitats and on existing landscape	mD		mD	1. Di 2. Ef 3. Do
Distribution of rock and spoil abstracted from tunnel		mD		
The creation of straight swathes through woodland	D	E		1. Ef 2. Di 3. Co 4. De
				1. Co
The creation of straight swathes through woodland	D	E		1. Go
Possible damage to the Antonine Wall and Forth and Clyde Canal		mE		2. Po
		4D6E	D2E	
		7D	1D1E	
Disturbance to existing commercial plantation in construction of secondary embankment	C	B		1. Di
Spoil disposal from tunnel	C			2. Ef
Downstream effects on the Keltie water and other associated burns	D		mE+	3. Ef
Effects on wildfowl and conservation management in area designated a SSSI			E	4. Lo
Drawdown effects on reservoir banks and bed				5. Ef
Effects of drawdown on reservoir banks and bed			E	1. Lo 1. Ef
Effects of altered flows and water composition in the Allan water on drainage, pollution and fisheries	D		mE+	1. Ef
Disturbance from construction of intakes, discharge points and aqueduct river crossings on Ardoch & Allan Waters		Do+		2. Do
Mix of regulating water with existing flow			E	1. Cha
Changes in level in existing water course - consequent effects on surrounding water table and land drainage			E+	2. Ef
Effects on fishing of changed river regime and water composition			EO+	
Effects of changed level on riverside bird population			FO	
Downstream effects of abstraction on pollution and wildlife			EA+	1. Lo
Trapping of smolt and parr on intake screens			mE	2. Di
Disruption during construction in river crossings - especially Teith and Forth		mDo+		1. Di
Disposal or landscaping of tunnel residue	B	mE		2. Di
Creation of straight swathes through woodland		E		3. Do
				1. Co
The creation of straight swathes through woodland	D	E		1. Go
Possible damage to the Antonine Wall and Forth and Clyde Canal		mE		2. Po
		4D4E	1D2E	
		2C 5D	2D3E	1C
Removal of existing varied habitats			mEO	1. Lo 2. Lo 3. Ef 4. Lo 5. Ef 6. Ef 7. Ef 8. Ef
Effects of changed river regime on banks, riverside habitats and fishing			mE+	1. Ef
Changes in level in existing water course - consequent effects on surrounding water table and land drainage			mE	2. Cha
Effects on fishing of changed river regime and water composition			mDO	3. Ef
Effects of lessened flows on Falls of Clyde - longer periods of reduced flow	E		mE+	1. Ef
Downstream effects on river pollution and sewage disposal. Reduction of dilution for purification schemes			mE+	
Disturbance to river during construction		mDo+		
Effects of lessened flows on river weed and fishing	E		mE	
Creation of straight swathes through woodland	B	E		1. Di
Disposal of tunnel spoil	B	mD		2. Do
Crossing of SSSI				
Loss of existing habitats.			mEO	1. Lo 2. Re 3. Ef
Creation of straight swathes through woodland	D	mD		1. Do
Crossing of Nethan Gorge SSSI and AGLV	D			2. Di
Effects of construction on river		Do+		1. Ef
Creation of straight swathes through woodland - Jock's Burn SSSI	D	E		1. Do 2. Ef 3. Ef
		SD3E	mE	
		5D	7E	

OVERALL WEIGHTINGS

EXISING TAY SCHEME

	A	B	C	D	E
EXTREME					
MAJOR					
MINOR					

ENVIRONMENTAL REVISED SCHEME

	A	B	C	D	E
EXTREME					
MAJOR					
MINOR					
NONE					

EXISTING FORTH SCHEME

	A	B	C	D	E
EXTREME					
MAJOR					
MINOR					

ENVIRONMENTAL REVISED SCHEME

	A	B	C	D	E
EXTREME					
MAJOR					
MINOR					
NONE					

EXISTING CLYDE SCHEME

	A	B	C	D	E
EXTREME					
MAJOR					
MINOR					

ENVIRONMENTAL REVISED SCHEME

	A	B	C	D	E
EXTREME					
MAJOR					
MINOR					
NONE					

HOW TO READ THE CHART

The Chart sets out the key issues identified in the study in such a way that their effects may be compared both within and between the three schemes. The object of the chart is not to crudely tot up these impacts but rather to illustrate the mix of problems and opportunities presented by each scheme, thus allowing a more qualitative assessment to be made.

The Chart is divided horizontally into the Tay, Forth and Clyde schemes. Within each scheme the sub areas are listed and against each are listed the key issues for that sub area. Key issues are grouped under visual, ecological, existing use and potential use headings. Against each heading there are three columns marked "Rev. Clas" C & U. C indicates impacts incurred during construction. U indicates impacts incurred during the long term use of facilities. "Rev Clas." indicates the change in classification which could be brought about within the scheme by design or by extra expenditure.

Within these columns each issue is given a classification indicating the degree of permanence of its impacts.

    A = long term benefit.
    B = short term benefit.
    C = No benefit or disbenefit
    D = Short term reversible damage.
    E = Long term irreversibel damage.

A further small letter code is given where the impacts are assessed as extreme (E) or major (M). Where no further letter code is given the impact is considered minor.

Certain impacts which have downstream consequences are coded with an arrow. ($\downarrow$)

We have also indicated in the diagram the effects of "designing out" or otherwise reducing or eradicating impacts. The revised classification indicates the character of the impact once this has been done. Those impacts coded with a black dot (●) are unavoidable and cannot be reduced or eradicated. The revised mix indicated at the bottom of the column indicates the character of a scheme once changes have been made and consists of the black dotted impacts and those in the revised classification column.

On the far right of the diagram the overall results of each sheme in its original and its adjusted form are indicated. (Note that the division into construction and use is dropped for these diagrams.)

Figure 14.4 Summary Bar Chart of EIA of Alternative Schemes for Water for Central Scotland.
Source: CSWDB, 1979, *Water for Central Scotland; The Way Ahead*, prepared by Percy Johnson-Marshall & Associates Ltd. This material is included merely to demonstrate the layout of the Environmental Impact Statement.

tion of Figure 14.4 reveals the Tay to be the least damaging scheme in environmental terms.

Water resource planners were thus faced with the familiar environmental dilemma of the most cost-effective scheme being most environmentally damaging and the least-impact scheme being most expensive. This forced a re-examination of the situation. The demand forecasts on which the three schemes were based were re-examined with a view to incorporating new developments since they were first derived five years before: namely, the regionalization of water management allowing the sharing of existing surpluses, the better estimation of trends in demand and more efficient management of existing resources, and a change in the economic outlook for different parts of central Scotland, specifically a deepening recession in the traditional heavy industry areas of the west paralleled by an upturn in economic activity related to the on-shore processing of North Sea oil and gas in the east. Briefly, these two sets of changing circumstances led to a substantial revision of the target quantity of water that a new source of supply was expected to meet, downwards from 200 million gallons per day to 100 million gallons per day, plus an expected shift eastwards in the centre of gravity of demand.[32] This new target allowed the redesign of the Tay scheme, significantly reducing its cost (to approximately £62 million) whilst maintaining its favourable environmental rating.

Thus the principal role of environmental impact assessment in this case was to force a rethink on the part of water planners. This having been undertaken, it was found that the least damaging scheme would also be acceptable on grounds of cost. If no procedure of EIA had been adopted, central Scotland may have not only suffered environmental damage needlessly but also been saddled in future years with an over-elaborate and poorly located water-resource development. The Tay scheme is now firmly established as the next major new source of future water supply for central Scotland although construction is not expected to begin for several years yet.

It seems that EIA is indeed useful in water resource planning but there are some difficulties in the application of the procedure. The most important of these can be illustrated by referring to another planning exercise in the UK. Following a national planning exercise for England and Wales the regional water authorities set about implementing the respective parts during the 1970s. One such part was the reconstruction of Haweswater reservoir in the Lake District to convert it from giving supplies directly, to one of regulating the river Lune for downstream abstraction of a greater supply.[33] (See Figure 14.5.)

Six different possibilities for the redevelopment of the Haweswater reservoir appeared feasible. One involved no change in the existing reservoir, two involved a minor raising of the height of the existing dam and shoreline, and a further three involved the construction of a new higher dam just downstream resulting in a significantly higher shoreline for the existing reservoir. The simplest scheme (the first) involved the construction of a reversible aqueduct from Haweswater to Tebay on the River Lune through which excess run-off could be drawn from the Lune for storage at Haweswater and later released in times of lower natural flow. The second scheme involved a minor raise of Haweswater to accommodate Lune water storage plus water transferred from the Upper Eden catchment to the north east, the latter to be sent on its way south when required.

The third scheme also involved storing water from two sources, this time

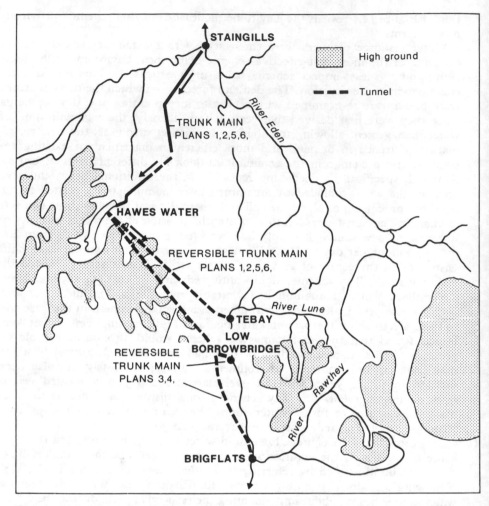

Figure 14.5 Alternative Schemes of Further Development Based on Haweswater

the Lune at Barrowbridge to the south of Tebay and even further south, from a major tributary of the Lune, the Rawthney, from which water for storage would be pumped north at appropriate times for later release. The remaining variants involve a higher dam at Haweswater. Scheme 4 is the large dam version of Scheme 3, Scheme 5 is a larger version of Scheme 2 and Scheme 6 a larger version still of Scheme 2, the difference between the two concerning the sizes of aqueducts and pumps from the Eden.

The yields and capital costs of each scheme were calculated as in Table 14.2. Clearly the cost of a new dam is considerable and the costs of pumping storage water from the south to the north is surprisingly less than from the north to the south.

Each variant was the subject of an environmental impact statement, that for Scheme 2 being reproduced as Figure 14.6. This serves to illustrate the main points of difficulty in applying EIA. First, the significance of impacts, although

Table 14.2: Alternative schemes for the further development of Haweswater. *Source:* North West Water Authority, 1978, Environmental Appraisal of Four Alternative Water Resource Schemes, pp. 30–33

	Intakes	Reservoir volume	Gain in available supplies	Headworks capital costs	Headworks present value unit costs
Scheme 1	Tebay & Staingills	84,700 Ml	215 Ml/day	£29·7m	£69 per Ml
Scheme 2	Tebay & Staingills	98,000 Ml	300 Ml/day	£41·6m	£79 per Ml
Scheme 3	Low Borrowbridge & Brigflatts	98,000 Ml	265 Ml/day	£39·9m	£89 per Ml
Scheme 4	Low Borrowbridge & Brigflatts	140,000 Ml	365 Ml/day	£64·8m	£71 per Ml
Scheme 5	Tebay & Staingills	156,000 Ml	600 Ml/day	£69·5m	£85 per Ml
Scheme 6	Tebay & Staingills	202,000 Ml	800 Ml/day	£92·9m	£89 per Ml

presented in a simple manner is clearly a matter of subjective judgement: Is the loss of 25 hectares of agricultural land comparable with the flooding of Sites of Special Scientific Interest (SSSI) at Naddle Low and Martindale Forest? But more than this, Table 14.3 is a compilation of the significant impact profiles of all six variants. Which is least damaging?

Can the differences between these schemes in terms of environmental impact be easily assessed? The answer must be in the negative. A major difficulty of the laudable comprehensiveness and multidisplinary concern of EIA is that

Table 14.3: Codings for summarising the environmental impact of alternative schemes of water resource development based on Haweswater. *Source:* North West Water Authority, 1978, Environmental Appraisal of Four Alternative Water Resource Schemes, pp. 55–57

Environmental facet	Scheme 1	Scheme 2	Scheme 3	Scheme 4	Scheme 5	Scheme 6
Naddle SSSI*	l/a/ir/lt	l/a/ir/lt	l/a/ir/lt	s/a/ir/lt	s/a/ir/lt	s/a/ir/lt
Martindale SSSI*	–	l/a/ir/lt	l/a/ir/lt	–	–	–
Fishery potential	l/b/r/lt	l/b/r/lt	l/b/r/lt	l/b/r/lt	l/b/r/lt	l/b/r/lt
Algal growth	l/a/r/st	l/a/r/st	s/a/r/st	s/a/r/st	s/a/ir/lt	s/a/ir/lt
Inter-basin transfer	–	l/a/r/st	s/a/r/lt	s/a/ir/lt	s/a/ir/lt	s/a/ir/lt
New dam	–	l/a/ir/lt	l/a/ir/lt	s/a/ir/lt	s/a/ir/lt	s/a/ir/lt
Extended reservoir	l/a/ir/st	l/a/ir/lt	l/a/ir/lt	s/a/ir/lt	s/a/ir/lt	s/a/ir/lt
Other works	l/a/r/st	l/a/r/st	l/a/r/st	l/a/r/st	l/a/r/st	l/a/r/st
Land lost	l/a/r/st	l/a/ir/lt	l/a/ir/lt	l/a/ir/lt	l/a/ir/lt	l/a/ir/lt
Holdings working	–	l/a/ir/lt	l/a/ir/lt	l/a/ir/lt	l/a/ir/lt	l/a/ir/lt
Cropping patterns	–	l/a/r/st	l/a/r/st	l/a/r/st	l/a/r/st	l/a/r/st
Existing recreation	l/a/r/st	l/a/r/st	l/a/r/st	l/a/r/st	l/a/r/st	s/a/r/lt
Local economy	l/b/r/st	l/b/r/st	l/b/r/st	l/b/r/st	l/b/r/st	l/b/r/st
Historic buildings	–	l/a/ir/st	l/a/ir/st	l/a/ir/lt	s/a/ir/lt	s/a/ir/lt
s/a/ir/lt						

* SSSI = Site of Special Scientific Interest.
Coding is ordered as follows: scale/value/reversibility/timescale of impact.
a = adverse, b = beneficial; ir = irreversible; l = local impact; lt = long term; r = reversible; s = strategic impact; st = short term.
The best possible case is l/b/ir/lt, the worst possible is s/a/ir/lt.

Figure 14.6 Extract of EIA for Alternative Schemes of Development based on Haweswater.
Source: North West Water Authority, 1978, Environmental Appraisal of Four Alternative Water Resource Schemes, p. 56

PHYSICAL ENVIRONMENT

Area and Description of Impact		Nature and Extent of Impact	Significance
ECOLOGY			
Statutory/Notified Sites affected by proposals	Naddle Low Forest SSSI	2-3 ha flooded[2] New tunnel portal at Wallow Crag	L,A,IR,Lt
	Martindale Forest SSSI	1-2 ha flooded	L,A,IR,Lt
Ecological Zones: Conservation Status[3] and %age of total Survey area affected	High	3.1 ha 0.4%	L,A,IR,Lt
	Medium	6.8 ha 0.8%	
	Low	4.6 ha 0.5%	
Effect on Reservoir and River Ecology	Potential Fishery	Could be stocked with trout	L,B,R,Lt
	Algal Growth Potential	Some potential for increased rate of growth	L,A,R,St
	Inter-River Transfer	Low order of risk to ecology of Upper Lune	L,A,R,St
LANDSCAPE			
Impact on existing landscape caused by:-	Dam Raised by 3 metres	Local changes at dam site	L,A,IR,Lt
	Reservoir TWL raised 3 metres	Minor change at reservoir head	L,A,IR,Lt
	Other Works Tunnel Aqueduct	Intermediate tunnel portals	L,A,R,St
Scope for restoring/modifying landscape formed by:-	Dam (concrete)	Limited	—
	Reservoir	Limited — drawdown range 10 metres +	—
	Other Works	Considerable	—

LAND USE AND ECONOMY

AGRICULTURE		Nature and Extent of Impact	Significance
Total area of agricultural land lost		25 ha	L,A,IR,Lt
Best quality land as %age of affected area		3%	L,A,IR,Lt
No. of farm holdings affected		one + Common grazing rights for 9 others	L,A,IR,Lt
No. of farmhouses/buildings affected		None	
Annual production from affected farm holdings	Milk None Beef 29,000 kg Mutton/Lamb 155,000 kg Wool 8,460 kg	Loss of 10 hectares of bottom land but otherwise of very limited effect	L,A,R,St

Effect on existing recreational activity and levels of use	Fell Walking/Climbing	Temporary disturbance to existing activities through construction	L,A,R,St
	Picnicking/Strolling		
	Fishing		
Recreation development potential and levels of use	Water Area	No change in existing levels of use	
	Land Area		
	Average Summer Use	150 people 50 cars	
	Peak Summer Use	300 people 100 cars	

TRANSPORT/COMMUNICATIONS AND UTILITIES

Diversion/Relocation of major routes and communications	none required	

LOCAL ECONOMY

Jobs Lost	None	
Temporary Jobs Provided	Say 600 Man/years	L,B,R,St
Permanent Jobs Provided	Say 3 or 4 (Pump House and Maintenance)	

LOCAL COMMUNITY

Communities affected by construction:-	Reservoir Works	Burnbanks, Bampton	L,A,R,St
	Aqueduct Works	Isolated Farms	L,A,R,St
	Diversionary Works	None	
	Construction Traffic	Brigflatts, Low Borrowbridge	L,A,R,St
Communities affected by operation:-	Reservoir Works, etc.	None	
	Recreation Activity	None	
	Recreation Traffic	None	

HISTORIC AND CULTURAL

Historic or Cultural Sites affected:-	Listed Buildings	None	
	Historic Sites/Buildings	3 scheduled Ancient Monuments destroyed	L,A,IR,St
	Archaeological Sites		

Notes: 1 This figure is included in the area of High Conservation Value described in (2)
2 Vegetation types affected:
High = Deciduous Woodland
Medium = Wet Flush Grassland, Permanent Pasture, Mixed Woodland, Gorse
Low = Bracken, Dry Upland Grassland.
3 Grassland which could be improved.

Key:

L	=	Local
S	=	Strategic
A	=	Adverse
B	=	Beneficial
St	=	Short Term
Lt	=	Long Term
R	=	Reversible
IR	=	Irreversible

it produces an information overload which is difficult to comprehend even when simplified in the British manner shown here. In this situation, there is a real danger of key issues being swamped in a fog of detailed information, fact, opinion and judgement.

Similar critical points have been made of EIAs in US water resource planning. The US Army Corps of Engineers WRAM procedure in particular has been criticized as suffering from the inherent drawbacks of all methods producing alphabetic or numeric scores for impact, i.e. confusion through over-elaborate notation and the inherently subjective judgements that go to make up the seemingly precise array of detail that systems of EIA produce.[34]

These are familiar criticisms of BCA, and as with BCA there are few post-audit studies to evaluate the effectiveness of EIA procedures. One such study was conducted by the University of Utah's Institute for Social Science Research on Natural Resources in 1974.[35] A post-audit analysis of a Weber Basin Project in Utah compared its original planning aims with impacts that actually followed the scheme's completion. Major unanticipated impact was found covering land-use changes and law enforcement problems. The same Utah team looked at both the US Water Resource Council and US Army Corps of Engineers guidelines for EIA and assessed the extent that they might have described the actual pattern of impact. Again, only a limited correspondence between actuality and impact assessment was found.[36]

More positively Hill and Ortolando[37] surveyed water planning agencies in the US to assess the effects of NEPA on both the planning procedures of water agencies and the decisions reached. Specifically, questionnaire survey of personnel within the Army Corps of Engineers and the Soil Conservation Service revealed that the most significant effect of statutory EIA had been an increase in cooperation between and consultation with other agencies, local administrations and the public. Much more detailed consideration was now given to the comments of others, particularly other agencies. Nevertheless, the effects on the final decisions reached were said to be insignificant, with additional measures of mitigation being the main result of the procedure. If this is generally so, the results of EIA must be disappointing. Indeed, as expressed in Chapter 9, one unfortunate and unforeseen effect of environmental legislation such as NEPA may have been to occupy everybody, planners, public and protestors, with procedural matters rather than the issues of good water-resource planning.

14.4.3 Water Pollution Control Policies

At the beginning of this chapter it was argued that a commonly identifiable trend in water management is the development of holistic river basin planning. The most sophisticated function of such an approach is the control of water quality. In this section, policies to this end are examined. As in other fields of resource management there are a number of possible approaches to the problem of water pollution, and in many countries policy reflects a mixture of several strategies as a result of historical evolution and as a response to the particular policy context of that country. One thing common to all countries is the natural desire on the part of manufacturers, farmers and communities to avoid extra costs consequent on requirements to control pollution. Clearly pollution control costs represent a threat to profits and capital investment for other purposes, and hence indirectly to employment in capitalist countries. In centrally planned economies there are equally strong pressures to meet production quotas within budgets and to direct investment to increasing production. The essential problem of pollution control is to strike a reasonable balance between the social costs of a polluted environment and the private and public costs incurred in controlling it.

The principal mechanisms available for the control of water pollution are: (a) a licence system where the quantity and quality of acceptable discharges of waste are laid down and it is made illegal to exceed the specified limits; (b) a charge system where charges are laid down according to a scale related to the quantity and quality of effluents so that a strong economic incentive is provided on the balance sheet of the pollution producing body to adopt measures of treatment and control; (c) a subsidy system whereby grants or other means of assistance are provided to reduce the social and external costs of waste production once and for all through the provision of treatment; and (d) a system of source agreements where practices and processes are agreed with major categories of pollution-producing activities such as municipal sewage treatment or the pulp and paper making, the universal adoption of which leads to significant reductions on polluting loads wherever individual plants happen to be situated. Finally, (e) it is possible to build one's way out of pollution problems through the construction of 'purification lakes', i.e. storage areas where polluted water may be treated or the natural processes of regeneration accelerated, or through the construction of clean water storage reservoirs for the purpose of diluting pollution downstream to acceptable levels. But use of such strategies is rare.

In the UK, as elsewhere, elements of all five strategies are to be found, but the principal thrust of policy is on licences that are location specific (a). In the United States the principal emphasis has been on source category agreements (d) and in France the emphasis has been on charges (c). Each of these systems is now reviewed in turn.

4.4.4 The System for Water Pollution Control in the United Kingdom

The system for controlling pollution in inland waters in the United Kingdom revolves around the legal requirement that each source of waste water must have the specific consent of the pollution control authority (Regional Water Authorities in England and Wales, River Purification Boards in Scotland). Consent to discharge may be conditional. Conditions may be reviewed at periods no shorter than two years. The dischargers must provide details of the place where the discharge is to be made, its nature, composition and temperature and the daily amount and maximum rate of discharge. The authority must respond within three months. Its decision as to permission or conditions may be the subject of appeal to the Secretary of State (for the Environment in England and Wales, for Scotland in Scotland).

In practice the bulk of waste water originates from sewage treatment plants (also under the control of regional water authorities in England and Wales but run by regional units of local government in Scotland). To ensure that the operation of sewage treatment works (STWs) is not disrupted by particularly difficult substances (such as paint), discharges to sewers from business premises and leading to STWs have also been subject to a system of consent control since 1974. Breach of consent conditions is illegal but, as Storey has shown,[38] in practice there have been very few prosecutions and those that have occurred have principally been directed towards the agricultural community, relating to the disposal of animal dips or silage liquor rather than more chronic problems arising with STWs or major industrial discharges. Instead of litigation, a policy of 'purification by persuasion' has been followed. The pollution control officers have attempted to persuade rather than threaten those responsible into making improvements to their processes or pre-treatment practices. Recourse to the law has been a last resort. This 'softly, softly' approach seems to have paid off. There has been a healthy and steady decline in the length of poor, grossly polluted inland water recorded since the full consent system was first introduced from 1961. The principal barrier to further improvement is the cost of rebuilding, replacing or installing treatment plants, particularly STWs, in the light of the high percentage of all waste waters diverted to them.

In 1970 £400 million was spent on improving sewage treatment works in England and Wales and a figure of £1000 million or so was put on the ultimate cost of bringing everywhere up to standard.[39] The money simply has not been available.

Since the mid-1970s, and in an attempt to maximize the efficiency of existing works, industrial sources of waste water have not only been subjected to consent conditions as to what is acceptable at STWs, but also required to pay charges related to the quantity and quality of their effluent, a substantial incentive to either build their own treatment plants where feasible or adjust their pollutant producing processes. The charge, payable per cubic metre of liquid wastes discharged to the public sewer, takes into account the expenditure involved in providing, maintaining and operating the sewers as well as the treatment plant and the disposal of 'sludge' residues from there.

The greatest danger of a consent system of regulation is that it will fall into general disregard and contempt as financial realities preclude satisfactory levels of compliance. This has been overcome in recent years by the addition of the trade effluent charging schemes, but there remains the difficulty of ensuring that regulated standards do not ossify and become, in effect, licences to pollute. A further problem is how to steadily improve the system of pollution control. In England and Wales this problem has been tackled by the recent introduction of 'River Quality Objectives' (RQOs) by Regional Water Authorities. They also help compliance with EEC regulations on the quality of drinking water, and help in the whole process of water supply planning which is at the heart of the institutional structure of water management in England and Wales.

RQOs apply to stretches of river on which consent conditions should be arranged and reviewed so that water of a certain quality is available. The introduction of an overall target means that consent conditions could be made more stringent so that the river may be used as a source of water supply or as a medium of transfer; conditions could be relaxed so as to make optimum use of natural regenerative powers whilst maintaining a high level of quality; or consent conditions may be relaxed so that the need for public expenditure on STWs and private capital investment, perhaps from a decreasingly competitive industry, is reduced.

Parker and Penning-Rowsell[40] report that it was fear of the latter that led the National Anglers Council to oppose the introduction of the concept of RQOs in 1978. They comment:

There is no doubt that this policy follows the appreciation of the impossibility of all Regional Water Authority sewage treatment plants meeting their own consent conditions.... The review was undertaken out of fear of prosecution of (Regional) Water Authorities by members of the public for not meeting their own consent conditions. Furthermore, the National Water Council indicated that the review implies that Water Authorities would not be expected to prosecute industrial discharges if occasional samples exceed the consent of conditions provided they are not outside the range of variation to be expected from well-run treatment plant. Water Authorities are expected to adopt an 'even handed' aproach as between their own and industry's discharges and would not expect private prosecutions in these cases. In essence this means that a little illegality will be tolerated and this fundamental change in policy prior to which discharges above consent conditions were illegal although prosecutions could be waived, will have to be tested in the courts.

.4.5 Water Pollution Control in the United States

Overall water quality objectives in the UK are a relatively recent development. More comprehensive are the objectives of the 1972 Water Pollution Control Amendments Act in the United States.

This Act set the objective of achieving clean water everywhere, able to support fish, wildlife and recreation. Prior to this Act, State pollution control authorities had been permitted to determine standards of water quality on a case-by-case basis depending on the projected use of the water under discussion. In effect this generally meant that the worst water was not improved since no higher use than a waste sump was envisaged.[41] The result of three years hard work in Congress, the Act represents a concerted attack on industrial and municipal polluters. Clean water was originally to be achieved by 1985 through establishing effluent standards for all major categories of discharges; permits would specify for each source a maximum level of discharge.

The overall guidelines were to be issued by the Environmental Protection Agency (EPA) for major classes of industry to publicly owned sewage treatment plants, so that by 1977 all STWs would have at least secondary treatment (biological treatment rather than simple sedimentation) and by 1983 the best practical form of waste treatment (including 'tertiary' processes of treatment to deal with non-organic elements). Industries were to install the best technology currently available for 1977, and by 1983 have the best technology economically feasible. Perhaps it was inevitable that there would be postponements. The 1977 Clean Water Act replaced the requirement for the 'best available technology' with 'the best conventional technology', a clause intended to be more stringent than 'best practical technology' but less stringent than 'best available technology'. The best practical technology was not required until 1984. New standards for toxic pollutants were delayed until 1987.[42]

The 1972 Act also said that all states had to develop a comprehensive and continuing process of water-quality management. It established several new levels of planning: the basin, the area-wide plan, and the facility plan. The basin plan would establish priorities for improvement and act as a basis for the issue of permits. For urban and industrial areas an area-wide plan would identify the new treatment plants required and establish patterns of operation and management. The facility plan would specify the details.

A special feature of the US 1972 Act is the emphasis on requirements for participatory democracy, in marked contrast to the UK. Section 107(e) requires provision for public participation in the development, revision and enforcement of any regulation, standard, effluent limitation, plan or programme established by the administrator of the EPA or state authority. This has led to a large number of information and publicity campaigns, seminars, workshops and public hearings on water pollution control matters.[43] Progress in implementing the dramatic intent of the Act has been delayed through court actions by major industrial interest groups challenging the fine details of EPA's atempts to discharge its duties. The exact definition of 'best practicable control technology' for 1977 and 'best available technology economically available' have proved particularly contentious. The American Petroleum Institute, the American Meat Institute, the American Iron and Steel Institute, the American Paper Institute and the Tanner's Council of America have all brought actions.[44]

But the further deterioration of surface waters seems to have been arrested and there are numerous examples of the successful rehabilitation of major problem rivers, such as the Savannah, the Hudson, the Detroit and the Connecticut. It is true, however, that cities have been slow to provide secondary treatment at municipal plants. As with the control of air pollution, the Reagan administration has cut budgets and staffing of control agencies to the point where actual decline in water quality may recur. The programme to set toxic effluent limits on industrial discharges appears to have been particularly badly affected.[45]

14.4.6 The French System of Water Pollution Control

A disappointing rate of progress is also reported for the system of effluent charges introduced in France in 1964.[46] A system of permits for water extraction and effluent discharge in France had operated since 1917, but in 1964 new autonomous river basin agencies (Agencies Financières de Bassin) were established to develop water plans and implement a system of charges for both abstraction and discharge. The effluent charges are calculated for industry by a formula relating charge to polluting load and for municipalities on the basis of a standard pollution equivalent per inhabitant. The total charge for a community is paid by the local water supply undertaking who then pass this on to individual households according to the quantity of fresh water consumed. The charges provide the finance for grants to improve treatment plants. Discounts are offered to industrial sources of pollution in recognition of approved pretreatment practices. Although in recent years the charges have steadily increased there seems to have been no corresponding increase in incentive to make further improvements to water quality. Since 1972 more and more emphasis has accordingly been put on voluntary agreements with industries of a particularly polluting nature on the regulatory pattern of the US 1972 Act.

Agreements (*contrats de branche*) have been concluded between the French Government and the pulp and paper industry (estimated to account for 20% of the industrial polluting load), the sugarbeet processes (16%), distillers (15%) and yeast manufacturers. Others have been concluded with specific companies or all the companies discharging into a particular river. For example, the agreement with the paper industry requires a sequence of effluent control measures beginning with the reduction of suspended matter. Between 1972 and 1979 over $75 million was to be invested by the industry in improving the quality of its wastes although 40% of this sum would be covered by grant-aid of one sort or another. In this way a quicker rate of improvement in the state of the country's rivers is envisaged.

Overall then, it seems that standard regulations for major sources of pollution, industrial or municipal, appear to be the most favoured water pollution control policy within the context of river-basin authorities. But the scale of investment required in universally establishing such regulated standards of treatment, sector by sector, appears inevitably to be a major constraint on the rate of improvement.

14.5 Conclusion

Overall, four themes have emerged in this review of water-management issues, institutional structures and policies. First and foremost, the importance of an appropriate institutional structure for the adequate planning and management of resources that have multiple uses has been continuously recognized in the thinking of water experts the world over. Secondly, water is a 'commons' (as discussed in Chapter 8), so that political impositions have had to be made that may threaten the financial viability of industry.' Policies have had to accommodate the vociferous objection of vested interests. Thirdly, a new interest by the public following a general increase in environmental awareness, now conditions the planning of water resources and encourages the adoption of measures of pollution control and more sophisticated appraisal of alternative plans. Finally, a general trend of increasing sophistication, moving from 'technical fixes' through 'administrative fixes' to 'behavioural fixes' has forced a change in attitudes to water, so that it is no longer regarded as a free good; planning replaces *laissez-faire*.

Summary of Part Two

Although resource management draws together the skills and knowledge of many disciplines, it is primarily a *political* activity. The role of political culture has permeated our discussion of problem identification, techniques employed in project appraisal and policy review and the attitudes and perceptions of 'actors' involved in the decision-making process. The rise of the environmental movement in the 1960s and the questioning of 'technical fix' solutions to resource-management problems has led to institutional responses to meet public concern. New government departments and agencies, using new appraisal techniques, have produced a more open, accountable system of resource evaluation with a greater degree of public participation than hitherto.

The extent of 'open' government and agency accountability relates to political cultures. The US is an example of the pluralistic model in which a liberal Freedom of Information Act, participatory decision making and political sensitivity regarding resource management issues has resulted in the most open system of policy review and project appraisal in the world. Other Western democracies, such as the UK, have a more élitist political culture, often lack a Freedom of Information Act and have a more closed decision-making system which is prone to secrecy and confidentiality. Participation is mainly by consultation; public comment is allowed only at a late stage in the evaluation process.

Many of the case studies in the preceding chapters drew upon examples from the UK and USA to highlight differences in approach to the solution of resource-management problems. The fairness of institutional procedures was questioned because of the 'routinization' of issues through the adoption of 'technical' or 'administrative fix' solutions. Indeed, the technical complexity of issues, for example in the field of energy management, has enhanced the role of 'experts' who are used to legitimize particular courses of action.

Although faults and flaws in institutional structures are found in all Western democracies, attempts have been made there to rationalize decisions so as to be broadly acceptable to all interest groups involved in policy formulation. This is far from being the case in the totalitarian régimes of the Eastern bloc and much of the Third World where there is little political accountability for resource management decisions, minimum interest-group activity or public participation and limited mechanisms for policy or project review.

Unlike the communist régimes of the Soviet Union and its satellites, most of the Third World nations have poorly developed or inadequate institutional structures to tackle their acute resource management problems. The tragedy of the 'freedom of the commons' is still evident throughout these lands. Whereas in the West, problems of overgrazing, deforestation, water pollution and soil depletion were deemed to warrant policy action through the establishment of regulations and the creation of agencies to enforce them, this level of institutionalization is absent from the less politically mature countries of the 'South'.

Indeed, in the case of some state agencies, corruption and bureaucratic mismanagement only aggravate the situation.

The United Nations, through a multitude of agencies, has sought to improve the institutional environment in these countries to foster better resource management practices. The UN, however, can act only as a catalyst. The political will must exist if well-intentioned UN initiatives are to be realized. Unfortunately, it is invariably lacking because of the unacceptable political ramifications of such measures.

Resource management is about power and politics, the rich and the poor, winners and losers. Policy is shaped according to the degree of power that vested interests can exert upon the decision-making process. In terms of international resource management, the 'Northern' nations have regained the power which they almost lost in the mid-1970s. The hopes of UNCTAD and UNCLOS for a better deal for the 'South' have evaporated. The Lomé Agreements, once heralded as a model for 'North–South' relations, are now in jeopardy. Lomé III may not be renegotiated. Although the 'South' has much of the world's oil and non-fuel mineral wealth it is still dependent upon the 'North' for financial, technical and marketing expertise. Consequently, at a national level, resource management throughout the 'South' remains linked to 'Northern' interdependence often at the expense of policies that would improve the livelihood of the majority of the population.

In the richer Western democracies, the election of conservative governments, such as those in the US and UK, with *laissez faire*, anti-regulatory, pro-development philosophies has had implications for resource management. Policy review and project appraisal procedures are being streamlined; regulations are being re-assessed and enforcement agencies are being subjected to expenditure cuts or 'politicking' to guide policy through. Conservation is under attack. Environmentalism is running out of momentum. Nevertheless, certain issues – the opening up of wilderness for development and nuclear power plant safety to name but two – remain high on the political agenda and will continue to warrant institutional accountability.

Notes

Notes to Chapter 1

1. For an elaboration of the view that resource-related international conflicts will be an increasingly important feature of international relations, see: D. Pirages, *The New Context for International Relations: Ecopolitics*, Duxbury Press, North Scituati, Massachusetts, 1978.
2. The Brandt Commission (Independent Commission on International Development), *North–South: A Programme for Survival*, Pan Books, London, 1980; The Brandt Commission, *Common Crisis: North–South – Co-operation for World Recovery*, Pan Books, London, 1983; M. Redclift, *Development and the Environmental Crisis: Red or Green Alternatives?*, Methuen, London, 1984.
3. The Brandt Commission, 1980, ibid, p. 32.
4. Secretariat for Future Studies (Stockholm, Sweden), *Resources, Society and the Future*, (translated by R. G. Tanner), Pergamon Press, Oxford, 1980, Chapter 2, Resources and Raw Materials Defined, pp. 11–38.
5. L. D. Stamp, *Our Developing World*, Faber, London, 1960, pp. 38–39.
6. E. W. Zimmerman, *World Resources and Industries*, Harper & Brothers, New York, 1933 (Revised 1951).
7. See for example: R. Weston, *Strategic Materials: A World Survey*, Croom Helm, Beckenham, Kent, 1984.
8. *The Global 2000 Report to the President*, Penguin Books, London, 1982, p. 217.
9. Quoted in C. Jenkins and B. Sherman, *The Leisure Shock*, Eyre Methuen, London, 1981, p. 10.
10. 'Yellowhammer in poster venture for Greenpeace', *Campaign*, 10 August 1984, p. 4.
11. W. Firey, *Man, Mind and Land*, Free Press, Glencoe, Illinois, 1960.
12. This often has heavy leanings towards Marxism; see for example: A. Gorz, *Ecology as Politics*, South End Press, Boston, 1980.
13. P. Lowe and J. Goyder, *Environmental Groups and Politics*, Allen & Unwin, London, 1983.
14. I. G. Simmons, *The Ecology of Natural Resources*, Edward Arnold, London, 1974.
15. D. H. Meadows, D. L. Meadows, J. Randers and W. W. Behrens, *The Limits to Growth*, Pan Books, London, 1974.
16. M. Mesarovic and M. Pestel, *Mankind at the Turning Point*, Dutton & Co, New York, 1974. H. E. Daley (ed.), *Toward a Steady State Economy*, Freeman & Co., San Francisco, 1973.
17. J. L. Simon, *The Ultimate Resource*, Martin Robertson, Oxford, 1981.
18. A. Madsen, *Private Power: Multinational Corporations and their Role in the Survival of our Planet*, Abacus, London, 1980.
19. For a traditional, perhaps even old-fashioned view of matters in the debate see: H. Robinson, *Population and Resources*, Macmillan, London, 1981.

Notes to Chapter 2

1. J. Passmore, *Man's Responsibility for Nature*, (2nd edn.), Duckworth, London, 1980.
2. T. R. Malthus, A Summary View of the Principle of Population, *in* G. J. Demko,

H. M. Rose and G. A. Schnell, *Population Geography: A Reader*, McGraw-Hill, New York, 1970, pp. 44–70.

3. R. Mitchison, *British Population Change since 1860*, Macmillan, London, 1977.

4. E. Pohlman, (ed.), *Population: A Clash of Prophets*, Mentor, New American Library, New York, 1973, Part 1, The Population Crisis 1930s Style, pp. 1–12.

5. S. J. Holmes, Will Birth Control Lead to Extinction?, *Scientific Monthly*, 34, 1932, pp. 247–251; quotation from Pohlman, ibid, p. 4.

6. J. J. Spengler, The Birth-Rate – Potential Dynamite, *Scribners Magazine*, 92, 1932, pp. 6–12, quotation from Pohlman, ibid, p. 5.

7. M. Chubb and H. R. Chubb, *One Third of our Time?: An introduction to recreation behaviour and resources*, John Wiley, New York, 1981, Part 1, The History and Importance of Recreation, Chapter 2, Historical Perspective, pp. 14–45.

8. H. R. Jones, *Population Geography*, Harper & Row, London, 1981; P. G. Marden, D. G. Hodgson and T. L. McCoy, *Population in the Global Arena*, Holt, Rinehart and Winston, New York, 1982; and R. Woods, *Population Analysis in Geography*, Longman, London, 1979.

9. Jones, ibid, pp. 88–158.

10. For a review of fertility statistics see Woods, op. cit., pp. 96–129.

11. G. J. Stolnitz, *The Demographic Transition*, in Demko, Rose & Schnell, ibid, pp. 71–78.

12. Jones, op cit, pp. 88–89.

13. Mitchison, op cit, pp. 27–28.

14. R. Andorka, *Determinants of Fertility in Advanced Societies*, Methuen, London, 1978.

15. Woods, op cit, pp. 37–61.

16. Jones, op cit, pp. 29–39.

17. T. McKeown, *The Modern Rise of Population*, Edward Arnold, London, 1976.

18. McKeown, ibid, p. 162.

19. J. A. Loraine, *Global Signposts to the 21st Century*, Peter Owen, London, 1979, Chapter 9, Population Still Dominant, pp. 152–174.

20. Ibid, p. 169.

21. Jones, op cit, p. 160.

22. D. H. Meadows, D. L. Meadows, J. Randers and W. W. Behrens, *The Limits to Growth*, Pan Books, London, 1974, p. 30.

23. R. Carson, *Silent Spring*, Penguin Books, London, 1965.

24. F. Graham, *Disaster by Default: Politics and Water Pollution*, Evans & Co., New York, 1966.

25. R. Rienow and L. T. Rienow, *Moment in the Sun: A Report on the Deteriorating Quality of the American Environment*, Ballantine, New York, 1967.

26. Ibid, p. 14.

27. Ibid, p. 285.

28. P. Ehrlich, A. Ehrlich and J. P. Holdren, *Human Ecology: Problems and Solutions*, Freeman, San Francisco, 1973; P. Ehrlich, *The Population Bomb*, Pan Books, London, 1971.

29. For a hindsight review of the Club of Rome see: A. Peccei, *One Hundred Pages for the Future: Reflections of the President of the Club of Rome*, Pergamon Books, London, 1982.

30. Meadows *et al*, op cit.

31. E. F. Schumacher, *Small is Beautiful*, Blond & Briggs, London, 1973.

32. E. Goldsmith *et al*, *Blueprint for Survival*, Houghton Miffin, Boston, 1972.

33. For a thoughtful review of the literature in this vein see: T. O'Riordan, *Environmentalism*, Pion, London, 1976; For a good summary of the whole debate see: S. Cole, The Global Futures Debate, 1965–1976, in C. Freeman and M. Jahoda, (eds.) *World Futures: The Great Debate*, Martin Robertson, London, 1978, pp. 9–50.

34. W. Leontief, *et al*, *The Future of the World Economy*, Preliminary Report, New York, United Nations, 1976.
35. Leontief, ibid, p. 48.
36. R. Heilbroner, The Human Prospect, *New York Review of Books*, January 1974, p. 23.
37. Ibid, p. 32.
38. M. W. Holdgate, M. Kassas and G. F. White, *The World Environment 1972–1982: A Report by the United Nations Environment Programme*, Tycooly International, Dublin, 1982.
39. R. Clarke and L. Timberlake, *Stockholm Plus Ten*, Earthscan, London, 1982.
40. The Cabinet Office, *Future World Trends: A Discussion Paper on World Trends in Population, Resources, Pollution, etc., and their Implications*, HMSO, London, 1976.
41. The *Global 2000 Report*, Penguin Books, London, 1981.
42. Ibid, p. 4.
43. H. D. S. Cole *et al*, *Thinking about the Future: a Critique of the Limits to Growth*, Chatto & Windus for Sussex University Press, London, 1973.
44. C. Freeman and M. Jahoda (eds.), op cit.
45. Ibid, p. 384.
46. Ibid, p. 386.
47. H. Kahn, *The Next 2000 Years*, Associated Business Programmes, London, 1977.
48. Ibid, (Abacus Books Edition, London, 1978) p. 164.
49. Ibid, p. 173.
50. J. L. Simon, *The Ultimate Resource*, Martin Robertson, Oxford, 1981, p. 285.
51. Ibid, p. 345.
52. K. L. Michaelson (ed.), *And the Poor get Children: Radical Perspectives on Population Dynamics*, Monthly Review Press, New York, 1981, p. 13.
53. H. L. Parsons, *Marx and Engels on Ecology*, Greenwood Press, Westport, Conn., 1977, pp. 26–35.
54. F. Sandbach, *Environment, Ideology and Policy*, Basil Blackwell, Oxford, 1980, Chapter 7, Technology and Environment under Socialism: the Case of China, pp. 183–199.
55. Michaelson, op cit, pp. 20–21.
56. Ibid, p. 21.
57. M. Mesarovic and M. Pestel, *Mankind at the Turning Point*, Dutton & Co., New York, 1974.
58. Ibid, p. ix.
59. T. Tinbergen, *RIO: Reshaping the International Order*, Dutton & Co., New York, 1976.
60. Ibid, (Signet New American Library Edition) pp. 180–181.
61. The Brandt Commission, *North–South: A Programme for Survival*, Pan Books, London, 1980.
62. M. Thatcher, in Friedrich Eber Foundation, *Towards One World: International Responses to the Brandt Report*, Temple Smith, London, 1981, pp. 104–110; quotation, p. 109.
63. Ibid, p. 105.
64. A. L. Mabogunje, The Dynamics of Centre-Periphery Relations: the need for a new geography of resource development, *Transactions of the Institute of British Geographers*, 1980, pp. 277–296; quotation, p. 281.
65. Ibid, p. 288.
66. The Brandt Commission, *Common Crisis. North–South: Co-operation for World Recovery*, Pan Books, 1983.
67. Ibid, p. 13.

Notes to Chapter 3

1. I. G. Simmons, *The Ecology of Natural Resources*, 2nd edn., Edward Arnold, London, 1981, p. 6.
2. Ibid, p. 238.
3. 1980 and 1981 figures will probably show a reversal of this trend due to the impact of policy measures and the continuation of the economic recession.
4. Shell Briefing Service, Energy in the Developing Countries, *SBS* January 1980.
5. United Nations *1979 Yearbook of World Energy Statistics*, UN 1981, Table 6, pp. 72–135 for a country by country comparison of per capita consumption.
6. Shell Briefing Service, Coal: energy for the future, *SBS*, May 1980, pp. 2–3; and Natural Gas, *SBS* No. 4, 1983, p. 3.
7. Ibid.
8. Ibid.
9. Ibid, p. 6.
10. J. Fernie, *A Geography of Energy in the United Kingdom*, Longman, London, 1980, pp. 51–52.
11. For excellent histories of oil industry developments, see: A. Sampson, *The Seven Sisters: the Great Oil Companies and the World They Shaped*, Hodder & Stoughton, 1980, 3rd ed.; T. Blair, *The Control of Oil*, Vintage Books, 1978; and S. M. Eraket, *OPEC and the Arab Israeli Conflict*, Unpublished PhD thesis, University of Bradford, 1984.
12. P. R. Odell in Chapter 2 of M. Saeter and I. Smart; *The Political Implications of North Sea Oil and Gas*, IPC Science and Technology Press, 1975.
13. Shell Briefing Service, The changing world of oil supply, *SBS*, p. 1, June 1980.
14. Ibid, p. 2.
15. Ibid.
16. The Japanese started this trend of direct-sales when they originally negotiated with the Iranian Government on the resumption of Iranian exports in March 1979.
17. T. J. Wilbanks, 'When will the next energy crisis occur?', conference paper presented at Association of American Geographers meeting, Washington DC, April 1984.
18. J. Fernie, op cit, p. 14.
19. Shell Briefing Service, Coal: energy for the future, *SBS*, May 1980.
20. Much of the future investment for coal expansion is being made by oil companies which see the US and Australia as politically 'safer' areas for investment than the more politically sensitive 'South'.
21. Carroll Wilson, *Coal – Bridge to the Future*, vol. 1 of the World Coal Study, MIT, 1980.
22. J. Winward, Not for burning, *Town and Country Planning*, July/August 1981, Vol. 50, p. 200.
23. President's Commission for a National Agenda for the Eighties, *Energy Natural Resources and the Environment in the Eighties*, US Government, Washington, 1980, p. 16.
24. D. J. Spooner, The geography of coal's second coming, *Geography*, January 1981, p. 39.
25. In the US new rail stock and maintenance programmes have enabled the railroad system to achieve new records in coal transportation, e.g. 12·5m tons were carried in the week ending 29 August 1981. Association of American Railroads, *Rail News*, 11 September 1981.
26. Mining International Services, *Keystone Coal Industry Manual*, McGraw-Hill, New York, 1979.
27. These include additional capacity from existing mines and planned new collieries.
28. One of the boom towns in the Powder River Basin of Wyoming.
29. House of Lords Select Committee on the European Communities, *European Community Coal Policy*, HMSO, 1983, p. xvii.

30. The higher figure would be equivalent to 13 m.b.d. of oil, around half OPEC exporting levels.
31. A. Granville and A. J. Venter, South Africa's coal industry expands, *World Coal*, 4 November 1978, pp. 52–53.
32. The Power Plant and Industrial Fuel Use Act 1978 required large users to shift from oil and gas to coal and other fuels.
33. C. Cunningham, A world full of coal, *New Scientist*. 7 May 1981.
34. For a detailed explanation of nuclear fission see W. Patterson, *Nuclear Power*, Pelican, 1976, pp. 75–77.
35. P. Beckmann, (L. G. Brookes reviews), The health hazards of not going nuclear, *Atom*, 244, February 1978, p. 20.
36. In 1977, three quarters of France's energy needs was met by oil with 71% of this oil coming from Middle Eastern States. See: *Town and Country Planning*, May 1979, vol. 48, p. 63.
37. Under President Carter, reprocessing was banned in the US. Hence, users of US enriched fuel required American authorization to reprocess this fuel.
38. In 1980, 12 'Southern' nations had commercial nuclear power plants in operation, on order or with a 'letter of intent' to build. They were Taiwan, India, S. Korea, Argentina, Brazil, Pakistan, Iraq, Mexico, Philippines, Peru, Chile and Uruguay. Egypt, Turkey and Libya are also planning nuclear energy programmes. See Jane House, 'The Third World goes nuclear', *South*, December 1980.
39. G. Hancock in The hatching of the nuclear bird, *New Internationalist*, 61, March 1978, claims that reactor sales were offered with lucrative credit arrangements. He also points out that no country should attempt to install a power plant that would represent more than 15% of its electricity and capacity. Hence only countries with 4,000 Mw capacity already installed should consider buying a 600 Mw reactor.
40. OECD Nuclear Energy Agency and International Atomic Energy Agency, *Uranium resources, production and demand*, OECD, 1979.
41. Department of Energy, Tidal power barrages in the Severn Estuary, recent evidence on their feasibility, *Energy Paper No. 23*, HMSO, 1977, p. 1.
42. In the US, the Energy Research and Development Administration (ERDA) has experimented with sodium sulphate (Glauber's salts) and sodium phosphate dodecahydrate in experimental solar houses.
43. See M. J. Pasqualetti, Geothermal energy and the environment: the global experience *Energy*, vol. 5, No. 2, 1980, for a more detailed account of geothermal power plants and their environmental impacts in specific countries.
44. See J. A. Johnson, Tidal Power: past, present and future, conference paper at AAG meeting, Washington DC, April 1984.
45. Severn Barrage Committee, *Tidal Power from the Severn Estuary*, vol. 1, HMSO, London, 1981, and G. Winter, 'Tidal power from the Bay of Fundy', *Geographical Magazine*, February 1979, p. 331.
46. In many cases in multiple-use schemes incorporating water supply regulation and recreational facilities.
47. *Popular Mechanics*, May 1978, p. 118.
48. US Department of Energy, *Solar Energy*, US DOE, 1979; and Shell Briefing Service, Solar Energy, *SBS*, December 1978.
49. It is estimated that world annual biomass production is more than ten times the world's consumption of energy. Shell Briefing Service, 'Energy from Biomass', *SBS*, February 1980.
50. Ibid. If the world's entire crop of maize, sugar cane, cassava and sweet sorghum were used for ethanol production this would meet only 6–7% of the world's oil demand.
51. Shell Briefing Service, January 1980, op cit.
52. See Fernie, op cit, p. 112. Countries in low latitudes would not require additional heat supplies to maintain the temperature of the digester for decomposition to take

place. Also, the move from mixed to specialist farming in many 'Northern' countries has prejudiced the development of biogas plants on farms. However, plants using sewerage offer potential for the future. The water hyacinth - one of the fastest growing aquatic plants - has unique attributes. The plant thrives in polluted water and can be used to purify water systems in addition to producing biogas.

53. Shell Briefing Service, January 1980, op cit.
54. See J. Fernie's review of W. Kovarik, Fuel alcohol: energy in a hungry world, in *Geography* vol. 68, Part 1, 1983.
55. *The Phoenix Gazette*, 16 October 1981.
56. Shell Briefing Service. February 1980, op cit.
57. For a detailed discussion on alcohol production from biomass in developing countries see H. S. Kohli, Renewable Energy: alcohol from biomass, *Finance and Development*, December 1980.
58. The US Programme has been criticized because of the adverse effects on food prices and Balance of Payments losses through diminished food exports, see: F. H. Sanderson, 'Benefits and costs of the US gasohol programme' *Resources*, No. 67, July 1981, Resources for the Future.
59. D. J. Harris and B. C. L. Davies, European Energy policy and planning: the role of the institutions, *National Westminster Quarterly Bank Review*, November 1980.
60. R. Goodman, Managing the demand for energy in the developing world, *Finance and Development*, December 1980.
61. L. Turner, Oil prices: the real impact on the Third World, *South*, October 1980.
62. Ibid.
63. Ibid.
64. R. Goodman op cit. It was hoped that a new energy affiliate of the World Bank would be created to permit a larger programme to be mounted but the US Administration opposed such a scheme.
65. The World Bank did not finance oil and gas projects until 1977 on the grounds that it would interfere with the operation of the oil majors.
66. In late 1981 the Strategic Petroleum Reserve contained sufficient oil to replace 40% of all US imports for 118 days.
67. 'Nuclear free zones' for both civilian and military nuclear facilities are being designated by many local governments throughout the world.
68. Planning World, *Town and Country Planning*, June 1980, p. 199.
69. See OECD, *World Energy Outlook*, OECD, 1977; Central Intelligence Agency, *International Energy Situation*, CIA, 1977; and the Workshop on Alternative Energy Strategies, *Energy Global Prospects 1985-2000*, McGraw-Hill, 1977.
70. P. R. Odell and K. E. Rosing, *The Future of Oil*, Kogan Page, 1980.
71. Lester R. Brown, No Fuelling: nuclear power is losing out to Firewood, *Arizona Republic*, 3 January 1982.

Notes to Chapter 4

1. C. Fortin, UNCTAD VI: prospects and approaches for Third World community producers, *Ceres*, November/December 1982, p. 20.
2. See: P. Rogers, World Debts, *The Guardian*, 30 December 1982. Brazil ($89bn), Mexico ($85bn), Argentine ($38bn) and Poland ($25·5bn) are the four largest debtors.
3. J. R. Blunden, *The Mineral Resources of Britain; a Study in Exploration and Planning*, Hutchinson, 1975.
4. The Materials Forum, *Strategic Minerals and the United Kingdom*, The Institution of Mechanical Engineers, 1981; H. G. Roepke, Changing sources of strategic minerals for the United States, *AAG Conference Paper*, San Antonio, 1982;

Carol Polsgrove, Strategic minerals, *Sierra*, July/August, 1982; R. Weston, *Strategic Materials: a World Survey*, Croom Helm, 1983.
5. N. Girvan, *Corporate Imperialism: Conflict and Expropriation*, Monthly Review Press, 1976.
6. The accuracy of consumption statistics is questioned by D. Humphreys in Measurement of mineral consumption, *Natural Resources Forum* 6, 1982, pp. 239–246, because of the problems of double counting between stages of production, namely mining, refining and manufacturing. He recommends the first processing stage as the appropriate cut off point to measure consumption in the unmanufactured stage. In a discussion on consumption production levels it is imperative that no confusion arises out of these different stages in the production chain.
7. R. Bosson and B. Varon, *The Mining Industry and the Developing Countries*, Oxford University Press, 1977, pp. 77–78, R. F. Mikesell, *New Patterns of World Mineral Development*, British–Northern American Committee, 1979, pp. 7–8, and L. Fischman, *World Mineral Trends and Supply Problems*, Resources for the Future, 1980, Chapter 1, pp. 23–133.
8. M. Tanzer, *The Race for Resources*, Heinemann, 1980, pp. 17, 18.
9. Ibid, p. 25.
10. She produced 50% of the world's lead from 1700–1850, 45% of the world's copper from 1820–1840 and 50% of iron ore production in 1890. See R. Bosson and B. Varon, op cit, p. 79.
11. Ibid, p. 85 and R. F. Mikesell, *New Patterns of World Mineral Development*, British–North American Committee, 1979, p. 85.
12. Mineral ores have high entropy in that even commercial deposits generally contain less than 1% pure mineral. Indeed, several 'bonanza' discoveries have yielded several minerals, for example, the South African gold and uranium mines. Present patterns of mineral development are therefore a function of past exploration activity and current political and technological conditions. It is outside the scope of this book to discuss the geophysical formation of ore minerals and their classification into primary, secondary and oxidized deposits. For a discussion on copper deposits see Kirk-Othmer, *Encyclopedia of Chemical Technology*, vol. 6, 3rd Edn., 1979, Wiley, pp. 819–827.
13. The Materials Forum, op cit, 1981.
14. J. M. Blaut, Geographical models of imperialism, *Antipode*, vol. 2, 1970, pp. 65–85.
15. R. I. Moore (ed.), *The Hamlyn Historical Atlas*, Book Club Associates, 1981, p. 77.
16. See: A. Mabogunje, *The Development Process: a Spatial Perspective*, Hutchinson, 1980, p. 82.
17. *South*, April 1981, p. 67.
18. R. J. Barnet, *The Lean Years: Politics in the Age of Scarcity*, Sphere Books, 1981, Chapter 6.
19. This includes 13 million tonnes or 14% for China. See: A. Kilgore, Record wheat crops will bypass the South, *South*, April 1981, pp. 63–66.
20. *South*, December 1981.
21. C. Raghavan, North's obstinate opposition blights jute negotiations, *South*, March 1981, p. 64.
22. S. A. Laukenlekas, Coffee producers lose more ground, *South*, March 1981, p. 72.
23. A. Manck, Tea disagreement, *South*, June 1981, p. 85.
24. C. Raghavan, North–South clash over cotton, *South*, July 1981, p. 80, 81.
25. Of the 84 million tonnes produced in 1981, 33 million was beet sugar, *South*, January 1982, p. 109.
26. Jane Robins and Oscar Rodriguez, Cashing in on the sugar boom, *South*, January 1981, p. 65.
27. A. Morris, Grim choice for sugar exporters, *The Guardian*, 29 September 1982.

28. The coefficient of variation is the ratio of the standard deviation of a series to its average, see D. L. McNicol, *Commodity Agreements and Price Stabilisation: A Policy Analysis*, Lexington Books, 1978, pp. 16–19.
29. L. Fischman, op cit, p. 25.
30. See D. Mezger, *Copper in the World Economy*, Heinemann, 1980, pp. 113–114. She argues that the multinationals gain from these wild fluctuations in prices at the expense of the others in the oligopoly because they can build up reserves when prices are low. The poorer countries rarely stockpile because of balance of payments difficulties and the smaller independents do not have the same diversification of supply in periods of low prices.
31. Independent Commission on International Development Issues (Brandt Report) *North–South: A Programme for Survival*, 1980, Pan, p. 144.
32. Ibid.
33. Bosson and Varon, op cit, p. 87.
34. M. Tanzer, op cit, p. 48.
35. It must be remembered that both Canada and Australia have become more nationalistic in attitude toward foreign investment in their countries in the 1970s and 1980s.
36. Both surveys quoted in R. F. Mikesell, op cit, p. 25.
37. C. Fortin, 1982, op cit, p. 21. For more detail on tariff structures see; *South*, May 1982, p. 9.
38. Council on Environmental Quality, *The Global 2000 Report to the President*, Penguin, 1982, p. 222.
39. Fidel Castro's speech to the non-aligned summit in 1983, quoted in *The Guardian*, 25 March 1983.
40. This list (Table 4.7) is not comprehensive. It can be argued that other producer groups have cooperated in order to achieve an improved bargaining position with transnationals/industrial nations. For example, in the earlier discussion of ICAs, Latin American coffee producers formed Pancafé a company which operated a buffer stock system. The company was dissolved on the negotiation of the International Coffee Agreement of 1980.
41. *South*, October 1981, and Z. Mikdashi, *The International Politics of Natural Resources*, Cornell University Press, 1976, pp. 114–117. See Tanzer or Girvan for further details of these nationalizations and the political response of the US Government.
42. The US Overseas Private Investment Insurance Corporation (OPIC) insures (for around 1% of the investment) against expropriation, wars, revolutions and impaired profitability due to contract or tax changes instigated by the host governments.
43. P. Croix, The other stocks, *South*, October 1980, pp. 66–67 and J. Friedland, Struggling producers lay siege to Washington's hoard, *South*, May 1983, pp. 72–73.
44. Friedland, Ibid.
45. Quoted in H. H. Landsberg, 'What next for US minerals policy', *Resources*, no. 71, October 1982.
46. US Bureau of Mines, 1976, World Bank Study, quoted in R. F. Mikesell, op cit, and W. Malenbaum, *World Demand for Raw Materials in 1985 and 2000*, McGraw-Hill, 1978. Two major reasons for the lower growth assumptions are the forecasts of reduced GDP growth rates in developed countries and the intensity of use (IOU) factor. Malenbaum argues that IOU of minerals begin to decline as economies pass through the post-industrial stage and demand 'lighter' goods.
47. R. F. Mikesell, op cit, p. 8.
48. H. Thomas, After all the energy problems – now minerals, *The Guardian*, 5 March 1980.
49. Council on Environmental Quality, op cit, p. 382.

Notes to Chapter 5

1. J. R. Tarrant, *Food Policies*, John Wiley & Sons, New York, 1980, pp. 182–192.
2. R. S. Love, Stability and growth in the world oilseed market, *Food Policy*, vol. 4, 1979, p. 35.
3. J. W. McAnuff, Towards a strategy for fish farming in the UK, *Food Policy*, vol. 4, 1979, p. 179.
4. Ibid, p. 184.
5. *Ceres*, June 1981, p. 22.
6. T. T. Poleman, World Food: Myth and Reality, p. 385 *in* R. Sinha (ed.), *The World Food Problem: Consensus and Conflict*, Pergamon Press, Oxford, 1978, pp. 383–394.
7. FAO (Food and Agricultural Organization of the United Nations), *The State of Food and Agriculture 1981*, Rome, 1982, p. 53.
8. Ibid, p. 54.
9. *Ceres*, March 1980, p. 5.
10. Poleman, 1978, op cit, p. 386.
11. FAO, op cit, p. 56.
12. FAO, ibid, p. 57.
13. D. Byerlee and E. Hesse de Polanco, Wheat in the world food economy: Increasing role in developing countries, *Food Policy*, Vol. 8, 1983, p. 71.
14. K. Abercombe, Intensive livestock feeding, *Ceres*, Jan–Feb 1982, p. 82.
15. E. Eckholm, *Losing Ground: Environmental Stress and World Food Prospects*, Pergamon Press, Oxford, 1976.
16. M. W. Holdgate, M. Kassas and G. F. White (eds.), *The World Environment 1972–1982, A Report by the United Nations Environment Programme*, Tycooly International, Dublin, 1982, p. 291.
17. G. M. Higgins, A. H. Kassam, L. Naiken and M. M. Shah, Africa's agricultural potential, *Ceres*, Sept-Oct, 1981, p. 19.
18. FAO, *Production Year Book 1975*, Rome, 1976.
19. D. Norse, Natural Resources, Development Strategies and the World Food Problems, *in* M. R. and A. K. Biswas (eds.), *Food, Climate and Man*, John Wiley & Son, New York, 1979, pp. 12–51, p. 18.
20. Ibid, p. 23.
21. Ibid, p. 30.
22. S. George, *How the Other Half Dies: The Real Reasons for World Hunger*, Penguin Books, 1976, p. 23.
23. J. G. Garcia, The Nature of Food Insecurity in Colombia, pp. 123–142 in A. Valdes, *Food Security for Developing Countries*, Westview Press, Colorado, 1981, p. 125.
24. Ibid, p. 133.
25. Ibid, p. 137.
26. E. P. Eckholm, *Down to Earth*, Pluto Press, 1982, pp. 23–24.
27. Ibid, pp. 26–28.
28. E. Saouma, A New Food Order for Africa, *Ceres*, Sept-Oct 1981, pp. 22.
29. Ibid, p. 24.
30. N. K. Nicholson and J. D. Esseks, The Politics of Food Scarcities in Developing Countries, pp. 103–143 *in* R. F. Hopkins and D. J. Puchula, (eds.), *The Global Political Economy of Food*, University of Wisconsin Press, 1978, p. 103.
31. Tarrant, op cit, pp. 48–50.
32. Ibid, pp. 87–93.
33. Ibid, pp. 95–107.
34. Ibid, p. 170.
35. A. Nove, Can Eastern Europe feed itself?, pp. 417–424 *in* R. Sinha (ed.), *The World Food Problem*, Pergamon Press, Oxford, 1978, pp. 47–48.
36. E. J. Clay, Food Aid and Food Policy in Bangladesh, *Food Policy*, May 1979, pp. 129–133.

37. Ibid, p. 130.
38. A. Sen, *Poverty and Famines: An Essay on Entitlement and Deprivation*, The Clarendon Press, Oxford 1981, pp. 141-145.
39. J. A. Gulland, Open Ocean Resources, pp. 347-377, *in* R. T. Lackay and L. A. Nielsen (eds.), *Fisheries Management*, Basil Blackwell, 1980.
40. M. M. Sibthorp (ed.), *The Noble Sea: Challenge and Opportunity*, Europe Publications, London, 1978, p. 14.
41. D. Cushing, *Fisheries Resources of the Sea and their Management*, Oxford University Press, 1975, p. 45.
42. J. L. McHugh, Coastal Fisheries, pp. 323-346 *in* R. T. Lackey, and L. A. Nielsen (eds.), *Fisheries Management*: Basil Blackwell, 1980, p. 342.
43. R. F. Hopkins, Food as a Global Issue *in* R. F. Hopkins, R. L. Paarlberg, M. B. Wallerstein, *Food in the Global Arena*, Holt, Rinehart and Winston, New York, 1982, pp. 21-23.
44. T. T. Poleman, A reappraisal of the extent of world hunger, *Food Policy*, November 1981, p. 243.
45. S. Ruttenburg, Climate, Food and Society, pp. 23-38, *in* L. E. Slater and S. K. Levin, 1981, p. 34.
46. Tarrant, op cit, p. 290.
47. Ibid, p. 282.
48. Ibid, p. 283.
49. Gulland, op cit, pp. 359-360.
50. A. Siamwalla and A. Valdes, Food insecurity in Developing Countries, *Food Policy*, November 1980, pp. 258-272.
51. A. Valdes and P. Konandreas, Assessing Food Insecurity based on National Aggregates in Developing Countries *in* A. Valdes, (ed.), *Food Security for Developing Countries*, Westview Press, 1981, pp. 101-121.
52. Ibid, p. 31.
53. Ibid, p. 32.
54. U. Lele and W. Candler, Food Security: Some East African Considerations, pp. 101-121, *in* A. Valdes, op cit.
55. Sen, op cit, p. 18.

Notes to Chapter 6

1. J. C. Hendee, G. H. Stankey and R. C. Lucas, *Wilderness Management*, Forest Service, US Department of Agriculture. Miscellaneous Publication No. 1365, 1978.
2. Marion Shoard, *The Theft of the Countryside*, Temple Smith, 1981, p. 147.
3. R. Nash, Chapter 3 *in* Hendee, *et al*, op cit.
4. A. Grainger, Reforesting Britain, *Ecologist*, vol. 11, No. 2, March/April 1981, p. 64.
5. E. M. Mnzava, Fuelwood: the private energy crises of the poor, *Ceres*, July/August 1981.
6. FAO, *The State of Food and Agriculture 1980*, FAO, Rome, 1981, p. 42.
7. D. Pimental, S. Chick and W. Vergara, Energy from forests: environmental and wildlife implications, *Interciercia*, vol. 6, no. 5, September/October 1981, p. 331.
8. *The Arizona Republic*, 3 January 1982.
9. Grainger, op cit.
10. Ibid, *Pulp and Paper*, August 1981.
11. Grainger, op cit.
12. I. G. Simmons, *The Ecology of Natural Resources*, 2nd edn., Edward Arnold, pp. 155-157, 1981.
13. R. Nash, op cit.
14. C. K. Leman, U.S.-Canadian outdoor recreation, *Resources*, October 1982, p. 17.
15. Ibid, p. 18.

16. C.K. Leman, U.S.-Canadian outdoor recreation, *Resources*, October 1982, p. 18.
17. Ibid.
18. M. W. Windhurst, Applied forest geography: general remarks and case studies, *Procedures of Applied Geography Conference*, Arizona State University, October 1981.
19. Grainger, op cit.
20. Council on Environmental Quality, *The Global 2000 Report to the President*, Penguin, 1982, p. 120.
21. Anon, Soviet exports falter as supply plateaus, *World Wood*, 11 September 1980.
22. FAO, op cit.
23. Grainger, op cit and Council on Environmental Quality, op cit.
24. R. A. Sedjo and M. Clawson, The World's Forests, *Resources*, October 1982.
25. Grainger, op cit.
26. Ibid.
27. R. Fontaine, What is really happening to tropical forests, *Ceres*, July/August 1981.
28. Mnzava op cit.
29. Shell Briefing Service, Energy in the developing countries, *SBS*, January 1980.
30. Sedjo and Clawson, op cit.
31. A. Grainger, The state of the world's tropical forests, *The Ecologist*, vol. 10, no. 1, January 1980, p. 50.
32. Ibid., p. 48.
33. N. Myers, *The Sinking Arc*, Pergamon Press, 1979.
34. Grainger, op cit.
35. Grainger, op cit, p. 61.
36. Council on Environmental Quality, op cit, p. 320.
37. Ibid, p. 321.
38. Grainger, op cit, p. 47.
39. Ibid.
40. *Arizona Republic*, September 1981.
41. Grainger, Reforesting Britain, op cit, p. 74.
42. *Arizona Republic*, September 1981.
43. V. Plumwood and R. Routley, World rainforest destruction – the social factors, *The Ecologist*, vol. 12, no. 1, January/February 1982.
44. Ibid, p. 7.
45. A. Grainger, Reforesting Britain, op cit, p. 18.
46. *The Guardian*, 28 October 1982.
47. Plumwood and Routley, op cit.
48. R. Nash, op cit.
49. J. Hendee *et al*, op cit, p. 69.
50. Friends of the Earth, *Ronald Reagan and the American Environment*, FOE, 1982.
51. R. Findley, Our national forests: problems in paradise, *National Geographic*, vol. 162, no. 3, September 1982, p. 311.
52. Friends of the Earth, op cit.
53. K. Parker, The Peak District National Park, p. 103 *in* A. Gilg (ed.), *Policies for Landscapes under Pressure*, Northgate Publishing, 1979.
54. *Christian Science Monitor*, 14 July 1981.
55. M. Blacksell and A. W. Gilg, *The Countryside: Planning and Change*, George Allen & Unwin, 1981, pp. 42, 43.
56. R. Nash, op cit, p. 29.
57. J. Annerino, Beyond the Rim, *Diversions*, Summer 1982, p. 26.
58. Although in some parts of the tropics, notably S.E. Asia, the use of manure and crop residues for biogas production has impeded agricultural productivity.
59. Council on Environmental Quality, op cit.
60. Ibid, pp. 318, 319.
61. Sedjo and Clawson, op cit.

Notes to Chapter 7

1. Cited in A. K. Biswas, *United Nations Water Conference: Summary and Main Documents*, Pergamon Press, Oxford, 1978, p. 48.
2. Ibid, p. 49.
3. Ibid, p. xiv.
4. United Nations, Water Development and Management: *Proceedings of the United Nations Water Conference*, Mar del Plata, Argentina, March 1977, Pergamon Press, Oxford 1978, vol. 1, pp. 1–46, p. 26.
5. Ibid, Resources and Needs, p. 27.
6. M. W. Holdgate, M. Kassas, and G. F. White, (eds.), *The World Environment 1972–1982*, A report by the United Nations Environment Programme (UNEP), Tycooly International, Dublin, 1982, p. 135.
7. E. Fano and M. Brewster, Financing the planning and development of water resources, *Natural Resources Forum*, 6, 1982, p. 292.
8. UN Water Conference, Resource and Needs, op cit, p. 31.
9. Fano and Brewster, op cit, p. 291.
10. Holdgate, *et al*, op cit, p. 133.
11. Holdgate, *et al*, ibid, p. 134.
12. UN Water Conference, Resources and Needs, op cit, p. 35.
13. Fano and Brewster, op cit, p. 292.
14. UN Water Conference, Resources and Needs, op cit, p. 35.
15. UN Water Conference, Economic Commission for Europe: Regional Report, vol. 2, p. 493.
16. ESCAP: The United Nations Economic and Social Commission for Asia and the Pacific, including Asian states from Iran eastwards, the Soviet Union, the United States and Australia.
17. UN Water Conference, op cit, vol. 2, Report of the ESCAP Regional Preparatory Meeting for the UN Water Conference, p. 401.
18. Biswas, op cit, pp. 38–39.
19. *The Global 2000 Report to the President*, Council on Environmental Quality, Penguin, Harmondsworth, 1981., p. 139.
20. Ibid, p. 157.
21. Ibid.
22. P. Beaumont, Water resource management in the USA: A case study of large dams, *Applied Geography*, 3, 1983, pp. 259–275.
23. H. D. Foster and W. R. D. Sewell, *Water: The Emerging Crisis in Canada*, Loromer & Co., Toronto, 1981.
24. Ibid, p. 19.
25. W. R. D. Sewell, Water across the American Continent, *Geographical Magazine*, June 1974, pp. 472–479.
26. Foster and Sewell, op cit, p. 20.
27. Ibid, pp. 30–32.
28. C. W. Howe. The effects of water resource development on economic growth: the conditions for success, *Natural Resources Journal*, 16, 1976, pp. 939–956.
29. D. Hart, *The Volta River Project: A case study in Politics and Technology*, Edinburgh University Press, Edinburgh, 1980.
30. Ibid, p. 44.
31. Ibid, p. 51.
32. Ibid, p. 58.
33. Ibid, p. 60.
34. Ibid, p. 101.
35. Ibid, p. 109.
36. Ibid, pp. 76–102.

37. M. Hafez, The Environmental Impacts of the Aswan Dam in UN Water Conference, *in* The UN Water Conference, op cit, pp. 1777-1785.
38. M. Kassas, Major Water Development Projects, pp. 215-235 *in* N. Polunin, (ed.), *The Environmental Future*, Macmillan, London, 1972.
39. UNICEF, Drinking Water Supply – A Field for UNICEF Assistance, pp. 847-856, in *The UN Water Conference*, op cit, pp. 848-852.
40. Intermediate Technology Development Group Ltd, Water for the thousand millions, *in* The UN Water Conference, op cit, pp. 1105-1162.
41. International Labour Office, World Employment Programme, Appropriate construction technology for water control and irrigation works in developing countries, *in* The UN Water Conference, op cit, pp. 819-846.
42. H. L. Parsons, *Marx and Engels on Ecology*, Greenwood Press, Westport, Connecticut, 1977, pp. 169-185.
43. J. Fullenbach, *European Environmental Policy: East and West*, Butterworths, London, 1981, p. 20.
44. Ibid, p. 13.
45. Ibid, pp. 28-29.
46. L. V. Cunha, W. L. Figueiredo, M. L. Correia and A. S. Goncalves, *Management and Land for Water Resources*, Water Resources Publications, Fort Collins, Colorado, 1977, p. 337.
47. N. A. Swainson, *Conflict over the Columbia: The Canadian Background to an historic treaty*. Institute of Public Administration of Canada, McGill-Queens University Press, Montreal, 1979.
48. J. V. Krutilla, *The Columbia River Treaty: The Economics of an International River Basin Development*, The Johns Hopkins Press, Baltimore, 1967.
49. Cunha, *et al*, ibid, p. 222.
50. United Nations, Mar del Plata Action Plan, *in* The UN Water Conference, op cit, pp. 329-330.
51. G. F. White. *Strategies of American Water Management*, University of Michigan Press, Ann Arbor, 1962. L. E. Craine, *Water Management Innovations in England*, Johns Hopkins Press, Baltimore, 1969.
52. W. R. D. Sewell, Water Resources Planning and Policy Making, Challenges and responses, *in* F. M. Leversedge, (ed.), Priorities in World Management, *Western Geographical Series*, vol. 8, University of Victoria, BC Canada, 1974, pp. 259-295.
53. Foster and Sewell, op cit, p. 82.
54. Biswas, op cit, pp. 8-9.

Notes to Chapter 8

1. For a brief account of the expansion of public administration in Great Britain see: R. G. S. Brown, *The Administrative Process in Britain*, Methuen, 1971, pp. 3-38.
2. C. Tugendhat, *The Multinationals*, Eyre and Spottiswoode Ltd, London, 1971; A. Madsen, *Private Power: Multinational Corporations and Their Role in the Survival of Our Planet*, Sphere Books, 1981; A. Samson, *The Sovereign State:* The Secret History of ITT, Hodder & Stoughton, 1973; A. Sampson, *The Seven Sisters: The Great Oil Companies and the World They Shaped*, Hodder & Stoughton, 1975; A. Sampson, *The Changing Anatomy of Britain*, Hodder & Stoughton, London, 1982, pp. 369-381; P. Marchak, *In Whose Interests: An Essay on Multinational Corporations in a Canadian Context*, McClelland and Stewart, Toronto, 1979.
3. L. F. Peter and R. Hull, *The Peter Principle*, Souvenir Press, 1969.
4. F. G. Castles, D. J. Murray, D. C. Potter, (eds.), *Decisions, Organisations and Society*, The Open University Press/Penguin Books, London, 1981.
5. J. G. March and H. A. Simon, *Organisations*, John Wiley & Co, New York, 1958.

6. D. Katz, R. L. Kahn and J. S. Adams, (eds.), *The Study of Organisations*, Jossey-Bass, San Francisco, 1980.
7. G. F. White, *Strategies of American Water Management*, University of Michigan Press, Ann Arbor, 1969.
8. L. E. Craine, *Water Management Institutions in England*, Johns Hopkins Press, Baltimore, 1969.
9. D. Okun, *Regionalisation of Water Management*, Applied Science Publishers, London, 1977.
10. B. Mitchell, (ed.), *Institutional Arrangements for Water Management: Canadian Experiences*, Department of Geography, University of Waterloo, Ontario, Canada, 1975.
11. For example, see W. R. D. Sewell and I. Burton, (eds.), *Perceptions and Attitudes in Resource Management*, Information Canada, Ottawa, 1971.
12. W. R. D. Sewell, Environmental perceptions and attitudes of engineers and public Health Officials, *Environment and Behaviour*, 1971, (3), pp. 23–59.
13. H. Kaufman, *The Forest Ranger: A study in Administrative Behaviour*, Johns Hopkins Press, Baltimore, 1960.
14. G. F. White, The choice of use in resource management, *Natural Resources Journal*, 1, 1961, pp. 23–40.
15. R. E. Kasperson, Environmental Stress and the Municipal Political System, pp. 481–496 *in*, R. E. Kasperson and J. V. Minghi (eds.), *The Structure of Political Geography*, Aldine, Chicago, 1969.
16. D. Braybrooke and C. E. Lindblom, *A Strategy of Decision*, The Free Press, Macmillan, New York, 1970.
17. A. Etzioni, Mixed Scanning: A Third Approach to Decision Making, pp. 217–229 *in* A. Faludi, *A Reader in Planning Theory*, Pergamon Press, Oxford, 1973.
18. W. R. D. Sewell and T. O'Riordan, The culture of participation in environmental decision making, *Natural Resources Journal*, 16, 1976, pp. 1–22.
19. F. Sandbach, *Environment, Ideology and Policy*, Blackwell, Oxford, 1980.
20. N. Wengert, Citizen Participation: practice in search of a theory, *Natural Resources Journal*, 16, 1976, pp. 23–40.
21. S. R. Arnstein, A ladder of citizen participation, *Journal of the American Institute of Planning*, 1969, 35, pp. 216–224.
22. Council for Science and Society, *The Big Public Inquiry*. The Outer Circle Policy Unit, London, 1979.
23. J. Tyme, *Motorways versus Democracy: Public Inquiries into Road Proposals and their Political Significance*, Macmillan, 1978.
24. C. Sweet, The CEGB and its Critics, paper at Conference, The Polytechnic of the South Bank, London, May 1981, The CEGB and the Public Interest. See also: A. Blowers, *Something in the Air: Corporate Power and the Environment*, Harper & Row, London, 1984, and M. Crenson, *The Un-Politics of Air Pollution: A Study of Non-Decision Making in the Cities*, Johns Hopkin Press, Baltimore, 1971.
25. R. Dahl, The Analysis of Influence in Local Communities, pp. 225–241 *in* B. J. Frieden and R. Morris, (eds.), *Urban Planning and Social Policy*, Basic Books, New York, 1968.
26. P. Lowe and J. Goyder, *Environmental Groups in Politics*, George Allen & Unwin, 1983.
27. Ibid, p. 62.
28. G. Hardin, The Tragedy of the Commons, pp. 288–298 *in* T. O'Riordan and R. K. Turner, *An Annotated Reader in Environmental Planning and Management*, Pergamon Press, Oxford, 1983.
29. Madsen, op cit.
30. K. Boulding, The Economics of the Coming Spaceship Earth, pp. 121–132, *in* H. E. Daly, (ed.) *Towards a Steady State Economy*, Freeman, San Francisco, 1973.
31. See, for example: W. J. Baumol and W. E. Oates, *Economics, Environmental Policy*

and the Quality of Life, Prentice-Hall, Englewood Cliffs, NJ, 1979; C. W. Howe, *Natural Resource Economics: Issues, Analysis and Policy*, John Wiley & Co, New York, 1979; R. Dorfman and N. S. Dorfman, (eds.), *Economics of the Environment*, Norton, New York, 1977; T. O'Riordan and R. K. Turner, (eds.), op cit, pp. 211–265, Economics and Ecology: Towards a new paradigm.

Notes to Chapter 9

1. See: R. G. Kasperson, Environmental stress and the municipal political system, *in* R. E. Kasperson and J. V. Minghi (eds.), *The Structure of Political Geography*, Aldine, Chicago, 1969, and C. J. B. Wood, Conflict in resource management and the use of threat: the Goldstream controversy, *Natural Resources Journal*, vol. 16, 1976.
2. C. J. B. Wood, op cit.
3. A. J. Downs, Up and down with ecology: the issue – attention cycle, *The Public Interest*, vol. 29, Summer 1972.
4. W. Solesbury, The Environmental Agenda, *Public Administration*, vol. 65, 1976.
5. W. R. D. Sewell and T. O'Riordan, The culture of participation in environmental decision making, *Natural Resources Journal*, vol. 16, 1976.
6. T. O'Riordan, *Perspectives in Resource Management*, Pion, 1971, p. 135.
7. R. Vicker, Exotic new technology used in oil drilling is leading to big success, a rise in reserves, *Wall Street Journal*, February 1982.
8. L. D. Stamp, The Land Utilisation Survey of Britain, *Geographical Journal* vol. 78, 1931; *The Land of Britain: its Use and Misuse*, Longman, 3rd edition, 1962; and *Applied Geography*, Penguin, 1960.
9. L. B. Leopold, *Quantitative Comparison of Some Aesthetic Factors among Rivers*, US Geological Survey 620, US Government, 1969; K. D. Fines, Landscape evaluation: a research project in East Sussex, *Regional Studies*, 1968; and D. Linton, The assessment of scenery as a natural resource, *Scottish Geographical Magazine* vol. 84, 1968.
10. L. B. Leopold, Landscape aesthetics, *Natural History*, vol. 78, 1969.
11. See: R. B. Linton, *Forest Landscape Description and Inventories: A Basis for Land Planning and Design* USDA, Forest Service Research Paper PSW-49, 1968; Visual vulnerability of forest landscapes, *Journal of Forestry*, vol. 72, 1974; E. H. Zuke, Evaluating the visual and cultural landscape, *Journal of Soil and Water Conservation*, vol. 25, 1970; and Cross disciplinary and inter mode agreement on the description and evaluation of landscape resources, *Environment and Behaviour*, vol. 6, 1974.
12. See: D. M. Knudson, A system for evaluating scenic rivers, *Water Resources Bulletin*, vol. 12, 1976; M. Chubb and E. H. Bauman, 'Assessing the recreation potential of rivers', *Journal of Soil and Water Conservation*, vol. 32, 1977; A. Gilg, The objectivity of Linton type methods of assessing scenery as a natural resource, *Regional Studies*, vol. 9, 1975; Assessing scenery as a natural resource, *Scottish Geographical Magazine*, vol. 92, 1976; and M. A. Anderson, The proposed High Weald Area of Outstanding Natural Beauty: the use of landscape appraisal in the definition of its boundaries, *Landscape Research*, vol. 6, no. 2, 1981.
13. D. Robinson, I. Laurie, J. Wager and A. Traill, *Landscape Evaluation: Report of the Landscape Evaluation Research Project*, Centre for Urban and Regional Research, University of Manchester, 1976; and D. J. Briggs and J. France, Assessing landscape attractiveness: a South Yorkshire study, *Landscape Research*, vol. 6, no. 2, 1981.
14. M. Powell, Landscape evaluation and the quest for objectivity, *Landscape Research*, vol. 6, no. 2, 1981, p. 17.
15. See: P. Bromley, The role of the public in landscape decisions: a case study in the Peak District National Park, *Landscape Research*, vol. 6, no. 1, 1981; and G. J.

Buhyoff, J. D. Wellman, H. Harvey and R. A. Frazer, Landscape architects' interpretations of peoples' landscape preferences, *Journal of Environment Management*,
vol. 6, 1978, for a discussion on this theme.
16. E. C. Penning-Rowsell, Assessing the validity of landscape evaluations, *Landscape
Research*, vol. 6, no. 2, 1981.
17. D. Lowenthal and M. C. Prince, The English Landscape, *Geographical Review*,
vol. 54, 1964; English landscape tastes, *Geographical Review*, vol. 55, 1965; and
Transcendental experience, *in* S. Wapner *et al.*, *Experiencing the Environment*,
Plenum Press, 1976.
18. P. C. Clamp, Evaluation of the impact of roads on the visual amenity of rural areas,
Research Report 7, Department of the Environment, 1976; and A. O. Grigg and
L. Huddart, Three surveys of visual intrusion of roads in rural landscapes, *Transport and Road Research Laboratory Report 861*, 1978, for the Department of Transport.
19. Penning-Rowsell, op cit.
20. J. C. Hendee *et al*, *Wilderness Management*, Forest Service, US Department of
Agriculture, Miscellaneous Publication no. 1365, 1978, p. 172.
21. A. Leopold, *Game Management*, Charles Scribner, New York, 1933; W. Dasmann,
A method for estimating the carrying capacity of range lands, *Journal of Forestry*,
vol. 43, 1945.
22. J. E. Ross, Natural limits to natural resources, in P. Dorner and M. A. El-Shafie
(eds.), *Resources and Development*, Croom Helm, 1980.
23. L. S. Fanaroff, Conservation and stock reduction on the Navajo tribal range, *Geographical Review*, vol. 53, 1963.
24. For a summary of this research see B. Mitchell, *Geography and Resource Analysis*,
Longman, 1979, Chapter 7.
25. T. O'Riordan, Planning to improve environmental capacity: a case study of Broad-
land, *Town Planning Review*, vol. 40, 1969; and R. C. Lucas, Wilderness perception
and use: the example of Boundary Waters Canoe Area, *Natural Resources Journal*,
vol. 3, 1964.
26. T. O'Riordan and W. R. D. Sewell, *Project Appraisal and Policy Review*, Wiley,
New York, 1981.
27. Ibid, p. 18.
28. T. O'Riordan, *Perspectives on Resource Management*, Pion, London, 1971, pp. 22–
37; and T. O'Riordan and R. K. Turner, (eds.), *An Annotated Reader in Environmental Planning and Management*, Pergamon Press, Oxford, 1983, Traditional
Cost-Benefits Analysis and its Critique, pp. 87–134.
29. B. D. Clark, R. Bisset and P. Wathern, *Environmental Impact Assessment: A Bibliography with Abstracts*, Mansell, London, 1980, especially, pp. 7–9, and S. K.
Fairfax and H. M. Ingram, The United States Experience *in* O'Riordan and Sewell,
op cit, pp. 29–45.
30. G. Wandesforde-Smith, The Evolution of Environmental Impact Assessment in
California, *in* O'Riordan and Sewell, op cit, pp. 47–76.
31. T. O'Riordan and W. R. D. Sewell, The culture of participation in environmental
decision making, *Natural Resources Journal*, 16, 1976, pp. 1–22.
32. R. E. Munn (ed.), *Environmental Impact Assessment*, Wiley, New York, 1979,
pp. 28–57.
33. L. B. Leopold, F. E. Clarke, B. B. Hanshaw and J. R. Balsey, *A Procedure for
Evaluating Environmental Impact*, United States Geological Survey Circular 645,
Washington DC, US Geological Survey, 1971.
34. R. M. Brown *et al*, A Water Quality Index – Crashing the Psychological Barrier, *in*
W. A. Thomas, (ed.), *Indicators of Environmental Quality*, Plenum Press, New
York, 1970, and N. Dee, J. K. Baker, N. L. Drobny, K. M. Duke and D. C.
Fahringer, *Environmental Evaluation System for Water Resource Planning*, Final
Report, Batelle Columbus Laboratories, Ohio, 1972.

35. Clark, Bisset & Wathern, op cit, pp. 104-107.
36. D. P. Beard, United States environmental legislation and energy resources: a review, *Geographical Review*, 65, 1975, pp. 229-243.
37. D. A. Dreyfus and H. M. Ingram, The National Environmental Policy Act: A view of intent and practice, *Natural Resources Journal*, 16, 1976, pp. 243-260; and R. A. Liroff, NEPA litigation in the 1970s: a deluge or a dribble?, *Natural Resources Journal*, 21, 1981, pp. 315-330.
38. Clark, Bisset and Wathern, Environmental Impact Assessment in Canada, op cit, pp. 365-368; and W. R. D. Sewell, How Canada Responded: The Berger Inquiry, *in* O'Riordan & Sewell, op cit, pp. 77-94.
39. Ibid, pp. 425-428.
40. Ibid, pp. 445-448.
41. T. O'Riordan and R. K. Turner, Planning and Environmental Protection, op cit, pp. 135-210; and Clark, Bisset and Wathern, op cit, pp. 393-397.
42. Council for Science and Society, *The Big Public Inquiry*, The Outer Circle Policy Unit, London, 1979.
43. G. Esler, The Nuclear Police, *The Listener*, 24 November 1983, pp. 5-6.
44. R. Gregory, The Cow Green Reservoir, *in* P. J. Smith (ed.), *The Politics of Physical Resources*, Penguin Books, 1975, pp. 22-65.
45. The Roskill Commission on the Third London Airport, *Report*, HMSO, London, 1971.
46. *The Surveyor*, 12 March 1981.
47. J. Catlow and G. G. Thirwall, Environmental Impact Analysis: *Research Report No. 11*, Department of Environment, London, 1976.
48. Department of the Environment, *Review of the Development Control System, Final Report (The Dobry Committee)*, HMSO, London, 1975; see also Royal Commission on Environmental Pollution, *5th Report, Air Pollution Control: An Integrated Approach*, Cmnd 6371, HMSO, London, 1976.
49. Stevens Committee, *Planning Control over Mineral Workings*, HMSO, London, 1976.
50. Leitch Advisory Committee, *Report of the Advisory Committee on Trunk Road Assessment*, HMSO, London, 1977.
51. N. Evans and C. W. Hope, Costs of nuclear accidents: implications for reactor choice, in *Issues in the Sizewell 'B' Inquiry*, vol. 3, Centre for Energy Studies, Polytechnic of the South Bank. These authors argue that an accident surcharge should be added to capital costs to act as an insurance premium against the economic effects of a major reactor accident.
52. The works of G. F. White and I. Burton, R. W. Kates and others involved in natural hazard research are summarized in B. Mitchell, *Geography and Resource Analysis*, Longman, 1979, Chapter 8.
53. D. J. Zeigler, J. H. Johnson and S. D. Brunn, *Technological Hazards*, AAG Resource Publications in Geography, 1983 gives a good review of risk estimation and policy responses to technological hazards.
54. N. C. Rasmussen, The Application of Probabilistic Risk Assessment Techniques to Energy Technologies, *Annual Review of Energy*, 6, 1981.
55. J. H. Bowen, Thermal Reactor Safety, *in* F. R. Farmer, *Nuclear Reactor Safety*, Academic Press, 1977, p. 181.
56. J. Fernie and S. Openshaw, Decision Making and Safety Issues in Nuclear Power Development in the United Kingdom, *in* M. J. Pasqualetti and K. D. Pijawka, (eds.), *Nuclear Power: Assessing and Managing Hazardous Technology*, Westview Press, 1984; Health and Safety Executive, *Canvey: An Investigation of Potential Hazards from Operations in the Canvey Island, Thurrock Area*, HMSO, 1978.
57. This methodology underestimates the relative risks involved. See: S. Openshaw, The siting of nuclear power stations in the UK, *Regional Studies*, 16, pp. 186-187. He shows that the risk of death for the whole population of a settlement close to a

nuclear plant is the same as the individual risk assuming that a catastrophic accident occurred, but the chances of the same population all being killed by a traffic accident is infinitesimal.

58. W. Ramsay, On Assessing Risk, *Resources*, October 1981.
59. P. Slovic, *et al*, Rating the Risks, *Environment*, 21 April 1979.
60. For a good review of project appraisal of hazardous technologies in the UK see: S. M. MacGill and D. J. Snowball, What use risk assessment, *Applied Geography*, 3, 1983.
61. B. Wynne, Public perception of risk, International Conference on the Urban Transport of Irradiated Fuel, London, 13 April 1983, Greater London Council, p. 12.

Notes to Chapter 10

1. Consumers have threatened not to pay their bills in Washington, Oregon, Idaho and Northern California; *Wall Street Journal*, 19 March 1982.
2. H. W. Henry *et al*, *Energy Management: Theory and Practice*, Marcel Dekker, 1980, p. 88, cites Chase Manhattan Bank which claimed in 1972 that a major reduction in energy use would harm the nation's economy and its standard of living.
3. G. Leach *et al*, *A Low Energy Strategy for the United Kingdom*, The International Institute for Environment and Development, 1979, p. 10.
4. P. Odell, Relative fuel costs and CEGB decision making, paper presented at a conference, The CEGB and the Public Interest, Polytechnic of the South Bank, 11 June 1982, where he showed that energy usage in the EEC had fallen 4·6% in 1980 despite 1% increase in GNP.
5. See California Energy Commission, *Electricity Tomorrow: Final Report to the Governor and the Legislature*, California Energy Commission, January 1981, pp. 18–21 for a discussion on forecasting models.
6. In general, a few categories of demand are chosen – residential, industrial, commercial and transportation, which are themselves a function of a small number of demographic and economic variables. It can be described as a 'best fit' model approach to extrapolating future demand.
7. The most often quoted example is the abandonment of the Kaiparowits project in South Utah by a consortia of South west utilities.
8. A. Lovin, *Soft Energy Paths: Toward a Durable Peace*; Ballinger 1977, and Re-examining the nature of the ECE energy problem, *Energy Policy*, 1979, p. 178. In the UK this approach was advocated by R. W. Todd and C. J. N. Alty (eds.), *An Alternative Strategy for the UK*, National Council for Alternative Technoloogy, 1978.
9. California Energy Commission, op cit; and US General Accounting Office; *Electrical Energy Development in the Pacific Southwest*, US, GAO, October 1979. At a seminar at Arizona State University in March 1982 on 'Planning for the West' it was stated that the Pacific North West states were advocating conservation, renewable and cogeneration technologies because of their cost effectiveness.
10. American Petroleum Institute; *Two Energy Futures: A National Choice for the 80's*, API 1981, p. iv.
11. The incidents include an IRA bombing at the Canvey Island petrochemical complex in Essex. Here, excavation plans were being drawn up in response to the likelihood of an accident. Health and Safety Executive, *Emergency Plans for Civil Nuclear Installations*, HMSO, 1982, specifies procedure in event of a nuclear accident.
12. *Wall Street Journal*, 4 February 1982.
13. *Financial Times*, 25 March 1981; and *The Guardian*, 18 March 1981.
14. The World's Largest Industrial Corporations, *Fortune*, 22 August 1983.
15. P. R. Odell and K. E. Rosing; *The Future of Oil: a Simulation Study of the Interrelationships of Resources, Reserves and Use*, 1980–2080, Kogan Page, London, 1980.

16. D. Gordon; Still only nibbling at energy conservation, *Building Services and Environmental Engineer*, November 1983.

17. The International 500, *Fortune*, 22 August 1983; and Monopolies and Mergers Commission, *Central Electricity Generating Board: a Report on the Operation by the Board of its System for the Generation and Supply of Electricity in Bulk*, HMSO, May 1981, p. 8.

18. O'Riordan, paper presented at the IBG Conference, Lancaster, 1980.

19. F. J. Calzonetti, M. S. Eckert and E. J. Malecki; Siting energy facilities in the USA: policies for the western states, *Energy Policy*, June 1980, p. 140.

20. R. E. Kasperson *et al*; Public opposition to nuclear energy: retrospect and prospect, *Science, technology and human values*, vol. 5, no. 31, Spring 1980, p. 18.

21. D. E. Dowall; US land use and energy policy – assessing potential conflicts, *Energy Policy*, March 1980, pp. 54–58.

22. M. Barrett, Environmental impact statements, *Omega*, vol. 7, no. 5, 1979, p. 436.

23. American Petroleum Institute; *Two Energy Futures: a National Choice for the 80's*, API, p. 95.

24. M. D. Devine, S. C. Ballard and I. L. White, Energy from the western states of the USA, *Energy Policy*, September 1980, p. 236. This article discusses BACT and other methods of minimizing environmental impacts in the western US.

25. J. V. Winter and D. A. Connor; *Power Plant Siting*, Van Norstrand Reinhold Company, 1978, and F. Calzonetti, op cit, p. 28.

26. Cited in J. Bellamy; Two utilities are better than one, *Reason*, October 1981, p. 29.

27. US General Accounting Office, op cit, p. 39.

28. H. J. Frank; Prospects for solar energy in Arizona: a progress report, *Arizona Review*, third/fourth quarter 1981, p. 24.

29. F. J. Calzonetti, op cit, p. 30.

30. D. Pearce *et al*, *Decision Making for Energy Futures*, Macmillan, 1979; and J. Rowan-Robinson and L. Edwards; The special inquiry, *Town and Country Planning*, March 1981.

31. M. R. Cupolos; The politics of energy, *Energy*, Special issue, 1978.

32. W. Patterson reviewing W. A. Rosenbaum's 'Coal and Crisis' in *Energy Policy*, December 1979.

33. P. J. Nyden, Mine disasters, *Phoenix Gazette*, 1 February 1982.

34. *The Economist*; 'Nuclear man at bay', 19 March 1977, pp. 12, 13.

35. Quoted in Colin Sweet, A Study of Nuclear Power in France, *Energy Paper No. 2*, Polytechnic of the South Bank, March 1981.

36. Ibid, pp. 3, 4.

37. The Royal Institute Forum was published as G. Foley and A. Van Buren, *Nuclear or Not?*, Heinemann, London, 1978. The relevant Benn statement is on page 114.

38. *The Guardian*, 28 October 1982.

39. The new SDP party in the UK is against any further development of nuclear power unless certain need, cost and safety considerations are met.

40. *The Guardian*, 5 November 1982.

41. US Department of Energy, *Securing America's Energy Future: the National Energy Policy Plan*, US Department of Commerce, July 1981.

42. B. Coffin; Nuclear power plants in the United States: current status and statistical history, Union of Concerned Scientists, 1983.

43. In April 1984 Public Service Company of New Hampshire eliminated stock dividends and stopped work on their Seabrook plant. Earlier in the year the Marble Hill plant (Public Service Company of Indiana) was cancelled and Limerick no. 2 (Pennsylvania Electric Company) was deferred.

44. For a detailed account of the history of TM1 2 see B. Keisling, *Three Mile Island: Turning Point*, Veritas Books, 1980.

45. *Arizona Republic*, 22 July 1982.

46. See M. Gray and I. Rosen; *The Warning*, W. W. Norton, 1982, for another review

of TM1 2, especially the NRC responses to the incidents before the accident and the accident itself.

47. *Wall Streeet Journal*, 26 February 1982.

48. American Petroleum Institute, op cit, p. 97.

49. House of Commons Select Committee on Energy (HCSCE); *The Government's Statement on the New Nuclear Power Programme*, HMSO, 1981, para. 96.

50. Sir Walter Marshall, formerly of the AEA, and Ian MacGregor, formerly of British Steel, are now Chairman of the CEGB and the NCB respectively. These appointments have been seen as methods to pilot through the PWR programme (Marshall) and to streamline the coal industry (MacGregor).

51. Monopolies Commission, op cit; and CEGB, *Statement of Case*, vol. 1, para. 11, London, 1982.

52. Department of Energy, *Proof of Evidence for the Sizewell 'B' Inquiry*, DoE, 1982, Tables C and D.

53. Monopolies Commission, op cit, para. 14.

54. HCSCE, op cit, para. 61.

55. S. Thomas, Worldwide nuclear plant performance revisited: an analysis of 1978–81 experience, *Science Policy Research Unit Occasional Paper no. 18*, University of Sussex, 1982.

56. Town and Country Planning Association, Sizewell 'B' Power Station Public Inquiry: *Statement of Case*, April 1983, p. 19.

57. HCSCE, op cit, para. 64; and Monopolies Commission, op cit, paras. 5.137 to 5.143.

58. Town and Country Planning Association, op cit, pp. 17–22.

59. J. W. Jeffery, The real cost of nuclear electricity in the UK, *Energy Policy*, vol. 10, no. 2, 1982; and A provisional critique of the CEGB's statement of case for a PWR at Sizewell, *in* D. Lowry and I. Gamble (eds.), *Issues in the Sizewell 'B' Inquiry*, vol. 3, 1982, pp. 20–23.

60. G. Gudgin and S. Fothergill, *The Economic Consequences of the Sizewell 'B' Nuclear Power Station*, Department of Applied Economics, Cambridge, 1984; and C. Sweet, Local Government and the Sizewell Inquiry, seminar on 29 May 1983 at South Yorkshire County Council, Barnsley.

61. Department of the Environment; *An Incident Leading to Contamination of the Beaches near the British Nuclear Fuels Limited, Windscale and Calder Works, Sellafield, November 1983*, DOE, 1984; and Nuclear Installations Inspectorate, *The Contamination of the Beach Incident at British Nuclear Fuels Ltd, Sellafield, November 1983*, Health and Safety Executive, 1984.

62. *Nuclear Engineering International*, January 1983, p. 6.

63. *The Guardian*, 12 May 1984; and F. Pearce, Sizewell: beware low-flying aircraft, *New Scientist*, 11 November 1983.

64. B. Ramberg; *Destruction of Nuclear Energy Facilities in War*, Lexington Books, 1980.

65. For more detail on siting and safety issues see J. Fernie and S. Openshaw, Policy making and safety issues in the development of nuclear power in the United Kingdom, Chapter 3 *in* M. J. Pasqualetti and K. D. Pijawka, *Nuclear Power: assessing and managing hazardous technology*, Westview Press, 1984; and UK nuclear power plants: a policy analysis, a paper presented to the AAG Conference at Washington DC, April 1984 by the same authors.

66. N. Evans and C. W. Hope, Costs of nuclear accidents: implications for reactor choice, *in* Lowry and Gamble, op cit, pp. 53–79.

Notes to Chapter 11

1. Council on Environmental Quality, *The Global 2000 Report to the President*, Penguin, 1982, p. 221.
2. For details of the London Metal Exchange's operations and the monopoly of price forecasting information in the 'North' see: *South*, June 1981 and *South*, October 1981.
3. R. J. Barnet, *The Lean Years: Politics in the Age of Scarcity*, Sphere Books, 1981, p. 137.
4. M. R. Wright (ed.) *Financial Times International Yearbook*, Longman, 1983, p. vii.
5. R. Bosson and B. Varon, *The Mining Industry and the Developing Countries*, World Bank, Oxford University Press, 1977, p. 29.
6. See M. Tanzer, *The Race for Resources*, Heinemann, 1980, p. 66, for a detailed, hypothetical example of the DCF method.
7. Ibid, p. 49.
8. Political risk is defined by W. C. Prast and H. L. Lax in Political risk as a variable in TNC decision making, *Natural Resources Forum*, 6, 1982, p. 185 as the probability that a project will be affected through changes in the political situation.
9. S. Blank, *Assessing the Political Environment*, The Conference Board, 1980.
10. Prast and Lax, op cit, p. 193.
11. R. F. Mikesell, *New Patterns of World Mineral Development*, British–North American Committee, 1979, p. 96.
12. R. C. Estell and R. O. Buchanan, *Industrial Activity and Economic Geography*, Hutchinson, 4th Edn., 1980, Table 15.
13. Tanzer, op cit, p. 173.
14. RTZ neveer accepted this diagnosis in public. For details of the case see C. Searle, Copper in Snowdonia National Park, *in* P. J. Smith (ed.), *The Politics of Physical Resources*, Open University Press/Penguin, 1975, pp. 66–112.
15. J. Berthelson, Cobalt on Gasquet Mountain, *Sierra*, November/December 1982, p. 56.
16. Friends of the Earth, *Ronald Reagan and the American Environment*, FOE, 1982, pp. 8–10.
17. The Sagebrush Rebellion is a political campaign by pro-development groups – mainly ranchers and miners – who want federal public lands turned over to states and/or private ownership.
18. Arizona Republic, 18 April 1982.
19. Arizona Republic, 7 April 1983.
20. R. F. Mikesell, op cit, pp. 16–19.
21. The largest are in the copper industry – CODELCO (Chile), ZIMCO (Zambia) and Gecomines (Zaire) – and in iron ore production – Vale do Rio Doce (Brazil).
22. D. Mezger, *Copper in the World Economy*, Heinemann, 1980, p. 153.
23. United Nations Secretariat, Two decades of mineral resources development: the role of the United Nations, *Natural Resources Forum*, 5, 1981, p. 20.
24. Ibid, p. 18.
25. Ibid, p. 28.
26. In 1978, UNDP-funded projects amounted to $18 million. Out of a total of 55 schemes, 24 were involved in exploration and 22 in institution building.
27. This includes the International Bank for Reconstruction and Development formed in 1945, the International Development Association established in 1960 and the International Finance Corporation created in 1956.
28. Bosson and Varon, op cit, p. 210; and Mikesell, op cit, p. 70.
29. World Bank, *Annual Report*, 1978, p. 21.
30. Z. Pysariwski, Law of the Sea: uncertainty follows the euphoria, *South*, August 1982, p. 62.
31. Ibid.

32. M. Rose, Seas – the assets, *New Internationalist*, May 1983, p. 27.
33. R. Gauhar and R. Manning, The Sea up for grabs, *South*, April 1981, p. 21.
34. R. Calder, *The Guardian*, 12 March 1981.
35. Gauher and Manning, op cit, p. 20.
36. Rose, op cit, p. 28.
37. A. McDonald, Mines in a lawless sea, *Geographical Magazine*, September 1982, p. 503.
38. *South*, November 1982.
39. A. Federman, Hitting the jackpot, *South*, May 1982, p. 9.
40. C. Raghaven, Unilateral action by G77 can stabilise prices, *South*, April 1982.
41. A. Federman, op cit.
42. C. Fortin, It's time to mobilise a united commodity front, *South*, December 1982, p. 73.
43. A. Federman, op cit.
44. M. Van Hatten, *Financial Times*, 31 October 1979.
45. A. Kilgore, North-South rift within STABEX, *South*, December 1980.
46. A. Hewitt, Safety net for minerals, *South*, May 1983, p. 74.
47. Ibid.
48. *South*, January 1982.
49. S. Islam, Stabex reform thwarted by Common Market, *South*, June 1982; and Commodity crisis tests Stabex, *South*, September 1981.
50. S. Islam, Stabex sour note as Brussels rings changes, *South*, October 1982.
51. A history of Kennecott up until the mid-1970s can be found in N. Girvan, *Corporate Imperialism: Conflict and Expropriation*, 1976, Monthly Review Press, pp. 79–85; and Kennecott Copper Corporation, *A brief background to Kennecott*, and *Bingham Canyon: the early years*.
52. Kennecott Copper Corporation, *Bingham Mine factsheet*, 1 January 1979.
53. It did integrate forwards into fabrication with the purchase of Chase Companies Inc. in 1929 and American Electrical Works in 1936.
54. M. Tanzer, *The Race for Resources*, Heinemann, 1980, p. 114.
55. Before 1964, Kennecott's share of profits was only 21%; the reduced tax rate after the agreement meant that Kennecott increased its share to 27% with only 49% ownership. See Girvan op cit, p. 84.
56. This incident was embarrassing for Anaconda, and the company fired many of its top executives. Eventually, on the fall of Allende and the accession of a military junta, Anaconda was adequately compensated for the expropriation.
57. The changing EPA air quality standards throughout the 1970s caused Kennecott much concern because of the design modifications which were deemed necessary to comply with the successive tightening of regulations. For detail on this issue see S. Dayton, Utah Copper and the $280 million investment in clean air, *Engineering and Mining Journal*, February 1979.
58. D. Mezger, *Copper in the World Economy*, Heinemann, 1980, pp. 178–198.
59. *The Guardian*, 15 September 1983.
60. D. Metzger, op cit, p. 194.
61. R. F. Mikesell, op cit, p. 54.
62. H. R. Wright, (ed.), op cit, p. 331.

Notes to Chapter 12

1. FAO, *The State of Food and Agriculture 1981*, Rome, 1982, p. 85.
2. Ibid, pp. 86, 87.
3. Ibid, p. 90.
4. Ibid, pp. 100–106.
5. Ibid, p. 100.

6. FAO, *The State of Food and Agriculture 1981*, Rome, 1982, p. 101.
7. Ibid, p. 102.
8. Ibid, p. 103.
9. Ibid, p. 106.
10. A. L. Mabogunje, *The Development Process: A Spatial Perspective*, Hutchinson, 1980, p. 116.
11. Ibid, p. 107.
12. Ibid, p. 113.
13. S. Barraclough, Agricultural Production Prospects in Latin America, pp. 459–476 *in* R. Sinha, (ed.), *The World Food Problem: Consensus and Conflict*, Pergamon Press, Oxford, 1978, p. 464.
14. Ibid, p. 465.
15. *Ceres*, January–February 1981, pp. 11–12.
16. A. R. Lamond, The UNCTAD Integrated Programme for Commodities and the world food problem, pp. 595–601 *in* R. Sinha, (ed.), *The World Food Problem: Consensus and Conflict*, Pergamon Press, Oxford, 1978, p. 595.
17. A. Valdes, *Ceres*, November–December 1982, pp. 13–18.
18. R. F. Hopkins, Food as a Global Issue, pp. 1–28, *in* R. F. Hopkins, R. L. Paarlberg and M. B. Wallerstein, *Food in the Global Arena*, Holt, Rinehart and Winston, New York, 1982.
19. R. L. Paarlberg, *in* Hopkins, Paarlberg and Wallerstein, ibid, p. 29.
20. Ibid, p. 33.
21. *Campaign*, Haymarket Publishers, London, 10 June 1983, p. 25.
22. R. R. Talbot, The four world food organisations: influence of the group of 77, *Food Policy*, August 1982, pp. 207–221, p. 207.
23. *New Internationalist*, February 1982, p. 11.
24. R. Burbach and P. Flynn, *Agribusiness in the Americas*, Monthly Review Press, New York, 1980.
25. Ibid, p. 108.
26. Ibid, p. 109.
27. D. P. Harman, Case Studies on the Multinational Corporation as a Food/Climate buffer, pp. 77–95 *in* L. E. Slater and S. K. Levin, (eds), *Climate's Impact on Food Supplies*, Westview Press, Colorado, 1981.
28. Ibid, p. 80.
29. D. Morgan, *Merchants of Grain*, The Viking Press, New York, 1979.
30. Ibid, p. 5.
31. Ibid, p. 6.
32. J. K. Bowers and P. Cheshire, *Agriculture, the Countryside and Land Use: An Economic Critique*, Methuen, 1983, p. 67.
33. Ibid, p. 32.
34. Ibid, p. 33.
35. European Economic Community (EEC), *The Agricultural Policy of the European Economic Community*, 3rd edn., Office for Official Publications of the European Communities, Luxembourg, 1983.
36. R. Body, *Agriculture: The Triumph and The Shame*, Temple Smith, London, p. 21.
37. Ibid, p. 28.
38. Bowers and Cheshire, op cit, p. 85.
39. Ibid, p. 2.
40. Ibid, p. 10.
41. Royal Commission on Environmental Pollution (RCEP), *Seventh Report, Agriculture and Pollution*, Cmnd 7644, HMSO, London, 1979, p. 10.
42. Ibid, p. 211.
43. Ibid, p. 212.
44. Ibid, p. 13.

45. Royal Commission on Environmental Pollution (RCEP), *Seventh Report, Agriculture and Pollution*, Cmnd 7644, HMSO, London, 1979.
46. Ibid, p. 17.
47. Ibid, p. 213.
48. EEC, op cit, p. 33.
49. J. P. Bhattacharjee, External Assistance for Food and Agricultural Development in the Third World, pp. 33–640 *in* R. Sinha, *The World Food Problem: Consensus and Conflict*, Pergamon Press, Oxford, 1978.
50. World Bank, *World Development Report*, Oxford University Press, 1982, p. 51.
51. J. R. Tarrant, *Food Policies*, John Wiley & Son, New York, 1980, p. 238.
52. R. B. Talbot, The European Community's Food Aid Programme, *Food Policy*, 1979, p. 273.
53. Tarrant, op cit, p. 262.
54. World Bank, op cit, pp. 86–87.
55. J. Gavan, The Calorie Energy Gap in Bangladesh and strategies for reducing it. Paper read at the conference on Nutrition Orientated Food Policies and Programs at Villa Serbelloni, Bellagio, Italy, August 1977. Quoted in J. Tarrant, op cit, pp. 167–170.
56. World Bank, 1982, p. 86.
57. Tarrant, op cit, p. 253.

Notes to Chapter 13

1. A. Grainger, The state of the world's tropical forests, *The Ecologist*, vol. 10, no. 1, January 1980.
2. M. L. Parry, Aerial Photographic Evidence of Moorland Change *in* A. W. Gilg (ed.), *Policies for Landscape under Pressure*, Northgate Publishing, 1979.
3. Sir John Cripps, Concluding Address, in A. W. Gilg (ed.), op cit.
4. Quoted in G. E. Cherry, *Environmental Planning, vol. II, National Parks and Recreation in the Countryside*, HMSO, 1975, p. 43.
5. Tourism and Recreational Research Unit (TRRU), *The Economy of Rural Communities in the National Parks of England and Wales*, TRRU Research Report no. 47, 1981, gives the international definition from the 10th General Assembly of the International Union for the Conservation of Nature, 1978, p. 39.
6. D. A. Ratcliffe (ed.), *A Nature Conservation Review*, Cambridge University Press, 1977.
7. For a more detailed account of the use of the Nature Conservation criteria see: B. Green, *Countryside Conservation*, George Allen & Unwin, 1981, pp. 196–202.
8. Quoted in J. C. Hendee, G. H. Stankey and R. C. Lucas, *Wilderness Management*, US Department of Agriculture–Forest Service, Miscellaneous Publications, No. 1365, 1978.
9. J. Baker, 'B.L.M. Wilderness Review', *Sierra*, March/April 1983.
10. J. C. Hendee *et al*, op cit, p. 103.
11. Ibid.
12. Ibid.
13. M. Clawson and W. F. Hyde, Managing the Forests, *in* W. McKillop and W. J. Mead, *Timber Policy Issues in British Columbia*, University of British Columbia Press, 1974, p. 180.
14. See: ibid; B. Dowdle, Comments and viewpoints, *in* McKillop and Mead, op cit; and J. P. Kimmins, How to provide for Environmental Protection, *in* McKillop and Mead, op cit.
15. S. J. Frissell and D. P. Duncan, Campsite preference and deterioration, *Journal of Forestry*, 63, 4, 1965, pp. 256–260.

16. L. C. Merriam and C. K. Smith, Visitor impact on newly developed campsites in the Boundary Waters Canoe Area, *Journal of Forestry*, 72, 1974, pp. 627–630.
17. R. C. Lucas, Wilderness perceptions and use: the example of the Boundary Waters Canoe Area, *Natural Resources Journal*. 3, 1964, pp. 394–411.
18. Quoted in Hendee *et al*, p. 176.
19. Ibid.
20. S. F. McColl and D. W. Lime, The wilderness area travel simulator applications to river recreation management, Paper at Interagency Whitewater Management Conference, Salt Lake City, 1976.
21. J. Hulbert and J. Higgins, BWCC visitor distribution system, *Journal of Forestry*, 75, 1977, pp. 338–340.
22. G. G. Gilbert, G. L. Peterson and D. W. Lime, Toward a model of travel behaviour in the Boundary Waters Canoe Area, *Environment and Planning*, 4, 1972, pp. 131–158.
23. I. G. Simmons, *The Ecology of Natural Resources*, 2nd Ed., Edward Arnold, 1981, p. 157.
24. R. and V. Routley, Destructive forestry in Melanesia and Australia, *The Ecologist*, vol. 10, no. 1, January 1980.
25. M. K. Muthoo, Better criteria for forest investment, *Ceres*, July/August 1981.
26. A. Grainger, op. cit, p. 31.
27. V. Plumwood and R. Routley, World rainforest destruction - the social factors, *The Ecologist*, vol. 12, no. 1, 1982, p. 11.
28. Quoted in Grainger, op cit.
29. Council on Environmental Quality, *The Global 2000 Report to the President*, Penguin, 1982, p. 323.
30. IUCN, UNEP and World Wildlife Fund, *World Conservation Strategy*, 1980.
31. See for example: I. Pollard, *The Conservation and Development Programme for the U.K.:* a response to the *World Conservation Strategy*, Kogan Page, 1983.
32. J. L. Elliot, TR's Wilderness Legacy, *National Geographic*, September 1982, p. 346.
33. Quoted in National Parks Service, *Index of the National Park System and Affiliated Areas (1979)*, Dept of the Interior, p. 4.
34. P. Wayburn, World Parks Conference: preservation, development and the Third World, *Sierra*, March/April 1983.
35. E. Abbey, *Desert Solitaire*, Ballentine, 1981, p. 55.
36. J. Hendee *et al*, op cit, p. 49.
37. P. Lowe, A question of bias, *Town and Country Planning*, vol. 52, no. 5, March 1983, pp. 132–134.
38. J. Hendee *et al*, op cit, pp. 79, 80.
39. Ibid, pp. 53–55, and C. K. Leman, U.S. - Canadian outdoor recreation, *Resources*, October 1982, p. 19.
40. S. K. Chauhan, Tree huggers save forests, *Development Forum*, September 1978, p. 6.
41. *The Guardian*, 17 June 1983.
42. V. Shiva, H. C. Sharatchandra and J. Bandyopadhyay, *The Social Economic and Ecological Impact of Social Forestry in Kolar*, Indian Institute of Management, 1983.
43. N. Vietmeyer, Tropical tree legumes: a front line against deforestation, *Ceres*, September/October 1979.
44. The name - *taungya* system - is derived from the Burmese for a technique in which tree seedlings are interplanted with agricultural crops.
45. M. Arnold, New approaches to tropical forestry: A habitat for more than just trees, *Ceres*, September/October 1979, p. 36.
46. Friends of the Earth, *Ronald Reagan and the American Environment*, FOE, 1982, p. 17.
47. Ibid. Average sales per annum in the late 1970s and early 1980s were around 11 billion board feet; the backlog amounts to 34 billion board feet.

48. R. Findley, Our national forests: problems in paradise, *National Geographic*, September 1982, p. 317 and J. Hooper, Privatisation, *Sierra*, November/December 1982, p. 35.

49. This process describes the designation of a 'primitive' area. Other roadless areas can be blocked by the Secretary of Agriculture at step 5, and no Presidential endorsement is required as the OMB is within the Office of the President. See Hendee *et al*, op cit, pp. 94–105 for details.

50. The 274 areas selected as WSAs accounted for 19% of the total areas and 23% of the acreage, J. C. Hendee *et al*, op cit, p. 105.

51. News section of *Sierra*, March/April 1983.

52. An estimate updating J. C. Hendee's calculations in 1978, op cit, p. 134.

53. For more discussion on these appointments in the National Park Service see R. Cahn, The National Parks System, *Sierra*, May/June 1983.

54. J. Hopper, Privatization, *Sierra*, November/December 1982.

55. J. Baker, B. L. M. Wilderness Review, *Sierra*, March/April 1983, p. 51.

56. Ibid., p. 54.

57. Friends of the Earth, op cit, p. 24.

58. R. Cahn, op cit, p. 52.

59. Office of Public Affairs, *Editorial Briefs*, vol. 9, no. 28, 21 July 1981.

60. E. Abbey, *Desert Solitaire*, Ballentine, 1981, p. 57.

61. M. Clawson, Park Visits in the Coming Decades: Problems and Opportunities, *in* H. Elliott (ed.) *World Conference on National Parks*, ICICN, 1974.

62. Friends of the Earth, op cit, p. 20.

63. T. O'Riordan, Part 3, Putting Trust in the Countryside, *in* Pollard, op cit, p. 175.

64. For more detail of the Scott Committee and the Dower and Hobhouse reports see: G. Cherry, op cit.

65. AONBs were deemed to be of high landscape, wildlife and recreational value but not to merit the same management attention as National Parks.

66. O'Riordan, op cit, 1983, p. 209.

67. Referred to in M. Anderson, Protecting the landscape, *Town and Country Planning*, vol. 5, no. 9, October 1982, p. 224.

68. TRRU, 1981, op cit, p. 75.

69. M. Blacksell and A. Gilg, *The Countryside: Planning and Change*, George Allen & Unwin, 1981, p. 23.

70. R. Body, *Agriculture: The Triumph and the Shame*, Temple Smith, 1982, pp. 1–25.

71. See Blacksell and Gilg, op cit, pp. 219–222 for a review of these reports.

72. Farmers applying to MAFF for grant-aided schemes must consult the NCC or the relevant National Park Authority/local authority. If the NCC objects to a grant-aided proposal and MAFF approves the scheme, the SOSE must decide, thereby influencing the direction of the management agreement.

73. Nature Conservancy Council, *Seventh Annual Report*, NCC, 1981.

74. O'Riordan, op cit, p. 212.

75. M. Anderson, op cit, quoting G. Wibberley.

76. M. Shoard, *The Theft of the Countryside*, Temple Smith, 1981, pp. 104–107.

77. P. Lowe, op cit.

78. O'Riordan, op cit, pp. 238–248.

79. Watt resigned in 1983.

Notes to Chapter 14

1. H. D. Foster and W. R. D. Sewell, *Water: The Emerging Crisis in Canada*, Lorimer & Co., Toronto, 1981, p. 21.

2. L. E. Craine, *Water Management Innovations in England*, John Hopkins Press, Baltimore, 1969. D. Okun, *Regionalisation of Water Management*, Applied Science Publishers, Ann Arbor, 1977. D. J. Parker and E. C. Penning-Rowsell, *Water*

Planning in Britain, George Allen & Unwin, London, 1980. E. Porter, *Water Management in England and Wales*, Cambridge University Press, Cambridge, 1978. W. R. D. Sewell and L. R. Barr, Evolution in the British institutional framework for water management, *Natural Resources Journal*, July 1977, pp. 359–413.

3. J. T. Coppock, W. R. D. Sewell and A. S. Pitkethly, *Institutional Adjustment in Scottish Water Management*, Geo Books, Norwich, 1985; A. S. Pitkethly, *Evolution of the Institutional Structure of Scottish Water Management, 1929–1977*, PhD Thesis, University of Edinburgh, 1980.

4. Okun, op cit, p. 19.

5. Central Advisory Water Committee, *Sub-committee on the Growing Demand for Water*, Final Report, HMSO, London, 1962.

6. Ministry of Housing and Local Government, *Taken for Granted, Report of the Working Party on Sewage Disposal (Jeger Committee)* HMSO, London, 1970.

7. Water Resources Board, *Water Resources in England and Wales*, HMSO, London 1973.

8. Royal Commission on *Local Government in England, 1966–1969*, Cmmd. 4039, 1969.

9. Central Advisory Water Committee, *The Future Management of Water in England and Wales*, HMSO, London, 1971.

10. G. Schramm, Integrated river basin planning in a holistic universe, *Natural Resources Journal*, October 1980, pp. 787–804.

11. L. V. Cunha, V. L. Figueiredo, M. L. Correia and A. S. Goncalves, *Management and Law for Water Resources*, Water Resources Publications, Fort Collins, Colorado, 1977.

12. Ibid, p. 20.

13. United Nations, Mar del Plata Action Plan, *in* United Nations, Water Development and Management, *Proceedings of the United Nations Water Conference*, Mar del Plata, Argentina, March 1977. Pergamon Press, Oxford, 1978, vol. 1, p. 293.

14. Report of the Administrative Committee on Co-ordination and the Environment Co-ordination Board, Present and Future Activities of the United Nations System in Water Resources Development, *in UN Water Conference*, ibid, p. 291.

15. Ibid, p. 291.

16. Foster and Sewell, op cit, p. 74.

17. UN Present and Future Activities of the United Nations System in Water Resources Development, UN Water Conference, op cit, p. 160.

18. Ibid, p. 260.

19. Ibid, p. 187.

20. Ibid, p. 188.

21. For a review of Benefit–Cost Analysis, see T. O'Riordan, *Perspectives on Resource Management*, Pion, London, 1971.

22. Q. Nguyen, The development of the Senegal River Basin: an example in international co-operation, *Natural Resources Forum*, 6, 1982, pp. 307–319.

23. J. Chadwick Day, Benefit-Cost Analysis and Multiple Purpose Reservoirs: A Reassessment of the Conservation Authorities Branch Deer Creek Project, Ontario, pp. 23–36 *in* F. M. Leversedge, (ed.), *Priorities in Water Management*, Weston Geographical Series, Vol. 8, University of Victoria BC, Canada, 1974.

24. Ibid, p. 26.

25. Ibid, p. 31.

26. B. D. Clark, R. Bissett and P. Wathern, *Environmental Impact Assessment*: A Bibliography with Abstracts, Mansell, London, 1980, pp. 59, 66.

27. B. D. Clark, K. Chapman, R. Bissett, P. Wathern and M. Barrett, *A Manual for the Assessment of Major Development Proposals*, HMSO, London 1981, Appendix F, pp. 238–249.

28. Ibid, p. 245.

29. Scottish Development Department, *Measure of Plenty: Water Resources in Scotland – A General Survey*, HMSO, London, 1973.

30. Central Scotland Water Development Board (CSWDB), *Water for Central Scotland: A Survey of Requirements, Resources and Schemes for Development*, CSWDB, Balmore, 1977.
31. Ibid, p. 127.
32. CSWDB, *Water for Central Scotland: The Way Ahead*, CSWDB, Balmore, 1979.
33. North West Water Authority, *Environmental Appraisal of Four Alternative Water Resource Scheme*, NWWA, Lancaster, 1978.
34. Clark *et al*, 1980, op cit, p. 49.
35. W. H. Andrews, G. E. Madsen and G. J. Legaz, *Social Impacts of Water Resource Developments: A Post Audit Analysis of the Weber Basin Project, Utah*, Research Monograph 4, Institute for Social Science Research, University of Utah, Logan, Utah, 1974.
36. W. H. Andrews, G. E. Madsen, C. W. Hardin and S. C. Campbell, *Social Dimensions of Water Resources Development*, Institute for Social Science Research on Natural Resources, University of Utah, Logan, Utah, 1976.
37. W. W. Hill and L. Ortolando, Effects of NEPA review on water resources planning, *Water Resources Research*, (12/6), pp. 1093-1100.
38. D. Storey, An Economic Appraisal of the Legal and Administrative Aspects of Works Pollution Control in England and Wales, 1970-1974, pp. 259-280, *in* T. O'Riordan and R. C. D'Arge (eds.), *Progress in Resource Management and Environmental Planning*, vol. 1, John Wiley, New York, 1979.
39. T. O'Riordan, The Role of Environmental Quality Objectives in the Politics of Pollution Control, pp. 221-248, *in* O'Riordan and D'Arge, ibid, p. 244.
40. D. J. Parker and E. C. Penning-Rowsell, op cit, p. 131.
41. G. Noble and E. L. Finey, Development of Water Quality Management Planning in the U.S., pp. 1-46, *in* J. L. Pavoni, (ed.), *Handbook of Water Quality Management Planning*, Van Nostrand Reinhold, New York, 1977, p. 9.
42. W. Harrington and A. J. Kupnick, Stationary source pollution policy and choices for Reform, *Natural Resources Journal*, 1981, p. 541.
43. C. C. Schimpeler, M. Gay and A. L. Roark, Public Participation in Water Quality Management, pp. 336-372 *in* Pavoni (ed.), op cit, pp. 338-342.
44. S. A. Taylor and S. Waylan, Federal Water Pollution Control Acts Amendments of 1972, *Natural Resources Journal*, 1979, pp. 511-519; and *Natural Resources Journal*, 1977, pp. 145-148.
45. Friends of the Earth, *et al*, *Ronald Reagan and the American Environment*, FOE, Washington, 1982, pp. 11-12.
46. P. Harrison and W. R. D. Sewell, Water pollution control by agreement: the French system of contracts, *Natural Resources Journal*, 1980, pp. 765-786.

Index